Middle and Secondary School Reading

Middle and Secondary School Reading

by

James W. Cunningham
University of North Carolina-Chapel Hill

Patricia M. Cunningham
Wake Forest University

Sharon V. Arthur
University of Georgia

Longman
New York & London

MIDDLE AND SECONDARY SCHOOL READING

Longman Inc., New York
Associated companies, branches, and representatives
throughout the world.

Developmental Editor: Lane Akers
Editorial and Design Supervisor: Judith Hirsch
Cover Design: Dan Serrano
Manufacturing and Production Supervisor: Maria Chiarino
Composition: A & S Graphics, Inc.
Printing and Binding: Book Press

Manufactured in the United States of America

9 8 7 6 5 4 3 2 1

Library of Congress Cataloging in Publication Data

Cunningham, James W
　　Middle and secondary school reading.

　　　Bibliography: p. 353
　　　Includes index.
　　　1. Reading (Secondary education)　I. Cunningham,
Patricia Marr, joint author.　II. Arthur, Sharon V.,
joint author.　III. Title.
LB1632.C8　428.4′07′12　79-27191
ISBN 0-582-28136-9

Dedication

For Cindie Cook

Acknowledgments

Thanks to Ernestine Windle for her typing, and to Harry Hultgren again, for his help in the early stages of the manuscript. Special thanks are due to David Moore for his editing skills and for his support and encouragement throughout.

Preface

MIDDLE AND SECONDARY SCHOOL READING is an appropriate text-book for developmental or remedial reading teachers, content-area teachers, or to prepare students for a graduation competency test in reading. The total approach of this book will be invaluable to a principal or secondary supervisor who wishes to improve the reading program in a middle or secondary school or a system of such schools.

A reading resource teacher who does not teach students but who works with teachers will find this book the only one available which actually models how such a job might be carried out. In short, each area of specialization is covered in depth and detail and each type of specialist can readily see how all parts of a complete reading program fit together and complement each other.

These benefits accrue because of the unique organization and composition of the book. Chapter 1 presents an overview of reading instruction in the form of answers to twenty commonly asked questions. Chapters 2, 3, and 4 outline and discuss the theory and practice of instruction in the areas of meaning vocabulary, comprehension, and study skills. In Chapter 5, the responsibilities of the content-area teacher to help students read assigned material, and ways of meeting these responsibilities, are described. A short section is also devoted to the specific reading demands of each content area. Chapters 6, 7, and 8 are written in narrative format. In these chapters, Connie Tent, a content-area reading specialist, endeavors to help teachers at Upton Hill Middle/Secondary School carry out the reading instruction required in their content areas. In reading Miss Tent's fictional account of her first year as a content-area reading specialist, one learns how principles of content-area reading can be applied on a day-to-day basis in real classrooms filled with real students. She demonstrates how one can successfully serve as a change agent working with teachers in a middle/secondary school.

Chapter 9 describes a program of instruction which integrates learning in the various language arts. Chapters 10 and 11 find Rita Wright, a middle school language arts teacher, reporting her progress in carrying out such a program. Chapter 12 introduces the unique specialty of diagnosing and remediating reading difficulties at the middle/secondary school level. In Chapters 13 and 14, the reader spends the year with Reed Moore who gives a blow-by-blow description of how he diagnoses, remediates, and "manages" his classes made up of the poorest readers in the school. Chapter 15 shows how what has been presented in the first fourteen chapters can be used to prepare students for a graduation competency test in reading, a test now a reality in many states. This last chapter makes the book especially timely regarding the needs of today's middle and secondary students and teachers.

Throughout the book are optional activities, "for the reader to do" and "for readers to do together." These activities may be assigned to students who read the book for a course, may be done by readers voluntarily, or may become in-class activities. These activities help students learn the principles presented at the application level.

At this point, we would like to say a few words about our experience of writing this book. We have all been successful classroom and remedial teachers and have worked with and taught many other teachers. We are certain that today's middle and secondary students of whatever ability can be taught in today's schools to be much better readers than they are; at the same time we know how difficult teaching can be. Writing this book has been a process of walking a tightrope: afraid on the one side of painting a too perfect picture of what is possible and on the other side of not painting a sufficiently optimistic picture of what competent, dedicated, confident, supported teachers can accomplish. You, the reader, must judge whether or not we have managed this balancing act.

In our model chapters, we have not attempted to produce a "cookbook," rather we have attempted to show how principles of instruction can be applied in everyday situations. We know that it is extremely difficult for almost everyone to do anything well unless they have seen and heard someone else doing it well first. This is true of swimming, riding a bicycle, repairing a carburetor and teaching reading. We are proud of our book because we feel that in addition to providing basic information about the reading process, it allows the reader to actually see a good school-wide reading program in operation for an entire year, with enough detail for a reader to become knowledgeable about all areas of middle/secondary reading.

Finally, we have tried to have fun as we worked at creating this book and have tried to write a book that is not dull and boring. Teaching has many problems but it is never mundane, and learning to teach should be an exciting process. We hope you will enjoy our book!

J.W.C.
P.M.C.
S.V.A.

Contents

Unit One
The Reading Process

1 Reading: Twenty Questions

"WHY DO WE SUDDENLY have a national reading problem?" "Isn't the problem really that today's children aren't being taught enough phonics?" "What does a 3.5 on a reading test mean?" "What can you do for a child who has dyslexia?" "Wouldn't reading instruction in grades 6–12 be unnecessary if reading were taught right in the early grades?"

Have you ever wondered about the answers to these or similar questions? Have you ever overheard or been involved in a discussion about reading, how it is taught, how it ought to be taught, what the current problem is? If the encounters we have daily in supermarkets, in restaurants, and at social gatherings are any indication, everybody is interested in reading and everybody has opinions about what the problem is and how it ought to be solved.

The focus of this book is on reading instruction as it can and should be carried out in grades 6–12. In the following 14 chapters, the theory and practice of teaching reading at these higher grade levels will be discussed in detail. After writing Chapters 2 to 15, and while discussing what information should be included in this introductory chapter (introductory chapters are always written last!), we realized that most of the "cocktail party" questions we are asked relate to issues of elementary reading instruction rather than to instruction at the middle and secondary levels. If, we reasoned, Jane Q. Public (and John!) is so interested in reading and has many questions for which answers are sought anytime she (or he) is confronted with an "expert," won't the readers of this text have many of the same questions? We then brainstormed questions and found that, indeed, each of us had been asked many of the same questions again and again. From this accumulation of questions, we eliminated those which related to middle and secondary instruction, leaving them to be answered later. We then eliminated three more. (Who ever heard of a game called "23 Questions"?) What remained were the "20 Most Commonly Asked Questions." We have tried to answer these in straightforward, "unjargony" language. We hope that some are questions about which you have always wondered and that, on completion of this chapter, with your "basic needs" satisfied, you will be ready to consider with us the topics of middle and secondary school reading in more depth. Herewith, then, the 20 common questions.

1. Why Do We Suddenly Have A National Reading Problem?

That the United States does have a reading problem is probably one of the few statements on which you could get majority agreement at any social gathering. One cause of this problem can be found in the area of society's expectations. We expect every child to learn to read. Not so very long ago in this country we claimed to have universal education—but not really! Many children did not come to school at all or came only until they were old enough to labor on the farms or in the mills. Other children did come to school longer and more regularly, but nobody really expected them to learn very much. These children sat at the back of the classroom and were held back year after year. This policy of nonpromotion finally ended when research showed that children who repeated a grade generally did no better the second time around. Presently our educational policy affirms a belief that, while all individuals will not learn at the same rate or to the same degree, all can and will learn if given good instruction at a level and pace at which they can experience success and progress. As a nation, we make a genuine effort to see to it that all children, rich and poor, rural and urban, normal and handicapped, well-behaved and unruly, well-fed-and-clothed and hungry-and-tattered, come to school and learn as much as they can while there. Consequently, the students who take achievement tests in the eighth grade represent all the children in this country, not just the fittest who have survived.

Another cause of the current reading problem can be found in the changed place of reading in our everyday life. Ironically, at a time when the reading demands of our society have become more complex and technical, reading as a pastime must compete for time with television, movies, Little League, and tennis lessons, among other activities. While we do not have suitable data from past years to make comparisons, most people agree that people in our society read less for entertainment than they did in previous generations. At the same time, people are required to read more in order to succeed in their jobs and to carry out their household chores. Virtually every occupation available to today's worker requires some reading; most require highly sophisticated reading ability. Less practice in reading *plus* more demand for sophisticated reading skills *equals* a reading problem.

2. Isn't The Problem Really That Today's Children Aren't Being Taught Enough Phonics?

English is not a language in which one letter stands for one sound. In fact, while there is some relationship between letters and sounds, this relationship is complex. The vowels present particular problems, because we have only 5 vowel letters to stand for 15 or more separate vowel sounds. Two sentences chosen from a newspaper article will illustrate the complexity of the vowel system in English.

Many of the 24,000 Americans in Iran stayed home Sunday following the assassination of the three executives of Rockwell International. American children were missing from playgrounds and sports fields.

If we consider only the vowel *a*, the above two sentences contain words in which the letter *a* stands for at least five different sounds:

1. m*a*ny — *a* has the sound of *e* as in b*e*d and m*e*n.
2. *A*mericans — *a* has the sound of *u* as in b*u*t and r*u*sh.
3. Ir*a*n —*a* has the sound of *a* as in c*a*n and t*a*p.
4. st*a*yed — *a* has the sound of *a* as in m*a*ke and j*a*il.
5. Internation*a*l — last *a* has the sound of *le* as in bott*le*.

Next, if we look at the vowel *e*, words taken from the same two sentences illustrate six distinct sounds:

1. th*e* — *e* has the sound of *u* as in b*u*t and r*u*sh.
2. Am*e*ricans —*e* has the sound of *a* as in d*a*re and ch*a*ir.
3. stay*e*d and hom*e* — *e* has no sound.
4. thr*e*e and fi*e*ld — *e* has the sound of *e* as in w*e* and ch*e*ap.
5. *e*x*e*cutiv*e*s — first two *e*'s have the sound of *e* as in b*e*d and m*e*ss; last *e* has no sound.
6. w*e*re — *e* has the sound of *e* as in h*e*r or *i* as in b*i*rd.

While the consonant sounds are more regular than the vowel sounds, examples from the same two sentences will illustrate that one consonant letter does not stand for only one sound. For example, *t* stands for one sound in s*t*ayed and spor*t*s, a different sound in *t*he and *t*hree, and a third sound in assassina*t*ion and interna*t*ional. The *f* in o*f* does not represent the same sound as the *f* in *f*ollowing and *f*ields.

These irregularities in letter-sound relationships are not the only ones which can be found in these two sentences, nor are they specific to these two sentences. If you want to prove to yourself that in English one letter does not stand for only one sound, choose any short paragraph from a book or newspaper, list the various letters, and then list the words in which these letters occur. A few frustrating minutes spent doing this should convince you that teaching children one or even two sounds for each letter will not solve their reading problems. In fact, many children who learn one sound for each letter are successful in the beginning stages of reading but become increasingly confused as they later encounter many words for which the sound they learned does not work.

Phonics instruction is carried out daily in almost every elementary school classroom. The system is complex and takes a long time to master. For those children who can master this complex system, the rules may help them in decoding an unfamiliar word. Yet many adults and children who do not know these rules are also good readers! A whole generation of people educated during the 1930s and 1940s learned to read by a "sight word" method. If your early memories of reading instruction conjure up visions of Sally, Dick, and

Jane, you were part of this generation of "sight readers" who memorized a large group of frequently used words, learned to use context (i.e., the other words in a sentence), and probably learned to compare and contrast unknown with known words. You don't need to know that *a* in stark is controlled by the *r* if, when you see the unknown word *stark*, you compare it with the known words *park* and *bark*. Teaching phonics rules is one way of helping children identify unknown words. Mastering these rules does not ensure successful reading, nor does failure to master these rules mandate overall failure.

3. What's a Basal?

Many different approaches can be used to teach reading. The most common is the "basal reader approach." A basal is one of a series of graded reading books. Basal readers are, and have been for many years, the most prevalent approach to reading instruction in America. Many of us went through several books with Sally, Dick, and Jane and their friends. Basals are considered anthologies; that is, a collection of several types of reading materials, including poetry, riddles, factual reports, plays, and stories. Stories predominate, however, and children generally receive their greatest amount of instruction from reading narrative materials. Basals generally begin with some type of reading readiness material such as a workbook, dittos that can be reproduced, a kit of materials, or some combination of these. First-grade basals generally consist of three or four softcover books called preprimers, a hardback primer, and a hardback first reader; the second and third grades normally have two hardback books each for use in the two different semesters. The fourth grade and above use only one reading book, as the amount of time spent on narrative reading decreases.

There are many different basal reader series, and each series presents the reading skills in a slightly different way. All basals include stories for the children to read. Some basals, however, include phonics rules and letter sounds very early in the program and limit the vocabulary used in the stories to words the children should be able to figure out, given the rules and sounds they have learned. This results in some pretty strange stories! Other basals teach rhyming patterns rather than phonics rules. These "linguistic" basals limit the words in the stories to rhyming patterns that have been mastered. Thus, there are sentences such as "Nat is a fat cat. Nat pats the rat." Other basals teach children some high-frequency sight words first; phonics rules or rhyming patterns are taught gradually as the program progresses.

4. What Are Sight Words?

Sight words are words children can immediately recognize and read on encountering them. A sight word is recognized within a half second. A goal of reading teachers is to make as many words as possible into sight words, so that word recognition itself is not a stumbling block in understanding what is being read. When teachers talk about sight words, they are often referring to a particular group of frequently used words such as *the, and, with*, and others. Since these words often are phonetically irregular and occur frequently in reading materials for readers of all ages, it is important that students be able to read them without hesitation. One major problem facing the teacher is that such words, though high-frequency, are not tangible or understandable in the way that most nouns and verbs are. Many children have a difficult time making associations for these words so that they can be easily recalled.

5. What Is Reading Level?

The term *reading level* generally refers to the level of the basal reader with which the child is being instructed. This instructional reading level is commonly determined by administering an IRI (Informal Reading Inventory) to each child. An IRI consists of selections from each of the books in the basal series. The teacher calls on each child, one at a time, to read the selection orally. After reading, the child is asked to respond to some comprehension questions about what has been read. General guidelines are that a child should not miss more than 5 words out of 100 and should be able to answer 75% of the comprehension questions. The highest level at which the child can meet both the oral-reading-accuracy criterion and comprehension criterion is considered that child's instructional level. Children cannot automatically be moved on to the book that follows the one they finished last year. If they don't read during the summer months, many children drop back an entire reading level. Before moving to the next level, these children need some review at the level they were at the previous term. Other children spend much of their summer vacation reading. Such children may be able to skip the next level! Another problem with automatically placing children wherever they left off is that a child, if misplaced as to level last year, is likely to be doomed to another year of frustration or boredom.

In addition to the *instructional level* (which is what "reading level" is generally used to refer to), each child has two other reading levels. The *independent reading level* is, as the name implies, that level of material the child can read independently, without instruction. For most adults, for instance, the magazines, novels, and "real world" materials such as brochures, advertisements, and recipes we read daily are independent-reading-level materials, easily grasped and usually enjoyable to read.

Frustration level, as the name implies, is the level at which reading material is so difficult that one becomes frustrated and cannot figure out what the content is. For young readers, material can be at their frustration level because there are too many words they can't figure out or because, even though they know all the words, they don't understand what they are reading.

6. What Does a 3.5 On A Reading Test Mean?

If a child achieves a score of 3.5 on a standardized reading achievement test, that score means, in the simplest terms, that the child performed as well as the typical student in the fifth month of third grade. That typical student in the fifth month of third grade may or may not be reading in the middle of a third-grade book. That "typical" child might, in fact, be reading in a book above or below third-grade level.

To be a little more technical, the 3.5 score means that you can be 66% sure that the child reads within one standard deviation (either way) of 3.5. If, for example, the standard deviation for that subtest were four months, then you could be 66% sure that the child read somewhere between 3.1 (typical child in first month of third grade) and 3.9 (typical child in ninth month of third grade).

Standardized tests were intended to provide indications of how well groups of children were progressing in reading. Across groups of children, the standard deviation equals out: some children score a little higher than their "true" level; some children score a little lower. Standardized tests were never intended to "tell" teachers or parents which book of a basal reading series a child could read in at instructional level. While some children are placed at basal reader levels on the basis of standardized test scores, this practice is an abuse and misuse of such scores—one that will result in many children being assigned to books so easy that they are at the child's independent level, or so hard that they are at the child's frustration level. An IRI along with teacher day-by-day observation is the only reliable way of placing children at the appropriate instructional level.

7. Ideally, Shouldn't All Fourth-graders Read At Fourth-grade Level?

That is impossible. Basal reading series are structured so that the *average* fourth-grader will have an instructional level in the fourth-grade book. All children are not average. Some fourth-graders have instructional levels in the fifth- or even the sixth-grade reader. If placed in the fourth-grade book, these children will be unchallenged and will not improve their reading skills. Other fourth-graders who have not progressed as fast as the average reader may have an instructional level in a third-, second-, or even first-grade book. While we would like to have all children be average or above in reading, placing them in their grade-level book will not achieve this end. In fact, if children are placed too far above their instructional levels, they may turn the pages of that book all year and, in May, be at the same instructional level as they were the previous September. Assigning all fourth-graders to fourth-grade books is as ridiculous as buying size 10 clothes for all 10-year-olds!

8. What's Wrong With Round-robin Oral Reading?

What do you remember about your own reading instruction? Do you remember sitting in a reading circle where each child took a turn reading a page or a paragraph aloud? Do you remember being bored and restless as the other children read the material you had already read? Do you remember feeling sorry for a child who always stumbled, got red in the face, and missed words? Do you remember being "called down" if you read ahead and "lost your place"? If any of this is familiar to you, you probably were taught to read using *round-robin oral reading*. Round-robin reading is not a recommended instructional practice because: (1) it emphasizes oral reading accuracy rather than silent reading comprehension; (2) it occupies time needed for skills development and comprehension-related activities; (3) it often makes children uneasy and anxious about the reading time; and (4) it is boring. Currently, most teachers ask the children to read the story together silently for specific comprehension purposes. When their silent reading is completed, children may "volunteer" to read short sections aloud to answer a specific question. If the story lends itself, children may be assigned parts and read the dialogue aloud. Teachers who feel children need practice in oral reading may pair the students and let each of them take turns reading a page to the other. Today's elementary teachers know and use many alternatives to round-robin oral reading.

9. What Is Language Experience?

Language experience is an approach used to teach beginning readers. In a language experience lesson, beginning readers are presented with a picture or some other experience to encourage discussion. The teacher leads the small group of children in discussing the picture or other stimulus. In the course of the discussion, meanings for words are developed, and speaking and listening skills are built. Next, the children dictate sentences related to the experience. The teacher records these sentences exactly as spoken by the children. In this way, the children use their own story as recorded on a chart to learn to read words that occur over and over in reading and writing. They also gain the essential understanding that writing is "talk written down" and that "what you say can be written and read by others."

10. What Is Individualized Reading?

The answer to that question depends on whom you ask. Individualized reading originally meant that children were not instructed with a basal reader in reading groups and with every child in a group reading the same page on the same day but, instead, were allowed to "self-select" their books (usually library or "trade" books), pace their own progress through the books, and confer with the teacher on completion of a book. The teacher, rather than teaching the children grouped according to ability, would then spend most of his or her time having individual conferences with children and meeting with skills groups — children grouped together because they needed work on a particular reading skill.

In the past decade, "individualized reading" has been used to mean an approach to reading in which the teacher assigns the children individually to workbooks and practice exercises of appropriate level. All children are expected to work at their own level and on needed skills. In this more recent individualized-reading approach, the emphasis has been on children working independently on reading skills, rather than on engaging in "real" reading—the reading of narrative stories and expository articles. Programmed instruction and criterion-referenced reading programs are typical features of the "new" individualized-reading approach.

In Chapters 9, 10, and 11, an "old" individualized-reading program is described as it functions at the middle school level. To distinguish this type of individualized-reading program from the more recent one, this "self-select, self-paced, conference-with-teacher, real-books" program will be referred to by its original name, "personalized reading."

11. What Are The "Reading Skills"?

Any complex act can be broken down into components. To drive a car successfully, one must be able to (1) start the ignition; (2) steer; (3) signal for left and right turns; (4) parallel-park; (5) read road signs; and (6) perform many other separate operations requiring distinct skills. The act of reading, too, has components, or necessary skills, some of which are as readily apparent as are the skills for driving a car. To read, everyone would agree, you must be able to (1) turn pages; (2) move the eye from left to right, then make a return sweep and move across each succeeding line from left to right; (3) identify in print the squiggles which are *written* words and which stand for known *spoken* words; and (4) associate meaning with what is being read.

The process by which one accomplishes these obvious skills, however, is not observable. Identification of a word takes place inside the mind of the reader, as does the comprehension of what is read. Different "experts" have different theories about how these covert processes occur. Based on these varied theories, long lists of component skills are compiled. These skills lists agree on the major, observable phenomena; all lists, for instance, include "identifying unknown words" as a skill. Some lists, however, would include such discrete skills as "recognizes the 'short *e*' sound" or "identifies the parts of a compound word." Reading skills are the elements that make up the complex act of reading. Since much of reading behavior is not observable, what "reading skills" are will depend on the particular theories held by the expert you consult about what goes on in the mind of the reader.

12. Why Do Some Children Fail To Learn To Read?

In an average American community, any method of teaching beginning reading will succeed for 75 to 80% of the children. No method will succeed in teaching *all* children to read. Some students who fail with method A would learn with method B; others who fail with method B would learn with method A. If any one of the major accepted methods of teaching reading is well implemented, most children will learn; but no method poorly taught will work. The ability, confidence, and dedication of the teacher are more important than are the materials or method. There are no teacher-proof materials; there are some materials-proof teachers.

Why do some children fail to learn to read? Perhaps their teachers use one-and-only-one method for all students. Perhaps their teachers fail to teach them that reading must always make sense or it is not reading. Perhaps their parents fail to read to them, tell them stories, and listen to them when they try to communicate—leaving them unsure of what reading is, what it is for, or even if it is worth learning. Perhaps their parents themselves fail to read for enjoyment and information, thus showing that reading is pleasurable, valuable, and worth any effort to learn. Perhaps the children have some undetected or uncorrected problem with their vision or hearing, causing them to miss crucial concepts or not acquire skills, or perhaps they were ill during the critical beginning stages of first and second grade to the extent that they fell behind. Children fail in reading either because the instruction they are given is poor or because they have physical or personal problems that prevent them from learning through regular instruction—or some combination of both.

13. Wouldn't We Have Fewer Reading Failures If We Began Reading Instruction In Kindergarten?

While it appears to make sense that beginning a difficult task earlier would allow more time to master that task, this is not the case with reading instruction. Success in beginning reading requires a level of physiological and attitudinal development that many children do not reach before the age of six. In order to succeed in beginning reading instruction, children must possess an understanding of what reading is and a desire to learn to read. They must be able to speak in sentences and understand an incredible number of sentence structures. In most classrooms, children must have the ability to sit and attend to instruction for at least 20 minutes at a time. Since reading instruction is usually combined with writing instruction, children must also have achieved a sophisticated level of fine-motor and eye-hand coordination.

Some children do come to kindergarten with all the prerequisite skills. These children should be given the opportunities, encouragement, and help to begin to learn to read. They also need continued opportunities to develop their manipulative, social, and language skills. For most five-year-olds, a kindergarten program that includes much storytelling, listening to stories read aloud, oral language experiences, and auditory and visual discrimination training will prepare them for a "flying start" in first-grade reading instruction. Some children are not really ready to begin reading instruction in first grade, but children and their parents *expect* they will learn to read in first grade. This general expectation means that a child who does not learn to read in first grade has "failed." If the expectation is moved back to the kindergarten level, more children will fail. A child can only be five years old once!

14. Wouldn't Retaining Children Until They Learn Prevent Reading Failure?

For generations, "keeping back" pupils was the popular practice in this country. Children were not passed to the next grade until they could complete the work at their current grade level. More recently, we have had a prevailing policy of "social promotion," in which children are passed from grade to grade as a matter of course. In this approach teachers are expected to meet each child's needs regardless of the ability level and reading level of the child. Many children have recently entered our secondary schools with inadequate reading, writing, and computational skills. This inadequacy is currently being blamed on the policy of social promotion, and many schools are returning to a "You have to make the grade to pass the grade" philosophy. What will be the results of this return to retention? Well, looking into my crystal ball, I see fewer students in secondary school with inadequate reading, writing, and computational skills. I also see fewer students in secondary school! Children who fail several grades, averaging three years for every two, are not going to continue in school in order to graduate from high school at age 24!

The research on which the social promotion movement was based demonstrated overwhelmingly that children are likely, with the same materials and teaching strategies that didn't work the first time, to do even *less* well the second year in the same grade. The solution to our reading problem is not to fail children and "send them around again." The solution is to teach them!

15. What Can You Do For a Child Who Has Dyslexia?

The term *dyslexia* implies there is something wrong with a child's brain that results in the child's inability to learn to read. This may be true for a very small percentage of our population. (While the exact percentage cannot be determined, it is certainly no higher than ½ percent!) Most children who fail to learn to read have no neurological impairment. The diagnosis of dyslexia is often made on the basis of an argument that goes something like this: "The child appears to be of average or above-average intelligence. He [most "dyslexics" are boys] can carry on a good conversation and listens very well. He can do math. His parents treat him well, provide him with stimulation and care about him. He has had special tutoring in reading and still can't read. He does seem to have some coordination problems. There must be some neurological impairment. He has dyslexia!"

The tragedy is that once a "diagnosis" of dyslexia has been made, even if based on the circular reasoning just described, that diagnosis is accepted. On numerous occasions, then, teachers and parents have explained away a child's failure to learn to read with—"Oh, Bill, he has dyslexia. It is so sad."

What you can do for a child who has been diagnosed as "dyslexic" is to demand to see direct evidence of neurological impairment. In the absence of such hard evidence, treat the alleged "dyslexic" as you would any other child having difficulty in learning to read. That is, try to discern and provide intensive instruction on the child's proper instructional reading level. Try an approach, for instance, that is drastically different from the one with which the child has failed. Most important, expect to see slow but steady growth. Most dyslexia is only terminal if you believe it is!

16. Why Is It So Hard To Teach Reading?

Reading is a complex act. To begin to read, children must be ready to read. This readiness means that their vision and hearing are adequate, their speaking and listening abilities are well developed, and reading is viewed as something that is fun and important, worth trying to learn how to do.

Once such overall readiness is achieved, children move into a stage during which the major focus of instruction should be on helping them learn to identify in print those words already in their listening vocabulary. Of course, this focus must not allow students to think that reading is just "saying the words." There are many ways to help children identify words. No one way will work for all words or for all children.

Before long, if children are progressing well in their ability to identify words in print, they will begin to meet many words which they can "say" but which have no meaning for them. At this stage, when they can say the words but don't understand what all the words mean, the focus of instruction should be on enlarging their meaning vocabulary. This comprehension stage is one that even adult readers never really leave. Each time we read material with unfamiliar subject matter, we must work at discovering the meaning of words. The comprehension stage of reading is not, however, the final stage.

If children are to become independent learners, they must learn to read so they can read to learn. A child investigating the subject of reptiles must first know where to find information about reptiles. Once appropriate books are located, he or she must use the index and table of contents to find the relevant pages. Once these pages are found, besides reading and understanding the printed text that tells about reptiles, the student usually must be able to interpret some charts, graphs, and maps requiring specialized "reading to learn" skills.

Finally, if children are eventually to become intelligent participants in our democratic society, they must learn to read critically. Reading with understanding is not enough to sort out the opposing views on complex issues confronting our society daily. As we read, we must also be able to respond to such questions as: Is the person who wrote this qualified to write about this topic? Are the conclusions supported by the facts? Which statements are facts and which are opinions? Does this information jibe with the other information I have on this subject?

Reading is a complex act, and teaching children to read requires a high level of knowledge and skill. To teach it well, teachers must first be aware of this fundamental complexity and then be able to teach each stage well. Since every classroom contains children who are in different reading stages, teachers must also be able to determine in which stage a child needs instruction and then juggle their time to provide this instruction for those who need it while keeping the other children meaningfully occupied.

17. How Can Someone Read The Words Right And Not Know What He Or She Has Read?

The difference between word identification and reading comprehension will become apparent as you attempt the following exercise:

A. Say these words to yourself or to someone else:

squares	interaction	cells
variance	sums	circumstances
degrees	within	combined
freedom	estimate	divided

B. Read this paragraph to yourself or to someone else. When you finish, cover the paragraph and explain in your own words what it means:

Under certain circumstances the within-cells and interaction sums of squares may be added together and divided by the combined degrees of freedom to obtain an estimate of the variance based on a larger number of degrees of freedom.[1]

If you were able to say the 12 words correctly, your word identification ability was good enough to allow you to read the paragraph containing those words along with some easier ones. If you were able to say the 12 words correctly but could not explain in your own words what the paragraph meant, your reading comprehension ability was not sufficient to allow you to read the paragraph with some understanding.

What do statisticians know that allows them to understand the paragraph? What else would you need to know — besides how to say the words — if you wanted to understand this paragraph about statistics? You would need to know the particular meanings of the words as they are used in the paragraph. You would need to be able to use the context to help you decide which meaning of a particular word was called for. You would need to know something about the subject being discussed. And you would need to read this complex material quite slowly.

Word meanings, use of context, general background information, and adjustment of reading rate are crucial abilities if a reader is to comprehend what is read. A system that merely teaches students how to say words is going to produce readers who cannot comprehend.

Any method of teaching beginning reading, whether "phonics only" or "look-say only" or a combination of both, must not teach children that reading is "just saying the words out loud." If they learn that definition of reading and believe it, they are doomed to failure in school and life. Middle and secondary school science and social studies teachers are not satisfied with students who can say the words only. They want students who can read the textbook silently and then answer questions about it and discuss the content intelligently. Employers are not satisfied with employees who can "say the words." They want employees able to read documents, memorandums, forms, etc., silently and respond sensibly to them. Saying most of the words right is necessary, but not sufficient for comprehension.

[1] Taken from George A. Ferguson, *Statistical Analysis in Psychology and Education.* New York: McGraw-Hill, 1971, p. 233.

18. Isn't Reading Comics And Series Books a Waste Of Time?

No time spent reading anything is wasted time. Anything we read helps in some way to strengthen our reading skills. Children who are receiving adequate reading instruction need time to practice those skills on independent-level materials. For practicing their reading skills with the fullest benefit and enjoyment, children need to read stories in which they miss very few words and understand almost all of what they are reading. For most of us, the novels we read, the newspapers and magazines we buy, and the daily contacts we have with reading recipes, maps, and traffic signs constitute these independent reading opportunities.

No child will continue to read series books (the "Hardy Boys," for example) and/or comics exclusively for the rest of his or her life. Children tend to outgrow the simplistic nature of these stories. But, although we want to lead them to discover other types of reading materials to develop a broader range of interests and information, allowing children to read series books and comics docs help instill the *habit* of reading. The child who can read but *doesn't* has no advantage over the child who *can't* read! If you are ever tempted to snatch away a Donald Duck comics and replace it with a piece of "good" literature, ask yourself if you would like someone to take away your current murder mystery and replace it with a Shakespeare sonnet.

19. What Can Parents Do To Ensure That Their Children Become Good Readers?

While most parents are not trained to provide systematic reading instruction, there are many things parents can do to assure their children success in reading and to help children who are having problems with reading.

Parents should have an early-in-the-year conference with their child's teacher, during which they should ask specific questions: "What level is my child reading on?" "How rapidly is my child progressing in reading?" "What approach to reading instruction is being used with my child?" If the child is reading below grade level and is having problems in reading, several other questions should be asked: "Is my child's problem with reading primarily one of identifying words or of comprehending what has been read?" "If the approach to reading instruction being used with my child is not working well, can another approach be tried?" "Is my child receiving special help from a trained reading specialist?" (Most schools now employ reading specialists trained to give help to children experiencing problems with reading.)

Parents should read to their children daily from interesting books. Research and common sense support the notion that children who are read to from an early age subsequently have more success in reading than children who are not read to. In addition to motivating children to want to learn to read, reading to them increases the store of words for which they have meanings. It may be years before children are able to read stories containing words such as *scuffed* and *sauntered*, but if these words have occurred in the stories read to them, they will have meanings for them in the stories they later read. Reading to children increases their meaning vocabulary and, eventually, their comprehension of what they themselves read. Parents should make sure that children have plenty of books to read. Each year thousands of exciting books are specifically written to appeal to children of all ages. These books can be found in school or public libraries or can be purchased at local bookstores, department stores, or supermarkets. Many suitable books are now available in inexpensive paperback editions.

Parents can have a "family read-in." Most of us lead increasingly busy lives, with seldom a quiet moment to sit down and enjoy a good book or an interesting magazine article. Consequently, today's children often do not see their parents reading, and many children do not view reading as an adult thing to do. While we may *tell* children that reading is important, our *actions* tell a different story. Many parents who have recognized that their children are not very motivated to learn to read have decided to "practice what they preach." In their homes, a certain ten-minute period is set aside each day during which television is turned off and all family members then at home read from a book, newspaper, or magazine of their own choosing. Parents who establish this nightly "read-in" as part of their busy schedule report that their children become more enthusiastic about reading when everyone is doing it and that *they* (the parents!) are finally getting caught up on their own neglected reading.

Parents can impress on children that reading is a survival skill in our society, though so much a part of our daily lives that we often do it without thinking about it. If I walk into your kitchen as you are fixing dinner and ask you what you're doing, you'll probably respond, "Cooking." If you're filling out an income tax form, you'll answer "Filling out this darn thing." If you're putting together a newly purchased infant stroller, you'll respond, "Trying to put this thing together." The fact that you were *reading* the recipe as you fixed dinner, *reading* the form as you filled it out, and *reading* the directions as you put the stroller together does not even occur to you. An integral part of our daily activities, reading is essential to survival in our complex world. Children should be helped to grasp this reality. As parents perform tasks that require reading, they should point out to children that reading is being used to help accomplish the goal. Parents can also provide opportunities for children to read recipes, forms, and directions. As you travel, you can let children read the maps, brochures, menus, and booklets that get you there, as well as fed, entertained, and sheltered. Mankind is instinctively motivated to survive. Children who see reading as essential to survival are soon motivated to learn to read.

20. Wouldn't Reading Instruction In Grades 6–12 Be Unnecessary If Reading Were Taught Right in the Early Grades?

We hope that you are already formulating an answer to this question. "Reading is complex. Children progress at different levels. You never stop learning to read if you continue to read unfamiliar and/or technical material. . . ." For a more comprehensive answer to the necessity for and place of reading in grades 6–12, read on!

2 Meaning Vocabulary

T HE IMPORTANCE OF relating meanings to words in order to achieve understanding while listening or reading cannot be overestimated. Research (e.g., Davis, 1968) and common sense again and again have affirmed that conjuring up appropriate meanings for crucial vocabulary is essential to comprehension. Consider some examples:

> He went to the party *in propria persona*.
> The avuncular man was having trouble with his sacrum.
> She painted all but her lunules.

These are simple sentences. The syntax is uncomplicated, and you have a general idea that "he" went to the party in some particular way, that a "certain" man was having trouble with "something that belonged to him," and that the girl (or woman) painted some "things" but not others. But you may not really know what the sentences are saying, since for most of you they contain some words for which you cannot conjure up any meaning. Your comprehension is consequently impaired. Consider some slightly different examples:

> The man put the lug on me.
> She had trouble doing the plow.

These are also simple sentences in which, for most of you, all the words have some meaning. Taken together, however, the familiar meanings do not make very much sense. Your comprehension, in this case, is impaired because you have encountered a multimeaning word for which you have a meaning referent that is not appropriate to the context.

17

When people talk about the importance of *meaning vocabulary* to reading and listening comprehension, they are not referring simply to words. A few more examples should illustrate this principle:

> In an analysis of variance, you must calculate the degrees of freedom.
> $\overline{AB} \cong \overline{CD}$
> N.Z. is ESE of Australia.
> The J.D. lost his B.V.D.s at U.R.I.
> The president of ASCAP is a member of CORE.

Phrases, symbols, abbreviations, initials, and acronyms all occur in the sophisticated reading material to which middle and secondary school students are exposed. Understanding their meanings is also essential to comprehension.

FOR THE READER TO DO:

Did you consult a friend or run to a dictionary to discover the meanings for the unfamiliar words, phrases, symbols, abbreviations, initials, and acronyms? If not, were you curious? If not, did you at least expect that the text would supply you with meanings for them later? Teachers who most successfully help students increase the depth and breadth of their meaning vocabulary stores are those who have a love of, curiosity about, and fascination for WORDS! If you fall into this category, you have the foundation on which to build a "bag of tricks" for teaching meaning vocabulary. If you fall into the other group, those outside this description, begin today to cultivate an interest in words. It is habit-forming and contagious! Try it, you'll like it!

How Many Words Do You Know?

Asking "How many words do you know?" is analogous to asking "How many people do you know?" If we ask you how many people you know, you will look askance at us and probably not respond, thinking we cannot really be serious in our question. If we persist, however, you might answer our question with a question. You might ask, "What do you mean by 'know'?" "What do you mean by 'know'?" is the dilemma that has confounded educators and researchers who have attempted to study the growth patterns and size of meaning vocabulary for children and adults. The lack of a definitive answer to "What do you mean by 'know'?" is one reason that, after many decades of research, there is still no definitive answer to other questions such as "How large is the average high school student's vocabulary?"

Burmeister (1978) suggests that knowing a word is like knowing a person. There are many people you barely know; perhaps only their names. Likewise, there are many words you have heard and would recognize as being "real" words as opposed to "made-up" words. If we measured the size of your "people store" by giving you a list of people (some real and some fictitious) and asking you to check the ones you have ever known or heard of, we would get a much longer list than if we gave you a multiple-choice people test on which, for each person, you had to choose an appropriate characteristic from four choices. We could further reduce the size of your people store if we asked you to write at least a page on each person you know.

Now consider the words you know. The size of your word store would be largest if our "measure" of vocabulary size was a list of words (some real and some made-up) from which you had to select those you knew or had heard. That amount would be drastically decreased if we gave you a multiple-choice vocabulary test similar to those given annually to students of all ages. Still, this quantity would be considerably larger than if we included only those words for which you could demonstrate a "rich understanding."

FOR THE READER TO DO:

Among the following list of "people," decide which you have "only heard of or known slightly," which you could correctly identify characteristics of on a multiple-choice test, and which you could write a page about. Then do the same for the words in the second column.

Paul Harvey	figure
Your mother	iambic
Your best friend	clock
Anwar El-Sadat	linguistics
C. S. Lewis	lie
Bugs Bunny	perdition

Another factor in the "What do you mean by 'know'?" dilemma is the existence of *receptive* and *expressive* meaning vocabularies. Measures of vocabulary size that use the receptive modes of listening and reading will result in a larger vocabulary size than measures that use the expressive modes, such as speaking and writing. All of us understand or "receive" many more words than we use in our own expression.

What Is a Word?

To demonstrate the complexity of the simple question "What is a word?", we suggest that you try to answer a parallel question: "What is a person?" Words, like people, are not unidimensional entities, the full substance of which can be expressed in a phrase or a sentence. Some words have several distinct meanings. The dictionary entry for these words—called multimeaning, or *polysemous*, words—is usually followed by several numbered definitions. The word *root*, for example, would be listed as having among its many meanings: (1) a subterranean plant part; (2) the part of a tooth within the jaw; (3) the base part of a word; and (4) a number that when multiplied by itself an indicated number of times gives a specified number. While these meanings are manifest in vastly different concepts, they share an essential commonality. The commonality around which the many meanings for *root* revolve might be stated as "a basic part, often covert, from which other parts, usually overt, emerge and grow."

To return to our analogy that words are like people, one might consider the many related meanings of a word to be analogous to the members of a family. People who share a last name often share some characteristics. These characteristics may be physical (red hair, big bones) or may be mannerisms, gestures, or idiosyncracies of speech. In some families, these resemblances are striking and easily discerned; in others, only the most astute observer would be able to detect family resemblances. So it is with words. The relationship between the many meanings for some words is apparent to everyone; other words reveal their kinship only to true philologists. Few middle/secondary school students are philologists; most require help and direction to perceive the family resemblances of words.

Returning to the dictionary listings for *root*, one discovers that, in addition to the numbered listings under the main entry, there are several other entries for *root*. A person who roots for the home team is called a rooter. Now, rooting for the home team may have at some former time been related to the more general meaning for *root*, but this is no longer apparent. In addition to having many distinct but related meanings, many words have several distinctly different, unrelated meanings. The *bear* in the forest does not *bear* fruit. Hat *checkers* in restaurants might wear *checkered* jackets and play *checkers* during off-hours. Thinking about all the Smiths and Browns there are in the world, one might make the analogy that, like people, some words with the same name are related and others can claim no kin. When teaching about the many meanings of words, teachers should encourage students to look for relationships between different meanings but also alert them not to expect to find such relationships invariably.

There is yet another, more subtle dimension to the question "What is a word?" Consider for a moment the "subterranean plant part" meaning for the word *root*. This is considered to be one meaning for the word. The idea formed in your mind, however, when you hear "The giant maple was unearthed by its roots" is very different from the idea conjured up by "Bury the roots of the tomato plant two inches deep." "The natives dug up, washed, and ate the roots" evokes a third, distinctly different idea. Anderson et al. (1976) have conducted research suggesting that, rather than form a general meaning for a word, readers and listeners "instantiate" a particular representation for a word. If I tell you "The 200-year-old grandfather clock was damaged beyond repair," you picture a different clock than if I tell you, "She looked at the clock and sighed, realizing the class had 45 minutes remaining." Different instantiations for a word denotation might be thought of as the different images each person presents to the people he or she interacts with. To my two-year-old son, I am "Mama." I am sure he instantiates me as that person who feeds him and plays with him and tries to get him to use the "potty" at home the way he does at the babysitter's. To my mother, I am her "grown" daughter, about whom she still worries. To my students, I am that person who drives a VW Rabbit and involves them in much simulation and nags them when they don't show as much ambition and dedication as future teachers ought to. The same person appears different in different contexts. Depending on their contexts, words are instantiated differently.

FOR THE READER TO DO:

Think of a word that has at least two distinct meanings and at least three related meanings. Write sentences to elucidate these meanings. For one meaning, write sentences that would evoke different instantiations.

So far in this section, we have been talking about the *denotations* of words—their "factual" or "literal" meanings. Words also have *connotations*, meanings which are not explicitly tied to a word but which might be inferred from it, depending on who is listening to or reading that word and on the context in which it is used. Let's return to our "people" analogy: Mary Smith has certain literal, factual, observable characteristics. She is 5 feet, 3 inches tall. She has short, brown, curly hair. She is 35 years old. She watches *Star Trek* reruns and reads long, lusty novels. These might be thought of as denotations for Mary Smith. Mention of Mary Smith's name at a large gathering of her acquaintances would conjure up these observable characteristics for many of them. It would also conjure up some connotations. At the mention of the name Mary Smith, one person might think "assertive"; another perhaps, "aggressive." Yet a third person might think "pushy." These are *not* observable facts about Mary Smith; rather, they are interpretations and opinions.

Recognizing that words have connotations as well as denotations is an important part of vocabulary instruction. When we say that we want our students to be "good critical readers" or "responsive listeners," we are often making a statement about the importance of the connotative meanings of words.

How Are Words Learned?

If you are following the logic of this treatise, you have probably predicted that we are going to suggest that one gets to know words in the same way one gets to know people. Indeed, you are not to be disappointed! Think of a person you know very well. Try to recall how you learned all the things you know about that person. You may be able to remember particular instances in which you learned specific bits of information. You may recall learning, perhaps, that your friend was allergic to chocolate on the evening of the day you spent making chocolate mousse. You may recall learning that he had an identical twin brother after jovially greeting his look-alike on a busy street. For the most part, however, you probably don't remember when, where, or how you learned all the things you know. You probably do realize that you got to know this person during many different encounters in many different contexts over an extended period of time. So it is with words. Most words are not thoroughly learned from one encounter (although it is possible to have such an intense single experience with a word that you remember it for the rest of your life, just as it is possible to have a short-lived but intensive "love at first sight" encounter with a person).

So, most of the people you know are people with whom you have interacted over a period of time. You have had firsthand or "direct" experience with them. Many words, too, are learned through direct experiences, which means that you actually experience the concept for which the word stands. You have direct experience with the word *tiger*, for example, by visiting a zoo or going on a safari in Africa. You have direct experience with weaving by weaving your own basket. Direct experience requires that the learner interact directly in some way with the word concept to be learned. Direct experience is how young children begin to acquire a spoken vocabulary, and it is by far the best route for getting to know a word.

Not all words can be learned through direct experience, however. Some words that one might experience directly are beyond the geographic or economic reach of the learner. Many words are learned through remote visual or vicarious encounters. Television, films, filmstrips, still pictures, maps, and other visual materials provide learners with the indirect experiences from which many words are learned. Do you know any people through indirect experience? Perhaps "know" is not the best word to describe the relationship most of us have with Walter Cronkite and Archie Bunker, but we certainly become acquainted with many people with whom we have not had face-to-face contact.

Do you "know" any people with whom you have had neither direct face-to-face experience or indirect experience? How about Louisa May Alcott or David and Goliath of the Old Testament? Do you "know" any people whom you have never seen live or in pictures but about whom you know a great deal because they are "friends of a friend," and you have heard them talked about for years? Do you have a great-uncle you have never met, of whom you have never seen pictures, but you feel you know? If so, you do know some people with whom you have never had direct or indirect experience. You know these people only through hearing or reading about them; you learned of them through symbolic interaction. Words, too, can be learned through symbolic interaction. New words are learned by being paired with known words. Many words must be learned symbolically: for example, there is no direct or indirect experience for the concept of federalism. It should come as no surprise that those words which must be learned without direct or indirect experience are the most difficult to learn.

FOR THE READER TO DO:

List three people and three words you have come to know through *direct* experience. Now, list three of each you have come to know through *indirect* experience. Can you think of any people or words you know but have had *neither* direct nor indirect experience with?

Which Words Should Be Taught?

Many teachers are overwhelmed by the apparent magnitude of the task of vocabulary development. Hundreds of thousands of words, most with a variety of related and unrelated meanings, exist to be learned. Many teachers teach no new words, because they know they can't possibly teach them all. While the question of which words a student ought to learn during his/her school career is puzzling, the question of which words a particular middle or secondary teacher ought to teach his/her particular group of students is more easily resolved.

Imagine for a moment that you have a good friend coming to town. He is unattached at the moment, so you want to arrange for him to meet some people during his stay. In the jargon of a few years ago, you intend to "fix him up." Who are you going to fix him up with? There are hundreds of thousands of people in the world with whom he might be compatible; but the number of people you know and have access to is much more limited. When you consider in more detail your friend's characteristics and those of all the "available" females, you will probably come up with a list of several possibilities.

Now, with which words should you "fix your students up"? Look at the material, the content, you intend to teach your students. The words you choose to teach should be those which you and your students can have easy daily access to, those which students need to know in order to listen and read with understanding, and those which the students are capable of learning. Herber (1978) suggests that teachers begin each unit by doing a content analysis of the essential information to be taught. Each concept to be mastered is listed, and under each, all vocabulary essential to learning that concept is listed. (For an example of content analysis, see Chapter 7).

A Review of Important Concepts

Before proceeding with the essence of this chapter—ways to provide instruction and practice in meaning vocabulary—here are some important principles to keep in mind about what words are and how they are learned:

1. Understanding and applying appropriate meanings is essential to reading comprehension.
2. Meaning vocabulary includes not only words but also phrases, symbols, abbreviations, initials, and acronyms.
3. It is impossible to make definitive statements about the size of a person's meaning vocabulary because words do not have "*a* meaning."
4. Most people's *receptive* vocabulary (words they understand while listening or reading) is larger than their *expressive* vocabulary (words they use in speaking or writing).
5. Many words have several different but related meanings, usually listed under a single dictionary entry.
6. Some words have several unrelated meanings, which are usually listed as separate entries in the dictionary.
7. As people read and listen, they particularize their general meanings for words—a process termed *instantiation*.
8. *Denotations* are factual, literal meanings of words.
9. *Connotations* are interpretations or value judgments attached to words.
10. Most words are learned through many different encounters in different contexts over a period of time.

11. Words are learned through direct experience, indirect experience, and symbolically.
12. The words that ought to be taught are those which students need to learn in order to understand the content they will be listening to or reading. In a content analysis, the teacher lists important concepts and then determines which words must be known in order to master or grasp these concepts.

Vocabulary Instruction and Practice

In this section, many strategies for teaching meaning vocabulary are described. It is important that a teacher know many ways to introduce words and to provide students opportunities to practice using them, because, as previously discussed, learning a word thoroughly requires many encounters in different contexts over a period of time. Some of these strategies are particularly applicable to whole-group, teacher-led presentations; others are practice activities that may be carried out by small groups, in pupil pairs, or individually. Small-group and pupil-pair activities are crucial to the long-term learning of a new word, since students must have opportunities to use the word if it is to become truly "theirs." Many of the instructional and practice strategies are further elucidated elsewhere in this book. For those treated in other sections as well, discussion of how to accomplish them is brief here, but page references for the more detailed description are listed.

Direct Experience

Whenever possible, students should be offered direct experience with the concept represented by the word or words to be taught. It is this direct experience that teachers are trying to provide when they arrange for field trips or guest speakers. Science teachers, when they arrange laboratory periods for their students, are attempting to provide such "hands-on" direct experience. The construction of models, simulations, and role-playing activities are other attempts at providing students with direct or face-to-face experiences. While it is true that it is not possible to offer students direct experience for every new word, it is also true that there are some words in each subject area for which direct experience can be provided. Think back to some of your own middle and secondary school experiences. Did you have one of those heart models you could take apart and reassemble? If so, you probably know what a right auricle and a right ventricle are. Did you participate in a mock trial, political convention, national election, or other simulated social/political process? Did you act out a scene from a Shakespeare drama or attempt to write poetry in iambic pentameter? It is just such "experiences" that we remember most vividly, and from these memorable experiences we learn words that become truly ours *because* we have experienced them.

Indirect Experience

When direct experience with a word is impossible, you should next consider the possibility of providing indirect experience. Indirect experiences are those in which we do not have face-to-face, hands-on interaction with the concept involved, but rather we experience it aurally and/or visually through an intermediary means. Television, films, filmstrips, film loops, slides, still pictures, and maps are examples of instructional vehicles for providing students with indirect experience with words.

What's That Thing? is an example of a teaching activity that uses direct or indirect experiences to teach the names of important nouns. The objects or pictures of objects are displayed, discussed, and labeled. After some practice, the labels can be removed, and students are then quizzed about whether they know "What's that thing?" This strategy is applicable to any subject for which there are the names of some tangible things to be learned. In a foreign language class, the list of things to which new names need to be attached is formidable. In a science class, there are beakers, graduated cylinders, flasks, burettes, and many other pieces of laboratory equipment. In an auto mechanics class, the parts of an engine require labeling. Positions on a soccer or hockey team are important "things" to be named in physical education classes. Instruments in a music class require names. In fact, it is hard to imagine a class in which there would not be many opportunities for the teacher and students to play *What's That Thing?*

FOR THE READER TO DO:

Find a book or other piece of reading material you might use in your teaching. From a beginning section or chapter of that book, identify words that seem essential to understanding major concepts. Make a list of 20–30 of these words. (Be sure to include multi-meaning words used in specialized ways!) Identify direct or indirect experiences you could provide for as many words as possible. Are there words for which you could use *What's That Thing?* Save this list of words for use with other activities in this chapter.

Learning Word Meanings Through Context

How are words learned when they are not learned through direct or indirect experience? Many new words are learned by a process of inferring something about the meaning of an unknown word from the relationship between the unknown word and the known words surrounding it in the sentences. Do you know what the word *jingo* means? Now consider these sentences:

> All he ever talked about was war. His country was the best country, and anyone who disagreed should be ready to fight in battle. He was really quite a jingo.

Now, what do you know about the word *jingo*? You still do not have a broad meaningful association with this unfamiliar word. (Remember, it takes many encounters with most words to make them your own!) But, based on the surrounding and related words, you probably have a better notion about what a jingo is than you did when you heard the word out of context, in isolation.

Your thoughts about the word *jingo* might include: person, sometimes male, patriotic, argumentative. Now imagine that several times in the following several days you read passages or heard conversations in which the word *jingo* occurred. Each time the context was different, and each time you gained a little more information about the meaning of *jingo*. You also discarded some features you might originally have attributed to *jingo*. Eventually you would have a rather full, precise meaning for this once-unfamiliar word. This word would now be part of your receptive vocabulary. If, after someone had just suggested that we invade some oil-producing nation and thus solve our energy problems with one decisive action, you found yourself retorting, "Boy, are you ever a jingo!" — *jingo* would have become a part of your expressive vocabulary.

Many new words are learned by meeting them again and again in different contexts. With each encounter, the meaning of the word is both broadened and made more precise. Enough encounters and opportunities for use result in the word becoming a "taken for granted" part of your vocabulary. If a teacher had to choose only one vocabulary teaching strategy other than direct and indirect experience, we believe that strategy should be *Learning Word Meanings Through Context*. A student who has learned 100 new words during the term of a course has 100 new words. A student who has learned 100 new words and who has also learned how to use context to derive meanings for unknown words has been given a tool that can be used to learn an infinite number of new words. *Learning Word Meanings Through Context*, a teaching strategy that begins by having the students totally dependent on the teacher and ends when they have become facile independent users of context, has three stages:

Stage 1: Teacher-created Context Clues

1. Select some words you have decided to teach based on your content analysis. These should be words for which many students will not have a meaning or else multimeaning words used in a specialized way.
2. For each word, write a sentence or two that gives clues to its meaning. Use different kinds of clues in your sentences. The clue about *jingo* was an explanation. Often, context clues take the form of appositives or contrasts or words in a series. (For examples of many different types of context clues, see page 133.) There are many different types of clues. Their labels are not important; what is important is that you use a variety of clues so that students will learn to interpret all different sorts of clues.
3. You are now ready for the lesson. Write the words on the blackboard *without* context-clue sentences. Tell students that these are some important words from the section they are going to be reading. They may know some of the words and not others. Or they may know one meaning for a word that will have an alternate meaning in their reading. Ask students to write down a meaning for *every* word. If they

know the meaning (or *a* meaning), they should write that meaning; if not, they should make up (yes, that's right — just make up!) a meaning. Have each student write something for each word. Once the students have written down something for each word, call on several volunteers to tell you what they have written for the words. Be sure the students understand that these are only guesses for the words. If a student thinks that he or she has the actual meaning for a word, that meaning should still be presented as a guess. Record two or three guesses for each word.

4. Now, write or display the sentence containing context clues that you made up for the words. Again, have students write a meaning for each word. Explain to them that this is still a guess and that their meaning may be sketchy. Students will quickly see the difference between guesses "pulled out of thin air" and their guesses based on context.

5. For each word, let students volunteer their "context-based" guesses. For each guess, have someone explain *which other words* in the context helped them to make the guess and *how* these other words helped. (Such explaining is crucial because it allows the students who do not know how to use context clues to "look into the minds" of those students who do know how.)

6. As each word is guessed from context and the reading behind the guess is explained, let a volunteer look up the word in the dictionary and read the dictionary definition to the class. If there are several definitions, decide which definition is appropriate to this context. Students should discover that while the context does not "tell the whole story" about a word, it does give important clues to its meaning.

7. Have students read the section which contains the words you have just taught. You should observe increased comprehension!

Stage 2: Textbook-available Context Clues.

After several days, weeks, or months of lessons such as described in stage 1 (the duration depends on the sophistication of the students), you should try to move students from dependence on your clues to dependence on the text clues themselves. To do this, from your list of "vocabulary I need to teach so that students can comprehend this material," select those words which are defined by the context of the textbook. Write these words and the page number where the context clue for each is to be found on the blackboard or on a ditto sheet. Proceed as in step 3 above to have students make "wild guesses" for the words, based solely on past knowledge and whim. Record several of these for each word; then, have students read the text. Explain that context clues for these words are found on the indicated pages. For each word, students should write down a meaning implied by the text-based context clues. When everyone has completed this assignment, proceed with steps 5, 6, and 7: context-based guesses should be shared, the reasoning for these guesses explained, and the dictionary definition for these words consulted.

Stage 3: Independence.

When your students become sophisticated users of text-based context clues, plan your instruction so that they learn to do what sophisticated readers do. Think for a moment about what you do when you happen on an unknown word in a book or magazine you are reading. You probably puzzle over the word for a few seconds, then continue reading, assuming the word will soon be explained by the other words—the context. This is often the case, and you read on. Occasionally, however, you meet a word that is never explained to your satisfaction by the context. If it is an important word, you may finally resort to consulting a dictionary. For most sophisticated readers, a dictionary is a resource of last resort!

How do you convey this idea through your teaching strategy, so that your students internalize this *context first, dictionary if necessary* approach to unknown words? In stage 3, list all the important words needed for comprehension of a text passage. Do not concern yourself with whether or not they are defined by text-based context clues or with the pages where these clues may be found. The student's task is to have appropriate written definitions for each word after reading the selection. For those words the context does not adequately define, students should consult a dictionary. As they carry out this lesson, observe what they do. They will try to define as many words as possible without consulting a dictionary (just as you do). They will consult a dictionary when necessary to find the *appropriate* definition (not necessarily the first or shortest one). (Remember, they have had much practice in choosing the appropriate definition as volunteers who consulted dictionaries during all those teacher-led context lessons.) When you get your students to this stage of independence, you will probably agree that, after direct and indirect experience, context-clue instruction is the most important vocabulary-building strategy.

The Dictionary

In the introduction to this chapter, an analogy between knowing a word and knowing a person was made. The most common vocabulary development activity in classrooms at all levels is to assign students a list of words to be looked up in the dictionary in order to write out a definition. This would be analogous to expecting that you might "learn" some people by being given a list of people, looking them up in a "people dictionary," and writing down some of their distinguishing characteristics. Would you actually know these people if this were the basis of your people learning? Would you recognize the very people for whom you copied down some features if you met them on the street two hours later? If you agree that this "people dictionary" activity would be a ridiculous waste of time and energy, consider this opinion when you are deciding how to teach your students essential vocabulary. Dictionaries are valuable resources. In the context-clue strategy, students consulted the dictionary to check definitions gained from context or to find an essential definition that was not supplied by the context. Dictionaries are valuable resources if students use them actively. "Actively," in this context, implies that students do something other than copy the meanings they find. A few such "active" dictionary strategies follow.

Multimeaning Detection. In *Multimeaning Detection*, students are given a list of words that have several meanings. These words are presented in sentences with only the word itself uncovered, but they are told the words have been used in sentences that determine the appropriate meaning for each word. Words used for this activity should include those which have a specialized meaning in the subject area being taught. The definition required by the covered-up clue sentence, however, should sometimes be the general one and sometimes the specialized one. Students look up the words and write down the particular definition for each word which they believe represents the meaning of that word as used in the hidden sentence. When students have written a definition for each word, the sentences should be uncovered. A point is awarded for each definition that was correctly (and luckily!) chosen from the several listed in the dictionary. Once students become proficient at this activity, let each student write the hidden sentence for one word. The student who writes the sentence gets one point for every wrong definition written by the other students. *Multimeaning Detection* is a learning activity that involves students in using dictionaries. It works especially well when students work together in pairs or groups to make up the clue sentences and try to outguess the other pairs or groups.

FOR THE READER TO DO:

Identify some multimeaning words. For each, write a sentence that determines which dictionary definition is appropriate. Show only the words to some friends and ask them to write a definition. Can you see how *Multimeaning Detection* would help students to be better dictionary users, more aware of the existence of multimeaning words and the importance of conjuring up the appropriate meaning?

Insult or Compliment? (Lake, 1971) Imagine that you overheard a conversation in which someone described you as "captious." Would you be insulted or complimented? Answering a forced-choice question involving some unknown or barely known words is the essence of *Insult or Compliment?* To prepare this activity, the teacher chooses a list of adjectives. (It is fun if all the adjectives begin with the same letter.) Some of the adjectives should be familiar to most students, but most should be unfamiliar or barely familiar. Students are presented with the list and told to imagine they heard someone use those adjectives to describe them. Their task is to put the adjectives in the "words I would be insulted by" or the "words I would be complimented by" category.

FOR THE READER TO DO:

Categorize these words as described above.

lithe	licentious	lascivious
languid	loquacious	ludicrous
luminous	lurid	lucid
laconic	luculent	lugubrious

If some of the above words were not familiar enough for you to classify them as insulting or complimentary, what did you have to do to make the choice? Yes, you probably consulted a friend or a dictionary. This is exactly what students must do. They consult a dictionary to find the meaning of words with which they are not familiar enough to categorize. They do not copy out the definition for these words; rather, they make a decision about these words as they relate to them personally. After all the students have decided whether the words are insulting or complimentary, a teacher-led discussion ensues. Many of the words may have been considered complimentary or insulting by everyone. For other words, some students may have considered them complimentary and other students may have considered them insulting. Such differing views present an excellent moment to discuss with students the idea that words have connotations as well as denotations.

Descriptive adjectives are not the only candidates for *Insult or Compliment?* type activities. Consider exotic foods like mousse, pasta, and quiche and a dual classification such as "Foods I would love to find I was having for dinner" and "Foods that would send me rushing to the local hamburger haven." Locations around the world might be categorized according to whether or not one would choose to spend a winter holiday there. In foreign language classes, the possibilities for this type of active dictionary practice are endless. (See page 94).

Is a Trapezoid the Bar a Trapeze Artist Practices On?   Is *treble* the part the soprano sings? Is a *mousse* a small furry animal? For this activity, the teacher constructs questions that can be answered "yes" or "no." The trick in constructing interesting questions is to use words that sound alike. Having a dictionary in hand as you construct the questions facilitates your task. Students are not required to copy out definitions. (In fact, they are not required to look up the underlined word if they already know the answer to the question.) Students are awarded a point for each correct answer. Bonus points are given to students who can explain why a correct answer is "yes" or "no" when a controversy arises.

These and the many other active dictionary exercises creative teachers can devise are like the context-clue strategy in that, in addition to furthering their acquaintance with the unknown words, students also learn to become independent, skilled dictionary users.

Prefixes, Suffixes, and Roots

Next to looking up words in a dictionary and copying their definitions, work with prefixes, suffixes, and roots is probably the most common form of vocabulary activity students are exposed to. Unfortunately, this work with prefixes, suffixes, and roots is often unrelated to words the students need to know in order to understand a particular reading selection. There are, however, relationships among words that are often revealed by parts these words share. Seeking out such relationships helps the learner to figure out what an unfamiliar word might mean and is an aid to recall when the word is later encountered. Often, however, the same word parts do not indicate any discernible relationship. Associating the prefix *mal*-with some notion of badness, evil, or inadequacy is useful when presented with such words as *malapropism*, *malign*, and *malnutrition* but fails to add to one's understanding of words such as *mallet*, *mallard*, and *malleable*. Most sophisticated readers and listeners are alert to the morpheme-based relationships of words but do not expect all words that share some word parts to share a relationship in meaning also. To return to our word/people analogy: if you meet someone named Paul Granowsky and you once knew an Ed Granowsky, you may wonder if and inquire whether there is some relationship between the two name-sharers. You would not be surprised, however, to find that the two Granowskys had never heard of each other!

How can middle and secondary teachers help students become aware of, and wary of, these similarities and relationships? Each time a content analysis is done, some of the vocabulary identified will have teachable prefixes, suffixes, or roots. Students should be introduced to these words by having their attention drawn to the identified word part. Rather than tell students what that word part means, teachers should help students to infer the meaning from words containing the same part that they already know. If *unicameral*, for example, was a word to be introduced, the teacher might ask students to list all the words beginning with *uni* they could think of (*unicycle*, *unicorn*, *unison*, *uniform*, and *unification*). Students would then give brief definitions for these known words and attempt to verbalize the idea that *uni* has something to do with one or oneness. Students might also list words such as *uninhibited*, clearly unrelated to the prefix *uni*, or *university*, in which the relationship is unclear. From such examples it would be pointed out that not all words with parts in common are related. This brief exercise, combined with many such experiences throughout the year (their occurrence determined by the need to learn words with shared parts), should result in improved learning and retention of targeted vocabulary and growing sophistication in the recognition and use of shared word parts.

FOR THE READER TO DO:

Remember that list of 20–30 words you chose, based on a content analysis of the beginning of a textbook or other reading material? Do any of those have a word part in common, the identification of which would aid students in learning and remembering that word? If not, can you think of such a word or find one in a later section of the book? For the word you find, plan an inductive lesson in which students will list other words having that part. List at least three related and three unrelated words students might come up with.

Structured Overview

Structured overviews (Barron, 1969; Earle, 1969) are diagrammatic representations of the relationships between related words and symbols. Once the words and symbols are identified, the teacher draws a diagram showing the interrelationship of the words and symbols. In presenting a structured overview to students, the diagram is *not* presented in its entirety; rather, the teacher builds the diagram with the students. As each word or symbol is placed on the diagram, it is explained and the relationship between it and the other words or symbols is discussed. Students are asked to recall their associations with the word, to think of examples, and to come up with their own way of remembering the word. The diagram is then displayed as a memory aid for future use. If you are somewhat "fuzzy" about what a structured overview is, this is probably because you have not had any direct or indirect experience with one. (For some indirect experience, study the structured overviews on pages 81 and 138.)

Words on the Wall

Words on the Wall is similar to the structured overview in that targeted words are introduced, explained, and used in various contexts. The words, however, are not arranged in any kind of diagrammatic way but instead are written singly on cards and placed on the wall or a bulletin board. A picture, sentence, or some other aid to meaning and memory may be included on the card. For symbols, abbreviations, initials, and acronyms, the translation in words is included on the card. This wall vocabulary grows as the year progresses. Keeping the essential vocabulary "right under the noses" of the teacher and students focuses continual attention on the words. Some words occur again and again as different topics are studied. As these words occur in new contexts, the teacher and students consider the other contexts in which they have already met the words. The depth and breadth of students' meaning vocabulary is constantly increased. A fringe benefit of the wall-vocabulary strategy is that students have a ready reference for spelling the key vocabulary to be used in their writing as well. Many teachers who use *Words on the Wall* give a weekly review quiz in which they call out definitions or read sentences with a blank to be filled in with one of the words. (More about *Words on the Wall* may be found on pages 93-94, and 124-126.)

Categorization

The ability to place words in categories and flexibly change words from category to category is an essential thinking skill. Categorization is also an aid to memory. If you are on your way to the store and we ask you to pick up a few things for us and begin to rattle off what we need, you will probably grab a pencil when it becomes apparent we are going to list more than five items. If we group some items together (bacon and eggs, peanut butter and jelly, chips and dip, for example), however, you can probably remember many more than five. Categorization as an aid to meaning vocabulary development helps the student to learn how the word fits with other known words and serves as an aid to retrieval. There are many categorization activities for students to become involved in. Here are a few to get you started:

List, Group, and Label   (Taba, 1967) This is a strategy in which students brainstorm a list of words for a specified topic. This brainstorming is usually done with the whole class. The teacher records the responses on the board or on large sheets of paper. Once there are a variety of responses (25 – 30 is a good number), students are asked to "make a group of some words that seem to go together in some way." Each student lists on a scrap of paper the words he or she thinks go together in some way. Students then devise a name or label for the group. The teacher leads the students in sharing their groups and labels and telling why they grouped certain words together. Throughout the *List, Group, and Label* lesson, the teacher accepts and encourages a variety of responses, groupings, and reasons for groupings. The content for a *List, Group, and Label* lesson evolves, of course, from the topic a teacher wishes to teach. From a meaning vocabulary standpoint, the goal is that students will come up with many of the important words associated with a particular topic and will expand their associations for these words. The lesson also serves a diagnostic function, in that the teacher can observe which important words no one volunteers and can plan lessons to teach these words.

Responses to the question "What are all the words you associate with the word *geometry*?" might result in this brainstormed list:

rectangle	triangle	circle	postulate
angles	theorem	isosceles	perpendicular
line	Euclid	diameter	radius
hypotenuse	intersection	ray	obtuse
congruent	acute	area	square
polygon	right angle	tangent	circumference
exterior angle	parallel	perimeter	equilateral triangle

A group made by an individual student might consist of *circle, triangle, rectangle, square*, and *polygon*. The label for this group might be "Polygons," and the response to the question "Why did you put all these together?" — "They are all closed figures." Another student might put *circumference, radius*, and *circle* together and label them simply "Things having to do with a circle." There are an almost infinite number of ways to group these words. As individual students share their groupings and reasons for groupings, the other students increase the depth and breadth of their "geometry" words and see new relationships among them.

Scavenger Hunt   (Vaughan, Crawley, and Mountain, 1979). Here is another categorization activity, for which the teacher divides the class into groups and provides each group with a list of words and several categories. The words should designate articles that students physically could find, draw, or trace pictures of. (Aha, you are thinking — indirect experience!) The group's first task is to place the words in the appropriate category. When this has been done and confirmed by the teacher, the group divides the list of words and decides who will bring a picture, drawing, tracing, or if possible "the real thing" for each. On the following day, the students bring their pictures or objects to class. Each team gets a point for each accurate representation. As in a real scavenger hunt, the team with the most points wins.

In a music class, students might be given a list of musical instruments and asked to classify them as strings, woodwinds, brass, or percussion. A social studies teacher might want students to classify countries according to the continent where they are found. (Traced outlines of the countries or pictures of activities in that country would be considered accurate representations.) An English teacher might provide students with a list of poets, and perhaps one of their poems would satisfy the requirements of the scavenger hunt. Application of vocabulary scavenger hunts in foreign language classes would be limited only by the amount of time the teacher could devote to this activity.

Feature Matrices   Words, like people, have features. Some of these features are shared with many other people; others are unique. Have you ever been fascinated by the notion that people are so much alike, yet each person is distinct? The *feature matrix* (Searfoss and Readence, unpublished paper) is a teaching strategy that helps students become aware of the relationships among words and the uniqueness of each word.

The teacher selects a category for the feature matrix that relates to the unit being studied. ("Flowering plants" might be the chosen category in a biology class. "Explorers" or "exports" might be the category in a social studies class.) Once the category is selected, students list five or six members of the category. These category members are listed down the side of the blackboard, overhead transparency, or chart paper.

The teacher then lists, across the top, five or six features that some members of the category share. Now teacher and students are ready to fill in the matrix together. (+ is used to indicate that the member has that feature; − indicates the member does not have that feature.) If our category were TV shows, the beginnings of our feature matrix might look like this. Can you fill in the missing pluses and minuses?

CATEGORY—TV SHOWS

Features

Members	Comedy	News	Afternoon	Evening	Science Fiction
Mork and Mindy	+	−	−	+	+
Happy Days	+	−	−	+	−
Star Trek	−	−	−	+	+
60 Minutes	−	+	−	+	−
All My Children					
Hollywood Squares					

Next, the students should expand the matrix, adding more members and more features. This is a good activity to do in pairs or small groups. When each group has an expanded matrix, it can trade with another group. Each group can then ask the other questions that focus attention on the shared properties and uniqueness found in the members of a category. If our matrix for TV shows were expanded, you might be able to ask "Which show is + soap opera, + afternoon, − 60 minutes long, and + NBC?" or "Which three shows are comedies?" One reads across the matrix to discover the unique combination of features for a word or concept and down the matrix to discover which members share which features.

FOR THE READER TO DO:

Choose a category that relates to something you may be teaching or that relates to general knowledge. (Beginning the feature matrix strategy with a popular topic such as "TV Shows" is motivating and helps students figure out how to do it with a very familiar topic. Later, they will do it more easily in less-familiar content areas.) Begin your feature matrix by listing five or six *members* going down and five or six *features* going across. Fill in the pluses and minuses. Give this feature matrix to several friends to expand. Let these friends ask, "What's the only one who . . . ?" and "What members all share . . . ?" questions. Notice how each person expands the matrix in a different way by adding different members and features. Explain to your friends how the use of feature matrices increases the depth and breadth of meaning vocabulary.

Capsule Vocabulary

Capsule vocabulary (Crist, 1975) is a strategy in which students listen to, speak, write, and read words related to a particular theme. These related words (12– 15) are selected by the teacher and presented to the students one at a time. As each word is presented, students share their associations with the word. The teacher, too, may add information about the word or may use the word in spoken context so that students can infer meanings associated with the word. When all the words are introduced, students are paired and given a limited time (3– 5 minutes) to try to use the words in conversation about the topic to which the words are related. Students then write a paragraph or two in which they use the "capsule" words. The teacher selects several of these paragraphs to read to the entire class. Capsule vocabulary uses both the receptive and expressive modes to teach new vocabulary and the relationships between these vocabulary words. (For more about how to teach a capsule vocabulary lesson, see pages 128-130.)

Phonetic Respelling

While just pronouncing the word without building a meaning for it will not aid a student's understanding of the word, students do need to know the pronunciation of words so they can rehearse the information they are learning. (There is evidence that rehearsal is an auditory process. Consider the way you practice a telephone number you have just gotten from Directory Assistance while waiting for the phone to get unbusy!) If the textbook you are using does not have the phonetic respelling of unusual words in parentheses following the word, teach students how to use the respelling key in a handy dictionary and then have them make memory cards with the respelling of difficult-to-pronounce words. Such practice will pay off as your students become gourmets (*gor-MAYS*) and connoisseurs (*kon-ǝ-SERS*) of your foreign-sounding terminology.

Practice and Review

Remember way back at the beginning of this chapter when the question of how words are learned was discussed, a major factor in determining whether and how well a word would be learned was the number and variety of encounters the learner had with the word. Most of the strategies discussed in the previous section were instructional strategies. Instruction implies some interaction with the instructor! In many of these strategies, students were acquiring a vocabulary-learning tool (context, word parts, dictionary) as they learned some new words or new meanings for old words. In addition to the instructional strategies listed in this chapter and others too numerous to be discussed, there are many ways of providing students with practice and review of key words. Some practice strategies are:

1. *Word banks.* Stacks of cards with the word, phrase, symbol, abbreviation, acronym, or initials on one side and the definition and word used in context on the other side. Many games can be played and categorization activities carried out with this constantly expanding, tangible store of important words.

2. *Synonyms.* Matching activities and other activities demonstrating the need for picking just the right word among many similar-meaning words.

3. *Antonyms.*

4. *Cloze activities.* Important words are left out and must be filled in by the students. Lists of words from which to choose may be provided if desired. The first letter or letters in words may be provided as additional clues.

5. *Crossword puzzles.*

6. *Analogies.*

7. *Concentration game.* Words can be matched with definitions or blanks in which they fit. Symbols, abbreviations, acronyms, and initials can be matched with the words they represent.

8. *Scrambled words.* Words should be unscrambled and then put back into the context of a sentence or matched with a definition, synonym, or antonym.

9. *AVE (Associative Verbal Encoding)* (Michelson, 1974). Students are given a limited time (30–60 seconds) to list all the words they think of when they hear a particular target word. Working in pairs as the teacher times the activity, one student says all the related words he or she can think of; the partner records a tally for each related word. The partners then switch roles, and a new word is presented.

10. *Multimeaning word practice.* Students need practice in determining the appropriate meaning for a multimeaning word and in "accessing" a new meaning for an old word. Students can be asked to write a sentence showing the *same* meaning of a word and another sentence showing a *different* meaning for a word. Exercises in which students have only a few words (5–6) and three or four times that many sentences with blanks require that students use the same word several times in several different ways. Pearson and Johnson (1978) suggest that students make up "hink hinks" (a quick diet involving complete abstention is a *fast fast*) and "hinky hinkies" (a lousy citrus fruit is a *lemon lemon*) for multimeaning words.

FOR THE READER TO DO:

You should now have a sound "theory" about how words are learned and the beginnings of a "bag of tricks" full of instructional and practice strategies for teaching meaning vocabulary. For the key words you identified earlier in this chapter, plan a series of lessons that should result in your students learning and using these words. Use a variety of instructional and practice strategies. (There are many, many more than the few described in this chapter. You can find these in reading, language arts, and subject-area journals as well as in textbooks.) For each strategy you choose, list the steps you will follow and the words you will use. Be sure to use each word in several different activities.

3 Comprehension

H AVING A CHAPTER entitled "Comprehension" in a book on middle and secondary school reading is a bit misleading. Every chapter in such a book could have "comprehension" in its title. While all reading has comprehension as its goal, reading in the middle or secondary school generally requires little else. Very little time is spent by middle or secondary teachers on word identification instruction or oral reading; students are expected to read silently and demonstrate comprehension by discussing orally or in writing, by applying, or by answering questions.

Every chapter in this book has an emphasis on comprehension, but this chapter is where one finds a concentrated analysis of what comprehension is and what some principles of comprehension instruction are. In the rest of the book, this analysis of comprehension will be assumed and the principles of comprehension instruction outlined here will be followed.

What Comprehension Is

In a traditional view of reading comprehension, it is often assumed that meaning lies on a page and that it must somehow be lifted from the page into the mind of the reader. The reader uses word identification abilities in decoding the words to arrive at their pronunciation, associates meaning with these identified pronunciations, groups these meanings together to comprehend sentences, groups these sentences together to comprehend paragraphs, and, finally, groups these paragraphs together to comprehend extended discourse. The emphasis, in this view, is on accurate word identification until it is mastered, since accurate word identification is felt to be prerequisite to associating meaning with words — which is, in turn, felt to be prerequisite to comprehending phrases, etc.

In recent years, it has become increasingly evident that such a *bottom-up* (as it has been called) explanation of comprehension cannot be true. In the sentence "The table was placed in the Appendix," it should be clear that, while *table* contributes to the meaning of the sentence, it is not possible to associate the appropriate meaning with *table* until the whole sentence has been comprehended. In the sentence "Eye red the sine be sighed the rode," it should be clear that readers do not simply use the pronunciation of a word to arrive at a meaning to associate with that word.

In order to understand how written language *is* comprehended by a reader, the contributions of the writer, the text, the situation (including a teacher), and the reader to the comprehension process must be considered. In recent years, sociolinguists have investigated situational factors affecting comprehension, while cognitive psychologists have investigated within-reader characteristics and within-text factors affecting comprehension. It would be impossible to outline here the findings of these investigations in any form related to traditional research or theory reporting, both because of lack of space and because of the need to build a great deal of background in these several disciplines to make these reports understandable. Fortunately, the mind has a great capacity to relate by analogy what is unknown to what is known and thus to shortcut the process of comprehension and learning. For this reason, an analogy suggested by Spiro (1979) will be extended to explain the comprehension process. (Spiro compared a text to a blueprint that a reader follows to construct understanding.) This extended analogy is an elaborate one, which you will have to concentrate on to follow. It is important to note, however, that the analogy is no more elaborate than the new, constructive view of comprehension that has resulted in recent years from interdisciplinary study of language and mind. This extended analogy will take into consideration each component of the comprehension process, from the writer to the reader's achievement of understanding.

An Extended Analogy

The Writer

A writer is like an architect. An architect does not directly build a building for a construction company, but produces a plan by which a construction company builds a building. A writer does not directly develop understanding for a reader; rather, a writer produces a text by which a reader develops understanding.

Writers work in different genres of writing, the way architects specialize in designing different types of buildings. In both cases, the product may be intended as primarily functional or primarily artistic or, more frequently, some combination of both qualities. The real comparison here, however, is that architects are not building buildings but are making plans that others can follow in building buildings; and writers are not somehow putting meaning into print but are making texts others can follow in developing their own meanings.

The Text

A text is like a blueprint or plan for a building. How much does a blueprint really tell the construction company about how to wire a building, how to install plumbing, how to paint, wallpaper, or install molding, etc? Yet these aspects of a building have a great deal to do with how the finished building looks and, in fact, how it is used. How much does a text really tell the reader about how to develop a particular concept, or a relation between or among concepts? The text cues the reader to go in particular directions, but the reader must know *how* to go in those directions; the text does not tell him or her.

Consider this sentence:

> She walked over to the phone and said, "Hello."

On the face of it, this sentence means something like —

> The female walked across the floor to the electric apparatus and said "Hello" to it.

The fact that none of you interpreted this sentence to mean that indicates that you probably used knowledge of the meaning of the word *phone* and the quotation "Hello" to cue the "telephone-answering" *script* or *schema* (Schank, 1975; Rumelhart and Norman, 1978; Anderson, 1978) from your memory. This schema probably contains the following organized collection of important information pertaining to how a phone is answered:

> A telephone, within hearing distance of one or more individuals, emits a loud ringing noise in several regular bursts, which is caused by electrical impulses coming through the wire. One of the individuals who hears this ringing moves from wherever he or she is to a position close enough to the phone to pick up the receiver/transmitter that is connected to the rest of the phone by a wire. Because a telephone generally makes a ringing noise when someone at a distance wants to transmit his or her speech from his or her telephone to the one ringing, the individual picking up the receiver/transmitter expects to find someone at the other telephone ready to deliver a message and, also, expects that person has his or her ear next to the receiver of the other phone, ready to listen to any speech transmitted to it. In our culture, a frequent and expected way of responding to a ringing telephone is to lift the receiver/transmitter to one's ear and mouth and say courteously into the transmitter, "Hello."

By comparing how much the writer provides with the one telephone-answering sentence and how much substantive background is provided by the reader in order to understand that sentence, the sentence can be seen as only a guide to the reader, who, at least in this example, does by far the lion's share of the comprehension.

The Reader

Imagine that the part of the mind which comprehends language functions like a construction company that follows architects' blueprints to construct buildings. The work of the company is actually carried out by individual employees and pieces of equipment organized together. The work of the mind during comprehension is carried out, analogously, by individual units of knowledge organized together in cognitive structures. The process of comprehending a written or oral text requires that the mind allocate the appropriate bit of knowledge to each aspect of the text as it is processed. The process of completing a construction job requires that the construction company allocate the appropriate employee or piece of equipment to each aspect of the job as it is performed. Unfortunately, the company has far too many employees and pieces of equipment to know offhand what each one is best at or capable of accomplishing. Instead, each employee and piece of equipment and, for that matter, each department and division in the company has a *job description*. This job description does not really describe the person or machine which fills it but, rather, the *qualifications* a person or machine must have in order to fill it. A woman who acts as foreman on a project, for example, may be a fantastic pianist, but the job description will not mention that, since someone else who has no musical talents may later fill that job just as well.

The analog of a job description in the comprehender's mind is a *schema*. A schema specifies the qualifications a unit of knowledge must have in order to fill or match that schema. In the same way that a construction company matches an aspect of a job to a particular employee by comparing the requisites of the blueprint or plan with the various job descriptions until a match is found, the mind matches an aspect of a text to a particular schema by comparing the features of the text to the various schemata until a match is found. If a match cannot be found, so that the job may be completed, the construction company develops a new job description for a person or piece of equipment.

Clearly, this extended metaphor of mind = construction company would break down if carried too far. A company is not finished with a job simply because it has matched all aspects of the job to different components of various job descriptions; the work these matches call for still needs to be done. With comprehension, however, the mind can be said to have comprehended when the matching of features to schemata is completed. Moreover, comprehenders always discard some features of a text as too insignificant to bother with — a luxury that most construction companies do not have with the construction jobs they undertake. Still, the similarities between construction company and mind may serve to illustrate tangibly how alike, at least in some respects, matching a construction plan to job descriptions and comprehending texts might be.

Situational Factors

In the building construction business, a whole host of factors can influence how the construction company develops the architect's building plans into an actual building. Many of these factors are outside the construction company's sphere of control and are not accounted for by the building plans or blueprints. Weather, for example, has a major influence on the construction business. Government regulations, building codes, and licensing agencies also have impact on how well and how fast a building should be built. For comprehension also, there are factors outside the reader and outside the text that can influence how well and how fast understanding is achieved. Teachers, peers, parents, and home and school physical surroundings can make reading comfortable or uncomfortable, pressured or unpressured, and may, in fact, encourage or force a change in how the text is followed.

Comprehension

Comprehension is a *process* during which a reader constructs understanding by following a writer's text just as a construction company constructs a building by following an architect's blueprints or building plans. Understanding is like a building, in that both are organized structures made of specific materials: buildings are made of girders, beams, nails, wires, etc.; understanding is made of concepts, relations, propositions, semantic networks, etc. Comprehension is as much a reflection of what readers have to construct their understanding from — that is, what they *bring* to it — as it is a reflection of the text. Smith (1978) has remarked that "the brain tells the eye more than the eye tells the brain." Anderson (1978) has written that "the knowledge a person already possesses has a potent influence on what he or she will learn and remember from exposure to discourse."

The Teacher

In this extended analogy, the teacher is presumed to play a role similar to that of a consultant to a construction company. Let us examine, for a moment, what such a consultant might do in an attempt to improve the operations of a construction company.

First of all, the consultant knows there is seldom just one thing to be done to improve the building that a construction company constructs. The consultant is open-minded about all areas of the construction business and the impact they can have on the final product. The building plans the construction company intends to follow will be examined. The resources the construction company has, with respect to building materials and know-how assumed by (but not provided in) the building plans, will also be examined. The consultant will not stop with finding out what resources are available but will also consider how they are organized for efficient use. The consultant will take into consideration what types of building plans the company *likes* to follow and what types of buildings the company *likes* to construct. Finally, the consultant will examine the impact of situational factors (including his/her own presence) and how the company copes with them. The consultant will then make recommendations and exert leadership so that modifications at one or more points can result in improved buildings and improved construction capability on the part of the company.

Like a successful construction consultant, the perceptive teacher knows there may be many reasons for a student's not gaining understanding from reading in general, or from reading a particular piece of writing. The teacher is open-minded and does not automatically attribute comprehension problems to any one cause. The teacher knows that readers do not, cannot, passively get meaning from a page of text, any more than a construction company can sit by passively while a blueprint turns into a building. The teacher examines and appraises the texts that students are expected to read, the knowledge and skills the students have or lack pertinent to those texts, their interest, and the situational factors (including his/her own presence) and how these affect interaction between reader and text. For purposes of a discussion of how the teacher goes about such examination, this extended analogy will be ended and more direct explanations will be used. Because the explanations will build on an understanding of the extended analogy, however, a final summary of that analogy is here presented in more graphic form:

Analogy: A "Constructive" View of Comprehension

a writer . . . . an architect
a text . . . . a building plan/blueprint
a reader . . . . a construction company
comprehension . . . . construction
understanding . . . . a completed building
a schema . . . . a job description
a teacher . . . . a construction consultant

Improving Comprehension

An act of verbal language comprehension involves a reader or listener, a written or oral text, and a task to be performed by that reader or listener in or with that text. The amount and type of information a person understands and retains from an act of comprehension depends on various characteristics of the person, the text, and the task. A reader who must devote all of his or her attention to identification of words, for example, because of a lack of automaticity in word identification ability (LaBerge and Samuels, 1974), will probably comprehend little, regardless of text or task characteristics. A text with poorly organized or structured paragraphs (Kieras, 1978; Haberlandt and Bingham, 1978) will probably limit comprehension, regardless of comprehender or task characteristics, unless the task itself somehow involves or results in improved paragraphs. A task that presents a written text to a reader at a rate of 15,000 words per minute will very likely limit comprehension, regardless of text characteristics, except for a small minority of the speediest readers!

Characteristics of a comprehender, text, and task interact with each other. Texts that use the specialized vocabulary of nuclear physics will limit comprehension only for those readers or listeners who lack knowledge of that vocabulary and the concepts it represents. Tasks that require multiple readings of a text will aid a reader who knows the language thoroughly in which the text is written more than a reader who does not.

What Teachers Should Know About Texts

Examine the following paragraph:

> The teacher had seriously considered quitting her job until she heard of psycholinguistics. "I will not quit without meeting him!" she said.

From this paragraph we delete the punctuation and capitalization:

> the teacher had seriously considered quitting her job until she heard of psycholinguistics I will not quit without meeting him she said

Next we delete the inflections:

> the teacher had serious consider quit her job until she hear of psycholinguistics I will not quit without meet him she say

And then the remaining tense and aspect markers:

> the teacher serious consider quit her job until she hear of psycholinguistics I not quit without meet him she say

Then the remaining function words:

> teacher   serious   consider   quit   job
>   hear   psycholinguistics   quit
> meet   say

And finally the word order:

> consider   quit
> hear   quit
> job   say
> meet   serious
> psycholinguistics   teacher

What remains? The content words — or, more precisely, the *concept* words. By eliminating punctuation, capitalization, inflections, other tense and aspect markers, other function words, and word order, the paragraph has been reduced to a list of meaning vocabulary. These words are readily definable by the concepts they can represent in various contexts, whereas *had* and *of*, two other words in the paragraph, are very difficult to define.

FOR THE READER TO DO:

In the example paragraph used above, notice which words were deleted when *function words* were removed. Without referring to a dictionary, try to define each. Why are they called "function words"? Then try to define several of the *concept words*. Why are they called "concept words"? Find *of* in the dictionary. What does *of* mean?

The concept words in a text are placed there by the writer to represent (Frederiksen 1975; Kintsch, 1974):

> objects (animate or inanimate): *teacher, job, psycholinguistics*
> actions (processive or resultive): *consider, quit, hear, quit, meet, say*
> attributes of objects

> manner of actions: *serious*
> location of objects or actions
> time of actions

It should be clear how the writer of the paragraph above could have included *attributes* of objects in his or her writing (the teacher could have been *young*) or included location of objects or actions (the job could have been at *Smith Middle School*) or included time of actions (the considering could have been done *late in the spring*). In any event, all texts (and all language, for that matter) tell of objects, their attributes and location, and of actions, their manner, location, and time. The writer assumes that the intended audience will be able to associate the appropriate concept (object, action, attribute, manner, location, or time) with each concept word.

But what of the other information on the page? Is the information we discarded from the above paragraph of no major importance? Let us restore the information deleted from the paragraph and, instead, remove the concept words:

> The _____ had _____ly _____ed _____ing
> her _____ until she _____ed of _____. "I
> will not _____ without _____ing him!" she _____ed.

This grammatical information (capitalization, punctuation, inflections, other tense and aspect markers, function words, and word order) conveys *relationships* between concepts rather than the concepts themselves. To illustrate this point, the same grammatical information can be used to signal the same relationships but with different concept words:

> The *tiger* had *anxious*ly *stopped lick*ing her *chops* until she *smelled* of *Rick*. "I will not *leave* without *eating* him!" she *grinn*ed.

Fortunately, it is not necessary for students to have labels for any of the various types of concept words or the various relationship information. In fact, the smallest children, without having the slightest notion of what a *noun* or a *preposition* is, can usually understand spoken language filled with *the*, *of*, actions, and objects. All that is required is that the reader have concepts and relationships that match most of those which the words and grammatical information in the text represent.

In addition to the content of clauses and sentences communicated through the use of concept words and relationships between them, texts also have *cohesion* and *staging* (Grimes, 1975). Cohesion is structured into a text by using two major devices: words that link clauses or sentences together (She was in the hospital *because* the car hit her) and anaphoric references (The *woman* loved to paint; *she* took lessons). Cohesion is how objects or actions in one clause or sentence are linked to objects or actions in other clauses or sentences.

Staging is like an outline of a text in which some ideas are coordinate with each other and other ideas are superordinate or subordinate to each other. Any text that can be outlined has ideas which are *leveled* or *staged*, so that certain statements which are superordinate are separated from those which are subordinate to them. For our purposes, a text can now be defined as:

A set of statements, made up of concept words and relations between them, which are linked together by cohesion and which are organized in a hierarchy with levels or stages.

What Teachers Should Know About Comprehenders

Consider the concept word for the object *clock*. What does it mean? Look up *clock* in a dictionary and consult the definitions for the noun form. Write a personal definition for *clock* and make it as complete as possible. Compare your personal definition with the following *schema* for *clock*:

Slots or Variables	Probable Values
a display for the current time	a clockface/a digital readout
a stem for setting the time displayed	plastic/metal
a power source	electric cord/winding stem/battery
an alarm	bell/buzz/none
a stem for setting the alarm.	same as stem for setting time/ separate stem/none

Look around the room where you are as you read this sentence. Try to find a clock. Whether or not you find one, think of how you accept or reject each object you see as being a clock or not. The recent work of the schema theorists in cognitive psychology suggests that you perceive and identify objects by comparing their distinctive features to various schemata you have stored and organized in your mind. In the room where you now are, you may have found a clock not exactly like any clock you have ever seen. It may have a strange shape or other unusual characteristics, but you still identify it as a clock if there is a sufficient match between the object you observe and the clock schema you have stored in your mind. When you achieve a match between what you perceive and a particular schema, you have *instantiated* that schema. Instantiation of a schema simply means that the slots or variables in the schema have been filled with particular values based on features of the object, action, time, location, manner, or attribute being considered or perceived.

FOR THE READER TO DO:

Choose an object and an action, as well as either a time, a location, a manner, or an attribute. Develop a schema for each as we did for *clock* in the example above. Consider how these three schemata would be used to perceive what they represent.

Once it is understood how schemata function in perception of the world, it becomes possible to consider how they function in language comprehension. Again, consider the spoken or written word *clock*. When you hear or see the word, it is not possible to instantiate the clock schema because you do not ac-

Figure 1. Pictures for clock sentences*

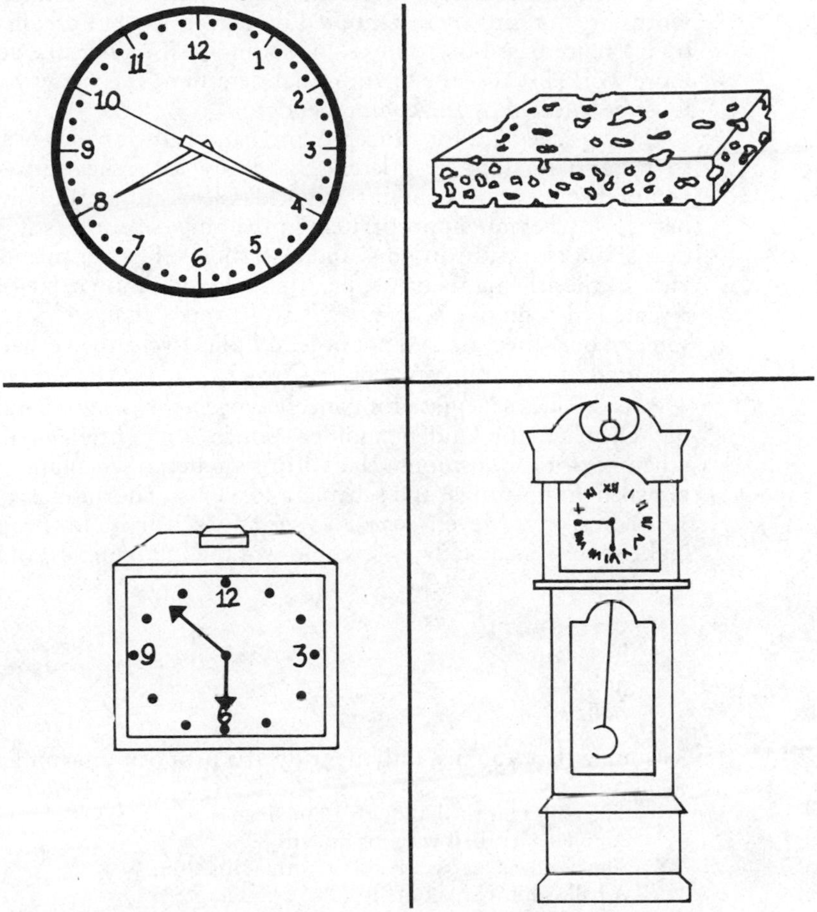

tually see a clock. But, if the word *clock* is in a linguistic context, something interesting happens. Compare these two sentences (Anderson et al., 1978):

Sally looked at the clock in her bedroom.
Sally looked at the clock in her classroom.

The definition of *clock* is the same in both sentences, and both sentences make use of the same clock schema. Yet pick the picture among the following four that best matches the first sentence; then pick the one that best matches the second. Are you surprised that, in each sentence, you instantiated *clock*? You instantiated or particularized your clock schema by using the words *bedroom* and *classroom* to suggest probable values for the clock schema slots. Your experience suggests that clocks for hanging in classrooms tend to have certain characteristics, whereas clocks found in bedrooms generally tend to have cer-

*Anderson, Stevens, Shifrin, and Osborn, 1978.

tain other characteristics. In language comprehension, therefore, concept words are not directly instantiated by perception but are, instead, instantiated by inference based on context. In reading or listening, the comprehender does more work, because the features that determine the values for the schema slots must be inferred by the comprehender.

Having schemata for concept words and being able to use linguistic context to instantiate slots by inference is really an indication of how much the comprehender knows about the world. Clearly, one can only instantiate his or her clock schemata appropriately in the above examples if one knows a good deal about clocks, bedrooms, and classrooms. For our purposes, we accept the view of the schema theorists, i.e., that all one's knowledge of the world is represented in cognitive schemata. It so happens that we have verbal labels for some of our schemata and not others. Collectively, the verbal labels we do have are referred to as our vocabularies.

Alas, besides schemata for concept words, the comprehender has other types of schemata for understanding spoken or written language. There are schemata for *propositions* (clauses or sentences), schemata for *logical relations* between propositions, and schemata for *texts* (Thorndyke, 1977; Mandler and Johnson, 1977; Meyer, 1977). To see how schemata for propositions function, make sense — as quickly as possible — of the following list of randomly ordered words:

> nine-iron
> hit
> golfer
> ball

Assuming that you instantly developed a proposition similar to one of these:

> The golfer hit the ball with a nine-iron.
> A golfer hit a ball with his nine-iron.
> The ball was hit by the golfer with a nine-iron.
> A ball is hit with a nine-iron by a golfer.

you made use of this proposition schema (Frederiksen, 1975):

> (animate object) *AGENT* (resultive action) *OBJECT* (inanimate object)
> *INSTRUMENT* (object)
> *GOAL* (proposition)

You instantiated this schema by filling the slots with concepts available to you in the randomly ordered list above:

> golfer *AGENT* hit *OBJECT* ball
> *INSTRUMENT* nine-iron
> *GOAL* to get the ball as close to the hole in the green as possible

The GOAL slot in the proposition schema had to be inferred by you, while the other slots could be filled in with the words in the list. In any event, instantiation of the proposition schema would have been accomplished more easily had the words been in the more customary word order (for English):

golfer
hit
ball
nine-iron

Moreover, had you been given the sentence "The golfer hit the ball with his nine-iron," assigning concepts to the various slots would have been instantaneous and effortless. Of course, a variety of proposition schemata exist; and in each case, one is selected that best fits the concepts and the surface appearance of the clause or sentence in which they occur. For example, in the sentence "Mary was hit by Jane," small children often assign *Mary* to the AGENT slot because of an incompletely developed understanding of how to divorce proposition schemata from the surface grammar of a sentence where word order is usually expressive of the active voice.

Schemata for logical relations between propositions (Frederiksen, 1975) are too complicated to discuss here. Suffice it to say that even when two or more propositions do not have an obvious logical connection, comprehenders are equipped with schemata for possible logical relations which they match to those propositions until one seems to fit.

Schemata for texts taken as a whole are also complicated matters to discuss, but one may suffice for an example. Stories have an overall plot structure, or "story grammar." It is suggested that if readers (or listeners) come in contact with enough stories, they will internalize this story grammar. These readers (or listeners) can then use this internalized story grammar to help them understand and remember a new story by anticipating and recalling basic structural elements of the plot such as "main character," "conflict," "resolution," etc.

What Teachers Should Know About Comprehension Tasks

When a comprehender is reading or listening to a text, there is generally a specific comprehension task assigned to that comprehender by a teacher or a superior, by a situation, or by him/herself. Although it is certainly possible to read whatever you pick up only for as long as you are interested, much of our reading has constraints on how it will be conducted, what will be gained from it, or what will be done by the reader after the reading is completed. And, though less formal, social and other constraints do exist on listening comprehension, particularly with respect to sermons, speeches, and lectures. (You generally cannot interrupt to ask questions or move nearer, for example.)

In middle and secondary school classrooms, comprehension tasks are of three major types: (1) tasks designed to result in the learning of specific content; (2) tasks designed to result in improved ability on the part of the student to perform those particular tasks; and (3) tasks designed to result in improved language comprehension ability.

Tasks designed to result in the learning of specific content are often tied to objectives, study questions, or study guides. In some way, students are informed of what they are expected to learn from what they will be listening to or reading. In addition, students may be guided to that information in the text by specific questions or activities.

Tasks designed to result in improved ability to perform those particular tasks are often marked by repetition. Students perform the particular task to be improved over and over again, in or with a variety of texts, until there is evidence the task has been mastered. For example, schools attempting to prepare their students for a standardized achievement or graduation competency test usually give them much practice with items that simulate those on the test to be given. If the test to be taken gives short paragraphs followed by several multiple-choice comprehension questions, each of which has five possible answers, the practice materials will have short paragraphs followed by several comprehension questions, each with five possible choices. The students will perform the task of selecting the best answer among the choices and marking it in the correct place on the answer sheet, over and over again until they seem to have mastered the task.

Tasks designed to result in improved language comprehension ability generally require the greatest variety, using materials that are of approximately the same level of difficulty, challenging but not frustrating for the students. A variety of tasks is used so that the students learn to attack comprehension of texts from all directions. No attempt is made to emphasize a particular task; rather, students are led to dealing with the many facets of texts. Sometimes they read to answer questions, sometimes to construct new endings, sometimes to develop new titles, sometimes to arrange major events in proper sequence, etc. Each task focuses the student's attention on one characteristic or component that texts have. It is assumed that a great deal of this kind of experience will improve students' overall text comprehension, both in awareness and ability.

Each of these three major task types can be designed in a variety of ways, depending on how much repetition, how much preparation for the task, how much time, and how much supervision/guidance/feedback are given by the teacher. In every case, however, a comprehension task is:

an assigned product to be achieved from or with the text

or

an assigned process for comprehending the text

or

both

Teachers may impose the assignments, the situation may impose the assignments, or a comprehender may impose them on him/herself.

Regardless of whether the task is an assigned process, product, or both, and regardless of the source of the assignment, it can be described as predominantly text-based or comprehender-based. A text-based assignment is one during or from which a comprehender is expected to gain a precise understanding of the text with little of the comprehender's own interpretations. When inferences are made, they are expected to be ones clearly authorized by the text. A comprehender-based assignment, however, is one during or from which a comprehender is expected to read creatively and critically, interpreting and inferring to gain implications of the text for the comprehender and judgments by the comprehender on the text. Assignments can differ widely as to how they fall on a continuum from text-based to comprehender-based.

FOR THE READER TO DO:

Using a textbook you have used or might use with students, develop six comprehension assignments or tasks: two which are text-based, two comprehender-based, and two which are approximately equally text- and comprehender-based.

Principles of Comprehension Instruction

In any comprehension task there is, to some degree, a match or mismatch between each comprehender and the text that person is attempting to understand. Assuming that a lack of accurate and automatic word identification ability or print-processing ability is *not* the source of most of these mismatches, there are four sources of a possible match or mismatch:

1. Does the comprehender have schemata for most of the concept words in the text?
2. Does the comprehender have schemata for propositions that match the relationships between concept words signaled in the text by the grammatical information?
3. Does the comprehender have schemata for logical relations between propositions that match the elements of cohesion in the text?
4. Does the comprehender have a text schema that corresponds to the staging pattern in the text?

The degree to which there is a match or mismatch between text and comprehender will affect how well, how fast, and how comfortably the comprehension task will be performed. How much of a mismatch there can be differs, depending on the type of comprehension task. Tasks designed to facilitate the learning of specific content can be accomplished in considerably more difficult material[1] than tasks designed to facilitate improvement in the tasks themselves. Tasks designed to raise general language comprehension ability must be performed with relatively easy material.

Tasks to facilitate the learning of specific content can use more difficult texts than the other two types of tasks when the student knows exactly what information he or she is seeking and has a reasonable idea of where that information is located. Study guides, study questions, purposes for reading or listening, stated objectives, etc., enhance the likelihood that students will learn particular content, even from difficult material, because the student can focus on the parts of the text relevant to the task and ignore the rest. On the other hand, if teachers expect students to learn specific content from a text but give them no guidance ("Read Chapter 5 for tomorrow"), either the text had better be a good match for the students' schemata or the content had better be easy, or both.

Tasks meant to result in improvement on the tasks themselves and tasks to raise language comprehension ability should only be performed by comprehenders working in or with texts at instructional level for this reason: When

---

[1] Difficult material is a text for which the comprehender lacks some of one or more of the four types of schemata the text requires.

reading or listening to texts that are too difficult, all readers/listeners behave like poor readers/listeners. Even very good readers can often be seen finger-pointing at the words or lip-moving and mumbling when negotiating extremely challenging texts. Even very good listeners can often be inattentive or easily distracted while hearing difficult texts being read or delivered. If we instruct students to perform certain comprehension tasks or to improve general comprehension ability in difficult material, what we may really be doing is giving them practice in how to be a poor comprehender. *With enough practice at the wrong instructional level, almost everyone can learn to be a poor comprehender!*

The first set of principles of comprehension instruction, then, pertains to matching materials to students. Generally, content-area teachers have audio-visual aids such as films, filmstrips, records, tapes, and transparencies they can use to supplement their texts, as well as library books at varying levels of difficulty that cover all or some of their course content. Even where content-area teachers feel compelled to use a difficult text with students for whom it is seldom a match, these teachers always have the option of selecting what sections of the text they will require the students to learn. Reading teachers should always have materials available across all levels of student reading ability. Therefore:

> Principle 1: *Regardless of grade level or readability level, a text is at instructional level for a comprehender only when there is a match between what the comprehender knows and what the text requires the comprehender to know.*
> Principle 2: *When attempting to improve students' comprehension ability or the ability to perform certain comprehension tasks, be sure that the students read or listen to material at or easier than instructional level.*
> Principle 3: *When attempting to teach students specific content using an oral or written text (including a lecture, of course), be sure that the students know the nature and approximate location in the text of the content they are to learn. (The more difficult the material is for the students, the more guidance required.)*

The second set of principles of comprehension instruction has to do with providing students with schemata they lack for reading or listening to particular texts. This discussion will follow the four sources of mismatches between comprehender and text mentioned above.

> Principle 4: *When students lack schemata for key concept words in a text, meaning vocabulary instruction is called for.*

Chapter 2 of this text provided guidance in how to supply that instruction.

> Principle 5: *When students lack schemata for propositions that match the relationships between concept words signaled in the text by the grammatical information, instruction in using grammatical information to discover relationships is called for.*

Because, in our experience, only remedial students at the middle or secondary school level have such deficiencies, we have placed a section entitled "Improving the Use of Grammatical Information in Reading" in the first remedial-reading chapter (Chapter 12).

> Principle 6: *When students lack schemata for logical relations between propositions that match the elements of cohesion in the text, instruction in following the reasoning through the text is called for.*

Inability to follow the reasoning through the text is generally an indication that students are having problems with other text areas such as vocabulary or grammatical information. A section of the first remedial-reading chapter (Chapter 12) has been devoted to techniques to improve student ability to follow cohesion.

> Principle 7: *When students lack the text schema that corresponds to the staging pattern in the text, lots of practice in whole-passage comprehension tasks with complete segments of that text is called for.*
> Principle 8: *Whole-passage comprehension tasks are those tasks which require students as a group to retell, reconstruct, or summarize a text and then to systematically compare and contrast their reconstruction with the original.*

In the remainder of the book, there will be little discussion of the constructive model of comprehension or of these principles of comprehension instruction as such. Elsewhere in the book, these principles will be applied to content area reading, middle school reading/language arts, and remedial-reading instruction for older disabled readers. The emphasis will be on practical understanding of reading instruction and the too often neglected area of program implementation. Comprehension, however, is the theme that ties all 15 chapters together. Throughout, Principle 9 should be uppermost in the reader's mind:

> Principle 9: *The teacher can reduce the mismatch between comprehenders and texts by supplementing or replacing the text, adding guidance to the task, and/or instructing the comprehender in handling difficult components of the text.*

4 Study Skills

STUDY SKILLS is a term used to refer to a wide variety of reading-related abilities. If you were to scan the pages of reading texts, indexed under "study skills" you would find discussions of such diverse topics as study habits, test-taking skills, locating information, using book parts, reading rate, and using maps, charts, graphs, diagrams, and tables. While these are important topics and useful skills, after completing the study skills section one is often unsure about what the goals of study skills instruction are and how these goals relate to one another. In order to give some focus and integration to the discussion in this chapter, study skills will be defined as those skills a person needs in order to use reading to solve a problem or investigate a topic. The cognitive question you should be asking yourself as you read this chapter is: "What skills other than the ability to comprehend and evaluate the printed word does a person need in order to *read to learn*?"

For many of you, the first time you were called upon to apply your study skills was when you were told to do a brief oral or written report or a "term paper" on some subject. Do you remember what you did? Did you rush to the library, grab the first encyclopedia, and copy down every other sentence? Did you scan the library shelves, find a book that seemed related to the topic, and begin reading on page one? A high school librarian I consulted about study skills confessed that she had "happened upon" the *Readers' Guide* while a sophomore in college and could not believe that anyone had indexed all those magazines so conveniently!

Many of us who can now do a report or a paper were never actually *taught* how. We learned by trial and error as we went along, because we had to. If your approach to using reading to investigate a topic is haphazard, "hit or miss," you will be unable to teach students how to approach and carry out the task systematically. In the authors' experience, because many undergraduates (and even a few graduate students!) do not know how to seek out and organize information efficiently, this chapter will have two strands of emphasis. The "For You as Student" sections will give the reader step-by-step instructions for doing a paper. The "For You as Teacher" sections will suggest to the reader how middle and secondary students can be led, one step at a time, through the process of doing a report. While it is not necessary for you to carry out the steps and actually do a paper in this organized fashion, it is recommended. If you do the paper as is suggested here, your active participation will increase the likelihood that you will (1) remember what you have done; (2) be aware of problems that may arise at each step of the process; and (3) recognize the value of instructing your students in this complex process.

So, for the remainder of this chapter, it will be assumed that you are going to write a paper on a topic. (It can be any topic—not restricted to the course for which you are reading this book on middle/secondary school reading!) Your first, often onerous task is choosing this topic.

Choosing and Narrowing a Topic

For You as Student

Assuming you are going to do your paper for this course, you have the entire field of middle and secondary school reading from which to select a topic for further investigation. Brainstorming is a good strategy for getting your mental wheels turning and thinking about what you would like to investigate. Brainstorming is best done with a large group of people—there are then many brains to put to work. Thus, if your whole class is going to do a paper for this course, let one class member record all the brainstormed ideas. If you are working alone, of course, you will have to brainstorm and record the list by yourself. Remember, when you brainstorm, the goal is to generate as many ideas as quickly as possible. Do not censor any ideas or hesitate to suggest ideas because they seem too narrow, too broad, or too ridiculous! Below are the beginnings of a brainstormed list of topics relating to middle/secondary school reading. Try to supplement it with 15 or 20 more of your own:

> **Middle/Secondary Reading Topics**
> Comprehension
> Reading in social studies
> Reading in auto mechanics classes
> Reading in music classes
> Meaning vocabulary
> Reading rate
> Helping the middle school remedial reader
> History of secondary reading
> Reading in science
> Inferential comprehension

Once you have brainstormed your list, you should have many ideas that you could investigate further. The next step is to choose one of the brainstormed topics. You may alter the initial topic somewhat, make it broader or narrower. You may want to combine two very broad topics, but in such a way that their combination results in a narrower unified topic. You might, for example, combine "Meaning vocabulary" and "Reading in science" to arrive at the topic "Improving meaning vocabulary in science classes." You might feel that this is still too broad a topic and want to narrow the field of science to physics or chemistry or biology.

Once you have chosen your topic, you should list as many questions as you can think of about the topic. For the topic "Improving meaning vocabulary in biology," you might list such questions as:

1. What meaning vocabulary is unfamiliar to the typical biology student?
2. Are there multimeaning words for which the student might have a general meaning, but not the appropriate one?
3. Do biology textbooks define the words by context?
4. What words are included in the glossary?
5. How can the glossary be used?
6. How can biology students be provided direct and indirect experience with new words?
7. Are there symbols, initials, acronyms, and abbreviations that should be taught?
8. Are there specialized phrases that need to be taught?

Now, take your list of questions and construct an outline in order to guide you in looking for specific information. Many terms used in the outline will become key words to aid you in finding information once the proper sources are located. Your outline for "Meaning vocabulary in biology" might look like this:

Meaning Vocabulary in Biology
  I. Identifying vocabulary to be taught
    A. Words
      1. New words
      2. Multimeaning words
    B. Symbols
    C. Initials, acronyms, and abbreviations
    D. Special phrases
  II. Usefulness of biology text
    A. Words defined by context
    B. Pictures and other graphics
    C. Glossary
  III. Strategies for teaching identified vocabulary
    A. Direct experience
    B. Indirect experience
    C. Roots, prefixes, and suffixes
    D. Context
    E. Glossary and dictionary
    F. Other

You now have your topic selected, narrowed, and outlined. Although the final paper may deviate greatly from your outline, constructing the outline gives you the direction you need to seek out sources and evaluate what information is relevant.

For You as Teacher

Now, switch to your teacher role and imagine you are about to assign your students an oral or written report or even a full-blown term paper. You have been studying a certain fairly general topic and now want your students to use their reading and study skills to investigate some subtopic further. How would you begin? Perhaps by having your students brainstorm as many different subtopics as they can think of. You can lead the whole class in doing this, or else can divide the class into groups of four or five and let each smaller group brainstorm independently. If the class is brainstorming in small groups, let each group record its brainstorming on graph or butcher paper. The completed lists of brainstormed ideas can then be displayed and compared. Many subtopics will occur on all or several of the lists; others will be unique to a single list.

Choose one topic from the brainstormed list, and then "model" for the students how to make a list of questions related to this topic. (Modeling is a very useful, often overlooked teaching strategy.) After you have modeled the list of relevant questions, choose a subtopic and let each group come up with its own questions. If you choose the same question for all the groups and lead students in comparing their lists, they will soon realize there is no *one* list of questions.

By now, students have watched you make a list of questions and participated in the group question-making, so it is time for each student to select a topic and list his/her questions. You should circulate among them and provide individual help as the students select their topic and list questions.

The final step is construction of an outline. The same "teacher model, group construction, individual construction" process should be followed. Students may need help with the number and letter subordination system required by an outline. Such instruction should be given, but with students (and teachers!) at all times keeping in mind that the outline is meant above all to give a clear sense of purpose and organization and as a source and reminder of key terms for later use. This primary study purpose should not be fogged out in a confusing miasma of numbers and letters. Teachers should collect outlines and make notes to or confer with those students who need individualized attention in order to select, narrow, and outline a topic.

FOR THE READER TO DO:

Choose a topic you might assign to students for further exploration. Make a brainstormed list of 20–30 subtopics students might think of. For one of these subtopics, list questions you would like to answer. Make an outline to guide your information search and synthesis.

Locating Information

For You as Student

You are now off to the library to try to gather information related to your topic. On your way to the library, think about sources where you are apt to find information. Books contain information, of course; and though there may not be an entire book written on your topic, there are apt to be sections of books that apply. For the topic "Improving meaning vocabulary in biology," for example, you will probably want to consult current textbooks on secondary or content-area reading. You may also want to consult current textbooks on science methods. In looking for information about science and meaning vocabulary, you will consult the index and table of contents of these books. So, on your arrival at the library, you will proceed directly to the card catalog. As you know, the card catalog is indexed by book author, title, and subject. Since you don't know which particular titles or authors you are looking for, you will consult the *subject index*, looking under appropriate headings (Reading — Secondary, Vocabulary, Science — Teaching, for example). For those books you wish to look at, you will record on an index card the library call number and all other essential information. If you are going to prepare a bibliography to accompany your report, you will probably want to enter the reference citation on the index card in the proper style so that you can have your bibliography typed directly from the accumulated cards. As you find each book, you will record information pertinent to your topic on this card. You will also make additional reference cards by checking through the sources listed in the books you found in your preliminary card catalog search.

Next, you might proceed to the encyclopedias. It may surprise you to learn that encyclopedias are not just multivolume sets of books about "every subject under the sun," such as you remember from your earliest library experiences. There are all kinds of specialized encyclopedias. Many are one- or two-volume encyclopedias, which are updated every five or ten years. Two encyclopedic works you ought to check if you are doing research related to education are the *Encyclopedia of Educational Research* and the *Second Handbook of Research on Teaching*. Using the index of these and other encyclopedias, you can find concise descriptions of the "state of the art" that serve as overviews and organizers for your research.

There are two other major sources of information: articles in professional journals and microfiche. Professional journals, like special-interest magazines, are published several times a year, are focused on a particular subject and readership, and contain articles written by qualified professionals in the field. The major reading journal devoted almost exclusively to middle/secondary school reading is the *Journal of Reading*. Many other reading journals, however, contain some articles on middle/secondary school reading. There are also journals in the various special content areas (*English Journal*, *The Science Teacher*, *Mathematics Teacher*, and *Social Education*, for example), which occasionally have articles on developing reading skills in each of those areas. Other journals (e.g., *Today's Education*, *NASSP Bulletin*) also have occasional reading-education articles. With so many different journals in which articles related to your topic might be found, you must have a systematic way to seek out articles likely to be of interest. Fortunately, there exist two major indexes of education-related articles: *Education Index* and *CIJE* (*Current Index to Journals in Education*).

Education Index is published monthly in paperback; each year's issues are then combined into hardback volumes. It has both a subject and an author index; in the former, articles in hundreds of education-related journals are listed under appropriate subject headings. Similar to *Education Index*, *CIJE* also contains a short abstract (summary) of each article. When using *Education Index* and *CIJE*, it is most expedient to make up an index card with the call number and bibliographical information for each article you wish to find. Beginning with the most recent volumes and searching back five years is probably sufficient for ordinary purposes. Most major articles published more than five years ago will be cited in the reference lists of more recent articles.

The knowledge explosion has resulted in a new source of information to be searched for education-related topics — microfiche. Microfiche is a small sheet of microfilm that can contain up to 60 pages of text. In 1965 the U.S. Office of Education founded ERIC (Educational Resources Information Center) which publishes *RIE* (*Resources in Education*), a monthly index and abstract of papers presented at conferences, reports of ongoing research studies, and reports of projects sponsored by local, state, and federal agencies. Much of this information is practical teacher-oriented material that will never appear in professional journals. In *RIE*, one can read a fairly detailed abstract. Many libraries now have collections of microfiche accessible to the reader who needs more information than is contained in the abstract. (Microfiche can also be ordered from ERIC.) While there is much current and often practical information contained in the *RIE* system, one caution should be given. Most professional journals are refereed; that is, the articles appearing in them have been reviewed and selected by members of an editorial advisory board composed of persons knowledgeable in the special field covered by the journal. *RIE* is not refereed. Consequently, mixed in with the valid, the well-thought-out and well-written, will be some "garbage." Critical reading skills are especially called for when reading *RIE* documents. Let the reader beware!

A final valuable source for the information seeker is the *Bibliographic Index*, a handy reference that lists by subject bibliographies which have been published separately or as parts of books or journals. All references included comprise at least 50 citations. A student who can locate a recent bibliography is way ahead in tracking down relevant resources.

For You as Teacher

Now, put your teacher hat back on and prepare to teach your students how to locate resources in the library. Your school librarian should assist you with this part of the study skills instruction. Most school librarians will be so delighted that you are willing to share the responsibility for teaching these essential skills that they will go out of their way to help you and your students! Basically, there are three types of materials your students need to know how to locate and use: (1) expository books, (2) magazines, and (3) basic reference works such as encyclopedias, atlases, almanacs, and dictionaries. While there are many ways of organizing this instruction in methods of locating sources, the following one-week plan is workable for most teachers:

MONDAY: Accompany your students to the library and have the librarian (or you yourself!) explain to them the major reference works other than the card catalog and the *Readers' Guide*. This process will be more meaningful if the librarian selects one of the topics being researched by the students and shows the students how to find information about this topic. (If you pick the topic of a less able student, he or she will be off to a flying start!) The several sets of encyclopedias available in most middle/secondary school libraries should be shown, and students should be told which are easier to read. (*The World Book Encyclopedia* is one of the easiest and most interesting. The difficulty of reading level increases as you read on in each entry; most opening portions of *World Book* articles are written at fourth-grade reading level! *Compton's Encyclopedia* is quite readable and contains many pictures with easy-to-read captions. *Britannica Junior* is easier than the *Encyclopaedia Britannica*, which is a more scholarly source. Its valuable information on many topics should be sought out by advanced students.)

In addition to the large multivolume encyclopedias, there are many one- or two-volume encyclopedias organized around a specialized topic. Students may be astonished to discover such intriguing resources as the *Encyclopedia of Auto Racing Greats*, *The Encyclopedia of Witchcraft and Demonology*, and *Bloodletters and Badmen* (American criminals). Other less curious specialized encyclopedias, such as *The Encyclopedia of Physics* and *Twentieth Century Authors*, are also available.

In addition to *The World Almanac*, most libraries contain the *Information Please Almanac* and *The People's Almanac*. *The Guinness Book of World Records* is a source of constant fascination to school-age and adult readers. In addition to the standard unabridged dictionaries, most libraries contain specialized dictionaries such as *Grove's Dictionary of Music and Musicians* and *Who Was Who in American Politics*. Other specialized multivolume sets include the *Scientific American Resource Library* (reprints from *Scientific American* in the earth sciences, life sciences, physical sciences and technology, psychology, and social sciences) and Time-Life's *This Fabulous Century* (eight volumes depicting the twentieth century in pictures and words).

In order for the whole class to see these sources and how a bibliographic index card is prepared for each source, you and the librarian may share the roles of displayer and cardmaker. The displayer uses an opaque projector to show the students how information is located by using the index and/or table of contents for each source and then to show the students the actual target pages. The cardmaker uses an overhead projector and writes down the essential information for each source. For each different type of reference, students make "model" cards, which they can later refer to when making their own set of cards. At the end of Monday's lesson, the whole class should know what reference books are available, where these are, how to locate the information once they have the book, and how to make cards for each reference. (That is a lot for one day, and if your students are especially unprepared, Monday's assignment might extend to Tuesday or even Wednesday!)

TUESDAY (or the day after completing the "Monday" activity): Divide your class into thirds. One-third will use this day to locate information in references shown yesterday and to make reference cards for their topic. Another third will go with you or the librarian to the card catalog and learn to use it efficiently. The final third will go with you or the librarian to learn to use the *Readers'*

Guide. (Many middle/secondary school libraries have the *Abridged Readers'
Guide to Periodical Literature*. This is set up just like the unabridged edition
but indexes fewer magazines, generally those most likely to be found in
middle/secondary schools.) Learning to use the card catalog and the *Readers'
Guide* to locate sources is a complex task that involves a variety of alphabetiz-
ing, key-word, abbreviations-reading, and indexing skills. Working with a
small group of nine or ten students, the teacher or librarian can let students
"crowd around" and observe closely just how to find the source, make the
reference, track down the right book or magazine, and find the information in
that source once it is in hand. After the students have observed this procedure
being modeled, they can then try to locate sources about their own topic. With
only nine or ten students, the teacher or librarian can provide on-the-spot
assistance and advise them individually.

WEDNESDAY AND THURSDAY: Switch groups so that all three groups have one
day to work with the encyclopedias and other standard reference books, one
day of supervised work with the card catalog, and one day of directed work
with the *Readers' Guide*.

FRIDAY: By now, the students should have located many sources and have made
many reference cards. Let them try to complete this locating process on Friday.
Provide individual help to students who need it, and check that reference cards
contain all essential information in the proper form. Review and reteach as
needed. Some students may begin making notes on what they have read if they
have located all their sources. Observe their reading and note-taking skills, and
you will get some notion of their needs for the next large block of instruction,
"reading and note taking."

Reading and Note Taking

For You as Student

Once you have located sources relevant to your chosen topic, your next major
task is to read and make notes on those sources. Since your time is undoubtedly
limited, you will want to do this in the most efficient manner possible. It is not
efficient to begin with the first word of an article or chapter and read along at
the same speed until you finish that selection. You may end up, after that large
investment of time, deciding the information was not really relevant after all or
realizing you already had that information. As you read information you think
might be pertinent, try this strategy:

1. Scan the selection by reading the headings, any graphics (maps,
    charts, graphs, tables, diagrams, or pictures), and the summary para-
    graph or paragraphs. If information appears irrelevant or redundant,
    put that source aside and go on to scan the next. If the information it
    contains appears relevant and not already known, proceed to step 2.
2. Skim the entire selection to get a general idea of what each section
    covers by reading the first and last sentence of each paragraph and
    just glancing at the rest of the paragraph. As you skim, make a mental
    note of which paragraphs you want to reread carefully.

3. Reread those paragraphs which seem most relevant and interesting.
4. Look at the outline you made and think about which subtopic the information you've read is most closely related to. Write that subtopic on your reference card. Without looking back at the information read, note down the important facts. You may do this in brief note, outline, or paragraph form, depending on which you prefer and the type of information you are recording. Refer to the original source only to check specific details or to copy a direct quote. (Quotes should be avoided unless necessary to convey the sense of what is being said. When you do quote, be sure to copy it exactly and to note the page numbers.) When you have made your notes, reread the applicable section and add or correct information as needed.
5. If the source you are reading contains information relevant to more than one subtopic, make a separate card for each. Put enough bibliographical information on *each* card so that you will know which reference is being cited on each. If information appears important but does not fit any of your subtopics, put it on a card labeled "General," "Miscellaneous," or simply "Fascinating."
6. Think about the information you have just recorded. Do you agree with it? Does it agree with other information you have read? Do you detect any bias? Do you have any personal experience that would confirm or deny what you have read? If it is a teaching strategy, do you think it would work? Under the heading "ME" on your card, note your own thoughts or opinions.

Repeat this step-by-step procedure for each of your sources. Time spent doing this will be more than repaid when you get to that final onerous step — writing the paper.

For You as Teacher

Your task now is to teach your students how to read and take notes. As in the other steps of teaching study skills, the most effective teaching strategy seems to be a combination of modeling and providing guidance as the students practice. You may want to have the whole class practice reading and taking notes on the same selection before you turn them loose in the library with the selections relating to their individual topics. Choose some informative material of which you have multiple copies, so that each student or pair of students can read the same piece at the same time. Make an outline about the topic. In choosing the material to be read and making the outline, divide the material into several sections. Then, so that students will have an opportunity to see that some material is not relevant and should be ignored once it is scanned, purposefully exclude from your outline some subtopics covered in the material. Also, try to choose selections with some graphic material (maps, charts, graphs, tables, diagrams, and/or pictures) so that you may guide students in interpreting such graphic data.

Begin the lesson by displaying the outline you have constructed and explaining to students that you are going to show them a system for reading and taking notes which will save them time in the long run and make writing the report or paper a much easier task. Make sure each student or pair of students (pairs may make the lessons go more smoothly, as partners teach each other) has the material to be read. Display a chart on which you have written the six steps to be followed: (1) scan; (2) skim; (3) reread; (4) notes for one subtopic; (5) notes for other subtopics; and (6) ME. Next to each, leave spaces to write in specifics about what to do in each step.

Select a section of the material to be read, and model for the students what is to be done for each step. As you complete each step, ask students to describe what you did and what reminders should be included on the chart next to that step. As you do each step, talk through what you are doing. Your dialogue for the scanning step, for instance, might sound like this:

> Okay, now I'm going to scan this selection to see if it relates to what I have on my outline. I am going to read each heading and look at every graphic as I go along. Okay, first heading, "Civil War Breaks Out," then "States Choose Sides." Aha! Here is a map of the states. I can see by reading this legend at the bottom that the gray states are Confederate and the blue are Union; the checkered states are undecided or neutral. Now a heading, "Brother Against Brother," and a picture of an unhappy mother. . . .

When you have completed modeling the scanning process, students should be able to tell you to record such information as (1) read all headings; (2) read all graphics; and (3) read the summary paragraph or legend on the chart. Continue this modeling and talking aloud about what you are doing for each of the six steps. As you model each step, stop and talk with the students about what you have done. Have them tell you in their own words what details to add next to each step on the chart.

FOR THE READER TO DO:

Make the chart described above, recording for each step the important points as you think students might remember them. Refer to steps 1–6 at the beginning of this section as you make this chart.

Next, lead the students through the steps on the chart. Stop after each step and talk about what they have done and why. The *why* is especially important, because the answers to that question will allow the students who understand the process to explain to those who don't what "goes on inside their heads." "Why did you decide this section was relevant to our outline?" "Why did you decide to read those two paragraphs?" "Why did you decide to put that in quotations?" and other "Why . . .?" questions will allow everyone to explore how this complex process of sifting and selecting, omitting and synthesizing, happens.

Also, as you proceed through the sections, discuss with the students the graphics that appear there. Graphics are placed in textbooks and magazines at substantial expense to the publisher because they are *supposed* to aid the reader in understanding the text. They do aid — but only if you can interpret them. Be sure your students are exposed to many kinds of graphs (bar, line, and pie graphs and pictographs are most common), charts, maps, tables, diagrams, and pictures. Take time to discuss each type and explain in words what it means. Pay particular attention to legends, symbols, and abbreviations. A bonus of this "graphics" instruction is that your poorer readers, once they know how to interpret them, can get a great deal of information from graphic aids even when they cannot plow through a lengthy or difficult text.

Provide students with much practice in actual note taking. Demonstrate for them how notes can be in brief comment, outline, or narrative form. After students have taken notes on a section, select someone who has taken concise, well-worded notes of the most important facts to transcribe them on the overhead projector. Ignore the expected students' protests and require them to take notes first without looking at the source, then to look back only to check for forgotten or incorrect details. Once they have learned to do this, they will never again be tempted to copy every other sentence in full.

Reading and note taking is a complex process that must be deliberately viewed by the teacher and students *as a process*. A process is something you learn to do and get better at as you do it but never do perfectly; there is no *right* way to do it. If you and your students can be *process*-oriented rather than *product*-oriented as you practice reading and note-taking skills, the students will undoubtedly get better at it. Progress, not perfection, must be the goal of this instruction. If the material you selected for them to practice reading and taking notes on is also material you want to cover with them, your reading/note-taking practice time will have been well spent, since they will surely have mastered that content by having studied it in the described manner.

When the students demonstrate some facility in reading and note taking, return to the library with them and the six-step chart for work on their chosen topics. Let them find their reference sources and practice the six steps as they make notes for their own paper or report. You and the librarian can provide individual help as needed.

Preparing the Paper or Report

For You as Student

If you have followed the approach and specific steps as outlined in this chapter, you won't believe how much easier the next paper you write will be compared to papers you have already done. Begin by taking your outline and, based on the information you have found, revising it. Sort out your note cards according to the subtopic each relates to. Gather up a dictionary, a handbook of grammar and punctuation, and a style manual and begin to write. First write a general introduction that tells what you intend to say and why. (Many of your "General," "Fascinating," or "Miscellaneous" cards may fit in here or else in the summary at the end.) Discuss each subtopic by referring to the notes you have on the cards for that subtopic. Your "ME" comments may follow the discussion based on that actual source or may come at the end of each subtopic. In conclusion, write a summary that reviews for your reader the major points you have made. (A renowned preacher credits his preaching success to the fact that he "tells them what he is going to tell them, then tells them, then tells them what he told them." Hence everyone leaves his church with a feeling of satisfaction and understanding.) Your bibliography can be easily completed by arranging the reference cards you have compiled in the manner prescribed by the style manual you are using and then typing the essential information from them in list form.

For You as Teacher

It is now time for your students to organize and prepare their reports. The form the report will take (brief oral or written report, "term paper," radio interview with a famous person, "You Are There" dramatization, debate, or other) should depend on the sophistication of your students. The specific instruction you provide for them will be determined by what form their reports will take. Regardless of the eventual form, however, the organizing and synthesizing process will be much simplified by having separate note cards for each subtopic. Lead the students in taking their original outline and modifying it according to the information they have been able to find. Show them how their "General," "Fascinating," and "Miscellaneous" cards can often supply interesting introductory and summary material. Provide them with modeling and practice in putting together the information from the cards for one subtopic. If a bibliography, footnote, or any other "exotic" appendage is required, be sure to provide students with a format for this and plan for a modeling practice session. Showing students how to use a dictionary to check spelling and capitalization, a handbook for grammar and punctuation conventions, and an editorial style manual furnishes them with useful tools — if they are ready to use such tools.

As you finish this chapter, you are probably thinking about what a complex task it is to master these "study skills," and about the investment of time and energy you will have to make in order to teach your students how to use reading to investigate and synthesize information about a topic. Think, for a moment, about your own study skills and how you learned them. If one or more of your middle/secondary school teachers had taken the time and made the effort to teach you the skills outlined in this chapter, would it have helped you? Study skills instruction is a part of reading instruction that must be carried out during the middle/secondary school years, since few students have enough sophistication in reading and writing to learn these skills during their elementary school years. The amount of time and energy that must be invested in acquiring them is large. But the return on that investment in your classroom in later months, and in all classrooms in later years, is equally large!

As a grand finale to this chapter, here is a list of questions (made up by students in middle/secondary reading methods courses) for evaluating and enhancing students' ability to locate information quickly and efficiently. These questions can be used before or after instruction in locating sources. A group-race format for finding the answers makes the process fun as well as instructional.

How Efficiently Can You Locate Information?

(Questions can be answered by sources found in most middle/secondary school libraries. Answers and possible sources are included.)

1. What is the capital and area of Jamaica?
   Kingston; 4,232 square miles
   (e.g., world atlas)

2. Which American presidents died on the fiftieth anniversary of the Declaration of Independence?
   John Adams and Thomas Jefferson
   (e.g., encyclopedia; almanac)

3. What was on the cover of *Newsweek* the week it contained an article entitled "Giscard's Soft Sell"?
   Caricatures of Ronald Reagan and Gerald Ford
   (e.g., *Readers' Guide; Newsweek*)

4. When was the composer of the oratorio *The Messiah* born?
   February 23, 1685
   (e.g., encyclopedia)

5. Where and when was the first child ever conceived outside its mother's body born?
   Oldham, England; July 25, 1978
   (e.g., *World Almanac*)

6. For what work did Ned Rorem receive a Pulitzer Prize in 1976?
   Air Music
   (e.g., *World Almanac*)

7. Of the many honors and offices held by Thomas Jefferson, which one does not appear on his tombstone?
   President of the United States
   (e.g., Jefferson biography)

8. What does the word "mollycoddle" mean? List three noun synonyms and three verb synonyms.
   1, *n.* a pampered darling; a spineless weakling; 2, *vt.* to treat with fond indulgence; to protect and cater to. Synonyms: *n.,* weakling, jellyfish, milksop; *v.,* baby, cater (to), humor
   (e.g., dictionary; thesaurus)

9. When and where was Doris June Waugh Betts born?
   Statesville, N.C.; June 4, 1932
   (e.g., *Who's Who in America*)

10. How far apart (miles) are Rollins College and Stetson University?
    30 miles
    (e.g., atlas; dictionary)

11. What is the capital of the state that *first* gave women the right to vote?
    Cheyenne, Wyoming
    (e.g., encyclopedia)

12. We are in the midst of a plastic surgery boom. Approximately how many such operations were performed in 1976?
    Approximately 1 million
    (e.g., *Readers' Guide*)

13. Josquin Des Prez, a great musician, is famous for what Mass?
    Pange Lingua Mass
    (e.g., *Grove's Dictionary of Music and Musicians*)

14. When was the first outbreak of Legionnaire's disease?
    Summer 1976, after American Legion convention in Philadelphia
    (e.g., *Readers Guide*)

15. During what dynasty or period did Confucianism become the state philosophy in China?
    During the Han Dynasty, 136 B.C.
    (e.g., encyclopedia)

16. Who holds the all-time, career, home-run record in major league baseball?
    Henry Aaron
    (e.g., *World Almanac*; encyclopedia)

17. What is the mythical county in Mississippi that William Faulkner created in his major literary works?
    Yoknapatawpha
    (e.g., biography of Faulkner; *Encyclopedia of World Literature in the 20th Century*)

18. Where was the Magna Carta signed?
    Runnymede
    (e.g., *World Almanac*)

19. Science fiction author Ray Bradbury claims that an ancestor who lived in Salem, Massachusetts in the 17th century may have influenced his writing career. Who was this ancestor?
    Mary Bradbury
    (e.g., *Twentieth Century Authors: A Biographical Dictionary of Modern Literature*)

20. What famous female made the cover of the first issue of *Ms.* magazine?
    Wonder Woman
    (e.g., *Readers' Guide; Ms.*)

21. What is the population of the city where the 1964 Olympics were held?
    11,622,651 (Tokyo)
    (e.g., encyclopedia; *World Almanac*)

22. What is the largest lake in Alabama?
    Guntersville
    (e.g., almanac)

23. Where are the islets of Langerhans?
    In the pancreas (cells that produce insulin)
    (e.g., encyclopedia)

24. Which are the five largest cities in the world?
    New York City, U.S.A.; Tokyo, Japan; Shanghai, China; Mexico City, Mexico; Paris, France
    (e.g., *World Almanac*)

25. In what county is Due West, South Carolina?
    Abbeville County
    (e.g., atlas)

26. What was Mark Twain's real name?
       Samuel Langhorne Clemens
       (e.g., encyclopedia; biography of Mark Twain)
27. Who was the first American Nobel Prize winner?
       Albert A. Michelson
       (e.g., encyclopedia; almanac)
28. What was the only major sport to originate in the United States?
       basketball
       (e.g., encyclopedia)
29. Who introduced lawn tennis into the United States?
       Mary E. Outerbridge
       (e.g., encyclopedia; tennis handbook; history of sports)
30. Where and when was the world's first successful nuclear power plant
    built?
       In a squash court under the west stands of Stagg Field at the
       University of Chicago
       (e.g., encyclopedia)

Unit Two
Reading in Content Areas

5 Content-Area Reading

ERHAPS NO ONE statement can engender so much resentment and hostility from secondary teachers as the oft-quoted "Every teacher is a teacher of reading." Secondary teachers are not reading teachers; they are science teachers or social studies teachers or career-education teachers or whatever. Attempts to make content-area teachers into reading teachers are doomed to fail because content-area teachers know they have a full-time job in teaching their own content area. The thesis of this and the following three chapters is that content-area teachers are *not* teachers of reading. They are teachers of their content areas. Reading is used by content area teachers to facilitate the students' mastery of that content. In fact, reading might be thought of as a "chest of tools." Specific reading and vocabulary skills are the individual tools in the chest. Each content-area subject requires specialized reading tools. The content-area teacher who assures that students can use the specific reading tools needed to master that content area is not a reading teacher but a "cost-efficient" content-area teacher. Time invested in assuring that students can adroitly use reading tools equals greater output of content-area learning. The content-area teacher does not "give up" part of the teaching time to teach some reading; rather, reading is "used" to teach more content.

The content-area teacher who wishes to use reading to "sneak in" more content learning has three major concerns: Can my students read the material I want to use to teach them? What technical and multimeaning vocabulary tools do they need? What special "reading tools" do they need?

Can My Students Read the Material?

As most teachers have observed, some textbooks and supplementary materials are harder to read than others. An "eleventh-grade textbook" does not necessarily mean that book is *written* at the eleventh-grade level; in fact, the eleven associated with a textbook generally means only that the book is written to be used in a course *taught* at the eleventh-grade level. The readability of the book might be considerably below or (more often) above the specified grade level. In many books, especially in books that are a collection of primary sources or of readings by various authors, readability may vary greatly from selection to selection within the book.

But what does readability mean? How do you determine the readability of a book? Many factors interact to make a book more or less readable. How interesting, up-to-date, and relevant a book is affects its readability. Whether the material is narrative or expository affects readability. The length and complexity of the sentences is an important factor. Language that is highly metaphorical seems more difficult to read. The number and frequency of long, unusual, or unfamiliar words that occur is also a factor.

When a book is reported to be at a particular readability level, however, the reader can assume that one of the many readability formulas has been used to compute its readability. These readability formulas generally consider two variables: (1) sentence length and (2) the number of long or unfamiliar words. A book that has been determined as being at the eleventh-grade level will generally have longer sentences and more long or unfamiliar words than a book computed to be at the ninth-grade level.

The Fry readability graph (Fry, 1977) has probably been most widely used by teachers. Raygor (1977) devised a readability graph in which the number of letters, rather than the number of syllables, is used to determine long words. Baldwin and Kaufman (1979) demonstrated that results obtained using the Raygor graph correlated well with results obtained using the Fry graph and that the Raygor graph was simpler and faster to use. (The Raygor readability graph and instructions are reproduced here with the kind permission of Alton L. Raygor.)

While it may be helpful to know the readability of a particular book, knowing that readability does not generally tell the teacher whether or not a particular group of students will be able to read the book. A book with a tenth-grade readability level that is intended for an eleventh-grade class may still be too difficult for a class in which most of the students actually read at seventh-grade level. In order to determine if a group of students can read a particular book, a teacher must put the book and the students together and see what happens! There are essentially two ways of doing this. The simplest and quickest way to determine whether students can read a book is to construct a *cloze passage* from a section of that book, have the students complete this cloze passage, score their completed passages, and use the established percentages to see whether they can read it. (Explicit directions for constructing and scoring cloze passages are found in Appendix A.)

A way that takes a little longer, which is less "scientific" but perhaps more accurate, is for the teacher to sit down for five minutes with each student, have the student read a paragraph or two aloud, and then ask him or her to explain what has just been read. Students for whom a certain book is too difficult will be readily identifiable, for they will stumble over *many* words and/or be unable to give a reasonable summary of what they have read. (Miss Tent demonstrates this strategy on pages 134-135.)

THE RAYGOR READABILITY ESTIMATE
ALTON L. RAYGOR—UNIVERSITY OF MINNESOTA

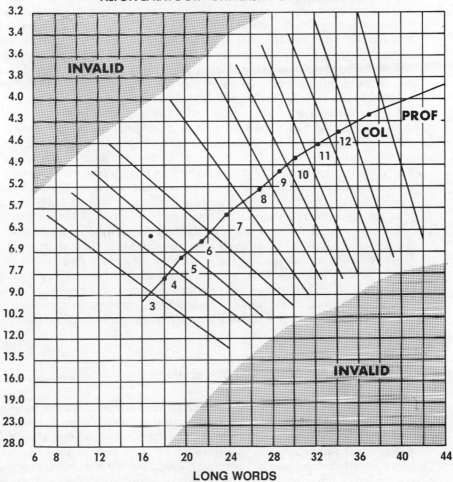

LONG WORDS

Directions:

Count out three 100-word passages near the beginning, middle, and end of a selection or book. Count proper nouns, but not numerals.

1. Count sentences in each passage, estimating to nearest tenth.
2. Count words with six or more letters.
3. Average the sentence length and word length over the three samples and plot the average on the graph.

Example:

	Sentences	6+ Words
A	6.0	15
B	6.8	19
C	6.4	17
Total	19.2	51
Average	6.4	17

Note mark on graph. Grade level is about 5.

Once the teacher has an estimate of which students can and cannot read a particular book, instruction based on that information can be planned. If a book is too hard for a majority of the students in a class, the students will not learn the content from using that book no matter how hard they try or study. The teacher who finds him/herself in this unfortunate (but not unusual) situation had best go looking for an easier text or some easier supplementary material or else prepare to do a lot of instruction in which the students view, listen, do, interact, and learn the content in this way.

In many classes, the teacher will find that many students can read the textbook and some cannot. The strategy of using a number of different texts and assigning general topics for reading and discussion is a good solution if this approach is feasible. Pairing a student who can't read the text with a friend who will read it to him or her works well for some teachers. Grouping the students into two groups and allowing those who can, to read the assigned parts of the text while the teacher gives instruction to the others, also works well. (See pages 122, 140 for a translation writing lesson in which students who cannot read the text construct their own "translated" text.)

Even those students who can read the text generally need instruction in the special vocabulary and reading skills needed for a particular content-area textbook. Reading an account of the Civil War requires a type of reading that would be totally inappropriate and unproductive when reading a chemistry experiment or an explanation in a mathematics text. Each subject has its own special vocabulary. Understanding and applying appropriate meanings for this vocabulary are essential if content-area learning is to be accomplished.

Teaching Technical and Multimeaning Vocabulary

There has been much research evidence to support the common sense notion that vocabulary knowledge is a major factor in reading comprehension. In general, students who have large vocabularies are better readers than students whose vocabularies are limited. Even students with large general vocabularies, however, are hampered when reading about a subject that has its own special vocabulary. Each content area has its own stock of vocabulary that is peculiar to it. Each content-area teacher must teach students to use with ease and facility the vocabulary tools needed in that content area.

Many content-area teachers, however, have difficulty in determining which words are special and peculiar to their content area. To the teacher who knows the subject so well, the "special" words have become "general" words. Herber (1978) suggests that teachers begin each unit by doing a content analysis of the essential information to be learned. Each concept to be mastered is listed, and then under each concept, all vocabulary essential to learning that concept is listed. Herber suggests that *all* essential vocabulary be listed, even if it appears to the teacher that much of it may already be known to the students. The teacher then spends time at the beginning of each unit teaching this essential vocabulary. Any vocabulary that is already known can be reviewed quickly, and most of the time can then be spent on vocabulary that is not known. (For an example of a content analysis, see pages 135-137.)

In identifying vocabulary that students must know in order to understand the concepts, teachers should be especially alert to words which have a general meaning but which are used in a specialized way in the particular content area being taught. Often, there is a link between the general and the specialized meaning that students do not generally see. In teaching multimeaning vocabulary terms, it is helpful to students if the teacher can help them discover the link between the two or more definitions. This makes learning the specialized meaning easier because it can be related to something already known. (On page 29, some ways of teaching multimeaning vocabulary are suggested.)

When teaching vocabulary, teachers should keep in mind that one definition for a word is almost never sufficient for learning that word thoroughly. Whether the student looks up the word and writes out a definition or the teacher hands out a prepared list of definitions, such passive reading of a definition does not fully teach the word. Words become meaningful to students when used in meaningful contexts several times. Under the different content-area headings in this and the next three chapters, suggestions will be made for teaching vocabulary in ways that render it usable and useful to the students.

Teaching the "Reading Tools" Essential to Each Content Area

FOR THE READER TO DO:

Gather together books from as many different content areas as you can find. Also, gather some novels, newspapers, and magazines. Examine these materials and try to determine the different reading skills required by the different kinds of reading materials. Does a mathematics text require students to follow a plot? Does a history text require reading to follow directions? Does a science text require a knowledge of characterization? In which books is the reading of diagrams an essential tool? Which books require the reader to be able to read bar graphs? flow charts? formulas? Try to list at least one essential reading tool for each type of material that is not essential for the others.

As carrying out the above activity will make evident, different content-area textbooks do require different reading tools. If a student is studying a content area for the first time or has never been given instruction in using the reading tools for a particular content area, it would be absurd to expect that student to know how to use those particular reading tools. In the following sections, the reading tools needed in each content area will be discussed. Teaching strategies for assuring that students can use these tools are briefly described in each section and then further elaborated in the next three chapters.

Reading in Mathematics Classes

To the uninformed, it might appear that a mathematics class would be the one place where a student's reading ability would not affect performance in the subject area. A glance at some mathematics texts, however, should soon convince you otherwise. Robinson (1975) defines three types of reading commonly found in and required by mathematics texts: (1) concept development; (2) principle development; and (3) problem solving.

Concept development refers to the development of meaning for a word or group of words (for example, *diameter, empty set, parallelogram*). For the mathematics teacher, concept development may be considered synonymous with teaching meaning vocabulary. Principles are generalizations that depend on the understanding of a number of concepts. Postulates, theorems, laws, and rules are examples of mathematical principles. Most mathematics texts contain explanatory sections on these principles. The most generally accepted intersection between reading and mathematics occurs in the solution of word problems. Students who do not read carefully and critically are often unable to solve word problems successfully even if they are able to perform the mathematical operations required.

FOR THE READER TO DO:

Select a mathematics textbook. Choose a chapter in that book and divide the prose material into four categories: concept development, principle development, problem solving, and other. What do you discover about the reading requirements of mathematics textbooks?

There are many activities a mathematics teacher can do with his/her students to improve their reading of mathematics materials. These activities will be discussed under three general headings: Teaching the Vocabulary of Mathematics, Walking the Students Through the Text, and Solving Word Problems.

Teaching the Vocabulary of Mathematics

Mathematics has a technical vocabulary that is unique to it, as well as a vocabulary which is used in a special way in mathematics but which also has a general meaning. *Diameter, parallelogram,* and *addend* are part of the technical mathematics vocabulary. *Problem, product,* and *root* are examples of everyday words that have a special meaning when used in a mathematics context. Effective reading of mathematics texts requires that students have clear, definitive meanings associated with both types of essential mathematics vocabulary. A mathematics teacher who wants to ensure that students have mastered that essential vocabulary will begin by identifying those words which are essential to a student's understanding and then giving direct instruction concerning them. There are many effective ways to give direct instruction in this vocabulary. A few to start with are:

1. Teach all mathematical symbols essential to understanding. Be sure that students can translate $<$ into its verbal counterpart "is less than." $\sqrt{16}$ must be read as the "square root of 16." 106,348 must be read as "one hundred six thousand, three hundred forty-eight." Construct exercises in which students must match symbols with their translation.

2. Have students make "memory cards" for essential terms. The word, phrase, or symbol is put on one side. On the back the student writes a definition and includes an example or a picture to aid memory. If all students have cards for the same words, many games can be played to review these words.

3. Make sure students know the specialized mathematical meaning for common words. Have students identify common words and state both their common and mathematical definitions.

4. Put the essential vocabulary "right under their noses." Select a word or symbol each day, and write it on a card. Develop meaning for that word through definition, example, and illustration. Tape the card to the wall or bulletin board. Try to remember to refer to this card whenever the word or symbol recurs in subsequent units.

5. Do a structured overview with related vocabulary. Create a diagram showing the relationship of various words and symbols to one another. Build the diagram with the students. Leave the diagram displayed as an aid to memory. (See page 137 for a step-by-step procedure for teaching a structured overview.)

6. When teaching a word that has a common affix or base word, teach the meaning of that word part. Knowing that *centi-* refers to *hundred* helps the student remember what a centimeter is and later aids in establishing a meaning for *centigrade*. If a student learns the meaning of *poly-* while learning the word *polygon, polynomial* will be learned more easily and remembered longer.

7. Teach context clues to meaning. Often in a mathematics text, new words are defined by the context in which they are used. This contextual definition is often directly stated: "A tetrahedron is. . . ." Illustrations often accompany this definition. Students should learn to look for these textual definitions and study carefully the accompanying illustrations. If an illustration is not provided, students should attempt to draw the figure described if a concrete illustration is feasible.

Walking the Students Through the Text

Reading a mathematics textbook is a very different process from reading the narrative "story" material most students are accustomed to. Each word, symbol, and numeral contains important information, which is usually not repeated elsewhere. A mathematical sentence such as:

$$20\% = \frac{1}{5}$$

takes only as much space as the words *run over*, but it takes considerably longer to read. This can be demonstrated by writing out the sentence:

Twenty percent equals one-fifth

$11^2 = 121$ must be read as *eleven squared equals one hundred twenty-one*.

Demonstrating the difference between the space required to write a sentence in mathematical symbols and that necessary to write it in words will often help students accept the fact that reading a page in a mathematics book will take longer than reading a page of similar length in a novel or a history text. Most students, however, are neither willing nor able to lead themselves through the slow, careful reading required for the explanatory sections of mathematics textbooks. Teachers can lead the students through the text materials in ways that force this slow, careful reading. Here are some suggestions for "walking the students through the text":

1. Teach students to interpret visual materials. Charts, graphs, diagrams, and illustrations are included in most mathematics textbooks to elucidate the written word. Unfortunately, many students tend to skip these graphic displays. When beginning a new section of text, *first* have students examine all graphics and see how much information they can gain from the graphics alone. Individually or as a class, have the students list what they think they have learned from the graphics. Then read the related prose material to verify what was learned from the graphics.

2. Help students set purposes for their reading. If a section is titled "Parallelograms," students should come up with questions such as: "What is a parallelogram?" "Is a square a parallelogram?" "How is the area of a parallelogram determined? These questions should be listed, and after reading the section, students should determine which questions were answered in the section read.

3. Have students read mathematics material with a pencil and scratch paper at hand. Important formulas should be noted. Definitions of unknown terms should be jotted down. Figures alluded to should be drawn. Writing, figuring, and drawing while reading assures a careful, deliberate study of the material.

These and other "walking through" strategies will aid the reader to comprehend and retain mathematical explanations only to the extent that students use them in their reading of mathematical text. Showing the students how to read the text probably will not result in their using a different, more appropriate writing style in making notes on their reading of a mathematics text. Demonstrating these "walking through" strategies again and again, however, each time a new section is to be read, will result in changing the students' approach to reading mathematical material. For their newly discovered careful, deliberate reading skills to become automatic, students should be walked through the materials as often as necessary.

Solving Word Problems

Ask any adult what they hated about math classes, and chances are you will get the answer "Word problems." Solving word problems requires very careful reading and interpretation, as well as a knowledge of mathematical formulas and operations and ability with precise calculation. In order to solve word problems, the reader must understand the meaning of the vocabulary used. Even if you can add and divide, you cannot find a batting average unless you are sure what an *average* is. Knowing how many pounds are in a ton, or decimeters in a meter, is essential to solving word problems containing these terms. Thus, the teaching of essential vocabulary is a must for successful solution of word problems.

Understanding the essential vocabulary is necessary but not alone sufficient for successful solution of word problems, however. Students must also be able to read with comprehension in order to determine exactly what the question to be answered is. They must be able to grasp what facts are given and, in many cases, to ignore extraneous information. Students must then decide which mathematical operations are required and in what order. Only then can they successfully carry out the mathematical operations to get an answer.

The best solvers of mathematical word problems always have an estimate beforehand of what the answer should be, to which they can compare the eventual results of their calculations. If the answer and the estimate are far apart, the problem solver knows that he or she has probably gone astray somewhere.

Miss Tent (see p. 161) leads the mathematics teachers at Upton High through a seven-step strategy for solving word problems:

Step 1. Read to get an overview.
Step 2. What facts are given?
Step 3. What is the question?
Step 4. What mathematical operations must I use?
Step 5. In what order should I do the above operations?
Step 6. What is a reasonable estimate of the answer?
Step 7. Solve the problem; compare the answer to the estimate.

The mathematics teacher who wants to assure that students proceed through the solution of a word problem systematically will list these or other steps on a transparency. Each time word problems are to be assigned, students will be lead through the solution of several problems, with the instructor listing their responses to the seven steps on the transparency. While students may not write down their responses to the seven steps for all the assigned word problems, the thinking process required should become automatic with repetition.

Reading in Science Classes

In the words of a tenth-grader trying to plow through his biology text, "Biology is hard enough without having a book written in a foreign language." To many students, trying to comprehend a science textbook, with its abundance of foreign-sounding terms, is like trying to understand a foreign language. Consider the following example:

There are five common types of antibodies: opsonin, agglutinin, precipitin, lysin, and antitoxin. The opsonins soften up the special covering, or capsule, of certain bacterial antigens. This seems to make the antigens more palatable to the phagocytes. The agglutinins cause the antigens to clump, so that more antigens can be eaten at once. Others, the precipitins, change toxins into solids, so the toxins can be engulfed more easily. Still others, the lysins, dissolve and destroy the antigens. And the antitoxins change the toxins to nonpoisonous substances.[1]

[1]Smallwood, William L., and Edna R. Green. *Biology*. Morristown, N.J.: Silver Burdett Co., 1974, pp. 400–1.

This short paragraph is only one from an entire textbook written in a similar manner. To the nonscientist, it does indeed look like a foreign language!

What can the science teacher do to enable students, many of whom are good readers in more familiar narrative material, to read their science texts with understanding? There are many ways a science teacher can help students read science material, but the first step down the path to better science reading is the hardest. Science teachers must make decisions about what concepts are essential for the students to learn and then must limit their teaching and the students' reading to material designed to build those concepts.

Herber (1978) originated the idea that content-area teachers must begin their attempts to improve reading ability by doing a content analysis and then making the hard decision that you cannot teach it all! To do a content analysis of a chapter or section of a science textbook, a teacher should read that section and list from three to five concepts which students must learn from that section. Under each concept, all vocabulary essential to learning that concept is listed.

Once the content analysis has been done and the essential vocabulary is listed, the science teacher leads the students to read with comprehension by teaching them the essential vocabulary and guiding their reading of the essential portions of the textbook.

Teaching the "Foreign Language" of Science

Many of the suggestions made in the vocabulary part of the mathematics section also apply to science. Reading science requires that students read numerals, symbols, and words at the same time. It is essential that students know how the symbol is translated into words and what each symbol means. Making memory cards and displaying the essential vocabulary on the wall or in some other always-visible place are as effective and essential for the science class as in the mathematics class. Science, too, has affixes and root words that are used again and again, the meanings of which students should learn as they learn the word.

Structured overviews (Barron, 1969; Earle, 1969), diagrammatic representations of essential vocabulary and its interrelationships, are especially important in science, where much of the information involves subclasses of general classes and the interrelationship of these subclasses. If, for example, the science teacher had decided, while doing the content analysis, that the information contained in the paragraph about the five types of antibodies and their functions was an essential concept to be learned by all students, a structured overview drawn to teach the terms and their interrelationships might look like the drawing on the next page.

In presenting a structured overview to the students, the teacher plans the complete overview ahead of time but presents it to the students piecemeal. Each word is written on the board or chart (which can be displayed for constant reference and review), pronounced, defined, and discussed by the teacher as the students watch and, whenever possible, contribute to the definition and discussion.

Because many scientific terms have been borrowed from other languages, they are like words in a foreign language since students often cannot pro-

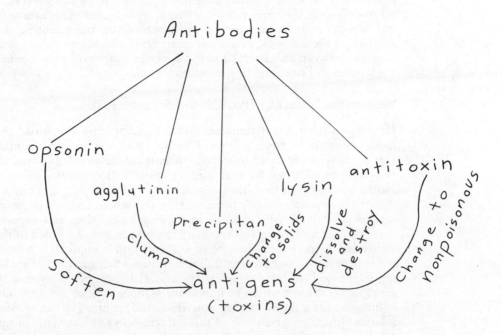

nounce them. While just pronouncing the words without building a meaning for them will not aid a student's understanding of the material read, students do need to know the correct pronunciation so that they can rehearse the information they are learning. (There is evidence that rehearsal is an auditory process. Consider the way you practice a telephone number you have just gotten from Directory Assistance while waiting for the line to get *un*busy!) Many science textbooks put a phonetic spelling of each new "foreign" term in parentheses immediately after its occurrence. Students should be taught how to use the key to pronounce the word, and instruction and practice should be devoted to this decoding skill early in the school year. Such practice will pay off as science students become gourmets (*gor*-MAYS) and connoisseurs (*kon-ə-*SERS) of scientific terminology. Teachers may also want to add these pronunciation aids to the words displayed on the wall or on charts. If a textbook you are using does not have such pronunciation aids, students can compile their own list of "foreign" terms and their pronunciations.

In addition to this direct teaching of vocabulary, science teachers will want to be sure their students can use the clues to meaning included in the textbook material. Pictures, diagrams, and other words in a sentence often illustrate and help define an unfamiliar term. Leading students to look in the textbooks themselves for the meaning of unfamiliar terms encourages them to become independent acquirers of new scientific vocabulary. (See the lessons on deriving vocabulary meanings through context taught by Miss Tent, pp. 131-134.)

Finally, the science teacher must be alert to general vocabulary used in a specialized way in the science curriculum. Many students who know what a *table* is do not know what a *water table* is. The term *energy* has some meaning for all students, but they may not know the accepted scientific meaning for energy nor see the connection between the general and the scientific definitions. Explaining the scientific definition to students and helping them see the relationship between the general and the scientific usage will promote better comprehension and retention of the material read.

Walking the Students Through the Science Text

Once the teacher has determined which concepts in a particular chapter are most important to teach and has identified and taught the vocabulary necessary for developing those concepts, students can be directed to read the particular sections of a chapter that contain information essential to the concepts. Nothing is more apt to confirm a student's lament that he "can't make head or tail of this science stuff" than assigning the whole chapter to be read. The teacher who makes this kind of broad assignment does not expect that the reader will comprehend and retain all the information included in the densely written chapter; nevertheless, most students find it impossible to sort out the really important from the trivial. Besides, the teacher has the advantage of having established (in mind at least) the essential concepts. Knowing these concepts makes determination of important sections a much simpler matter.

Imagine, for a moment, that you are a student in a secondary science class who has just been given one of those thick, heavy books with full pages and small print. As the teacher is passing out books and recording their inventory numbers, you begin to look through the book. There are some interesting topics and intriguing pictures, but for the most part, the book looks "really hard to read." Your teacher now gives you a general introduction to the first unit to be studied, does a structured overview with some related vocabulary and then proceeds to make the first homework assignment.

Next, to your amazement, you find yourself being led to peruse the titles, headings, pictures, graphs, and charts and to read the first and last paragraphs of sections. At the teacher's instruction, you close your book and write down what you have learned already. Though given only five minutes in which to do this, you fill half of a notebook page with scattered remembrances.

But the most amazing part of all is yet to come. Your teacher instructs the class to use their pencils ever so lightly to go through the text and put check marks next to certain sections. You are then guided to turn the heading for each of the sections checked into a question that you predict the section may answer. After you have practiced turning the headings of two sections into questions, have read those sections, and then closed the book and tried to recite what you were told in them (rereading when necessary), your teacher tells you that these checked sections contain the crucial information. "Read these sections very carefully," she instructs. "Take time to formulate questions from the headings, read the text, and then close your eyes and recite, rereading when necessary. As for the other sections, just read them adequately enough to follow the general train of thought from section to section. They, too, contain a lot of interesting information, but 'You can't learn it all, you know.' Tomorrow, we'll take some time to review the important sections."

The class bell rings, and as you leave the room, that new science book doesn't seem quite so heavy!

The strategy just described is a combination of "limited reading" and PQ4R (Preview, Question, Read, Reflect, Recite, and Review). Adapted by Thomas and Robinson (1977) from the SQ3R study techniques (Robinson, 1961), PQ4R helps students to read and study densely written material. (Miss Tent and Mr. Burner do some PQ4R lessons with his chemistry class; see pages 164-166 for the content and results of their experiment.)

Another useful teaching strategy for the science teacher is DR-TA (Directed Reading-Thinking Activity; Stauffer, 1969), which helps students to overview the sections to be read by scanning the title, headings, and all graphics. Students then make query predictions of what the text will be about, read to verify their predictions, make new predictions, and continue their active reading in this way (see pages 163-164).

Keeping in mind that students will read with comprehension and retention if they are familiar with the vocabulary, if the amount they must read carefully is judiciously delineated, and if they begin by interpreting all visuals, a teacher can develop many ways of leading students through the material.

Experimenting with Experiments

In the modern-day science class, only a portion of the learning occurs when the student and the teacher, or the student and the textbook, interact. Students learn concepts, as well as scientific processes, as they carry out activities and experiments in the laboratory setting. This laboratory experience requires reading of a different kind. Directions must be followed "to the letter" and in a given sequence. Measurements and calculations must be exact. Diagrams must be read and used to set up equipment. When a student scientist goes astray in the laboratory, it is often because he or she "read it wrong."

Thomas and Robinson (1977) report the results of some "how to read it" sessions conducted with high school science students. Students were given a reading guide, "A Scientist's Approach to Reading Laboratory Procedures," on which the steps for successfully reading and carrying out a science experiment were listed. Students were required to read the directions at least three times before beginning the experiment. The first reading is "once over lightly" to get a general idea of what will be done. During the second reading, the student is urged to read each step carefully and to stop after reading each step and try to "form a mental picture of yourself doing this step" (p. 390). The student's attention is also directed to the diagrams that often accompany the written directions. Any accompanying diagram should be carefully studied first, and all labeled parts should be identified. Then, each time the diagram is referred to in the text, the student should look back at the diagram to help "picture" the directions in his/her mind.

The third reading is another quick run-through to fix the procedures in the mind. While carrying out the experiment, the student continually refers to the directions to be sure the steps are carried out accurately and in the proper order.

In order to demonstrate to science students the importance and efficiency of careful reading and rereading of the experimental procedure before beginning an experiment, a teacher might one day give the students the directions and just let them read them and carry them out as they normally would. Students might then be given a checklist on which to record how successfully they carried out the experiment and whether they completed it successfully within the time limits allowed. A discussion will probably reveal their false starts, blunders, and the necessity of doing some steps over again.

During the next lab period, the instructor might lead the students through the steps described. (For a more detailed description, see Thomas and Robinson, 1977, pp. 388–98.) Again, let them carry out the experiment and complete the checklist. Most students will observe that the time spent in the reading-rereading process was well compensated by the efficient, scientific way in which they afterward carried out the experiment. If each time students are given written directions for an experiment the teacher will lead them through a careful reading and rereading of the procedures, both students and teacher will have a much more successful and satisfying experience with experiments.

Reading in Social Studies Classes

Currently there is no other content area so broad in its course offerings and so diverse in its reading demands as social studies. The state/U.S. history course is probably the only remnant of the once-universal civics, American history, and world history required courses. Replacing this narrow interpretation of social studies in most middle and secondary schools is a plethora of year-long, one-semester, and mini-courses designed to involve students in anthropological, social, economic, political, geographic, and historical concerns. After completing the usually required state/U.S. history course, in most schools the student can choose from courses as esoteric as "Ancient Civilizations," as topical as "Current Events," and as basic as "Survival Skills." The reading demands made of the social studies student and the reading-teaching demands made of the social studies teacher will vary greatly with the reading requirements for a particular course offering. Most social studies courses will require, however, that the social studies teacher teach the special vocabulary of social studies, adapt instruction to a variety of reading levels, and develop critical reading skills.

Teaching the Vocabulary of Social Studies

On first looking through a social studies text or listening to secondary students converse, one might conclude that the vocabulary of the social sciences is much more familiar to the average secondary student than is the "foreign language" used in the sciences. Anyone who watches the nightly TV news has certainly heard the words *amendment*, *constitutional*, and *democracy*. Even popular songs sing of *justice* and *equality*. Faraway places are often the setting for movies and television shows. A closer look, however, often reveals that the meaning associated with the words is shallow, indefinite, and sometimes erroneous. The same student who may use the term *democracy* cannot define the characteristics of a democracy or contrast it with other forms of government. *Angola* may be a familiar word, but most students could not locate it on a map or discuss its political ideology. Even *balance of trade* is recognized as a familiar phrase, but few adults could explain it adequately. The social studies teacher, then, has the task of building meaningful associations for many words that students think they already know!

In addition, social studies content utilizes a wealth of words borrowed from general use that have special usage in a social studies context. Being "cultured" is only remotely related to the *culture* of a particular society and has even less relationship to the *culture* used to grow organisms in a biology class. The president's *cabinet* is not the place where he stores his *china*. And *China* is not what mother serves *company* meals on. Nor is a *company* the same as people who come to visit.

How does the social studies teacher go about teaching overused and *under*-understood "media" words and other words having a common, familiar meaning and a specialized meaning in a social studies context? The first step, as in the solution to any problem, is identification. Only when the teacher has identified these "familiar" words can an attack on such "word-dropping" be organized. The social studies teacher who wishes to assure that students have full, resonant meanings for crucial social studies terms will begin by listing the concepts to be taught in a particular unit and, under each concept, the vocabulary crucial to developing an understanding of that concept. Rather than omitting those overused words as "words everybody knows," the astute social studies teacher will pay particular attention to such words in order to clarify their meaning.

Once this vocabulary is identified, the teacher will highlight these words in some way and then provide many opportunities for the students to use them. In most cases, a dictionary definition of the word is less than illuminating. (This author remembers looking up *existentialism* in the dictionary and learning that "existence precedes essence!") Most illuminating are examples of what a word *is* and *is not*! In developing the concept of *democracy*, for example, the instructor might lead students to read about the governments of various past and current civilizations and then classify each as "a democracy" or "not a democracy." Reasons for classifying each would have to be stated, and the class might begin with some clear-cut examples and move to some more equivocal ones. (This is a particularly good activity for small-group discussions, since the group must discuss the characteristics of a democracy in order to decide how to classify a particular government.)

To help students see that many general words have a specialized meaning in social studies, they should be sent on a hunt for such words and then required to make up an imaginary story about how the general word got the specialized meaning. (How did the president's top advisers come to be called his *cabinet*? What happens when we *table* a motion?) It does not matter whether or not the students' invented explanation reflects the true derivation of the meaning. Merely constructing the tale should be sufficient to fix the two meanings in the minds of most students and to alert them to the many social studies words with specialized meanings.

As often as possible, teachers should make use of direct experience to build difficult concepts. The class that goes through the process of devising a constitution and amending it will *know* the meanings of many government-related words they can now only *say*. When direct experience is impossible, indirect experience through the use of films and other audiovisuals is helpful. It is important, however, that the teacher direct the students' attention particularly to the concept or concepts being developed through the indirect experience of audiovisual materials.

Finally, students must be led to recognize that there are many words which they use but with which they associate little meaning. Beginning a unit by giving the students a list of crucial vocabulary for that unit and ten minutes to write down as many associations as they can make for each word often demonstrates effectively their need for vocabulary development with "familiar" words.

But They Can't All Read the Book!

This is perhaps the most often-heard lament of social studies teachers, especially in the required state/U.S. history course. In the introductory section of this chapter, ways of determining which students could read a particular textbook were discussed. There are a number of ways of adjusting instruction when not all the students in a class can read the textbook. Some suggested strategies are:

1. Use a variety of books and other print and nonprint material to teach the crucial concepts. Many teachers arrange their courses according to the unit approach to teaching. A topic for study is introduced. The teacher uses lecture, audiovisuals, group discussion, and any other relevant experiences to build some basic concepts, get the class interested in the unit, and suggest some questions for further investigation. Groups or individuals within the class then do reading and research to seek answers to the questions raised. The teacher and the librarian work together to provide the students with as much print and nonprint materials on as many levels as possible. Groups or individuals complete a report or project and share their results with the entire class. This is perhaps the most satisfactory way of handling the "many reading levels" problem. In addition to offering successful experiences for most of the students, it provides for the teaching of important inquiry, research, and reporting skills. Teachers who dare to teach in this way swear they would never return to "textbook teaching."

2. Have two or more basic texts that vary in reading level, and assign students to the one they can come closest to handling. This alternative method is a lot more feasible now than it was a decade ago. Many publishers, recognizing the need for materials written on an easier reading level, publish texts written at a lower grade level than that of the students for whom they are intended. This is especially true of textbooks intended for the U.S. history course, a requirement for most students. One publisher, Rand McNally, publishes two editions of its history text *The Free and the Brave* (Chicago, 1972). The Diamond Edition has the identical organization, scope, and illustrations of the regular edition but is written on an easier reading level.

3. When you assign the same text to the entire class to read, use a teaching strategy that allows even the poorest readers to learn the material if they listen attentively. The guided reading procedure (Manzo, 1975) is a technique in which students read a short selection, brainstorm their pooled remembrances, reread to verify their remembrances, and

then distinguish the main ideas of their remembrances from the supporting details. Students who could not themselves read the selection thus learn the content by listening. (See pages 118-120.)

4. Let those who are able read assigned portions of the text. Lead the other students in a "translation" lesson, in which they listen to the teacher read a section and then tell in their own words what they have heard. As the teacher records their remembrances on the board, students copy this record in a notebook. Over several lessons, they create a personal textbook they can read, to which they can refer for review.

5. Teach all students to read visuals. Social studies texts are full of maps, charts, graphs, and pictures containing a great deal of information. Even the poorest readers can often be taught to read and interpret these visuals. The visuals will then serve as a prod to memory and an aid for review.

Critical Reading Skills Are Critical in Social Studies

All teachers have the responsibility of encouraging their students not to just read and retain but also to react. The social studies teacher, however, carries a particularly heavy part of that instructional burden. By their very nature, inquiries into human conduct ranging across the ages and over continents are conglomerates of fact and opinion. Two historians examine the same events from their egocentric perspectives and report opposing accounts of those events. Two economists may have radically different opinions about the best way to fight inflation or provide for full employment.

A social studies teacher must demand that students know the source of all information they report. Looking at the date when a book was published and considering the qualifications and probable bias of a writer should become second nature to the young social scientist. Students should be taught how to analyze persuasive language and propaganda. *Was the writer reporting fact or expressing an opinion? Was vague or precise language used? Are the conclusions justifiable based on the evidence reported?* Students should be asked to consider these questions again and again as they investigate social studies topics.

Finally, teachers of social studies should always take the few extra minutes required to consider with their students some critical reaction questions: *Do I agree or not with this solution to the problem? Would this form of government be best for me? Do I consider this a humane way to behave?* Similar questions should always be the final step in the read/retain/react process. Years later, the information gained from reading will be forgotten, but the value judgments made as a result of reacting to the reading will continue to affect students in their daily work and interactions with others.

Reading In English Class

There is no teacher of whom more is expected than the English teacher. Traditionally, the English teacher spent half the year "exposing" students to a representative sampling of American and European literature and the other half teaching grammar and composition. It was assumed that the English teacher, along with teaching this content, would take a major part of the responsibility for increasing the depth and breadth of the students' vocabulary and developing their discussion and public-speaking skills.

When administrators and specialists, concerned by the apparently inadequate reading skills of today's secondary students, decreed that students should be given additional instruction in reading skills, the English teacher seemed the most likely candidate for this additional teaching responsibility. Few people stopped to consider that English teachers were no better trained than any other secondary teachers for assuming this responsibility, or that students might face their greatest reading difficulties when attempting to read the nonnarrative materials they encountered in science and mathematics classes. The job of teaching reading skills just seemed to fall "naturally" to the English teacher.

Today, in most middle/secondary schools, every teacher is asked to assume responsibility for teaching the special vocabulary and developing the particular reading skills needed for a particular content area. In addition to building those skills needed to read literature, the English teacher is usually given the responsibility for increasing the students' non-subject-specific vocabulary and motivating students to read widely.

Directing the Students through Literature

In some ways, the English teacher has an easier job of teaching those skills essential to reading in English classes than other content teachers have. Students who have learned to read in elementary school using a basal reader have had much practice in reading narrative, "story" material. Most current basal readers, in addition to a plethora of short story selections, also include some extended "novel-type" selections and some poetry. In addition, the English teacher is usually aware that, rather than merely being assigned to read a selection and answer some questions, students must be prepared to read the selection and then participate in group debate and discussion. Thus, a teaching strategy common to reading instruction, called DRA (Directed Reading Activity), is a natural for most English teachers.

A Directed Reading Activity consists of three stages. In the first stage, the teacher is preparing the students to read the selection. Since interest in the material read is a key factor in comprehension, some time is spent during the readiness stage of the lesson to pique the students' interest in what they will read. Often, the selection to be read in a literature class involves characters and situations far removed in time and place from the adolescent experience. Many English teachers, however, find they can make even ancient classics interesting and relevant by first helping students to realize that they have probably encountered parallel situations in their own lives.

In addition to arousing the students' interest in the selection to be read, the English teacher builds background for the selection, introduces unfamiliar or unusual vocabulary, and sets the purpose for reading by telling the students what they will do upon completion of the selection. Many English teachers find that reading aloud to students from the beginning of a play or story helps to get them "into the story." (This is especially important in classes where many students are poor readers or when the material to be read contains unusual names or archaic language.)

In the middle stage of the Directed Reading Activity, the students are actually reading the selection. Whether this reading is done a paragraph, a page, or a chapter at a time depends on the maturity of the students and the purposes set for reading. A teacher can aid the students' comprehension — and increase the probability they will be able to fulfill the purposes set for reading — by pointing out to them which parts of the assigned reading are crucial and must be read carefully and which can merely be skimmed. Especially difficult passages can be pointed out to the students with instructions such as: "Really try to figure out what is being said here" or "Do the best you can with this, but don't get bogged down; it is not crucial, and we'll discuss it later." Some teachers construct guides for difficult selections in which students are told how and for what information to read various portions of the selection. These guides may contain specific questions for the students to answer or page numbers with notations about how to read particular passages.

After the reading stage of the Directed Reading Activity is completed, the teacher leads the students to react and respond to the material that has been read. This reacting and responding stage can take many forms, such as discussion, debates, dramatization, or choral reading.

FOR THE READER TO DO:

Choose a literary selection you would like to teach to a group of English students. Plan a Directed Reading Activity around that selection. Remember that, in the readiness stage, you must pique interest, build background, preteach difficult or unusual vocabulary, and set purposes for the reading. In planning the reading stage, consider which parts are crucial and how large a chunk the students should be expected to read at one time. Finally, decide how you should structure the reaction and responding stage. If possible, teach this lesson to an appropriate group of students. (For some detailed examples of Directed Reading Activities, see Thomas and Robinson, 1977, pp. 325–75; and T. Pietras, "Teaching High School Literature: A Reading Skills Approach," *English Journal*, September 1976, pp. 44–47.)

Vocabulary Building

In addition to developing meaning for specialized words students encounter in their reading of literature, the English teacher has traditionally accepted major responsibility for improving students' general vocabulary. To many of us, English brings back memories of a thick alphabetically arranged book of words and their meanings. The number of words in the book was divided by the 36 weeks of school, and each week definitions were memorized, parroted back at the Friday "quiz," and never used again! Fortunately, this type of vocabulary "instruction" is rare in today's middle or secondary school. But unfortunately, some modern-day English teachers, lacking a substitute for the "memorize and test" teaching strategy, have stopped specific vocabulary teaching altogether.

FOR THE READER TO DO:

Look back over the last two paragraphs and try to remember or figure out how you learned meanings for many of the words contained there. Where did you learn, for instance, what *traditionally*, *encounter*, and *parroted* mean? Did you learn these words by looking them up in a dictionary? Did someone give you direct instruction in what these words mean? Did you memorize the definitions of these words?

There are, however, many effective strategies for improving and increasing students' meaning vocabularies. These strategies should reflect the way in which people learn words naturally. The meaning of most words used by adults and children was learned by hearing or reading the word again and again in different contexts. Each time the word was met, a new context shed additional light on the meaning of that word. Students should be given specific instruction in using the variety of context clues to meaning they encounter in their everyday listening and reading. (On pages 131-134, Miss Tent and Miss Stern use a "vocabulary meanings through context" strategy to teach students to use context clues to meaning.

Other words are learned because someone gave the learner direct instruction in the meaning of those words. A mother who answers that it means "too big for your britches" when Billy asks what *precocious* is (after his grandmother has labeled *him* precocious) is providing a sort of natural direct instruction in the meaning of that word. Likewise, the first-grade teacher who teaches students to associate various names with different animals and the mathematics teacher who teaches students what a parallelogram is are both providing direct meaning-vocabulary instruction. An excellent strategy for enlarging students' meaning vocabulary through direct instruction centered around topics of interest to students is the "capsule vocabulary lesson." In a capsule vocabulary lesson (Crist, 1975), students listen and talk and read and write words organized around a particular topic. (See pages 128-130 for a sample capsule vocabulary lesson.)

Many words are learned by applying knowledge of affixes and base words in order to decipher a meaning for an unfamiliar word. Most people who know what a *bicycle* is and what a *unicorn* is can decipher the meaning of the word *unicycle*. When teaching the use of morphology as an aid to understanding word meanings, the teacher should build on what students know rather than have them memorize an isolated list of words. Students who are given two minutes to write down all the words they can think of with *port* as a component can then pool their lists and quickly induce the meaning of the base word. Applying this meaning to other unfamiliar words demonstrates to students, in a way that memorizing individual meanings never can, the value of knowing the meaning for parts of words.

Finally, some words are learned by looking them up in the dictionary. This is usually a measure of last resort, but students should be taught to use the dictionary efficiently and effectively so that they have this tool to use when needed. Fortunately, dictionary instruction does not have to be deadly dull! In fact, there are many exciting activities that allow students to (1) learn the meanings of new words; (2) view the dictionary as a valuable resource; and (3) enjoy dictionary activities!

One popular "parlor game" meets all three of these criteria and is adaptable to English classes. In this "dictionary game," students choose or are given by the teacher an unusual word. They then write the word and four definitions for that word on a card. Of the four definitions, three have nothing whatever to do with the word and are solely the product of the maker's imagination. One is an actual dictionary definition for the word, copied verbatim from the dictionary. When all students have the card with their word and its four definitions completed, each reads his or her word and definitions. The remainder of the class vote (using every-pupil-response cards with 1, 2, 3, and 4 on them) on which definition they think was the true definition. The maker of the definitions gets one point for each incorrect vote!

Another dictionary activity that ensures student involvement is the "classifying game." Instead of being asked to write definitions for a group of words, students are given a group of words and asked to classify them in two or more categories. A list of foreign-sounding foods (*mousse, caviar, quiche,* for example) might be classified as "foods I would love to find that I was having for dinner tonight" or "foods that would make me want to make a quick trip to the local hamburger haven." For adjectives describing people, students might sort them into "words I would be flattered by if I overheard someone use them about me" and "words I would be insulted by." Lake (1971) suggests many other activities for making dictionary work exciting and relevant to students.

FOR THE READER TO DO:

Make a list of 10 descriptive adjectives not likely to be known by the average student. It is especially fun if these words all begin with the same letter (*fatuous, fastidious, fascist, frumpy,* for example). Have some students divide the words into "words I would be flattered by" and "words I would be insulted by" categories. Observe how actively they use their dictionaries as they do this. When the students have finished, compare lists. Discuss and acknowledge differences of opinion.

One caution must be given to all teachers about to embark on the task of broadening students' meaning vocabulary. Students must constantly be reminded and shown that most words do not have a single, fixed meaning. A *play* read in English is different from to *play* after school, and still different from a *play* on words. It is easy to ask students, "What does that word mean?" But many students, having heard that question year after year, have come to believe that words have only one meaning. In building meaning vocabulary, care must be taken that words are always used in the context of at least a sentence and that students recognize that the context must be considered when determining meaning for the word. (On page 108, Miss Tent helps the Upton Hill teachers to realize that words have different meanings in the different content areas.)

USSR (Uninterrupted Sustained Silent Reading; McCracken, 1971) is the most valuable weapon in the arsenal of the teacher who wishes to assure not only that students *can* read but also that they *do*. In many English classes (and indeed, in other content-area classes!), each day or week a time is set aside when everyone reads something of his or her own choosing. Sometimes called RSVP (Reading Silently — Very Pleasurable), this sustained reading time gives students a chance to practice their reading skills and to develop broader reading interests. The role of the teacher in this sustained reading activity is to (1) set a model for the others by reading as the students do; (2) make a variety of books and magazines available in the classroom; and (3) see that time is devoted to sustained reading on a regularly scheduled basis. No records or reports of any kind are required of students. The only requirement is that students spend the time reading. Teachers who have tried a regularly scheduled time for USSR often report they would never give it up: "The students love it, and it's the only quiet time in my whole day."

Reading in Foreign Language Classes

When one of the authors taught her first course in middle and secondary reading and language arts, there were several foreign-language teachers in the class. For many assignments, these teachers were requested to try with their own classes some of the teaching strategies they learned. To the foreign-language teachers, I apologized: "I'm not quite sure how all this relates to teaching French, Spanish, or German. You'll just have to try what seems like it might work. Later we'll have a conference, and if these strategies are not adaptable to your foreign-language teaching, we'll adapt the assignments accordingly."

To my amazement, these teachers reported that the strategies I was teaching them to help students read better in their content-area subjects were especially effective in foreign-language classes. These strategies are discussed under three general headings: vocabulary improvement, listening comprehension improvement, and reading comprehension improvement.

Teaching the Vocabulary of a Foreign Language

As every foreign-language teacher and student recognizes, learning the new vocabulary is the first and the biggest hurdle in the race to master a foreign language. Five strategies that foreign-language teachers have adapted and used will be discussed.

In a foreign language, as in English, the meaning of many words can be learned by reading the other words in a sentence or the surrounding text passage. These context clues to the meaning of words are often ignored by foreign-language students, who tend to "overuse" their dictionary needlessly by looking up every unfamiliar word. Thomas and Robinson (1977) suggest teaching foreign-language students how to use specific types of context clues and when to rely on context clues. Their suggestions include relying on context clues when the meaning they give you "clicks" with the rest of the passage and when only an approximate meaning for the word is needed. They further suggest that students be taught *not* to rely on context but to look words up when (1) the word is a key word; (2) a precise meaning is required; (3) context clues are insufficient; (4) many nearby words are also unknown; and (5) the word has been seen many times before, so that its occurrence is obviously frequent enough to require direct learning.

A direct vocabulary teaching approach is the *List, Group, and Label* strategy originated by Hilda Taba (1967) as a social studies unit opener. In this strategy, students are asked to brainstorm words that answer a particular question. A French teacher, for example, who wished to review with students the names of foods they had learned could ask them to *"Nomez, s'il vous plait, les choses on peut manger."* The students would then respond in French with the names of things to eat, and the teacher would list these foods on the board. When the board was filled with words, the teacher would ask the students, "Write down some foods that seem to go together in some way." Students would then volunteer to read the names of the foods in their group, explain (in French) why they grouped them, and give the group a name or a label.

There are numerous such questions that can elicit many vocabulary words to be reviewed. Students might be asked, for example, to name "all the animals they can think of" or "all the places one could visit in a particular country." In addition to reviewing specific vocabulary, students are also engaged in trying to formulate labels and reasons for their groups and to express these in the new language. They also benefit from listening to the other students' explanations.

FOR THE READER TO DO:

Think of three questions other than the ones suggested in this chapter which could be used for a *List, Group, and Label* lesson in a particular language. If possible, teach this lesson to a group of students. While the responses of the students will not be perfectly formed, consider how actively they are trying to use the language. How does this parallel what children do as they first learn to talk?

Words on the Wall is a good vocabulary development strategy for the core vocabulary—that is, words used again and again that students must learn in the very beginning in order to communicate at all. In this foreign-language teaching strategy, core words (10 per week) are displayed alphabetically on a wall or bulletin board. When the words are first placed there, they are pronounced and used in context and their English translation are given. Students are then given a test in which the English translation is called out: they must quickly find and write the foreign word. This test, which should only take about three minutes, is then self-graded. Each day, the students take this quick quiz and grade their own responses. At the beginning of the second week, 10 new words are added. Again, these words are pronounced and used in context, and their translation is discussed. The test proceeds as before, except that now the teacher gives the English translation for any 10 of the accumulated 20 words. If 10 words are added each week during a 36-week term, the students will have a "wall vocabulary" of 360 high-frequency words. They can quickly translate these words and can write them as well as read them. Foreign-language teachers who use this strategy report that it is a great aid to students, especially in the beginning foreign-language courses.

Capsule vocabulary is also effective in foreign language classes. In this strategy, the teacher selects approximately 15 related words to teach the students. The words are introduced orally, written on the board, and used in context (both foreign language and English), one at a time. After listening to this introduction, students make a list of the 15 words. At a signal from the teacher, students arrange themselves in "talking pairs" and are given a set time (5–10 minutes) to try to use all 15 words in conversation. (One partner talks while the other partner checks off the words used; then they switch talking and checking roles.) Next the students are given 10 minutes in which to write, trying to use as many of the 15 words as they can. Volunteers are afterward selected to read what they have written.

FOR THE READER TO DO:

Come up with a list of 15 words you would like to teach to a particular foreign-language class. If possible, teach a capsule vocabulary lesson with these words. How does this strategy help students to learn the vocabulary being taught and become better users of the language?

Finally, a dictionary activity adapted from the classifying game discussed in the English reading skills section of this chapter is a most effective vocabulary introducer. Students are given a list of words and asked to classify them in some way. Words for a "things I would like to have for supper" versus "things I would not want to have for supper" classification activity would include some foods and some other things (old shoes, perhaps!). A list of adjectives could be classified as "flattering" or "insulting." There are nearly as many different classifications as there are names of objects, actions, and descriptors to be learned. Students who use a dictionary to classify the words are actively and personally involved and are much more apt to remember the translations they find.

Improving Listening Comprehension in a Foreign Language

Students who are going to read with comprehension in a foreign language are greatly aided by learning to listen with comprehension. Two teaching strategies, Directed Listening Activity and Guided Listening Procedure, have been adapted and used by foreign-language teachers to improve their students' listening comprehension.

A Directed Listening Activity has three stages. In the readiness stage, the teacher prepares the students to listen by (1) establishing motivation; (2) building background; (3) introducing new vocabulary; and (4) setting purposes for their listening. A teacher who was about to read to students a selection about railroad transportation in Germany might: (1) have students discuss what they know about railroad transportation in the United States; (2) show a map of Germany and point out important rail lines; (3) introduce new vocabulary by writing each word on the board, then have the students pronounce the word, give its English translation, and use the foreign word in the context of several sentences; and (4) ask students to listen to the reading so that they will be able to list five characteristics of the German railroad system.

In the middle stage of a Directed Listening Activity students are actually listening to the information. Following through with the example above, the teacher would read to students the selection about German railroads. (Often it is helpful to break a long selection into several shorter sections. For each section, the teacher can introduce new vocabulary and set a purpose for listening.)

Finally, after listening, the students do something to follow up the purposes set for listening. For the example of the German railroad system, students might be asked to contribute one of the five characteristics they had listed. The teacher would then list the pooled characteristics on the board. Students might then be asked to discuss, in talking pairs, the differences between the U.S. and German railroad systems.

FOR THE READER TO DO:

Plan a Directed Listening Activity. Remember to build motivation and background, introduce vocabulary, and set purposes for listening during the readiness stage. For the actual listening stage, decide whether you want the students to listen to the whole selection at once or only a portion of it at a time. For the followup, try to plan an activity that builds on the purposes set for listening and involves the students in further thought and discussion.

Another strategy that can be effectively used in a foreign-language class to improve listening comprehension is the Guided Listening Procedure. In a Guided Listening Procedure, students are asked to "listen to remember everything." The teacher reads a short selection (for not more than 5 minutes) and tape-records the reading.

After listening to the teacher's reading, students tell the teacher what they remember as the teacher lists their pooled remembrances on the board. When no more information can be recalled, students listen to the taped reading to see whether any of the information on the board needs to be amended or additional information should be added. Finally, students decide which of the items listed on the board are main ideas and which are supporting details. A short quiz tests the students' comprehension and memory. (For an example of how to conduct a Guided Listening Procedure, see pages 138-139.)

Improved Reading Comprehension in a Foreign Language

If you were to go through the preceding section on improving listening comprehension in a foreign language and substitute the word *reading* for *listening*, you would have outlined two valuable reading comprehension strategies: the Directed Reading Activity and the Guided Reading Procedure. Teachers can direct and guide their students' reading of foreign-language texts in the same way they direct and guide their listening. Using lessons designed to improve listening comprehension and reading comprehension will result in great improvement in most students' learning of—and attitude toward—a foreign language.

FOR THE READER TO DO:

List the steps in a Directed Reading Activity and a Guided Reading Procedure. (Note that in a Guided Reading Procedure, the students do not reread the whole selection; rather, they skim it for incorrect or missing information in their initial comprehension.) If possible, teach a Directed Reading Activity or a Guided Reading Procedure to a group of students.

Reading in Art, Music, and Physical Education

At first, the combination of art, music, and physical education may seem incongruous, but these subject areas do share many characteristics in their interrelationship with reading. In art, music, and physical education, students spend much of their time *doing* rather than *reading*. In many of these classes, in fact, students are not required to read at all. Sometimes, however, rather than *doing* art, music, or physical education, students are learning about these disciplines. And such history, theory, or appreciation courses do require extensive reading and specialized reading skills. Finally, art, music, and physical education offer attractive and highly motivating opportunities for teachers to inspire students to read.

Reading While Doing

Most students in physical education and art activity classes are required to do very little reading as they carry out their activities. Musicians, however, generally are required to do some reading, at least in the printed music scores. For instrumental music, students are required to read directions (*allegro* or *sotto voce*, for example). In choral music, both performance directions and the texts of songs and other larger works are necessary reading. For whatever reading is required while carrying out the physical, artistic, or musical activity, teachers should ensure that students can read and understand the meaning of the technical vocabulary used. Vocabulary activities suggested in any of the preceding sections can be adapted to physical education, art, and music.

Reading While Learning About Art, Music, and Physical Education

Often, in addition to the active, "doing" courses, teachers of these content areas find themselves teaching courses *about* art, music, and physical education. Such history, appreciation, theory, and general culture courses require the same kind of specialized reading skills as are required by the other academic content areas. In fact, these courses could be, and often are, considered "academic." As in all the other content areas, if students are to read with comprehension, vocabulary specific to the topic as well as general vocabulary with a specialized meaning in the particular content area must be taught.

FOR THE READER TO DO:

Choose some text material in the area of art, music, or physical education. Determine which vocabulary is probably unfamiliar to students and which vocabulary is general vocabulary used in a specialized way. Referring to the vocabulary sections for other content areas, plan at least three strategies for teaching this vocabulary.

In addition to teaching vocabulary, teachers also need to direct and guide the students' reading of the text. The Directed Reading Activity (outlined in the English reading skills section; see pages 88-89) and the Guided Reading Procedure (see pages 118-120) are two specific strategies applicable to art, music, and physical education as well.

Much of the reading in books about art, music, and physical education requires both the reading of text and extensive use of diagrams and illustrations. These visuals, intended to aid and enlighten the student, are in reality often ignored by the student reader. Students should be specifically directed to acquire as much information from the visuals as possible. The Directed Reading-Thinking Activity, in which students are required to predict what the text will say (based on their study of the title, headings, and illustrative material), is a particularly good strategy to use with texts containing much illustrative material. (For a sample Directed Reading-Thinking Activity, see pages 163-164.)

An effective strategy for demonstrating how much can be learned from illustrative material alone is to give students just a few minutes to study the illustrations and then make a list of everything they have learned from them. Students who are asked to do this kind of quick preview when each reading assignment is made will be amazed at how much can be learned from the visuals and will probably develop the habit of studying the visuals first.

"Turning Students On to Reading"

In their book *Improving Reading in Every Class* (1977), Thomas and Robinson have included some excellent examples of how teachers can use their students' interest in art or physical education to inspire reluctant readers to read. (The music teacher could do the same!) The physical education coach ("Sandy" Patlak) reported on in their book, who collects books about sports and sports heroes, encourages his students to check out the books and read about their favorite sports and stars. During quiet times, the coach gives "book talks" to his students and invites them to share information learned from their sports-related reading.

The art teacher (Robert Erickson) described by Thomas and Robinson keeps a closet filled with art books in his art room (many of which he picks up at Salvation Army stores and equally inexpensive places!). He uses these art books to provide examples of various media, styles, and effects for students. When they have questions that occur in the course of their "doing" art, Erickson tries to steer students to appropriate sections of the art books. According to Erickson, even reluctant readers will check out an art book when art is something they are vitally interested in.

Reading in Career Education Classes

Perhaps no other teacher in the secondary school faces as varied a group of students in each class as does the teacher of the various career education subjects. The traditional image of the "vocational" student has been of an academically unmotivated student taking "shop" courses in order to avoid the "academics." This is no longer the case — if it ever was! Today's secondary students enrolled in career education courses include many college- and technical-school-bound students interested in vocational pursuits as vocation or avocation. They also include some students who see career courses as a refuge from heavily text-book-oriented academic courses.

As the image of the students has changed, so has the course content. No longer can reading be considered an adjunct or an "extra" in this content area, something the less able students can get along without. Courses in auto mechanics can require the reading of repair manuals that make biology textbooks look simple. Wiring diagrams in an electricity "primer" require meticulous reading of both the picture and the text. Food and nutrition classes often require as much skill in reading to follow directions as does the chemistry class next door. The poor reader will find no haven in today's career education courses.

While many students in career education courses would prefer to be told or shown what to do than to read how to do it, such instructional practice is, in the long run, unfair to the student. Career education is closely tied with current technology, a technology that is constantly producing "new and better" products and ways to do things. Today's career education student *must* be able to read in order to keep up with the changing demands that will be made "on the job." The major special reading demands made on the student in career education classes are rooted in the extremely heavy load of technical vocabulary and the necessity of being able to read and follow a set of directions accurately.

Teaching All That Technical Vocabulary

Every "trade" has its jargon, and the proficient practitioner of that trade must read and talk that jargon. Most vocational subjects have an advantage over academic subjects in that the terminology to be learned is often concrete, tangible, and demonstrable. Unlike the biology class, where the student must learn foreign-sounding names for unknown substances, and the social studies class, where a student must develop meanings for abstractions, the career-oriented class offers vocabulary that can be pointed to or done. In many career labs and workshops, the student is inundated with reading. All tools and utensils are labeled with their correct name; parts of machines are labeled. Diagrams showing various jobs to be done are likewise profusely labeled. In these learning environments, students learn to read and understand the essential vocabulary as they work firsthand at the various jobs.

Lab and workshop instructors attuned to the reading needs of their subject and the reading problems of their students teach vocabulary as they teach the manual skills. Students in these classes often construct their own "job box," with a key word on one side of an index card and a definition, diagram, or illustration on the other side. Occupational glossaries are also used in these classes, because teachers of career classes realize that the vocabulary needs of their students will change and increase as the students become practitioners. A student who knows where to look for an explanation of an unknown term is assured of greater success "on the job."

In addition to teaching unfamiliar words, career education teachers must assure that their students know the important abbreviations, symbols, or codes used in their chosen occupation. Because these are frequently overlooked by both teachers and students, a "botched" job is often the result. Finally, teachers must alert their students to the specialized meaning of many general terms. Because these words look familiar to students, they often "sneak up on them" in an unfamiliar usage, and the bewildered student does not even recognize the reason for the confusion.

FOR THE READER TO DO:

Choose a textbook, job sheet, or manual in a particular career area. Look first for technical vocabulary that is crucial to successful implementation of a task. How would you ensure that students could read and understand these technical terms? Could you provide direct experience with this terminology for them? How could you help them visualize the meaning for a word? Next, look for general words (*fold, cast, dog,* etc.) used in a specialized way. After alerting yourself to these "sneaky" words, plan ways of alerting your students to them.

Following Directions

Most adults who have spent the better part of Christmas Eve and the next morning trying to assemble some "simple-to-assemble" toy realize that reading to follow directions is a demanding and difficult task. Much of the reading required in career-oriented classes is of this kind. Students must learn that the time spent in a three-times-over reading of directions is often more than compensated for by successful accomplishment of a task first time around. Some career education teachers report that, at the very beginning of the semester, they give students sets of directions to follow without any instruction in how to read and follow them. They then sit back and watch as the students plunge ahead after only a cursory reading. Not surprisingly, most of the students cannot carry out their assigned task successfully, and after much moaning and groaning, teacher and students sit down and discuss the need of a careful, step-by-step reading of the entire procedure before beginning.

In the next lesson, the teacher leads the students through three readings of their directions. For the first reading, they are given very little time (3 – 5 minutes) and asked to get a general notion of what they will do. Next they read each step carefully, stopping to study each accompanying diagram or illustration. Unfamiliar terms are identified, and an explanation is found or given for these. Students are told to try to visualize themselves carrying out each step and to imagine what the final product will look like. The third reading is again a quick one, just to "set" the whole procedure in mind. Students then carry out the task with the directions in front of them, to make sure that all measurements are accurate and all steps are done in the specified order. The results of this lesson are then compared with the results of the generally disastrous first lesson. Most students will admit they were more successful after their careful reading.

Teachers who lead their students through a "reading to follow directions" lesson do not stop with one lesson. Often, with the students they make a list of the steps to be followed in reading a set of directions, and each time directions reading is required, they remind students of the steps. (For a detailed account of how to help students read to follow directions in career education classes, see Thomas and Robinson, 1977, pp. 460–466.)

6 A Year of Content-Area Reading (September-October)

F OR THE NEXT three chapters, you will follow Connie Tent as she carries out her daily struggle to help content-area teachers teach the reading skills essential to their content areas. You will be introduced to Mr. Topps (the principal), to Upton Hill Middle/Secondary School, and to many of the teachers who teach there. (Later in the book you will have extensive contact with Reed Moore, the remedial reading teacher, and Rita Wright, a middle school language arts teacher.) The narration of teaching successes and failures in the next three chapters serves a dual purpose.

For the teacher of any content area, the chapters should permit a glimpse of what content-area reading instruction looks like as it is carried out on a day-to-day basis. Diagnosing student needs and reading material demands, planning for instruction, implementing teaching strategies, organizing for instruction, and evaluating the products and process of instruction can be viewed within the context of actual classroom instruction. Although Miss Tent works with teachers of a particular content area as she demonstrates a particular strategy, in most cases the teaching strategy is not confined to that content area but is applicable to other content areas. As you are reading, think of your own chosen content area and substitute, perhaps, biology or mathematics for French or social studies. Think about how a particular strategy, with alterations as necessary, might work for you.

The second purpose of these three chapters is to serve as a model for a person who becomes a high school content-area reading specialist. It is becoming more and more common throughout the United States to have such a staff member employed to help content-area teachers implement appropriate teaching strategies. Often, the content-area reading specialist is someone with a master's degree in reading who has taken a course in content-area reading in order to learn how to help content-area teachers. For the person who is or aspires to become a content-area reading specialist, the successes and failures of Connie Tent should provide entertainment, inspiration, and the harsh realization that being a content-area reading specialist is no easy task.

Many of the teaching strategies mentioned previously in this book are demonstrated in the next three chapters. We hope this narrative format will provide you with a "picture in your mind" of how teaching strategies and organization can be implemented in a content-area classroom. Now, as you begin reading, put on and "walk in the shoes" of Connie Tent and the content-area teachers.

The Faculty Workshop

Miss Tent arrived at Upton Hill Middle/Secondary School at 7:30 in the morning. "What an eerie place this is without any students or teachers," she thought as she walked down the hall toward the library where her workshop would be held. It was hard for her to imagine that within 48 hours over 1,000 students and 60-plus teachers would be streaming through these deserted halls on their way to the first day of classes. "I just hope I can do something with the teachers today that will make the first day of school in their classes this year different from last year," she mumbled to herself as she flicked on the lights in the library and surveyed the room arrangement she had finally decided on at 5:30 yesterday afternoon.

If the truth be told, Miss Tent was looking forward to the beginning of classes. During the past three teacher workdays she had been very busy trying to find space in her tiny cubbyhole for mounds of teaching materials and preparing for this morning's workshop. In an effort to learn all the teachers' names, she had gone to chat with many of them and had borrowed copies of their textbooks. Most of the teachers had been friendly enough, but she sensed that they were unsure of the role of a content-area reading specialist and were not at all convinced that Upton Hill needed one. Mr. Gramm, the elderly math teacher, had commented that he thought the high pupil/teacher ratio was the teachers' main problem and that additional teachers would ease their workload and solve the whole problem of individualization of instruction. Vera Stern, the head of the English department, had asked Miss Tent if she thought the school needed another remedial reading teacher like Mr. Moore. Miss Tent was hoping that this morning's workshop with the secondary teachers would begin to convince them of her potential usefulness for them. Consequently, she had devoted much time, energy, and thought to what she would do and how she would do it.

Fortunately, conducting workshops was something that no longer frightened Connie Tent. Partially, it was practice that had helped her overcome her fear. While working as curriculum coordinator at Moore Elementary School, she had chaired and conducted in-service and faculty meetings on a regular basis. More crucial, however, was her increasing conviction about how in-service ought to be conducted. She had always known that lecturing to teachers would have the same effect on them as it had on their students. In fact, teachers were usually not as polite as their students. When faced with a long lecture, many would fall asleep or read the morning newspaper. On the other hand, sessions that a good friend of hers had labeled "pooled ignorance," in which participants shared ideas and jointly evolved curriculum, were usually equally dull and unproductive.

When conducting in-service with teachers, Connie firmly believed in the old adage "Practice what you preach." If you believe that teachers should involve students in active learning, then your in-service must involve the teachers as active learners. If you believe that experiencing something affects the learner in a way that talking about something cannot, you must arrange for teachers to experience. If you believe that reading instruction must be guided and focused, then what teachers do in an in-service must be guided and focused. If you believe in a variety of learning activities—whole-group, small-group, and individual—you must demonstrate for teachers how to have a variety of activities and how to move learners from one activity to another.

All this Miss Tent had learned, and by following her "Practice what you preach" motto, she had conducted many successful in-services. Those in-services, however, had been conducted primarily with elementary teachers, and Miss Tent's only concern about how this morning's session would go was that she was not very experienced with secondary teachers—or with secondary students, for that matter. For that reason, she had thought long and hard before accepting this job Mr. Topps had offered her. In fact, she had been on the verge of accepting an elementary reading specialist's job in a city several hundred miles away rather than this content-area reading specialist job when she had met Rich Mann and soon decided that several hundred miles was a long way to travel every weekend!

"Good morning, Connie," said Mr. Topps. "It isn't often that anyone besides Dusty beats me to school. You aren't nervous, are you? I know that it will go well. I appreciate your taking this job and consider it my responsibility to see that you have a chance to be successful at it. I certainly had to argue long and loud enough with the school board members to get this position funded, and I don't intend for it *not* to work!"

"No, I'm not nervous about today," replied Miss Tent. "But I am still a little concerned about how to get into the classrooms to work with the teachers. Some of them seem to think that if I were another classroom teacher and lessened their pupil/teacher load a little, I would do more good. Others think I should be a remedial teacher like Mr. Moore. Today I'm going to demonstrate some of the strategies I can teach them to use. At the end of the session, I'll ask the teachers to let me know how I can help them in their classrooms. Even if I get only four or five teachers initially, word will get around to the others if the work I do with them is really helpful."

Mr. Topps nodded his head in agreement and turned to greet the other staff members, who were now entering the library. When most of the teachers were there, he began the meeting by reminiscing with the teachers about some of the humorous and not-so-humorous incidents that had happened at Upton Hill Middle/Secondary School in the two years since he had come there as principal. He reminded the teachers of the faculty meeting at which he had played a tape of students reading, or at least attempting to read, the school code. It was about six weeks into the school year, and he was at the end of his rope, trying to decide what to do about the endless stream of discipline problems passing through his office every day. Finally, while lecturing one boy who had already been sent there twice that week, he pointed to the chart displaying the school code of rules. "Read rule number four," he instructed the boy. The boy stuttered and stammered, unable to read "*There will be no fighting anywhere on the school grounds.*" Mr. Topps had been appalled. He knew that many of the students could not read their textbooks, but he also knew *that* sentence could be read by almost any second-grader at Merritt Elementary School. The following day, as the discipline problems streamed into his office, he sat each down with the tape recorder and asked each culprit to read the school code. Only two of the 27 severe discipline problems could fluently read the school code. That afternoon Mr. Topps had played several portions of the tape at the weekly faculty meeting. From then on, reading had become a priority at Upton Hill! Consultants had been brought in to conduct workshops with the teachers, and the parents' aid had been enlisted to help convince the school board to fund a remedial reading teacher. Mrs. Bennett had worked hard with the 90 remedial reading students she saw each day and had made some visible progress with most of them. These 90 students, however, represented only a small percentage of the students with reading problems at Upton Hill. Many other students were not being helped at all, and the 90 students Mrs. Bennett worked with were still having great difficulty in other subjects because they couldn't read their textbooks.

"Toward the end of last year," Mr. Topps continued, "I decided that if we were really going to give reading help to all the students who needed it, we'd need at least four remedial reading teachers, and even then the students would not be able to progress fast enough to keep them from falling behind in their other subjects because they couldn't read the textbooks. A content-area reading specialist who could work with you teachers to help you adapt your instruction to the reading abilities of your students, and at the same time improve your students' reading of material in your content area, seemed to be the only feasible solution to our problem. Convincing the school board of this need was not easy, and finding a competent person for the position was even harder. I have somehow managed to accomplish both, however, although the school board has funded the position only on a one-year trial basis. Miss Tent, whom most of you have met, is unusually well qualified to be our content-area reading specialist. She has taught both first and fourth grades and has worked as an elementary school curriculum coordinator. She has her master's degree in reading education from State and has been a consultant for several school systems. Last year she worked as a consultant to social studies teachers at Urban Middle School. I guess the only qualification she lacks for this job is experience teaching secondary school students, but I know that you teachers will be able to help her adapt her ideas to older students."

Mr. Topps then completed his introduction and turned the morning's workshop over to Miss Tent. While Miss Tent was relieved that the fact that she hadn't taught students above elementary school level had come out (it had to eventually!), she was somewhat disheartened by the knowing nods and raised eyebrows around the room. She plunged right in, however, convinced that what she had planned for the morning would soon have the teachers involved and active. She intended to point out, at the workshop's end, that the teaching strategies she had used with them were applicable to middle, secondary, and elementary students and that, while minor adjustments for age and sophistication levels were necessary, a sound teaching strategy could be adapted to learners of all ages.

"All of you know," began Miss Tent, "that many of your students can pronounce words but get very little meaning from what they read. It is hard for adults to realize what it means to be able to read all the words and yet not understand what was read. In order to really know something, I believe that you must have experienced it." With those terse introductory remarks, Miss Tent turned on the overhead, displaying a selection from an advanced statistics book. "Please read this passage so that you can explain to me the advantages and disadvantages of fractional factorial designs."

> FRACTIONAL FACTORIAL DESIGNS HAVE MUCH IN COMMON WITH CONFOUNDED FACTORIAL DESIGNS. THE LATTER DESIGNS, THROUGH THE TECHNIQUE OF CONFOUNDING, ACHIEVE A REDUCTION IN THE NUMBER OF TREATMENT COMBINATIONS THAT MUST BE INCLUDED WITHIN A BLOCK. A FRACTIONAL FACTORIAL DESIGN USES CONFOUNDING TO REDUCE THE NUMBER OF TREATMENT COMBINATIONS IN THE EXPERIMENT. AS IS ALWAYS THE CASE WHEN CONFOUNDING IS USED, THE REDUCTION IS OBTAINED AT A PRICE. THERE IS CONSIDERABLE AMBIGUITY IN INTERPRETING THE OUTCOME OF A FRACTIONAL FACTORIAL EXPERIMENT, SINCE TREATMENTS ARE CONFOUNDED WITH INTERACTIONS. FOR EXAMPLE, A SIGNIFICANT MEAN SQUARE MIGHT BE ATTRIBUTED TO THE EFFECTS OF TREATMENT *A* OR TO A *BCDE* INTERACTION. THE TWO OR MORE DESIGNATIONS THAT CAN BE GIVEN TO THE SAME MEAN SQUARE ARE CALLED *ALIASES*. TREATMENTS ARE CUSTOMARILY CONFOUNDED WITH HIGHER-ORDER INTERACTIONS THAT ARE ASSUMED TO EQUAL ZERO. THIS HELPS TO MINIMIZE BUT DOES NOT ELIMINATE AMBIGUITY IN INTERPRETING THE OUTCOME OF AN EXPERIMENT.[1]

Immediately the teachers began to laugh nervously. Several commented that it looked a lot like the book used in an educational research course they had taken at State. Most did not seriously attempt the task. When all had had time to read, Miss Tent turned off the overhead and asked Mr. Battle to explain what he had read. He laughed and said "Search me!" Mrs. Cash, the economics teacher, and Mr. Burner, the chemistry teacher, likewise declined to explain to the group what they had read. Finally, Miss Tent asked the stumped teachers if they had "read" the paragraph as instructed. They replied that they had "read the words."

"Well, perhaps you just can't remember what you read," commented Miss Tent as she turned the projector back on. "Now, with the passage in front of you, explain it in your own words." Again there were nervous laughs, and the three teachers in turn declined to explain what they had read. "Well, perhaps," said Miss Tent, "you don't know all the words."

Miss Tent instructed the group to listen as one of their members read the

[1]Roger E. Kirk, "Classification of ANOVA Designs," in Kirk, *Statistical Issues* (Belmont, Calif.: Wadsworth, 1972), p. 256.

paragraph aloud and then try to decide whether that reader seemed to know what was being said in the paragraphs. Miss Werth volunteered and read the paragraph aloud. She pronounced every word correctly and read with great expression. When she had finished, the teachers agreed that Miss Werth seemed to understand what she was reading. She had read all the words correctly, emphasized the appropriate words, stopped at appropriate junctures, and had very smooth intonation. But in response to Miss Tent's inquiry, Miss Werth confessed she "didn't understand a word of it."

The group of teachers was quiet and thoughtful as Miss Tent led them to realize that comprehension entails more than being able to pronounce the words with appropriate expression. The teachers at first said that they had no meanings for the words used but, upon reflection, had to admit that they did indeed have some meanings for all the words. "Blocks are what children build with . . . or the area in which you live." "Confounding is fooling someone." "Factorial is like one factorial(1!)." The teachers concluded that the words used in this statistics selection were multimeaning words for which they had one or two general meanings but which also had a specialized meaning in a statistics context. The specialized use of common words, plus their lack of background information about the subject, had made the teachers incapable of understanding this paragraph. Miss Stern also noted that many of the sentences were long and complicated. On a chart that Miss Tent had attached to the wall was printed: "What makes comprehension impossible?" In answer to this query, she listed: (1) lack of background information; (2) specialized use of vocabulary, and (3) long, complicated sentences.

Next Miss Tent projected a transparency on which the following passage was printed:

THE PALEOCORTEX OR ALLOCORTEX IS PHYLOGENETICALLY OLDER, AND INCLUDES THE HIPPOCAMPUS, THE PYRIFORM LOBE, AND THE OLFACTORY BULB AND TUBERCLE. THE JUXTALLOCORTEX INCLUDES THE CINGULATE GYRUS, PRESUBICULUM AND FRONTO-TEMPORAL CORTEX. THE NON-CORTICAL TISSUE OF FIRST IMPORTANCE INCLUDES THE AMYGDALOID COMPLEX, THE SEPTAL REGION, THALAMIC AND HYPOTHALAMIC NUCLEI, AS WELL AS THE CAUDATE AND MIDBRAIN RETICULAR FORMULATION. THE ISOCORTEX, OR NEOCORTEX, IS FURTHER DIVIDED INTO EXTRINSIC AND INTRINSIC AREAS. THE EXTRINSIC HAVE PROJECTIVE FIBRES FROM THE THALAMIC RELAY NUCLEI AND FIBRES FROM OUTSIDE THE THALAMUS, WHILE THE INTRINSIC PROJECT SOLELY FROM THE THALAMIC RELAY NUCLEI TO THE ISOCORTEX.[2]

After giving the teachers sufficient time to read the paragraph, Miss Tent turned the projector off and asked for someone to explain what was read. Again, there were nervous laughs and no volunteers. Miss Tent then turned the projector on once more, directed the teachers to number their papers from one to five, and asked the following questions:

1. What is another name for paleocortex?

[2]F. H. George, *The Brain as a Computer* (New York: Pergamon Press, 1973), p. 286–87.

2. Besides the amygdaloid complex and the septal region, what else of first importance is included in the non-cortical tissue?
3. Where is the fronto-temporal cortex?
4. What four structures does the paleocortex include?
5. Which tissue is phylogenetically older?

Without hesitation, the teachers wrote answers to these "comprehension" questions. Miss Tent then read each question to them again, and the teachers gave the answers in confident chorus. "Marvelous," replied Miss Tent. "You were all able to answer the comprehension questions, so you must have understood this passage." Of course, they hadn't understood it, and Miss Tent led them to discover how one can answer *wh-* transformation questions (who? what? when? where? which?) by drawing on their knowledge of the syntactic structure of language. Such ability to answer questions is not necessarily indicative of true understanding. Miss Tent then told them about a fourth-grade boy named Charlie, who could always answer the questions at the end of the social studies chapter but who could never answer the same questions on a test. She had assumed he had a poor memory or was not studying for the test, but she now realized there was another possible explanation. Imagine that the question he was trying to answer was: "What is the capital of Rhode Island?" Imagine further that the student had no meanings for the words *capital* and *Rhode Island*. He was smart enough, however, to realize that the questions at the end of each chapter usually followed the sequence of the chapter, so he searched through the text until he found a sentence that said: "The capital of Rhode Island is Providence." He then wrote the word *Providence* on his paper in answer to the question and went on to the next: "When did Roger Williams settle Rhode Island?" The answer to this *wh-* transformation question was found in the text sentence "Roger Williams settled Rhode Island in 1636." In this way Charlie correctly answered most of the questions at the end of the chapter. Since he still didn't know meanings for the words *Rhode Island*, *capital*, *Providence*, *Roger Williams*, and *settle*, his answers were meaningless to him.

Miss Tent then asked the teachers how they might do if tested in a few days on information from the medical selection about which they had just answered five questions correctly! The teachers got the message. Several agreed that they had had students like Charlie and had never thought that a student might be able to answer questions even if he or she did not understand what was being read.

Next, Miss Tent asked the teachers what made this medical selection impossible for them to comprehend. Lack of background information was again listed as a factor. The sentences, although long, were not difficult to understand because they were not structurally complicated. The vocabulary, again, was seen as a major impediment, but this time the teachers had no general meanings for the words. The special vocabulary was termed "technical jargon," and this factor was added as number four to the list of factors that can make comprehension more difficult.

To bring this session of the meeting to a close and help teachers apply what they had learned to their own subject areas, Miss Tent wrote a number on the board and asked each teacher to turn to this page in one of the textbooks she had asked them to bring to the meeting. When all had done this, she asked them first to look for any technical jargon — words peculiar to a particular subject — and make a list of these terms. Next, they looked for words that have a general meaning but are used in some specialized way in their subject area. They then counted the number of words in the longest sentence on that page, and decided whether that sentence was structurally complicated. Finally, she asked them to look at any graphic material on that page and state what one would have to know in order to interpret it. The teachers then got together according to departments and made a chart listing all this information. The chart made by the science teachers looked like this:

SCIENCE

Technical Jargon		Words Used in Specialized Way
microscope	cerebrum	carbon
cellulose	pons	schools
xylem	cerebellum	organ
phloem	medulla	skeleton
carbohydrate	lymph	chambers
synthetic	neurons	properties
fibrovascular	galaxy	building blocks
topology	chloroplast	digest
insulin	photosynthesis	tissue
diabetes	nitrogen	stage
species	amino acids	series
estrogen	proteins	state
ovary	minerals	root
hemoglobin	cytologist	sound
oxyhemoglobin	contour plowing	colon
pancreas	irrigation	base
bladder	root cap	plain
hydrosphere	membrane	cape
lithosphere	nuclear	pole
chemical		matter
		mine
		iron
		culture
		graft
		power
		cell

Graphics — illustration of brain
          diagram of frog's heart and internal structure
          flow chart
          graph
Longest sentence — 40 words

FOR READERS TO DO TOGETHER:

Complete the activity just described by Miss Tent. Each person should choose a subject area of interest and survey one page of text to answer the questions: (1) What technical jargon is used? (2) What specialized vocabulary is used? (3) How long is the longest sentence? (4) Are the sentences structurally complicated? (5) What graphic material must be read? Working with the other people in your general subject area, make a chart compiling this information. Compare the charts from the various subject areas. What can you conclude about the difficulty of reading content-area texts?

As the teachers munched doughnuts and drank coffee during the break, they surveyed the charts made by the various groups. Miss Tent was delighted to see that the lists on the charts were extensive and that many of the teachers were so surprised to discover the reading difficulty presented by all their textbooks. After the break, Miss Tent handed them the following *cloze passage* (see definition below) to complete. She instructed them to put in each blank the one word they thought had been omitted. With a few groans, the teachers settled down to this task as Miss Tent hung the charts they had constructed.

FOR THE READER TO DO:

Complete this cloze passage by putting in each blank the one word you believe was originally there.

A *cloze passage* is one in which words have been systematically deleted and replaced by blanks. Cloze passages may be used to determine a student's instructional reading level as _____ as to assess the _____ ability to comprehend or _____ a particular passage. This _____ has been used successfully _____ readers, fourth grade through _____ .

To construct a cloze _____ , choose a 300-word _____ . Leave the first and _____ 25 words of the _____ intact. Beginning with the _____ word in the passage, _____ every fifth word and _____ it with a blank _____ there are 50 blanks. _____ blanks should be of _____ length. Before administering the _____ test, one should direct _____ readers to complete each _____ with the exact word _____ think has been deleted. _____ test should have no _____ limit, and students should _____ no help. Tests should _____ be collected and scored, _____ correct only those answers _____ match the original word (_____ are correct if the _____ believes the correct word _____ intended, but synonyms are _____ be marked incorrect).

Students _____ correctly complete 44–57 _____ of the blanks may _____ expected to adequately comprehend _____ material after some instruction. _____ passage may be said _____ to be at their "instructional _____ ." If a student is _____ to successfully complete 44 _____ of the blanks, the _____ is too difficult for _____ even with instruction and _____ should be tested in _____ material. If a student _____ com-

pletes more than 57 _____ of the blanks, he _____ be expected to read
_____ passage without instruction. The _____ may want to test
_____ in more difficult material _____ find an instructional level.

It took the teachers nearly 20 minutes to complete the cloze passage. When
they had completed it, Miss Tent read them the entire passage with the original
words in the blanks (see Appendix A), and the teachers checked their own papers. As Miss Tent had expected, there were cries of outrage at her unwillingness to accept synonyms, many of which were "better" than the words originally put there by the authors. Miss Tent was able to explain to the teachers,
however, that accepting synonyms would present a tremendous scoring and interpretation problem. "If we score passages counting only exact replacements
as correct," she queried, "would each of you scoring the same text come up
with the same score for a student?" The teachers agreed that they would and
realized that there would be less agreement in their scoring if they accepted
synonyms. "What I would accept as correct, Miss Stern would never accept,"
Mr. Lucky pointed out. The teachers chuckled. As Miss Stern squirmed and
frowned, Miss Tent realized that the English teacher must be known to have a
penchant for "just the right word."

"Now," Miss Tent continued, "If we counted synonyms as correct, what
would happen to the percentages for determining instructional level?" The
teachers agreed that these percentages would have to be higher, but no one
knew how much higher, and several teachers contended it would vary with the
passage and with the scorer. Miss Tent explained that these percentages had
been established by determining the average percentage scores obtained on
cloze passages by students who could read those passages at an instructional
level. If synonyms were counted, it was impossible to know what the percentage range for instructional level would be, since this would vary among passages and scorers.

Miss Tent had intended to have each teacher construct a cloze passage from
a textbook but, realizing she had only an hour and a half left, decided she
couldn't possibly do that besides the Guided Reading Procedure, which was
essential. She therefore hurriedly explained to them the concept of instructional level: it was the level of material a student could understand if given
some guidance and direction in reading that material. She pointed out to them
that every reader has an instructional level, an independent level, and a frustration level. The frustration level, she noted, had been experienced by all of them
that morning when trying to read the statistics and medical excerpts. The independent level was the level at which most adults did most of their reading —
newspapers, magazines, novels, or their own subject-area textbooks. These
were all independent-level reading for most teachers. Instructional-level materials that teachers read might include educational research studies in their field
and some of the textbooks assigned in their graduate courses at State.

"For students for whom a textbook is at the frustration level," Miss Tent
emphasized, "no amount of guidance and direction will enable them to read
that text with understanding. Those students need another text or structured
listening activities. In a few minutes I will teach you two specific ways to struc-

ture listening activities for such students. For students who are at instructional level in a textbook, however, there are many ways you can guide them through the material so that they can read it meaningfully. If you want to find out on the very first day of school which of your students can read the text independently, which can read it with guidance and instruction, and which cannot read it even with guidance and instruction, follow the simple instructions in the cloze passage you just completed to construct a cloze passage for your own textbook. Give this test to the students and then grade it, sorting the tests into three piles as you grade (independent level, instructional level, frustration level.) Do not, however, return these tests to your students. I was just barely able to explain to you why synonyms don't count, but your students would never understand it! While a few students will be incorrectly placed by using the cloze test and criteria, you will quickly learn who they are as you work with them and can adjust your expectations for them. This afternoon and tomorrow, I'll be glad to help you construct your cloze tests, and once you have scored them, I'll be glad to help you plan instruction based on the results. Now, let's take a quick stretch break, and then, as promised, I'll teach you some structured listening activities."

FOR THE READER TO DO:

Choose a textbook in a subject area of interest to you. Construct a cloze test from a passage in that textbook. Administer the test to students and, on the basis of the results, determine for which students the textbook is independent, instructional, or frustration level.

Once more the group reassembled, and Miss Tent realized with concern that she had less than one hour left. "Why do I always plan twice as much as I can possibly do?" she asked herself as she passed out copies of an *NASSP Bulletin* article, "Improving Listening in Content Area Subjects." She told the teachers she was going to demonstrate a teaching strategy with them that they could use with students to guide their reading, and at the same time teach them two listening comprehension strategies to use with students who could not read the text or who needed to improve their listening comprehension ability. She then asked them to read the *NASSP Bulletin* article to remember everything! Somewhat skeptically, the teachers began to read the article. Miss Tent, nearly worn out at this point in the meeting, smiled at the wink Mr. Topps gave her as he, too, settled down to read the article.

FOR THE READER TO DO:

Do as the Upton Hill teachers are doing. Read the article "Improving Listening in Content Area Subjects" to remember everything!

Improving Listening
in Content Area Subjects

Patricia M. Cunningham
James W. Cunningham

**The ability to listen attentively and critically, the
authors state, is crucial. In the following article they
describe two techniques for improving listening
skills.**

Mr. Blackard teaches history. He is qualified to teach history, desires
to teach history, and is employed to and recompensed for teaching history. He has neither the time, nor the training, nor the responsibility to
teach anything else.

One day, however, Mr. Blackard began to wonder if he was transmitting his subject matter in the most efficient, economical way. If he
could use some teaching strategies that improved his students' history
learning and increased their facility with language, he thought, he and
his students would be twice rewarded. Mr. Blackard did some research,
and made some remarkable discoveries!

Why Not Teach Listening?

The ability to listen attentively and critically is crucial to success in all
academic areas as well as in everyday living. Studies have found that
students are expected to listen for over half of their school day and that
the amount of time required for listening increases in the higher grades
(Wilt, 1950; Nichols and Stevens, 1957). Study after study has demonstrated that listening abilities can be improved with direct instruction
(Hogan, 1953; Hollow, 1955; Edgar, 1961; Devine, 1961; Lundstein,
1963). Unfortunately, this direct instruction is seldom given except in
the context of a research project!

Three explanations are commonly offered for the lack of instruction
in listening. They are:

1. Listening is seen as a maturation process that just naturally gets

*Patricia M. Cunningham and James W. Cunningham are assistant professors at
the University of North Carolina, Chapel Hill.*

better as the child gets older. (Most high school teachers will dispute this point.)
2. There are few guides, manuals, or other structured programs to direct listening instruction.
3. Improving listening is everyone's job and consequently is attempted by no one.

While these three explanations are probably valid, there is a fourth explanation that also merits consideration: Teaching listening is analogous to teaching reading comprehension. Instruction in reading can be divided into decoding (figuring out what the squiggles say) and comprehension (figuring out what the squiggles mean). Many teachers believe comprehension to be synonymous with thinking, and frankly admit they don't know how to teach it.

In listening, the decoding function is assumed. Children are expected to be able to hear and reproduce the oral input. (If they have difficulties in decoding this input, they are promptly referred to the speech therapist or other specialist.) Instruction in listening is instruction in comprehension.

While there are differences between listening and reading (listeners cannot control their listening rate or make regressions; must adjust to dialectical differences, and cannot generally relisten), techniques that improve reading comprehension should result in increased listening comprehension. In the remainder of this article, two techniques for improving listening in content subjects will be described. These techniques will not take time away from content teaching; will improve the student's learning of content; and will increase the student's general language facility.

Directed Listening Activity

The concept of directed reading is a mainstay of good reading instruction. While there is disagreement as to the exact number and order of steps, most experts agree on at least three stages: a readiness stage, a reading-recitation stage, and a follow-up stage. Within these stages the following activities should take place:

1. The Readiness Stage
   a. Establish motivation for the lesson.
   b. Introduce any new or difficult concepts.
   c. Introduce any new or difficult words (five per lesson is a maximum).
   d. Set purposes for listening.
2. The Listening-Reciting Stage

a. Students listen to satisfy the purposes for listening set during readiness.

b. The teacher asks several literal and inferential questions that relate to the purposes set during readiness.

c. The students volunteer interpretive and evaluative comments about the lesson. Some class discussion may ensue.

d. If there are errors or gaps in the students' understanding of the lesson, the teacher directs the students to relisten to certain parts of the lesson.

3. The Follow-Up Stage:

a. The teacher provides opportunities for and encourages students to engage in activities that build on and develop concepts acquired during the lesson. These may include writing, reading, small group discussions, art activities, etc.

Here are some examples of directed listening activities taught in content-area classes:

Mrs. Cowen used a directed listening activity in her tenth-grade home economics class. During the readiness stage, Mrs. Cowen motivated the students to listen by presenting facts and figures on the rising cost of beef, both in dollars and in pounds of grain needed to produce it. She then introduced the terms: complete and incomplete protein, animal and vegetable protein, and grams. The purpose set for listening was: Listen to determine which protein foods are complete and which are incomplete.

During the listening-reciting stage, Mrs. Cowen talked to the students about the protein value of food compared to dollars and grain costs. To satisfy the purpose set for listening, students classified 12 foods as complete or incomplete proteins.

As a follow-up to this lesson, students kept a one-week record of the foods they ate that contained protein. They then classified these into complete and incomplete protein, and animal and vegetable protein. Finally, they estimated the cost in dollars and grain for each person's total protein intake.

* * *

Mrs. Jason teaches an eighth grade remedial math class. She introduced the basics of the metric system with a directed listening activity. After establishing motivation for the lesson by explaining that our nation will soon be adapting this measurement system, Mrs. Jason introduced the words liter, gram, and meter, and the concept of volume. She set purposes for listening by asking the students to listen for answers to the following questions: How did the meter originate? Which is larger—a liter or a quart? a meter or a yard? a gram or an ounce?

During the listening-reciting stage, Mrs. Jason described an American trying to survive in Paris. As he travelled and shopped he discovered some relationships between American units and metric units. Mrs. Jason then questioned the students to see that they had fulfilled the purposes set for listening and provided further explanation where necessary.

As a follow-up, Mrs. Jason distributed metric-converter slide rules and the students converted yards to meters, quarts to liters, and ounces to grams.

Guided Listening Procedure

The guided listening procedure is based on and adopted from the guided reading procedure developed by Anthony V. Manzo (1975). This procedure differs from the directed listening activity in purpose and procedure. The purpose of the guided listening procedure is to improve students' long-term recall. Whereas the directed listening activity can be varied and used frequently, the guided listening procedure follows set steps and should not be used more than once every two or three weeks.

In the guided listening procedure, the teacher selects some material for the students to hear. The teacher may give a lecture, a selection, or play a record, or tape. The selection should not exceed 10 minutes of total listening time. The teacher then proceeds through the following nine steps (the first eight steps can be completed in a 50-minute period or less if the listening selection is 10 minutes or less).

1. The teacher sets the major purpose: "Listen to remember *everything.*"
2. The teacher lectures, reads, or plays a recorded selection. If the teacher is lecturing, she records her lecture.
3. The teacher reminds the students that she asked them to listen to remember everything. She then writes everything they remember on the board. (She may have two students perform this task.) During this stage the teacher accepts and writes everything the students contribute. She makes no corrections and asks no questions.
4. The teacher reads everything listed on the board, directing the students to look for incorrect or missing information.
5. The students listen again to the tape, record, or reading to correct wrong information and obtain missing information.
6. The information on the board is amended and added to as needed.
7. The teacher asks the students which ideas on the board seem to be the main ideas, the most important ideas, the ones they think they should remember for a long time. She marks these items.
8. Now that the students have mastered the literal level of the selection, the teacher raises any inferential questions she feels are vital for complete understanding.
9. The teacher erases the board and tests short-term memory with a test that is not dependent on reading or writing skills. (Oral true/false or multiple-choice items will do.)
10. Test long-term memory with a similar test containing different items several weeks later.

There is no need for the teacher to grade these tests; rather, the students should be allowed to exchange papers or grade their own. They may then record their scores and chart their own growth in short and long-term listening retention. Two separate graphs, like the model shown in the figure, could be kept in the students' notebooks.

	GLP #1	GLP #2	GLP #3	GLP #4	GLP #5
1					
2					
3					
4					
5					

QUESTIONS CORRECT

The following examples are taken from actual guided listening procedures taught in secondary content subjects.

Mr. Fred used the guided listening procedure with his junior high school general music class. After being instructed to listen to remember everything, the class listened to a record on classical music. Two students then wrote everything the class remembered on the chalkboard. After reviewing the information on the board, the students relistened to the record and corrected some misinformation. Mr. Fred then helped the students determine the main ideas, which he then circled. In order to apply what they had learned to contemporary culture, Mr. Fred asked the students if they saw any parallels between the development of classical music and the development of hard rock music. After erasing the board, Mr. Fred gave a five-item true/false test. The students exchanged papers, graded the tests, and recorded them on their graphs. Two weeks later, Mr. Fred gave a long-term memory test over the same material. These scores were recorded on the long-term recall graph.

* * *

Mr. Garry used the guided listening procedure in his eleventh-grade communications electronics class. After preparing the students by asking them not to take notes but to listen to remember everything, he lectured to them about basic vacuum tube action, illustrating key points with drawings on the board. He then wrote all their comments on the board and played a tape recording of his lecture. Students added much information to that already on the board and corrected some misconceptions. After marking the student-determined main ideas, Mr. Garry asked students why the basic vacuum tube theory was crucial to communication electronics. A short-term matching test was followed a week later by a long-term test.

A Happy Ending

Mr. Blackard continues to teach history, but his students are listening better, understanding better, and learning more history. He often pauses between classes to think, "And I thought I would have to teach less history to improve their listening."

Language is the medium by which content is transmitted. Improving student language ability can only benefit the learning of that content.

References

Devine, T. C. "The Development and Evaluation of a Series of Recordings for Teaching Certain Critical Listening Abilities." Doctoral dissertation, Boston University, 1961.

Dixon, Norman R. "Listening: Most Neglected of the Language Arts." *Elementary English,* March 1964, pp. 285-288.

Edgar, K. F., "The Validation of Four Methods of Improving Listening Ability." Doctoral dissertation, University of Pittsburgh, 1961.

Hogan, Ursula. *An Experiment in Improving Listening Skills of Fifth and Sixth Grade Pupils.* Master's thesis, University of California at Berkeley, 1953.

Hollow, Sister Mary Kevin. "Listening Comprehension at the Intermediate Grade Level." *Elementary School Journal,* December 1955, pp. 158-61.

Lundstein, Sara W. *"Teaching Abilities in Critical Listening in the Fifth and Sixth Grade."* Doctoral dissertation, University of California at Berkeley, 1963.

Manzo, Anthony V. "Guided Reading Procedure." *Journal of Reading,* January 1975, pp. 287-291.

Nichols, Ralph G., and Stevens, Leonard A., *Are You Listening?* New York: McGraw-Hill Book Co., Inc., 1957.

Wilt, Mirian E. "A Study of Teacher Awareness of Listening as a Factor in Elementary Education." *Journal of Educational Research,* April 1950, pp 626-36.

From the *NASSP Bulletin,* Vol. 60, No. 404, December 1976, pp. 26-31. Reprinted by permission.

Within 10 minutes, most of the teachers had completed reading the article. Miss Tent asked those who had finished to put the article inside their notebooks and instructed those who had not finished reading to continue reading until they had. She then told the teachers that she was going to list the ideas they remembered on some pieces of chart paper. "In fact," she remarked as she looked at the clock and realized it was 11:25, "let's have several of you be recorders, so it will take us much less time to make our list." Miss Stern, Miss Werth, and Mr. Topps volunteered to record, and on the charts they listed what the teachers remembered.

Mr. Battle remembered that "a Guided Listening Procedure should not be used every day." Miss Cook contributed "in a Directed Listening Activity there are three stages: readiness, listening-reciting, and followup." Mr. Gramm remembered that "a Guided Listening Procedure helps improve long-term memory." After the initial two or three suggestions, other remembrances came quickly, and even with three recorders, it was hard to write down the information as fast as it was recalled. Finally, when the teachers had exhausted their remembrances, Miss Tent numbered the list. As she did so, she read each item on the list, asking teachers to think about whether, given the information they had just read, each item was correct or not.

When she had read all the items on the list, Miss Tent instructed the teachers to take a minute to go back to the article and check on any information listed on the charts they believed might be incorrect. Mr. Battle said he believed that No. 27 was wrong. "It said a Guided Listening Procedure could be completed in a 50-minute period, not a 60-minute period," he explained. Miss Tent asked him to read the part of the article that told him that, and Mr. Battle did so. After verifying the correction against the text in this way, Miss Tent corrected item No. 27. No other corrections were needed, but several teachers did add information they thought was important that had not been put on the charts originally.

Next, Miss Tent asked the teachers to listen as she read the items on the charts one last time. This time their purpose in listening was to sort out the main ideas from the details. "While we can all agree and verify that all this information was stated in the article, we may not all agree on which ideas are the most important ideas, the main ideas, the ones we would like to remember from this article," she explained. "We as a group would probably choose more main ideas than any of you would choose individually. Let's go ahead, however, and pick out seven or eight main idea statements. I'll circle those you tell me to." Mrs. Baker said that, to her, No. 4 ("Listening skills can be improved if they are taught") and No. 7 ("Improved listening will result in increased content learning") were important, and Miss Tent circled those two statements. Other statements were suggested for their importance and circled, until nine had been identified as the main ideas of the article.

As Miss Tent was removing the charts from the board, she asked the teachers how they might use Directed Listening Activities and Guided Listening Procedures in their classes. Several teachers felt that these types of activities would be particularly appropriate for classes with many students who could not read well enough to read the textbook. Other teachers felt that all students would profit from some direct instruction in listening. Miss Werth thought that the Guided Listening Procedure would be a very effective way to teach her home economics classes to listen to a set of directions. All in all, the teachers seemed enthusiastic about these two listening comprehension strategies.

Miss Tent told the teachers that there was just one more quick step in the Guided Reading Procedure she was demonstrating with them. On a sheet of paper, the teachers numbered from 1 to 5, and Miss Tent read five true/false statements to them. Each teacher then checked his or her own paper as Miss Tent read the correct answers. Most teachers got the answers to all five questions correct.

"Now," said Miss Tent, "I have just led you through a Guided Reading Procedure, which is a technique you can use with your students. The Guided Reading Procedure was developed by a Professor Anthony Manzo from the University of Missouri at Kansas City, who addressed a seminar I attended at State last summer. His theory is that many children do not comprehend a lot of what they read because they don't have many stored facts to which they can compare, contrast, and relate the information being read. He suggests that if Guided Reading Procedures are done every two weeks, with a delayed retention test in the intervening week, after several procedures students will begin to develop a mind-set to try to remember more of what they read. About the fourth time they sit down to read a selection with the direction 'Read to remember everything,' a little voice inside their heads begins to say, 'Hey, now I am going to remember this stuff well enough this time so that I can do as well on the test a week from now as I do on the one today.' This is when, Tony hypothesizes, you will begin to see some improvement in long-term memory of information read. Over the course of a year, it is hoped this mind-set to remember what you read will transfer to material being read at times other than during Guided Reading Procedures. As this continues, readers increase their store of facts with which to think about what they are reading."

Miss Stern interrupted Miss Tent as she was finishing her last sentence, to ask: "This is a very interesting idea, and I know my English students don't have very much literature-related trivia in their heads, but if I had my entire class do this Guided Reading Procedure, five or six of the students wouldn't be able to read the simplest selection I could find. What do I do with them?" Miss Tent had anticipated this question and was pleased that it was Miss Stern who had asked it. Miss Stern was certainly the person to win over in the English department. She looked around the room, singled out a group of five teachers, and inquired, "Imagine that you five couldn't read the article I just gave you to read, would you have learned the information contained in that article?" Mr. Battle genially remarked that everyone knew coaches couldn't read, and Miss Tent then realized that she had inadvertently singled out Will Wynn and the other coaches, who were seated together at the rear of the library. Fortunately, the group laughed good-naturedly, and it appeared that no feelings were hurt. Miss Tent repeated her question to the group as a whole: "Well, we all assume these coaches can read as well as play ball, but what if they couldn't? Would they have learned the information about listening comprehension strategies I wanted to teach you?" The group agreed that, if the coaches had listened as the other teachers were stating their remembrances and while Miss Tent read all the items on the chart twice, they would indeed have learned the information, even though they couldn't read the article. Miss Tent then asked, "Could they have done well on the true/false test I gave you after you had read the article?"

Again the group agreed, and Miss Tent could tell they were beginning to appreciate the value of a Guided Reading Procedure.

Mr. Battle summed it up for everyone, when he said, "Now, Miss Tent, are you telling me that if we do Guided Reading Procedures with our classes, even the students who cannot read the material will learn our content and that, if a test does not require them to read, they can do well on it? If so, that's a strategy I, for one, plan to use!" Other teachers nodded their heads, and Mr. Topps announced that it was five minutes past lunchtime and that Miss Tent had proved her worth under fire today. He said he hoped her fellow teachers would be calling on her to demonstrate this and other strategies in their classrooms. After handing out a sheet on which she had listed the steps of the Guided Reading Procedure, Miss Tent was last seen in animated conversation with Miss Werth and Mr. Sherk.

FOR THE READER TO DO:

Make your own handout on the Guided Reading Procedure by revising the steps described in the article the Upton Hill teachers read. Compare and contrast Guided Listening Procedure and Guided Reading Procedure.

September   At the end of the faculty workshop, I thought I was really on my way toward a super year. What a disappointment this month has been! It all started on the morning following the faculty meeting, when I found on my desk a stack of social studies books accompanied by this note:

> Miss Tent,
> Your workshop was the most interesting one I have attended! I am most interested in trying out the strategies you taught us. Here are the social studies texts I use. Would you please make me cloze passages for them?
>
> W. W. Battle
>
> P.S. – I need 100 copies of each, Monday if possible.

Well, I didn't know what to do. I certainly didn't think it was my job to construct cloze passages for his textbooks! On the other hand, I didn't want to discourage Mr. Battle from using the cloze test or appear unwilling to help him. While many of the teachers told me how much they enjoyed the in-service and how much they had learned, only Miss Werth and Mr. Sherk actually asked me to work with them and their classes. I decided the thing to do was to make one cloze passage, take this down to Mr. Battle, and then work together with him to make the others. When I had one typed and ready, I headed for Mr. Battle's room. He was nowhere in sight, and Mrs. Epock told me he was attending a meeting of the local teachers' association. He would be gone all day. I spent the rest of that morning making cloze passages for Mr. Battle!

On Monday the students arrived to begin the term. All day I was busy helping Mr. Topps and Mr. Rule, the guidance counselor, register new students and get classes scheduled for them. I did get a chance to go by Mr. Battle's room and was pleased to observe that the students were working diligently on the cloze passages I had made. On Tuesday morning, I found those same cloze passages back on my desk with a second note from Mr. Battle:

Miss Teat,

Since you don't have any classes, would you please score these for me? I could do it over the weekend, but I'd like to know as soon as possible which kids can read the book so I can begin to plan my lessons!

You're a doll!

W.W. Battle

At first I wanted to take that huge stack of papers right down and throw them at him. I did not, however. Actually, I didn't have anything I had to do that day. Still, no one besides Miss Werth and Mr. Sherk had asked me for help, and they wanted me to wait until their classes were settled. I knew that if I went to the office I would have to help with the "getting the year started" chores. "Oh, heck, why not?" I mumbled as I settled down to the enormous stack of tests.

That afternoon I took them down to Mr. Battle. In each of his classes, he had some students who could read the book at an independent level, some who could read it at an instructional level, and some who could not read it at all. Mr. Battle informed me that this just went to prove what he had always believed: "We should track these kids, so that we don't have all these different abilities in one room. We used to do that here before Mr. Topps came. Maybe it wasn't good for the self-concept of the slower students, and maybe they created problems when they were all together all in one room, but at least you could teach the other students who could read the book." I was just beginning to suggest some ways of dealing with the different reading levels he had when we were interrupted by a voice on the intercom asking Mr. Battle to come to the office and talk to a teacher. Mr. Battle patted me on the back, thanked me for all my help, and said he didn't blame *me* for the crazy way they set up the classes and left. I have tried several times to talk with him and help him plan instruction for the different levels. He is always very nice—and in a very big hurry to get somewhere!

So I made and scored all those cloze tests, and as far as I can tell, he is not doing anything any differently, based on the results of the tests. As if that weren't bad enough, several other teachers heard that I had constructed and scored his cloze tests and brought me their books to do the same thing. What could I do? I spent the first week of school making and scoring cloze tests!

I have worked with Miss Werth this month, and that has been very exciting. A second-year teacher in the home economics department, she is enthusiastic and eager to learn. I have worked with her almost every day in her third-period class, an introductory home economics course. In this class, she has several students who are practically nonreaders and who attend Mr. Moore's remedial reading classes. Miss Werth has found Directed Listening Activities and Guided Listening Procedures to be especially effective in the "foods" unit they are now doing. For these lessons, she often uses magazine articles about food preparation and serving. The students relate well to this "real-world" reading material, and the pictures really help them understand what is being said. Since the order in which you do things is crucial to successful cooking, Miss Werth does many Directed Listening Activities in which the purpose set for listening is to "Listen so that you can put

DLA

these steps [e.g., for making carrot cake] in order." The students are introduced to vocabulary and taken through the listening-reciting stage of a Directed Listening Activity
one day. The next day, they carry out the instructions to create the food. This activity is a
natural and functional followup for the directed listening.

Translation writing   Last week, I demonstrated a translation-writing lesson for Miss Werth. For part of her
foods unit, Miss Werth attempts to give the students an understanding of the role of vitamins and minerals in maintaining good health and of the vitamin and mineral content of
various foods. To teach the translation-writing lesson, we selected from one of Miss
Werth's texts a three-page section describing the functions of the different vitamins. I
asked the students to listen as I read the selection, so that when I finished they could tell
me what I had read. I told them we would compile their "translation" of what I read and,
from these collective translations, would construct a textbook jointly authored by them,
for their later personal reference and study.

I then read the three-page selection one paragraph at a time. When I finished each
paragraph, I stopped and asked the students to tell me what the paragraph said. As they
did so, I recorded this information on a chart. I then reread the paragraph to them and let
them reread their translations of that paragraph. Often, after the paragraph was read the
second time, we would revise what had been originally written on the chart. It took longer
than I had expected to complete this activity, and we were forced to finish the last two
paragraphs on the following day.

When we had finally finished, I let volunteers read portions of our translated text. I then
typed it and ran off copies for the students. I also constructed several exercises based on
the translated text, which the students could complete. One exercise consisted of several
true/false comprehension questions. In another exercise, I left out a key word in each
sentence and had the students try to fill in that word. They then checked their filled-in
copy with the original.

For another exercise, I scrambled the sentence order, and the students had to reorder
the sentences to make a sensible composition. There was much arguing about the results of this one, and we finally had to conclude there were several possible orderings that
were as good as the original. For the most part, the students enjoyed the dictation of the
selection and the ensuing activities, and they certainly did learn the information about vitamins and minerals. Miss Werth says she is covering less this year, but the students are
learning what she teaches. She is going to do another translation-writing lesson with
them next week. Eventually they will have created a textbook they can read and review.

FOR THE READER TO DO:

Choose a student or a group of students who are having difficulty reading their textbook.
Do a translation-writing lesson with them as Miss Tent did with Miss Werth's home economics class. Using the translated text, make some comprehension exercises for them
to complete. Do several such lessons and compile their translation into a self-created
textbook.

My work with Mr. Sherk's class has not been so successful. Actually, the lessons I have
taught have gone quite well. The problem is that Mr. Sherk himself has not been there to
observe my "demonstration" lessons! After the faculty workshop, Mr. Sherk came up to
me and said he thought some of his general mathematics students might be having difficulty reading the directions and word problems in their textbooks. He asked if I would

come in and see whether I thought this judgment was accurate and then help him decide what to do about the problem.

Math diagnosis

I spent several hours reviewing the first chapter in the book and creating for the students some exercises that would tell me how well they could read the text. One diagnostic activity was a list of symbols that had to be matched with their verbal translation. This was simply a test of their knowledge that "=" is read as *equals*, "%" is read as *percent*, etc. I chose the symbols from those used in the first chapter of the text. I also devised an activity in which students had to match written numbers to their verbal counterparts: for example, 1,000,000 was matched to *one million*; 256,780 was matched to *two hundred fifty-six thousand seven hundred eighty*. In the final diagnostic activity, I chose some of the word problems in the chapter and asked students questions that would indicate their understanding of what they were being asked to do. Their task was not to solve the problem, but simply to understand what was given and what was being asked for.

During the second week of school, I administered these diagnostic activities to two of Mr. Sherk's general mathematics classes. As the students were completing the activities, I asked individuals to read a short portion of the explanatory part of the text and then explain in their own words what had been read. I explained to Mr. Sherk that he would very quickly learn to tell which students could read their text with comprehension and which couldn't. My plan was that, for these two classes, Mr. Sherk and I would listen together as each student read and explained a few sentences in the text. We would then, separately, rate each student by starring the names of those who could definitely read the text, putting a minus next to those who could definitely not read it, and putting a question mark next to those about whom we were not sure. I thought that by separately rating each and then comparing our ratings, Mr. Sherk would see that, in most cases, our judgments were the same; thus he would gain confidence in his ability to determine which students could read the textbook and which couldn't.

Unfortunately, things didn't work out quite that way. I went into Mr. Sherk's class and got the students started on the diagnostic activities and then explained to Mr. Sherk that I wanted each of us, separately, to rate each student and then compare our ratings. He said he thought that was a marvelous idea but that first he had to take care of some business in the office for a few minutes and, if I would start without him, he would return "pronto." Pronto, it turned out, was almost two full class periods later. When he returned, he was very apologetic and explained that he had been detained and just couldn't get away. With much effort, I smiled and said I knew how that could happen. I then gathered up those three sets of diagnostic activities for two classes of 30-plus students and the sheets on which I had rated each student on oral reading and retelling. "I'll score these, and then we'll have a conference to talk about what to do with those students who can't read the text." Well, Mr. Sherk's intuition that many of his general mathematics students could not read the text was certainly correct. In fact, I found only seven students in both sections who performed well on all three diagnostic activities and on individual oral reading.

FOR THE READER TO DO:

Select a mathematics textbook. Make some diagnostic activities, like those described by Miss Tent, in which you diagnose the student's ability to read symbols, numbers, and word problems. Choose an explanatory paragraph for individual students to read aloud and explain. If possible, administer these diagnostic activities to a group of students. Which of them need reading instruction in order to comprehend their math textbook?

Armed with this evidence, I went to my scheduled meeting with Mr. Sherk during his planning period. We planned several lessons on vocabulary and reading word problems that I would demonstrate with his second-period class and then he would teach to his third-period class. So far, I have taught two of these lessons. Both times, Mr. Sherk has managed to slip out of the room on some urgent business as I taught the demonstration lesson! Each time he is very apologetic and seems so sincere! If this happens one more time, however, I've had it! Mr. Topps came into Sherk's class the other morning while I was demonstrating for no audience. He observed the lesson and was very complimentary. I wanted to talk to him about my problem but was afraid to appear as if I were carrying tales.

All in all, this month has been a disappointing one. The workshop went exceptionally well, and many of the teachers have used cloze tests in order to decide whether their students can read their textbooks. Some are now much more sympathetic toward those students who cannot read the book and are trying to teach vocabulary and do directed and guided listening lessons with their students. However, they don't seem to want me in their classrooms. I must be able to demonstrate some alternate teaching strategies if I am going to have an effect on the way they teach and on their students' learning. I am scheduled to have a conference with Mr. Topps next week. Perhaps he can give me some advice on how to get into more classrooms.

October

Looking back over this month, the most positive thing I can think of is that it got better as it went on! On the first day of October, I went into Mr. Sherk's class to teach a lesson on solving word problems. Soon after I started, he slipped out again. I got very angry, and I think the students sensed what was happening. They became quite hard to manage, and I felt as if I were being given the substitute-teacher treatment. I managed to stay there and teach the lesson. When the period ended, I left Mr. Sherk a note in which I explained that I was hired to *help* him improve his students' reading abilities, not to teach his class for him! He was very apologetic that afternoon after school, but I haven't been back in his classroom since. I feel bad about this situation and wish I could have thought of some other way to resolve it, but I cannot continue to be used as a substitute teacher!

After terminating my work in Mr. Sherk's classroom, I had only Miss Werth's class in which to work! The days were very long, and I learned a lot of home economics. Miss Werth is having such success with her "academically unmotivated" students by using Directed Listening Activities, Guided Listening Procedures, and translation writing with them. She is eager, however, to help these students so they can at least read some simple recipes. In a cookbook intended for young children, she found several that she thought were clearly written and easy to follow. Together, we looked at the recipes and identified the words that were crucial to reading these simple recipes and occurred over and over again in most recipes. (*Teaspoon, tablespoon, cup, half, quarter, mix, beat, sift, eggs, milk, baking power,* and *shortening* were just a few of the 55 words we identified as a core vocabulary for reading simple recipes.) I suggested to Miss Werth that we use the *Words on the Wall* strategy to teach her students to read and write these core words. To

Words on the Wall

begin with, we selected 15 of the 55 words and wrote these on half sheets of construction paper. I began by explaining to the students that there were some words it was crucial that they be able to recognize rapidly when reading a recipe, and that it would help them in copying recipes from their friends or from magazines if they could spell these words without any trouble. I told them that they would spend the first five minutes of each home economics period learning to spell these core words. At first, there were sighs and groans, and I was reminded that spelling is not an "academically unmotivated" student's favorite pastime. I ignored their protests, however, and continued with the lesson. Taking the 15 words one at a time, I had a volunteer read each and tell me what it meant. For concrete words such as *teaspoon* and *shortening*, I had a student find that object or material and display it for the group. We discussed the difference between *teaspoon* and *tablespoon* and looked carefully at the differences in the words. *Baking powder* and *baking soda* were also discussed, and we matched the word on my card with the label on the container.

As each word was identified and its meaning attached to it, I had one of the students place these words in random order above the blackboard, I asked students to number from 1 to 15 on a sheet of paper for a spelling test. Again, there were groans and complaints. Again, I ignored them. When the papers were finally numbered, I proceeded to call out the words. Of course, these were the 15 words displayed on the wall, and the students at first throught it was a joke that they could copy the words off the wall for the test. They completed the "test," however, and I then had them exchange papers and grade each other's as I called out the word and pointed to the appropriate word on the wall. All but one student got 100 percent of the words correct (Emily had confused tablespoon and teaspoon!). Miss Werth then recorded their grades in her grade book. The conversation that followed went like this:

CAROLYN: Miss Werth, you mean these here grades gonna count on our report cards?

MISS WERTH: Well, yes Carolyn. I don't see how you can be a very good cook if you can't read and write the words that are used again and again in recipes. So learning to spell these words will help you to cook! We will have a spelling test at the beginning of every class, and the averaged grade for all these tests each week will count the same as one of your daily assignments.

SUE: Yes, but we got to look at the words when she was giving us that test. That wasn't no test!

MISS WERTH: Well, I admit that it wasn't very hard today. But each day I am going to call out the words faster and faster, and each week I am going to add ten words. In five weeks I will be calling out 15 words, but those 15 will come from a total of 55 words on the wall. It will get harder if that's what you want!

The other students told Sue to hush. The bell rang and 27 happy, "academically unmotivated" students bustled out to their other classes. At the beginning of each class for the rest of the week, Miss Werth had the students number their papers from 1 to 15 and write out each word as she called them out. She called out the words in a different order and a little faster each day. By Friday, Miss Werth observed that most of the students no longer looked up at the wall as the words were called out; rather they wrote the word as Miss Werth called it out and then looked up at the wall to check the spelling. The students were learning to spell the words!

On Monday of the following week, Miss Werth added 10 more words to the 15 already on the wall. She did this as she had observed me doing it. She took one word at a time, made sure the students could read it, had the students define the word, and, whenever possible, showed a tangible object or material represented by the word. The Monday lesson took most of the period. On the other days, it took only a few minutes at the beginning of the period to call out the 15-word spelling test and have the students check each other's papers and record the grades. This week, Miss Werth has added the last 10 words to the wall vocabulary. They are finishing up their unit on foods. They have read and followed many simple recipes. Presently, they are making some recipe file boxes and copying favorite recipes on cards. Yesterday, when I was in her class, I observed that most of the students were writing the 15 words Miss Werth was calling out from the wall vocabulary of 55 words without even looking up at the wall very often. They were all very proud of their spelling test grades. Emily informed me that after that first test, she had never missed another word and that she liked home economics class best of all!

GRP   I was finally able to track down Mr. Battle, and I taught a demonstration Guided Reading Procedure in his state/U.S. history class. I used a selection from a magazine that described historical sites of interest around the state. The lesson went very well. All the students got at least four of the five true/false questions right on the quiz and seemed to enjoy the lesson. They especially enjoyed being allowed to go back to the article to point out untrue statements listed by the other students. Actually, they wanted to correct these untrue statements as soon as the students said them, but I wouldn't let them. "You'll have a chance in a few minutes," I told them, "to go back to the article and justify your corrections. For now, we are just going to list what everyone says. If you think something isn't right, wait until we return to the article. Then you can prove your point by reading aloud the part that makes you think a statement is untrue." When we got to the step where I told them to listen as I read the items listed to see whether there were any they thought were incorrect or only partially correct, they were eager to skim the article and find the part that proved their point. When a student told me, "No. 31 is not right; the state museum is in the western corner of the state, not the eastern corner," I had that student read me the part verifying that. After he had read aloud the corroborating section, I made the correction in No. 31. In this way, the students observed I was changing items on the list not just because another student thought it was incorrect, but because the information in the article proved it so.

The only problem I had with the Guided Reading Procedure was when it came to the part where the students indicated which statements they thought were the main ideas. They wanted to circle them all. I understood why this was happening. There were several items on the list that all the students could agree were main ideas. There were also several items, however, that were only important to one or two students. But when we determined main ideas as a group, the combined number of main ideas that were important to any class member was quite large. I didn't know what to do about this at the time, but I think I solved the problem last week while doing a Guided Reading Procedure with Miss Stern's class. This time, anticipating the problem of almost all the ideas being designated as main ideas and knowing that would bother Miss Stern, I asked the students to listen as I read all the items on the list and to write down on a scrap of paper the numbers of the five items they considered the most important, the main ideas, what the story was mostly about. I read the items one at a time, and the students wrote down five numbers. Actually, many of the students had their five numbers written down before I was halfway through the list and then complained that some items in the latter part of the list were also main ideas. I told them they could change some they had already written down for the others, but in all they could not have more than five. After some juggling, most students were able to list just five items. I then went through each numbered item and had the students raise their hands if they had written that number down. I checked those items where the majority of the students raised their hands. In this way, we identified 7 main ideas from the 38 items listed on the board. These items were indeed the main ideas, and most students were pleased to see that most of the items they had selected did indeed turn out to be the main ideas. It was also interesting to note that many of the items were not chosen by anyone; these were clearly lesser details.

I have tried to find Mr. Battle and tell him about this way of determining main ideas, but he is always so busy, I can't ever seem to find a few minutes to talk with him. He seems concerned about how his students are reading the material, but I can't ever pin him down long enough to plan some other teaching strategies with him.

It was Mr. Topps who managed to get me working with Miss Stern and her English classes. We had our conference a few weeks ago, and I told him how concerned I was about being able to work with the teachers. "Maybe it was a mistake," I suggested, "to go only into those classrooms where I was invited. But I am so convinced that a teacher has to want your help before you can make any real difference in the way that teacher teaches. I thought that the teachers who did ask for my help would see I was a help, not a threat or a supervisor or a critic, and that these teachers would spread the word so that, little by little, most of the other teachers would come around."

"So, far," I confessed, "I have really only worked with Miss Werth, Mr. Battle, and Mr. Sherk, although I have helped several others construct cloze passages for their text-books." (I didn't tell him that, because I couldn't find him to plan with, I had only worked with Mr. Battle's class once, or that I was no longer working with Mr. Sherk's classes, or that I didn't really *help* the teachers construct the cloze passages but constructed and graded them myself!)

Mr. Topps was very supportive. "No, Miss Tent, I don't think you made a mistake. You can't force yourself on anyone, and I believe that word will get around. It may just take a little longer than we thought it would. Middle and secondary teachers *are* different from elementary teachers. They have a particular subject area that most of them love and want to teach. They have a hard time understanding and accepting the fact that they must teach their students the tools to learn their subject. I know, however, that they were impressed by the faculty workshop you did with them. Even Miss Stern remarked on how effectively you had gotten across to them what it feels like to be able to read the words and not understand what you are reading. In fact, I'm surprised she hasn't asked for your help. She was one of the most supportive and vocal teachers when we were trying to convince the board of education to allow us to hire a remedial reading teacher."

"But that's part of the problem," I interrupted. "I think she thinks that I should be another remedial reading teacher. She may be right, you know. I have spent some time in Mr. Moore's room ('not having anyplace else to go,' I thought), and he is really making a difference with those kids. Maybe that is what I should be doing."

As I was finishing that sentence, Miss Sills, Mr. Topps's secretary, interrupted to tell him that R. R. Rowe, the school board chairman, was in the office and needed to see him immediately. Mr. Topps apologized to me for having to cut our conference short. "Don't worry," he said, "it's all going to work out. Just keep doing a bang-up job with the teachers you're already working with. I'm going to see Miss Stern this afternoon, and I'll drop a hint or two about asking you in. I'm sure she meant to do it and just forgot."

His hint was obviously successful, because the next day Miss Stern was in my office when I got there in the morning. She asked me if I would demonstrate a Guided Reading Procedure with her kids, and, of course, I agreed. We found a short selection on social conditions in Dickens's day, and I taught the lesson during which I managed to solve the main-idea dilemma. The lesson was quite successful, and since then I have helped Miss Stern set up a program of Sustained Silent Reading in her class and have demonstrated a capsule vocabulary lesson.

After I had taught the demonstration Guided Reading Procedure in Miss Stern's class, she and I had a long talk about "today's students." "I have taught English for 27 years," she related, "and the students are less knowledgeable each year." As we talked about this phenomenon, I tried to get Miss Stern to be more specific about what she meant by "less knowledgeable." I reasoned that if I could find out specifically what she meant, I might be able to find some ways of helping her that would really solve her particular concerns. One thing I have learned, in working with teachers at any level, is that you can't just teach them a bunch of effective teaching strategies and expect that to change their teaching behavior. Teachers, like learners at any age or level, have specific needs, and if you can determine what these needs are and then teach them some specific strategies to relate directly to their concerns, then you can have a permanent effect on their teaching practices.

As we talked, I realized that when Miss Stern said, "They are less knowledgeable," she really meant they are less well-read and their general vocabulary is more limited. I agreed with her that today's students probably read less and that, since many words are learned through the context of reading, their meager vocabularies are probably directly related to a paucity of reading in their lives. I suggested that I would like to work with her on increasing the amount of reading that students did and on some direct methods for increasing their meaning vocabularies.

USSR

I then told her about USSR (Uninterrupted Sustained Silent Reading; McCracken, 1971) and about the success I had had with my fourth-graders by setting aside a specified time each day for children to read material of their own choosing. I further told her that I knew Mrs. Wright was doing USSR with her language arts blocks and offered to teach her class one period, so that she could go and observe USSR in action in Mrs. Wright's class and talk with her about setting it up. I suggested that, while she was observing, I would do a capsule vocabulary lesson with her students; if successful, I would then demonstrate this vocabulary-building strategy for her on another day. I could tell Miss Stern was a bit dubious about USSR, but she agreed to go and observe. Mr. Topps had obviously hinted *strongly*!

Capsule vocab.

On the day Miss Stern went to observe, I taught a capsule vocabulary lesson in her class. I was a little nervous because I had never taught one of these lessons before; I had only read about it in the *Journal of Reading* (Crist, 1975). "Well, at least if it flops Miss Stern won't be here to see it," I consoled myself as I began the lesson. I began by giving the students a little pep talk about the importance of a good vocabulary, that the only way to really learn a word is to use it frequently in speaking and writing. We talked about how embarrassing it is to use a word incorrectly, and the students understood what a malapropism is when I reminded them of some that Archie Bunker had committed. I then told them researchers had determined that words were most easily learned and recalled when the speaker had many associations for a word and when that word had been experienced in listening, speaking, reading, and writing.

Noticing that the students were looking a bit skeptical, I decided to forego the rest of my introduction and jump right into the activity. In her *Journal of Reading* article, Crist had identified nine areas that college freshmen indicated they talked about most. I chose the subject of money from this list and used the 15 words identified by Crist as money-related: *affluent, austerity, avarice, facilitate, fiscal, indigent, liquidate, lucrative, niggard, opportunist, ostentatious, parsimonius, pecuniary, pittance,* and *squalid* (p. 148). I then talked to the students a little bit about money, inviting them to participate as they were willing. As I used one of the words in the money "capsule," I wrote that word on the board. I tried to use each word naturally in the context of our discussion, but at times it was a little artificial. I then had the students make a list of the 15 words and reviewed with them the meaning of each word as it related to money. "Now," I said to the students, "I want you to talk about money to the person who sits across the aisle. You have five minutes in which to talk. See how many of these money words you can use in the course of your conversation. Each person will check off the words as his talking part-ner uses them. You have five minutes, starting right now," I said as I set my timer for five minutes.

At first they were a little slow to talk, but as they saw the time running out and got into the spirit of the "game," most pairs got into animated, if fairly artificial, conversation. When the buzzer sounded at the end of five minutes, most pairs continued talking, trying to get a few more words into their conversations. I then had each person tally the number of words the partner had used. Most of the students had used almost all the words.

"For the last part of today's lesson," I said hurriedly, looking at the clock, "you have ten minutes in which to write a composition on the subject of money. Your goals are to try to make sensible compositions and to use as many of the money-related words as you can." The students quickly got out pen and paper and began to write. The quiet intensity was broken only by occasional chuckles as students found ingenious ways to get three of the words into one sentence. Miss Stern walked into the room just before the bell rang to signal the end of the period. She looked somewhat surprised to find all the students ea-gerly writing. When the bell rang, several students moaned and tried frantically to finish sentences. I collected their papers as they left, except for those who said they wanted a chance to finish them and would bring them to class tomorrow! Of course, Miss Stern was amazed at their willingness to do any unrequired writing. I gave her a copy of the Crist article and told her about how I had done the lesson. "The article doesn't suggest using a timer," I explained, "but I always find that kids enjoy trying to beat the clock."

We then read some of the compositions the students wrote. Miss Stern expressed con-cern about the poor grammar and spelling used, but she was impressed with the number of *money* capsule words they had used and with their demonstrated knowledge of how to use these words. I told her that the grammar and spelling worried me, too, but "you just can't work on everything at once, and the purpose of this writing activity was to give the students a writing experience with the words." She agreed, if somewhat hesitantly, that when writing under a time limit, as the students were, you have to overlook some of the mechanical things.

We then talked about her observations in Mrs. Wright's class. She was most impressed. "I couldn't believe it," she marveled. "Those students all read for nine minutes. It was so quiet in that room, you could have heard a pin drop. Mrs. Wright gave me a new adoles-cents' fiction book to read, and I got so interested in it, I'm taking it home to finish to-night," she said as she showed me a copy of *And All Between* by Zilpha Keatley Snyder (1976). "Why don't you save it to read here while you and your students have USSR?" I coaxed. "Well," she said, "I would like to do it, but I just don't know where the time is go-ing to come from. The periods are too short as it is, and you can see by looking at those compositions that no one has taught these students any grammar and spelling. I wish they would read at home as we did when we were young."

I waited quietly for Miss Stern to resolve her dilemma. "But, I guess they won't. You are right; you only become a reader by reading, and I know it will help enlarge their vocabu-laries. Tomorrow I'll start having them read for the first ten minutes of every period. You just can't do everything, and I have complained and worried for too long about the fact that students these days just don't read not to do something about it that I think will work. I'll need some books, though. Rita told me that USSR would work if you had a variety of good books in the room at many different reading levels and if you did it consistently for a set period of time every day, with the teacher setting a model for the students by read-ing as they read." I promised Miss Stern I would try to round up some books for her. I thought I could borrow some high-interest/low-vocabulary books from Mr. Moore, and

USSR

Miss Turner, the librarian, had just gotten in a new supply of current adolescents' fiction paperbacks. "I'll find some books for you and bring them in this afternoon," I told her as I left. "Oh, and I almost forgot, I'll be in tomorrow to finish up the capsule vocabulary lesson on money. The last step is to read some of the compositions to the class."

"Well, if you come during the first ten minutes, bring a book you want to read," replied Miss Stern. "*Everyone* in my class *will* be reading during the first ten minutes, or they won't be in here! I guess I'd better go out tonight and buy a timer. Rita said it helps to keep the USSR time consistent each day, and I'll need it to teach capsule vocabulary lessons, too. With the money I've taken out of my own pocket to buy teaching supplies over the last 27 years I could retire!"

I left Miss Stern's room more optimistic than I had been since coming to Upton Hill. "I'm not going to ruin my good mood right now by worrying about how I will ever convince her that teaching grammar doesn't improve students' writing one bit," I resolved.

FOR THE READER TO DO:

The other topics identified in the Crist article (1975) as topics that college freshmen talked about most were: family, study, politics, sleep, personality, sports, sex, and entertainment. Choose one of these and decide on approximately 15 words that most high school students might have heard but probably do not use in their own speaking and writing. List the steps in a capsule vocabulary lesson. If possible, teach this capsule vocabulary lesson to a group of students.

7 A Year of Content-Area Reading (November-February)

November I believe Miss Stern is my first real convert! Miss Werth is enthusiastic and committed, but this is only her second year of teaching and her teaching practices and beliefs are not very well established. She is a zealot but not technically a convert. Miss Stern is a convert! She does capsule vocabulary lessons with her students on a regular basis and has been especially pleased that they have become so interested in words. Last week, they did a capsule on religion, and she challenged the students to bring in religion-related words to use in the lesson. They found so many that it was difficult to limit the lesson to a manageable 15 words. Miss Stern also challenges her students to use the words they learn in their capsule lessons in other speaking and writing. Many of the students are attempting to use these words, and several have come across words they recently learned during sustained silent reading. Miss Stern was justifiably concerned, however, that the number of words she could directly teach her students was quite limited when compared with the thousands of words they would need to know. She and I agreed that adults who read learn most of their "advanced" vocabulary by seeing and hearing words over and over again in various contexts and inferring meanings for the words from those contexts. While this process of learning the meanings of new words from context is automatic in good readers, poor readers do not automatically make use of these context clues to meaning. I promised Miss Stern that I would try to find some suggestions for the direct teaching of vocabulary meanings through context.

What I found was disappointing. Most textbooks and articles on reading instruction defined the various types of context clues to meaning but did not suggest ways of helping students actually use the context to deduce meaning. Several workbooks had exercises in which students had to read sentences and then decide whether the context clues were explanations, definitions, appositives, metaphors, examples, or contrasts. While these are the major types of context clues, it does not necessarily follow that being able to identify and name them will result in the student's being able to use them. In fact, it seems to me that we spend far too much time in education trying to teach labels and categories and

131

far too little time trying to teach students actually to use whatever the labels and categories represent. I saw this occur all too often when teaching fourth-graders. Many of my fourth-graders could tell you whether a vowel was long or short and could quote both chapter and verse of phonics and grammar rules, but they would not apply these rules when sounding out a word or writing a composition.

Vocab through context

I became determined to find or develop some activities that would teach students how to use context clues to obtain meaning rather than merely to recognize and label the different types. I planned my activities so that students would first learn to use the context clues within a sentence and later learn to use the context of longer discourse.

I began my first lesson by giving the students in Miss Stern's class a list of 14 words and asking them to write a definition or a sentence that illustrated the meaning of each word. The students complained vigorously when they looked at the list of words, protesting that they had never heard of these words before and that it "wasn't fair." I assured them that I was not going to record a grade for this test, but that I did want to see which words they knew and which they didn't. We would compare their scores before and after I taught them some special ways to figure out what words mean without using a dictionary. After several minutes, I collected the pretests. Most had not known the meanings of any of the words. A few knew the meanings for *droned* and *perambulated*.

Next, I showed them a transparency on which I had written six words in sentences which gave clues to the meanings of the words. Over the transparency I had clipped a sheet of construction paper with holes cut in it so that only the word in each sentence whose meaning I wanted the students to decipher was visible. As I displayed each word, I asked if any of the students knew what that word meant. If no one had a possible meaning for the word, I asked students to guess what it might possibly mean. At first the students were very hesitant to make guesses, but when they realized that it was impossible to really know the meaning, they got into the spirit of the lesson and came up with some ingenious, albeit totally ridiculous, suggestions. For *laconic*, Billy suggested that it might mean "crazy." Carol thought that *laconic* might be a "cone-shaped fish"! For *manticore*, Carlos suggested it was the "core of a manti fruit," but Priscilla argued that it was really a "man's heart"! This blind guessing was fun, but it was also meant to contrast with the guessing they would do when the construction paper shield was removed and the rest of the sentence or sentences were visible.

After the students had guessed at the meanings of the six words and we had listed their guesses on the board, I uncovered the first sentence, which now read:

> Pepe's great-grandfather often told him tales of a giant manticore, an animal with the head of a man, the body of a lion, and the tail of a dragon.

The students enjoyed this activity, and we then talked about how they had discovered what a manticore was. They observed that "the sentence tells you what it is." I pushed them to explain how the sentence tells you what it is and, finally, was able to get them to verbalize that because *manticore* was followed by a comma and a phrase, that phrase told what a manticore was. They did not use the label "appositive," and I saw no reason to introduce it into the conversation. Next I showed them the two sentences for the word *laconic*:

> Bertha and Bridget were twins, but you'd never know it from listening to them. Bridget talked constantly, but Bertha was laconic.

Again I questioned the students about how they knew what *laconic* meant, until they explained that "since you couldn't tell they were twins from listening to them, they must be opposites. If Bridget talks constantly, then Bertha must hardly talk at all."

In this fashion, we went through the remaining four sentences. The students decided what they thought each word meant based on the clues in that sentence, and then explained exactly how the context had helped them figure out the meaning. We then wrote our definition for each word next to that word on the board. To conclude the lesson, six volunteers looked up the words in a dictionary to see whether our inferred definitions were accurate. The students were pleased to discover that they had indeed come close to the dictionary definition in all six cases. We did note, however, that often the context does not give you a complete definition for a word but only a partial meaning for it as used in that context. Later, Miss Stern taught three more lessons following the same steps I had followed for the original lesson. On Friday, I went back and returned to the students the pretest they had taken on Monday. I told them that, this time, Miss Stern would be recording a grade for their test and that I had some sentences I thought would help them. I then gave them a mimeographed sheet on which the 14 words were used in sentences that gave clues to their meanings. The students' task was the same as that on Monday: Write a definition or a sentence that illustrates the meaning of each word. This time, however, the students went right to work. They were so proud of their accomplishment. Miss Stern was even prouder!

FOR THE READER TO DO:

Here is the list of sentences Miss Tent used to posttest the students. The italicized words are those for which the students must write a definition or a sentence illustrating the meaning of the word. Explain how you figured out the meaning of the words.

1. The frightened soldiers locked, bolted, and *snecked* the gate to the city.
2. Some patients *perambulated* around the grounds all day, while others sat and never moved.
3. The general was *implacable*. He never forgave them, he never gave up, he never told them anything, and he never stopped being loyal to his country.
4. They were mean, cruel, and *truculent*.
5. Mrs. Smith believed in God, but her son was a *pyrrhonist* of the purest kind.
6. A *gynarchy* is a government run by women.
7. The pioneer *excised* the tree limb. First he cut almost through with an ax and then finished the job with a saw.
8. The little girl's face was as *fervid* as a stove.
9. The *pandowdy*, a pudding made with apples, was the best he had ever had.
10. Everywhere Bob looked, he saw thousands of cedars, pines, and *tamaracks*.
11. At times I wonder why some things are easy and others are so *arduous*.
12. His foot sunk deep and wet in the soft, *paludal* ground.
13. His voice *droned* on like the hum of a bumblebee.
14. All he ever talked about was war. His country was the best country, and anyone who disagreed should be ready to do battle. He was really quite a *jingo*!

Presently, I am working with Miss Stern's class on activities that teach them to use context to infer a meaning for a word when the context is longer than a sentence or two. For these lessons, I use short selections from a literature anthology. I write several words on the blackboard and ask the students what the words might mean. Sometimes, when the students have no idea of the meaning, they make wild guesses, as they did in the earlier context lessons. I then have them read the several pages that contain these words and ask them to use the surrounding words as clues to the meanings of the unknown ones. With this particular English content area, I find that it works best to put the students in groups of three or four to complete this activity. One student reads the selection aloud; then all students participate in deciding what the words mean. The group next writes a definition or a sentence that illustrates the meaning of each word. They look up the words in the dictionary to verify their meanings. In addition to entirely unfamiliar words, I also include words for which the students might have a general meaning but which are used in a specialized way in a particular story.

FOR THE READER TO DO:

Find a passage in a textbook that contains some unfamiliar words and some familiar words used in a specialized way. Identify those words for which the context provides some clue to their meanings. Using this material, lead a group of students through the teaching procedure just described by Miss Tent.

When I was in Miss Werth's classroom last week, I noticed that she had started a new wall vocabulary. This time she selected words used in sewing pattern directions. As they work through their clothes-construction unit, the students are learning to read and write these words which are essential to sewing.

I have spent quite a bit of time in Mr. Moore's class this month. He is really working with the hard-core reading problems and is having a lot of success with them. Last week, while I was there, Coach Wynn came in. He and Mr. Moore and I talked a long time about several of the football players who are in Mr. Moore's program and who are having a great deal of difficulty with their academic subjects. "It's funny," Coach Wynn remarked, "but I have coached here for six years now, and I never realized that many of my boys were such poor readers. I knew they didn't study and didn't make good grades, but now I realize they actually had reading problems. In fact, it wasn't until I realized that almost one-third of my football team comes in here for remedial reading instruction that I really began to understand their problems. I wonder if you two can think of anything I can do to help them. I don't know anything about teaching reading, but contrary to the remarks made at the faculty workshop, Miss Tent, some coaches can and do read!"

I promised Coach Wynn I would try to think of some ways he could help his players improve their reading, although I didn't really know what he could do. Later that day, I passed by Mrs. Epock's history class. There, with the textbook open in front of them, sat three of the football players who were in Mr. Moore's class. "I am sure there is no way those boys can read that book," I muttered to myself.

Assessment   The next day, I determined to do something about it. I told Mrs. Epock I wanted to carry out an experiment to see how many of her students could function with their texts. I then set up a table and two chairs outside her classroom door. One by one, the students from her last period came out. I told each that I was conducting an experiment to see how hard their history text was for high school students to read. I then had each student read one paragraph for me and tell me in his or her own words what the paragraph said. That afternoon, I played the tape for Mrs. Epock. At first she appeared skeptical and then a little hostile. "It's not *my* fault they can't read," she protested. "I don't know how to teach them to read." As she talked, I continued to let the tape play. Student after student stumbled over the paragraph in the history textbook. Many could not read it at all; others could read most of the words but could not tell what they had read. When I was sure that the point was made, I stopped the tape. "I know that it's not your fault these students can't read the text, and I know it's not your job to teach them to read. But can you imagine how frustrating it is for these students to be faced, day after day, with a book that makes no sense to them? I'll tell you what—if you'll show me what you want to teach these students for the next two weeks, I'll come in and teach this class for you. The only thing I ask is that you observe my teaching and reserve judgment until the two weeks are over." Mrs. Epock agreed. She really didn't have much choice!

Well, now I have broken my resolve about going only where I'm asked. I surely hope I can do a good job of teaching those students for the next two weeks. Why did I have to go and do this during the two weeks just before Christmas vacation?

December

Content Analysis

December is the shortest school month and, to students and teachers, seems like the longest. That certainly has been true for me this December. I have spent most of my time teaching or preparing to teach Mrs. Epock's class. After agreeing to let me teach her class for two weeks, she showed me what she wanted to teach them: two chapters on American government. To my question about which concepts in the chapter she specifically wanted to teach, she responded, "Well, all of it!" I was going to argue that you can't teach it all but decided, instead, to try to make a case for this only after teaching the unit. I sat down with the textbook and following Herber's (1978) advice, tried to determine the most important concepts and the vocabulary essential for learning those concepts. It was indeed quite difficult to limit the concepts and the resulting vocabulary to a reasonable number. There was such an incredible amount of information in those two chapters. I persevered, however, and finally came up with these five concepts and associated vocabulary:

1. Our government is a representative democracy based on a constitution.
   dictatorship
   direct democracy
   representative democracy
   republic
   elections
   vote
   constitution
   Bill of Rights
   amendments
   citizens

2. Local, state, and national governments have three branches: executive, legislative, and judicial.

local	congress
city	justices
town	national
county	executive
major	branches

        council
        judges
        courts
        state
        governor
        legislature
        national
        president
        vice president
        cabinet
        senate
        house

3. Government's main function is to pass laws and enforce the constitution.
        government
        function
        laws
        enforce
        constitution
        committees
        bills
        veto
        unconstitutional

4. In a representative democracy, the people elect their representatives.
        representative
        democracy
        elect
        representatives
        vote
        election
        political parties
        Democrats
        Republicans
        candidates
        primary
        nominating convention
        delegates
        campaign
        inauguration

5. Who the people are who hold important local, state and, national office (local, state, and national officials' names).

Of course, Herber emphasizes that it is the responsibility of the content-area teacher to do the content analysis and decide what is to be taught. The reading specialist can then help the content-area teacher do a process analysis and determine the processes students must go through in order to learn the content. I knew that Mrs. Epock was not ready or willing to do this yet. I could only hope that my two-week unit would be successful enough that she would see the need to limit the content covered and use some teaching strategies that would help the students learn the content. Then, perhaps, she and I could sit down together, she could tell me what concepts she wanted to teach, and I could help her decide on appropriate strategies.

Having done the content analysis by determining crucial concepts and vocabulary, I decided how I would teach these concepts to Mrs. Epock's class. This decision was a difficult one to make because I had to ensure that I taught in such a way that the students understood the concepts and in such a way that Mrs. Epock would feel she could teach. My own preference would have been to group the students into three groups: students who could read the textbook independently and do some project research in the library; students who could read the textbook if I gave them some instruction including introducing difficult vocabulary and setting purposes for their reading; and students who could not read the text even with instruction and who would need to learn most of the content by listening and discussing. I could easily have grouped the students based on their taped readings and retellings, but I knew that Mrs. Epock would not see this plan of instruction as one she could implement. One basic difference between elementary teachers and secondary teachers is that elementary teachers are accustomed to having groups and individuals engaged in different activities according to interest and ability. Many middle and secondary teachers, however, are not comfortable with this kind of organization. Again, I compromised what I believed was ideal with what I thought Mrs. Epock would be impressed by and willing to attempt. "I'll do some grouping," I resolved, "but most of the activities will be listening activities in which all the students can participate and from which they can all benefit. Later, perhaps, I can help her feel comfortable with groups and individuals doing different things."

Structured Overview

For my first lesson, I presented a "structured overview" (Barron, 1969; Earle, 1969) of government in the United States. I took as many of the words from the vocabulary listed under each concept as were appropriate and built a chart to show the relationship of these terms to one another. When I actually taught the lesson, I created the structured overview chart with the students. Beginning with *government*, I wrote each word on a sheet of chart paper and explained it in relation to the other words. I encouraged the students to help me construct and fill out the chart by asking them questions as I went along. In this manner, I had the students explain which is the executive branch at each level of government, what a primary is, who U. S. citizens are, and so forth. Building this structured overview with the students took almost all of one class period, but it was worth doing. The students truly had an overview of what we were going to be studying, and their active participation in building this overview generated much interest in the unit. In addition, we kept the chart with the overview on it in full view as we worked through the unit. Each time I used one of the words on the chart, I tried to remember to point to it in order to reestablish for the students the relationship between that word and the other words on the chart.

FOR THE READER TO DO:

Choose a topic and decide on some crucial terms for understanding that concept. Make a structured overview showing the interrelationship between the words. Miss Tent's structured overview of government is shown here as a model.

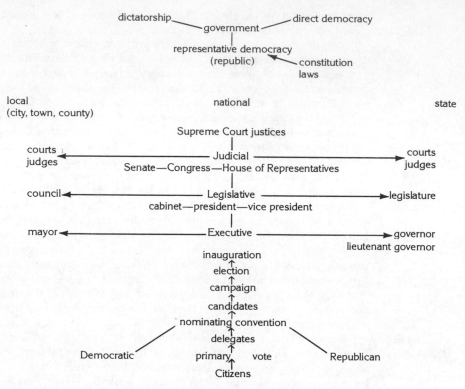

For homework that night, the students were asked to find all the names they could of people who held executive, legislative, or judicial office at the local, state, and national levels. Newspapers, television news programs, and parent and friend interviews were suggested as resources for completing this assignment. To motivate them to complete this assignment, I pointed out to them the bulletin board on which I had tacked sheets of colored paper. On the three sheets going across the top of the bulletin board, I had written the words *executive*, *legislative*, and *judicial*. On the three sheets going down the side of the board, I had written *national*, *state*, and *local*. I had blank sheets of paper in the appropriate places on which to write the names of the appropriate office-holders. I told the students that each blank sheet represented a particular person and that we would write as many names as they could discover on the appropriate sheets during the following day's lesson.

That next day we completed most of our chart showing the *Who's Who* of local, state, and national government. We discussed officeholders known to the students personally or by television appearances. We compared the number of female and male office-holders and the number of minority group members who were officeholders. From this springboard, we discussed the term *representative*. Was our government really representative? Why was there an over-representation of white males? What actions had been taken in recent years to make government more representative? The concept of representative, at least, was one the students were acquainted with.

GLP   For the third lesson, I used a Guided Listening Procedure in which I read aloud a short section from their textbook on the United States Constitution. As I was reading the selection, I tape recorded it, then proceeded through the steps, having the students recall everything they had listened to. We relistened to the tape to correct wrong information and add missing information. Finally, we identified main ideas. The students enjoyed writing down the numbers of five main ideas as I read the list to them and then raising their hands to show which numbers they had chosen. They were pleased and somewhat surprised to discover that there were some ideas that almost everyone had selected. As we were determining the main ideas in this way, I noticed that Mrs. Epock, who had been sitting at the back of the room grading papers during each of my three lessons, had stopped her grading and was observing the enthusiastic responses of her class with a puzzled, but I think pleased, expression. However, as I gave the students the five-item true/false quiz covering the essential points of the information they had just listened to and then had the students exchange papers to correct each other's quizzes, Mrs. Epock scowled. All the students got at least four answers correct, and most got all five right. As the bell rang and the students began to file out, one student hollered: "Hey, let's be sure and leave our tests with Mrs. Epock so she can record them. This is the first one I've passed all year!" The students concurred noisily and handed their papers to a stunned Mrs. Epock as they left the room.

"I really don't know what to do," Mrs. Epock began. "I must admit that they are enthusiastic and they seem to be learning, but they are not learning as much as they need to and I can't see how I can give them good grades when they are not working up to level. You really did spoonfeed them the information today, and the items on your test were easy. Some of the students can do a lot more than this, I know. But then, for many of them, they are doing all they can. I just don't know the right thing to do."

I responded to Mrs. Epock and tried to let her know that I understood and shared her concern. "Yes, I know how you feel," I began. "There are some students in here who can read the textbook and who could have learned more information than I presented to them today, but those students did learn the essential points I wanted to cover and they did enjoy the class. It is hard to plan two lessons for every class," I added in an attempt to find some common ground on which we could agree.

"Well, I certainly agree with that," Mrs. Epock responded. I then took the opportunity to show Mrs. Epock the essential concepts and vocabulary which I had selected from the textbook section on government. "I know there is a lot more content than this in those chapters," I explained, "but you simply can't teach it all well, and it's crucial that these students develop an understanding of how our government works and what the responsibilities of citizens in a representative democracy are."

By the time I had finished my last statement, Mrs. Epock's next class was in the room and needing her immediate attention. "We'll talk some more about this," I assured her as I hurried out the door.

DLA The rest of the government unit went quite well. I used a Directed Listening Activity in which I read a section of the text that explained how bills were first suggested, discussed in committees, voted on by the Senate and the House, vetoed or signed by the president, and sometimes reviewed for constitutionality by the Supreme Court. I set the purpose for listening by telling the students that we were going to have a demonstration of how a bill became law and that they would all play the parts of various legislative, executive, and judicial officials. I handed out a copy of a proposed law requiring that all high school students in the United States pass a test certifying that they can read, write, and compute at a functional level before being allowed to graduate from high school. I read the law to them several times and told them that they would be required to take different sides and different roles in the passage of this law. "In this box," I explained, "I have written the names of senators, representatives, the president, vice president, secretary of Education and Supreme Court justices. When I have finished reading the explanation of how a bill becomes law, each of you will pick a card from this box. The card will tell you who you will be and what your position on this bill is. You are not allowed to tell anyone else what it says on your card. We will then transform this classroom into a Capitol setting and see if our bill becomes the 'law of the land.'"

The students listened attentively as I read the section that explained the steps in a bill becoming a law. We listed the steps on a flow chart to which we could refer as we were trying to resolve the issue of functional literacy and a high school diploma. Just before the class ended, I let each student select a card telling who that student would be in tomorrow's class and what that person's responsibility was. Friday's class was loud, lively, and relevant. The bill got out of committee in both the House and the Senate, was passed by both houses, and was vetoed by the president on advice from the secretary of Education and the vice president. The veto was overridden by a one-vote margin and became law. A citizens' action group, however, questioned the constitutionality of the law, and the Supreme Court justices had the final say. The vote of the justices was five to four. Appropriate majority and minority reports were filed!

Vocab,
Direct
Experience

During the second week of the unit, I used a Guided Reading Procedure with the students using a selection from an elementary text that described in simple dramatic terms the meeting of the Philadelphia group that drafted and passed the Constitution. I also used a Directed Listening-Viewing Activity with a film on the election process. I asked each student to watch one specific character in the film and be ready to list all the things that person did as part of the election process.

Differ-
entiated
instruction

On Wednesday and Thursday, I divided the students into two groups. One group contained all the students who I decided (on the basis of their taped reading and retelling) could read the textbook at an independent or instructional level. The other group included those students who could not read the textbook even with instruction. I began the class by discussing the meaning of the word *equal* as used in the Constitution. By using everyday examples of individual abilities in sports, music, woodworking, and so forth, I led the students to agree that *equal* does not mean equally good at all things and that treating everybody equally does not mean treating everyone the same at all times, but means helping each person achieve his or her potential and trying to provide people with what they need to achieve that potential. This discussion took longer than I had planned but was worth the time invested. I explained to the students that some of them could read the textbook better than others and that I was going to let a group of them do some reading in order to practice and learn from their reading while I worked directly with other students who had difficulty reading their text. Most of the students understood and accepted the rationale for the differentiated instruction.

I introduced words which the students would meet in their reading or listening and which I thought they might not have an understanding of. To the group who would read the textbook, I made an assignment to read and complete some short-answer questions. I asked the remaining 12 students to gather around a table at the back of the room. I could tell that although they accepted my "rap" about equal not necessarily meaning same, they would have preferred to have been on the other end of the equality continuum. I proceeded to explain to them that we were going to write a textbook that they could read. Their job would be to listen as I read each paragraph to them and then to tell me the main ideas of that paragraph. I would then record their "translated" version on some chart paper, and they would copy this information into their notebooks. I then proceeded with the translation-writing lesson as I had done in Miss Werth's classroom. We finished the actual writing the next day, and the students completed several comprehension exercises using their translated "text" as a source.

Translation
writing

It was the next to the last day for our unit on government. I sat down that afternoon and discussed with Mrs. Epock what we had done. She admitted that she had been skeptical about what I would be able to accomplish, but she could now see that the students had indeed actually learned more than they would have had they been reading the text, responding to questions, and engaging in post-reading discussion.

"I see what you did, and I see that the students did learn, but I'm just not sure I know how to teach that way. And what about all my other classes? I have another section of state/U.S. history and several semester electives. I don't see how I can possibly do this with all my classes."

"Now hang on," I interrupted her. "I will work with you to plan your lessons for this class. It's the one you are most concerned about, and you just can't do everything at once. I'm sure the students who take social studies electives are better students and better readers than the students in these required U.S./state courses. If your other section of this course has students with reading difficulties, you can plan for both sections at the same time. Right now, however, I need your help. I have worried all week about how to evaluate the students' learning of the content I have taught them this week. I want to evaluate them fairly, and I don't want to penalize those students with poor reading and writing skills."

Mrs. Epock and I then constructed some test items which we both thought would fairly evaluate what the students had learned without penalizing students for their reading and writing deficiencies. To evaluate the students' understanding of the concept that "our government is a representative democracy based on a constitution," we described several of the world's governments and asked students to indicate which type of government a described country had by circling *dictatorship*, *direct democracy*, or *representative democracy*. To evaluate their learning of the concept that "local, state, and national governments have three branches—executive, legislative, and judicial," we read them several responsibilities of various officials and had them write down the title of the person who would carry out that responsibility. To evaluate the concepts that "government's main function is to pass laws and enforce the constitution," and that "in a representative democracy, the people elect their representatives," we listed the steps in the "becoming-a-law" and election processes, scrambled the order of these steps, and had students rearrange the steps. When we gave the test, we first read the scrambled steps to the students to be sure they could read them. As they were rearranging them into the proper order, we offered reading help as needed. Finally, we evaluate the objective that stated that students would know the names of persons presently holding important local, state, and national offices. We gave the students a matching task in which they were required to match each person with the office he or she held. Again, before the students began we read the persons' names and the offices and volunteered reading help as needed. The lowest score obtained by any student was a 78. "I'm convinced," remarked Mrs. Epock as we graded the tests. "But you're going to have to help me do it. Maybe we could get together sometime between Christmas and New Year's."

Mrs. Epock and I set a date to meet during the vacation and to plan the next unit. Rich will be away during that week visiting his family, so I will have plenty of time to work. I also plan to meet with Coach Wynn during the vacation. I have found some super ideas for ways he can motivate his players to read. It looks like it will be a busy new year!

January

What a busy month this has been! I did meet with Mrs. Epock during the Christmas break and helped her plan her next unit. We began by identifying the concepts she wanted to teach and the vocabulary essential to those concepts. This was a very difficult process because, while Mrs. Epock realized she couldn't teach it all, she still wanted to! Eventual-

Evaluation

ly, we did narrow it down to six concepts, however. As we selected the essential vocabulary for learning these concepts, we found that many of the words essential to the government unit (*citizen*, *democracy*, *constitution*, and so forth) were also essential to this colonial period unit. We included these words again, however, in our essential vocabulary. These words *were* essential, and we could not assume that the students remembered them.

I then helped Mrs. Epock make a structured overview that included many of the words listed under the six concepts. She wanted to make her structured overview chart in advance and then present it to the class, but I convinced her that it would be most effective if she wrote the words on the chart one at a time as the students watched. In this way, they could see the rationale for the interrelationship between the words, and she could elicit responses to each word from them. While she agreed, I could tell that she still wasn't very comfortable with this strategy, so I volunteered to teach this introductory lesson with her second-period state/U.S. history class, then she could do it with her last-period class. This pattern of her watching me teach a lesson in the morning and then teaching it herself in the afternoon worked well, and we followed it for most of the lessons in the unit. Mrs. Epock observed my teaching but she did not want me to observe her teaching. I can only assume that the lessons she taught went well, based on her reactions and the demonstrated learning of the students.

The teaching strategies we used in this unit were repetitions of the strategies used in the other unit. We used a Guided Reading Procedure and a Guided Listening Procedure.

DL-VA We also used a Directed Listening-Viewing Activity in which the students viewed a film after we had introduced several unfamiliar words and set purposes for their viewing. For this particular film, we wanted to focus attention on family interaction in colonial days. After attempting to help the students understand the terms *nuclear family*, *extended family, apprenticeship, parsimonious*, and *spinster*, we told them that while there were certain "universals" in human existence, there were also certain elements of life—particularly family life—that had changed drastically since colonial days.

"Watch the film," I instructed the students, "so that when the film is over, we can list on this chart some universals of family life and on this other chart some ways family life today is drastically different from family life in colonial times. Also, as you watch the film, try to decide what the advantages and disadvantages of colonial and modern-day living are as they relate to families." When the film was over, we made our lists of family universals and contrasts.

Group discussion I then assigned the students to groups of four or five, appointed a recorder who had good writing ability in each group, and gave the groups ten minutes to brainstorm ideas on one of four topics. These topics I had previously written on the tops of eight sheets of paper. So two groups each brainstormed ideas on: advantages of colonial family life; disadvantages of colonial family life; advantages of modern family life; and disadvantages of modern family life. During the next day's lesson, we compared what the various groups had written, and discovered, in several cases, that something considered to be an advantage by one group was considered a disadvantage by another group. Tina's group thought that having lots of relatives around would be an advantage of colonial family life; Burt's group saw it as a disadvantage. From this springboard, we had a lively discussion on values and value judgments.

FOR THE READER TO DO:

In a directed lesson—be it a directed reading lesson, a directed listening lesson, or a directed listening-viewing lesson—the procedure for planning and carrying out the lesson is the same. When planning the lesson, the teacher decides which concepts in the story or tape or film are apt to be unfamiliar to many of his or her students. The teacher also decides what the students should learn from reading or listening or listening/viewing. Keeping in mind that "you can't learn it all," the instructor sets purposes for the students in order to focus their attention on the concepts he or she has determined to be crucial. In teaching the lesson, the instructor introduces and builds meaning for unfamiliar words, and then lets students in on the purpose for having them participate in this lesson. After reading or listening or listening/viewing, the instructor follows up the purpose in some way.

Choose a story, tape, or film. Identify the unfamiliar concepts contained in the material. Decide on purposes for having the students participate in the directed lesson and on a way to follow up those purposes. If possible, teach this directed lesson to a group of students.

Cloze

Toward the end of the unit, we again divided the students into two groups based on their ability to read the textbook. (I constructed a cloze test and administered it to Mrs. Epock's second-period class. This procedure was a lot faster than listening to all the students read and retell a paragraph, and it placed all but two students appropriately.) Sammy had only answered six items on the cloze tests. These six he got correct. When I put him with the group that would do translation writing, he objected furiously. "I can read that book" he argued. "What makes you think I can't?" I explained to the students about the cloze test and about how I had used it to determine the ease with which they could read the text. Sammy's reply was, "Well, I didn't do that test because I just wasn't sure what should go in those blanks. But I can read the book." I assured Sammy and the rest of the group that the cloze test was not infallible and that anyone who wanted to read the book and complete the assignment given to the other group rather than make a translated text with me was free to do so. Sammy and two other boys joined the students who were working with the textbooks. Sammy could, indeed, read the book, but I don't believe the other two could. They sat there, however, and plugged away at it. Mrs. Epock and I agreed that "you can lead horses to water, but you can't make them drink!" We hope that as the year goes on and the students realize they are not penalized for their inability to read the text, these two boys will be willing to work where they can succeed.

Carolyn, who had scored 40 percent correct on the cloze test, also had a very hard time reading the text. She didn't say anything during this unit, but during the next unit, when Mrs. Epock divided the class into the two groups, Carolyn asked to join those who were doing the translation writing. Mrs. Epock agreed, of course. How she ever did that well on the cloze test is beyond us. Mrs. Epock swears she can barely read the translated text right after they complete it!

Once again, all the students passed the test Mrs. Epock and I constructed to evaluate their learning of the concepts taught in this unit. While Mrs. Epock is still concerned that she is "spoonfeeding" the students and that they are not "learning it all," she does see that they are learning the essentials. Most importantly, the attitude and behavior of the students in her last-period class, who have now had two successful experiences, have improved markedly. Mrs. Epock must be talking to the other teachers about what she is doing, because I got another note from Mr. Battle the other day. Maybe this time he really intends to follow through on his good intentions.

Dear Connie,

Help! I am about to throw in the towel with my U.S./state
history students. Can we talk about my despair tomorrow
during my planning period?

You're a lifesaver,

W. W. Battle

Motivation

Working with Will is the most exciting thing I have done this month. We got together during the Christmas break, and I showed him the section on physical education in the Thomas and Robinson (1977) text, *Improving Reading in Every Class*. The authors of this text suggest that while the actual teaching of reading skills may have little or no place in some subjects such as physical education, teachers such as the coach, who are popular with and admired by students, can motivate them to read.

Will thought the ideas suggested in this chapter were great, and we spent a lot of time together during the Christmas vacation gathering up materials for his bookshelf and reading and discussing the various sports-related books so that Will could do book talks with his boys. While Will was impressed by my knowledge and enthusiasm about reading instruction, he found my ignorance about sports and sports heroes astonishing. His enthusiasm for sports does appear to be contagious, however. He took me to several basketball games, and I even found myself reading the sports section of *Time* magazine last week!

When we returned to school after the holidays, Will set up his sports-related books in several stacked orange crates in a corner of the gym. After some vigorous physical activity, Will would have a five-minute rest break during which he did book talks with the boys or read them a portion of a book he particularly liked. After several days, a few students brought in books about sports which they had enjoyed. Coach Wynn encouraged them to tell about the books and, usually, these books were quickly borrowed by other students. The students also wanted to borrow the books Coach Wynn had collected, and, not wanting to set up an elaborate check-out system, Coach Wynn set up a trading system. To start with, each boy was allowed to take one book. When he was finished with that book, he traded it for another one. Once the boys started trading books, Will's supply of books was quickly depleted. By then the boys were really interested in the sports books, and Coach Wynn asked them to contribute some books to the collection. He also had one of the paperback book company representatives come to all his classes to display and talk about the multitude of sports-related books his company had. Students were then given the opportunity to order these books and many did. Coach Wynn is hoping that after the books arrive and the boys have read them, many of these books will be donated to his shelf and ensure a constant supply of sports-related reading material on various levels.

The success of Coach Wynn's motivational activities was evident yesterday when I was in Miss Stern's room during USSR time. I counted eight sports-related books being read by the boys and three by the girls. In fact, the girls, who are finally beginning to be treated equally in the school sports program, have recently asked Ms. Ball, their physical education teacher and softball coach, if there aren't some sports stories about women sports heroes. While there are far fewer of these, there are some, and I have promised Ms. Ball I will try to help her locate some. When I was thinking about this job and how I could get teachers involved and committed to helping their students read better, I never imagined that my biggest reading booster would be the football coach! Another stereotype laid to rest!

February   This has been one of those months when I never knew from one day to the next what to expect. Actually, the beginning of the month was fairly normal. I planned and worked with Mr. Battle in much the same way that I did with Mrs. Epock. The lessons I taught were quite successful. Mr. Battle has a talent for leading the students in discussions and through strategies such as Guided Reading Procedures and Directed Reading Activities. His biggest problem is committing the time it takes to identify the crucial concepts and vocabulary, plan his teaching strategies, and develop evaluation measures that determine if concepts have been mastered in a way that does not penalize students with poor reading and writing abilities. He complains that one planning period a day is not enough. Of course, he is right, but there is nothing I can do about that. There is just no simple, time-saving plan for teaching so that all students have the opportunity to learn the material. I did point out to him, however, that a lot of what he has to do this year, he will not have to repeat next year. I am encouraging him to concentrate his "teaching-every-student" efforts this year on the U.S./state history course which all students are required to take. Next year he can begin to look at the teaching strategies he uses in the semester electives he teaches. While these electives contain some students who have limited reading and writing ability, the number of these students is small compared to the number in the required courses.

Ms. Ball now has her bookshelf set up and is doing book-talks with her girls, encouraging them to read books about sports and stories about sports heroes and heroines. I never realized until I began combing the public library and backyard rummage sales for sports-related books (and specifically books written from a female perspective) how few books address themselves to girls. Ms. Ball's motivational program is not quite as successful as Will's program is. While some of the girls are very interested in sports, others have already developed well-formed reading habits. Their interest, currently, seems to be more boy- and teenage-problem related than sports related. Maybe I can convince Ms. Ball to broaden the scope of books she has available, but I doubt it. She is a sports enthusiast and wants "her girls" to be the same way. Sometimes she is less than patient with their normal adolescent interests.

Actually, the month started to take a strange twist on Valentine's Day afternoon. I went to the health spa that afternoon as I do most afternoons when I can find some time and any energy. Miss Yung, a middle-school language arts teacher, was there. I smiled and nodded at her and then began my situps. As I was struggling to complete the second set of 20, Miss Yung came over and sat down on the board next to mine. She began her situps and I finished mine, lying there a few moments luxuriating in having that part of my exercise completed.

Suddenly, she stopped and turned to me, "I don't suppose you could help me," she said.

"Of course, if you want me to. Do you need something?" I asked.

"Yes, I need something," she responded, "but I don't know what. A new career, I'm beginning to think. Teaching sure isn't what I thought it was going to be. I had no idea the students would be so uncooperative."

Normally I try to avoid thinking about and, especially, talking about school problems when I am at the spa. Exercising is supposed to relieve tension, not increase it! I could tell however that Miss Yung wanted to talk. I had heard the rumors that her classes were out of control, so I responded in such a way that she could continue talking if she needed to.

"Well, this is your first year, isn't it? The first year is seldom a joyous one. When I think of some of the things I did my first year, I shudder! But things got better. Is there a specific problem or a specific group you teach which presents more problems for you?"

"They are all problems for *me*," she responded, resuming her situps. I could tell that she didn't want to talk anymore and, somewhat relieved, I told her that if she did want to talk, I was always available. She smiled and thanked me and I went over to the bar to do my leg lifts.

Later, as I was dressing after my sauna and shower, Miss Yung came into the dressing room. She looked so dejected, I just had to make one more attempt. "What do the kids do that annoys you the most?" I asked. The tears began to flow as she described the students in one of her language arts classes. "At first it was just a few who wouldn't do what I told them to do, but now it is just a few who will! I had to fail almost half my students when semester grades went home. Mr. Topps has scheduled a conference with me to talk about it, and I must have had 50 calls from parents. I know that if a lot of students fail, it is the teacher who is failing, but I just don't know what to do. I have tried to make the assignments easier and easier, but it doesn't seem to matter. They just won't do them. I even tried a behavior modification, token-reinforcement system that my ed psych professor had guaranteed would work, and it didn't. They just didn't seem to care about getting points to win the prizes I had bought. In fact, they got a lot worse after I tried that and it failed."

As Miss Yung talked on, I realized that things were even worse than I had suspected and that she would probably be run off before the year was out. I could tell that she liked the kids, or at least had liked them before she let them take over her class. We talked for almost an hour. Mostly, I tried to help her to feel better and to realize that this had happened to other first-year teachers who had survived and become good teachers. "I'll drop by your classroom tomorrow," I promised as I rushed home to meet Rich!

He was already there when I arrived and so was a beautiful Valentine flower arrangement. "Oh, you shouldn't have! They're beautiful," I blurted out before I realized, by observing the expression on his face, that he hadn't!

"They came a few minutes ago. I guess you have an admirer who is also a football nut." He smiled, but I knew he wasn't amused! I then realized that the arrangement was in a football-shaped container and that Will must have sent it. "If only I hadn't stayed to talk to Miss Yung for so long," I thought. "I would have been here when it came!"

"It must be from Coach Wynn, the football coach at school," I hurriedly explained. "I have helped him out a lot, and he has been trying to cure my ignorance of sports. I tried to sound casual as I explained, but I was amazed and delighted that Will had been so thoughtful, and I guess my pleasure showed. The evening was a disaster and ended with our deciding not to see one another for a few weeks. I hardly slept that night, worried about losing Rich and yet annoyed at his pettiness and jealousy. Mixed with these emotions was my pleasure and curiosity concerning the meaning of this gesture from Will. "He's just saying 'thank you,'" I tried to convince myself, as I lay in bed wide awake at 3:00 A.M.

Classroom management

First thing the next morning, I went into Miss Yung's classroom. I stood at the back of the room ostensibly looking at some materials. She was right. Things were out of control and nobody was doing anything—anything constructive, that is. Miss Yung was standing at the front of the room, valiantly trying to teach them the mechanics of writing a good composition. Two boys at the back of the room were arm wrestling. A table of girls giggled and whispered the whole time Miss Yung was talking. One student was throwing spitballs at the table of giggly girls, and several students were obviously engaged in trying to complete homework for other classes. Finally, Miss Yung gave up her attempt to instruct and assigned them to write a composition on "What Valentine's Day Means to Me." There were moans and groans and lots of "I ain't got no paper, Teach," as Miss Yung walked around the room, prodding students to begin, and reminding them that many of them had failed English last semester and that these compositions would be part of their nine-week's grade.

Miss Yung then called up one of her reading groups. The students came up with their books and papers and were fairly cooperative with Miss Yung as she had them check the work they had completed the day before. I guessed, correctly, that this was her top reading group. While she was meeting with the group, however, the remainder of her students were doing anything but writing the assigned composition. Most students did scribble something down, and a few even seemed to be trying to write a good composition. It was hard for the more cooperative students to work, however, with the bedlam all around them.

When Miss Yung finished working with her top group, she called another group to meet with her. Several of the more obstreperous students reluctantly gathered up their basal readers and joined Miss Yung at the front of the room. I noticed that these boys (not a girl in the group!) were all reading in a 3^1 basal reader. The lesson was a disaster. Miss Yung tried to do a Directed Reading Activity with the students, but they paid very little attention. When they wouldn't read the story silently, she resorted to having them take turns reading it orally.

You can imagine how well that went over! The one who was reading stuttered and stammered, as he tried to read something that was obviously at his frustration level. The others "messed" with one another and laughed at the one doing the reading. It was so awful I had to leave the room. "Well, I told her I would help, and I don't know if I can," I muttered to myself as I made my way down the hall. Not watching where I was going, I almost collided directly with Will. He just smiled and winked as he avoided the collision and hurried on to the gym. As concerned as I was about Miss Yung, I had to smile at the good-natured Coach Wynn!

All during that day, as I went in and out of other classrooms, I thought about Miss Yung and what she could do to get back in control of her class. I considered actually going in and teaching the class for her for awhile but decided that that would be a lose-lose situation. If I succeeded in settling the class down and getting them to work and cooperate, Miss Yung would see it as something I could do but she couldn't. The students would know that I had had to come in and bail her out, and they probably would not transfer their appropriate behaviors to her. If I was not able to get control of the class, Miss Yung would observe my failure and decide the situation was hopeless. The word would quickly spread through the school that Miss Tent had been run off by a middle-school class. No, I definitely should not take over the class.

What could I help Miss Yung to do, then, that would enable her to regain control of the class? I considered teaching her to conduct classroom meetings (Glasser, 1969) in which she would lead the class in discussions about school and language arts and the necessity of gaining certain skills, but I decided that she was too defeated to exert the kind of confident leadership essential to the success of the classroom meeting strategy. That may be a strategy she can use later, I mused, when she has regained some control and has most of the students working and cooperating.

As I was visiting in Mrs. Wright's classroom that afternoon, I was struck by the vivid contrast between the way in which her language arts class functioned and the way Miss Yung's functioned. I then began to make a list of the differences between the two classrooms:

1. Mrs. Wright acts like a leader. She gives the students a lot of freedom and

choice, but she also gives them direction and expects them to behave appropriately.

2. In Mrs. Wright's class, every student has assignments he or she can complete. No student is on frustration level, as many of the students in Miss Yung's bottom reading group were.

3. Mrs. Wright has a lot of variety in the types of activities her students are engaged in. She does some listening, group-writing, and discussion activities in which the whole class is involved. She has some small groups that are together for a specified length of time to work on a particular skill or a project spurred from common interest. All students complete some individual reading and writing assignments.

4. Mrs. Wright has a reasonable number of clearly stated rules. She demands that these rules be followed but does not hassle the students about lots of little things (pencil sharpening, quiet discussions, gum chewing, and so on.)

5. The activities Mrs. Wright has the students engage in are, for the most part, interesting. Her writing center contains many pictures, story starters, interesting objects, and so forth. Students play games to review reading and writing skills.

6. Mrs. Wright always has some activities for the students who complete their work. There is a different art project each week in the art center. There are a variety of games that the students can play (checkers, chess, *Sorry,* etc.) Puzzles, books, and popular magazines are available in the "relaxation corner." Students are also allowed to "just talk" to one another when their work is completed.

7. In Mrs. Wright's class, pupil work is prominently displayed. Pupils seem to take pride in what they accomplish.

I was just finishing the seventh item on the list when Mrs. Wright signaled the group that they had three minutes to complete whatever they were doing and meet her in the "interaction corner" to share some things they had accomplished during the day and make plans for tomorrow. She then set her timer for three minutes, and they all rushed to beat the clock. The students put up the materials or games they were working with. Students who had assignments that needed checking put their folders in Mrs. Wright's "in" box. As the students were scurrying around trying to finish up, Mrs. Wright circulated and saw to it that things would be put back and ready for her next class. When the timer sounded, the students and Mrs. Wright met in the "interaction corner" where they sat on the rug. Mrs. Wright led them in a ten-minute "summing-up" activity. She shared with them several new creations from the art center and some samples of writing completed that afternoon in the writing center. She congratulated students who had achieved certain goals that day and complimented those whom she had observed working exceptionally well, either alone or with a partner. She then had the pupils role play the traditional at-home "well, what did you learn in school today?" scene. Several children played the part of students in her class; others played the role of parents, grandparents, and older brothers and sisters. The students really had a ball doing this activity and were quite "hammy" in their portrayals. Finally, Mrs. Wright observed that some of them had been a little sluggish about getting started on their assigned work. She reminded them that she expected them to "work hard" and "play hard" in her room and asked them all to help each other tomorrow by getting down to business immediately and by refusing to be led away from the task.

That class of students left as the last class of the day filed in. I noticed how Mrs. Wright stood by the door to greet each student as he or she entered. She shared a quick personal remark with many of the students and jostled a few of them affectionately. "Sam, how's that new baby? Does he sleep all night yet? Billy, I saw your name in the paper last night—what a celebrity! Can I have your autograph? Carol, you got your hair cut. It's cute!" were among the overheard comments as Mrs. Wright greeted each student and handed him or her a folder containing their week's assignments and schedules. Students began USSR immediately after the final bell rang. Mrs. Wright and I read during the pre-scribed time as well.

As the children began to get their materials together to get to work, Mrs. Wright wrote the names of those she wanted to meet with next to the time she would meet with them. She then wrote the remaining times on the blackboard, and students who wanted to have individual conferences with her signed up for a specific time slot. Fifteen minutes into the period, all the students were working, and Mrs. Wright was just beginning one of her "quickie" skills groups. I added to my list:

8. Has a summing-up time during which she recognizes the students' accomplishments and helps them realize what they have learned.
9. Greets each student in a friendly manner while handing him or her a folder. (She likes them and expects them to get right to work!)
10. Waits until all students are "settled in" to begin working with a specific group or individual.
11. Keeps her groups or individual conferences to a maximum of ten minutes.

I probably could have written down many more good teaching practices Mrs. Wright used, but, as I was frantically scribbling down the last several, I began to realize what it was I must help Miss Yung do. I returned to my office and looked over the list. I made a list of what Miss Yung would have to do and how I could help her do it.

What	How
Act like a leader. Get some confidence. Expect the students to behave.	Completely change the present environment and *modus operandi*. Rearrange the room. Change the schedule. Have new expectations. Say over and over again to herself: "I am the teacher and thus the leader in this classroom. I have made some mistakes, but I am on the right track now and, day by day, the students will begin to cooperate and follow my leadership."
Assign students work in material at instructional or independent level. Give assignments the students *can* successfully complete.	I will help test children and get them placed in appropriate material. I will borrow some high-interest/low-vocabulary books from Reed and see if I can round up some self-instructional reading kits.
Have a variety of whole class, small group, and individual activities for students to engage in.	Begin with individual activities now because students won't pay any attention to whole class activities and will need direct supervision for awhile on

their individual activities. She should not leave them unsupervised to work with small groups for awhile.

Have no more than six clearly stated rules. Expect these to be followed. Do not pick at the students about other minor things.

Work with class *later*, once they are cooperating more, to draft a set of rules.

Have an area of the room where students can go when they complete their work. Have some things they like to do there.

I will help Miss Yung set up an area and collect stuff to go there.

Show in some tangible way that the students' work is valued and that students are making progress.

Arrange to display student work. Help Miss Yung devise some progress charts.

Have a summing-up time at the end of each period.

Greet the students as they enter and have their assignments and schedule in a folder. Make daily assignments first— move later to weekly assignments.

I will help Miss Yung set up folders and make reasonable assignments. Some assignments everyone will complete; some will be completed by many students. Others will be individually completed.

When you begin working with small groups, wait until all students are settled in. Keep small group work and individual conferences to a maximum of ten minutes.

Help Miss Yung plan small group instruction and individual conferences *later*.

I was just completing this list when Miss Yung walked in for our prescheduled after-school conference. She looked so dejected that I had second thoughts again about my ability to help her. I rallied, however, as I reminded myself that she had to begin to believe she could be a leader and a good teacher and that the students would follow her leadership. Mustering as much enthusiasm and confidence as I could, I began, "Well, Lee, I have been busy thinking and planning all day, and I think I have come up with a plan that will work. It will take a lot of time, planning and energy to get started, but I will work with you. I think we can have your classroom and your attitude completely transformed by next Monday morning. Here's what we need to do."

I then explained to Miss Yung that the scientific principle which states that matter is always in motion and never at rest applies equally to classrooms. "There is always a momentum, a cycle, in the interaction that takes place in a classroom. Right now, for some reason, the momentum in your classroom is pulling things in the wrong direction. Somehow you have to interrupt the cycle and begin it spinning the other way." Miss Yung looked skeptical, but I plunged forward! "To achieve this change, you must drastically change the environment and approach you have used thus far in teaching. Normally, a balance of whole class, small group, and individual activities is ideal during a 90-minute language arts block. You have been doing whole class activities, however, and the students have not been paying very much attention, so, for the time being, you will quit any attempts at whole class instruction.

"You can only do effective small group instruction when the members of the class who are not in the group are meaningfully and independently engaged in other activities. Starting Monday, each student in your room will have a folder in which are listed the activities and assignments to be completed that day. I will work with you to find materials on which your students can work independently and to test them to make sure that they are appropriately placed in that material. I will also help you set up a writing and listening center and create the materials to go into that center. What are you doing this weekend? I think we should get the key from Mr. Topps and spend Saturday rearranging your classroom. When the students come in on Monday, they will see that it is the beginning of a new era in Miss Yung's class." As I talked, I even began to believe it could be done!

The next morning I spent on a "materials hunt." I borrowed a set of high-interest/low-vocabulary novels from Mr. Moore and found a multilevel reading kit in the bookroom. From Mrs. Wright I borrowed a set of booklets on various comprehension skills at different reading levels. In Miss Yung's closet, I found another multilevel kit of materials and a large supply of basal readers at different levels. During lunch, Miss Yung and I looked at the instructional levels Miss Yung had determined by giving a group informal reading inventory at the beginning of the year. Based on these, we decided that the ten students in her top group should take the placement test for the more difficult multilevel kit that focuses on the development of comprehension and study skills. Students in her middle group would take the placement test for the easier multilevel kit.

Of course the students in the low group were the problem, and Miss Yung admitted that she knew several of them were practically nonreaders. However, she didn't know what to do with them and the 3^1 basal was the lowest level book she could find. "Besides," she explained, "even if I had had something lower, I couldn't have handled another group. If no one has been able to teach these students to read so far, I was sure that I couldn't." We decided to let four of the students in the lowest group take the placement test for the easier multilevel kit. The other six children I would work with individually and try to find some materials they could work with independently.

When Miss Yung's students burst noisily into her classroom after lunch, Miss Yung calmly handed all but the six students I was going to work with the appropriate placement test with their names already written on it. She wrote on the board: "This is a test to see where you need to work in some new material we will start next week. If you have a green booklet, you have 35 minutes to complete this test. If you have a blue booklet, you have 50 minutes. I will record the remaining time in five-minute intervals on the board."

I took the six students who didn't have a booklet to the back of the room with me. Ignoring their protests, I handed each of them one of the lowest-level skills booklets that I had borrowed from Mrs. Wright. "You are each to complete one of the exercises in each of these booklets," I instructed them. "On this sheet, I have written your name and, for each booklet, the number of the exercise I want you to complete. Write your answers on this sheet of paper. When you complete the assigned exercise in the booklet you have now, return that booklet to me and get another. I have pencils here for anyone who needs them." I then assigned the six boys to sit at specific desks at the back of the room and begin work. "I will help you if you can't figure out what to do," I promised. Since there were seven booklets and six boys, I had one extra to start with. When the first boy completed the assigned exercise in his booklet, I swapped him the booklet I had for his. I then swapped his with the next boy who finished, and so on.

Meanwhile, the rest of the class had settled down and were taking the placement test assigned to them. Miss Yung was writing the remaining time for each group on the board. She looked somewhat disbelieving at the calm and concentration prevalent in her

Placing
students in
materials

classroom, and I winked at her to let her know we were, indeed, going to break the cycle and get the momentum moving in a positive direction.

That afternoon we graded the placement tests. All but one of the students we had tested could work in the kit for which they were tested. This student had been tested in the higher-level kit and needed to be tested in the easier-level kit. Drawing on my past experience with using these placement tests, and wanting to be absolutely positive that every student could succeed in the assigned material, I counseled Miss Yung to begin the students two levels below the level indicated by the test. "They will move up quickly," I assured her, "and will start out with a very positive attitude because they will all do very well."

For the six students whom I had tested in the comprehension skills booklets, three showed by their performance on the sample exercise that they could work well and profitably in these materials. A fourth student did very well on all the sample exercises and probably could have started in the second level of these booklets, but Miss Yung and I agreed that his confidence was so minimal that he would profit for awhile from completing some work which was very easy for him.

Nonreaders   The other two students, Jeff and Bill, were, for all practical purposes, nonreaders. "I guess that is why they are causing me so much trouble," Miss Yung hypothesized. Miss Yung and I then went down to Mr. Moore's room and talked to him about these students. Both were in his program and thus were not in Miss Yung's classroom for the whole 90-minute block of time. Mr. Moore indicated that he was working with Jeff and Bill on building a basic sight vocabulary and on using consonant substitution and context clues to identify unknown words. He indicated that the two boys had made tremendous progress since coming to his class and showed us some of their language-experience stories. He then agreed to send each of these two boys back to the classroom every day with something they could complete in the classroom and have Miss Yung check. "I am glad you have come," he commented as we were leaving. "If we can both work with these two, I believe we will have them to a point where they can read something independently by the end of the year!"

During the first 30 minutes of Miss Yung's class the following day, Miss Yung took the group of students working in the higher-level kit, and I took the group working in the easier kit. We explained how to work in the kit, how to record answers on answer sheets, and how to check and record their scores. We then gave each student an answer sheet on which we had written the level at which each student was to begin. Each student then completed two of the skills cards at that level. Miss Yung and I gave help as needed and assured ourselves that each student could, indeed, be successful with the assigned level.

We then helped students check and record their scores at a checking table set up at the back of the room. We allowed the students to use only the colored pencils placed there specifically for checking, and one of us double-checked what the students had done. While the other students were thus engaged, the four students who would work in the comprehension skills booklets completed two exercises in the booklet we had assigned them to. They also were shown how to check and record their score. Bill and Jeff were in Mr. Moore's class during this time. Because we had made sure that every student could successfully complete the assigned exercises, all students did well. Miss Yung then showed the students an enjoyable film for the remainder of the class period and her second successful class came to a close.

The class period for the following two days continued as it had on Tuesday. Miss Yung and I made sure that every student knew what to do, how to check and record the score, and how to get out and replace the materials. We circulated among them to keep the students working, ignored the few who were obstreperous, and concentrated on helping, encouraging, and complimenting those students who were cooperating. We stayed by the grading table to make sure each student carefully checked his or her answers and initialed each exercise as it was finished. During the remainder of the period, Miss Yung showed them a film or filmstrip we knew they would enjoy. By Friday, the class entered and left in a much calmer state, and Miss Yung and I both began to believe our plan might work!

Centers

On Saturday, Miss Yung and I transformed her classroom. We set up a listening center at which we placed a tape recorder and ten desks. I then helped Miss Yung tape record five directed listening lessons which would each take the students approximately 20 minutes to complete. We set up a writing center with five different writing activities that could accommodate ten students. For one activity, the students were given examples of cinquain poetry, then allowed to select words from the noun, verb, adjective, and phrase boxes and create from these words their own cinquains. In the noun box we put little cards on which we had written the names of 20 animals. In the adjective box were 40 words which described animals. In the verb box were 50 words which told things animals did. In the phrase box, we put 30 phrases that could apply to animals. If the students chose to complete this activity, they used the cards to create three different cinquains about animals. They copied these cinquains on a sheet of paper and then wrote at least one original cinquain describing an animal not among the original 20, using their own words, not those from the boxes. We anticipated that most students would take two or three 25-minute periods to complete this activity.

Other activities put into the writing center included several mimeographed cartoons without captions for which the students needed to write captions, some story starters which the students could use as a jumping-off point for writing a story at least three paragraphs long, and some cards on which were written the names of three unrelated objects. Students were required to write a story that related all three objects in some way. A final, very popular activity was the magazine monster project. A boxful of magazines, paste, and scissors were provided. A sample magazine monster I had constructed was on display. The monster's head, body, appendages, and other physical characteristics were created by cutting advertised products from magazines and making each product a part of the monster. My monster had a can of cleaning spray for a head and a giant box of soap for his body. Several bars of various hand soaps made up his arms and hands, and his legs were made from various scrubbing cleansers. I named my monster Mr. Scrubby and wrote a story about him escaping from the dark cupboard in which he was always stored. Creating that writing stimulus was the most fun I had had in months!

FOR THE READER TO DO:

Create five stimulus activities that you could put in a writing center. Remember to allow for the varying writing abilities of your students by having activities requiring different levels of sophistication. If possible, duplicate these stimulus activities to share with others.

Finally, we set up the reading center. In the reading center we placed the multilevel kits, the comprehension skills booklets, and a variety of books and magazines we found and borrowed. In the reading center we included the high-interest/low-vocabulary novels I had borrowed from Mr. Moore. We also moved the checking-grading table into the reading center. At the back of the room we put the rug, a beanbag chair, and several pillows. On a tall bookshelf which separated this area somewhat from the remainder of the room, we displayed puzzles, games, comic books, magazines, and other recreational materials. We used tall refrigerator cartons to somewhat close off the listening and writing centers which were on opposite sides of the room.

After a break for pizza and liquid refreshment, we returned to Upton Hill to complete our final task—setting up folders for each student that contained the week's assignments and schedules. Each student was required to complete a Directed Listening Activity and two exercises in the assigned skills kit or comprehension booklets each day. In addition, each pupil was required to read at least 50 pages in a self-selected book and complete three activities in the writing center each week. From these three activities, each student was required to choose one to edit, rewrite, and submit in polished form. We assigned the students to three groups of ten each and to a specific time to complete the taped Directed Listening Activity. We made sure that each group contained a variety of good and poor students and tried to arrange to have the nucleus of trouble-makers assigned to different listening times. In this way, we hoped to minimize the disruptions, since one of the obstreperous students would be at the listening center or in Mr. Moore's class almost all the time. (The whole quartet was never together at one time!) We also wrote the name and level of the reading skills exercises they should complete and check, and left two spaces for each day in which they could write in their score. In another space we left a place for the student to record the title and the author of the book being read and a space to indicate the pages completed. Finally, there was a space in which the five writing center activities were listed. The students were to check the three they chose to complete and circle the one they chose to edit, rewrite, and hand in.

Setting up these folders took quite a long time, and Miss Yung wondered how she would ever find the time to do this for each student in all four language arts classes. She felt much better when I explained that we were getting it all planned out for every student this week—and probably for another week or two—but when she had the students working and cooperating, they would be able to set up their own folders each Monday. "You will give them a mimeographed sheet with the skeleton filled in, and they will copy their listening comprehension times and writing activities from the board. They will also fill in the name and level of the kit they are working in. For a few weeks, however, we must be absolutely certain they can come right in and have no excuses not to get right down to work!"

As we were finishing the folders, Will came in. "I couldn't believe it when I saw lights up here," he said. "What are you two doing here on a Saturday night? I should think you would have something more exciting to do. A bunch of us got awfully hungry yelling for the Upton Hill Bears to win tonight's basketball game, and now we're going out to eat and celebrate. You just have to come along!"

8 A Year of Content-Area Reading (March-June)

March   I can't believe what has happened in Miss Yung's class. Our transformation has really worked and much sooner than I had thought. On the Monday after the Saturday spent transforming Miss Yung and her classroom, the students clamored in. They seemed to have forgotten the four quiet days they had spent in Miss Yung's classroom the previous week and sounded like the same old class again. The transformed room, however, and a calm Miss Yung sitting in a chair in the "relaxing corner" handing out folders as they came over to find out what was going on, had a quieting influence on them. When most of the students had come over and Miss Yung had handed them their folders, she began to talk to them in a very quiet voice. Ignoring the six students who were horsing around at the other end of the room, she explained: "As you can see, I have spent most of the weekend here rearranging the room and setting up a new program for you. I know that we have had some problems in here, partly my fault because I was a new teacher and partly yours because you took advantage of that." A few students snickered and others looked embarrassed. "But that is over now," continued Miss Yung. "Today is the beginning of a new year in this classroom. All slates are wiped clean, and we are going to start over again."

"As you look around the room, you see that we have a listening center. Look in your folder and you will see the time that you are assigned to the listening center. Each day this week at that time, you will go to the listening center, listen to the tape I have made, and complete a listening comprehension exercise that follows the taped story. Before class ends each day, you will all bring your listening comprehension answer sheet here, and I will read the appropriate answers to you. You will check your own papers, and I will double check them. Each person who pays attention while in the listening center and who honestly checks his or her own paper will receive a grade of 'satisfactory' for that day's listening activity."

"On the other side of the room you see a writing center. In this writing center there are five activities. Each of you must complete three of these five writing activities sometime

155

during this week. You must then choose one of the three activities and get a friend, or me, to help you proofread and edit your writing. When I collect your folders on Friday, each person who has completed three writing activities and edited and rewritten one of these, will receive a grade of 'satisfactory' for the week in writing."

"At the front of the room you see the reading center. In the reading center I have placed the skills kits and booklets along with a variety of 'free reading' books. Each of you is required to complete two of the skills exercises each day and to read at least 50 pages each week in a book of your own choosing. Completing this work will result in your achieving a grade of 'satisfactory' for the week in reading. As of right now, I am giving each of you a fresh start. Many of you received a grade of 'unsatisfactory' in language arts for the first semester. That grade will no longer count. From now on, for the remainder of the year, your grade will be based solely on your completing the assigned listening, reading, and writing activities in your folder. Later, I will make some extra credit project assignments for those who wish to work for a grade of 'outstanding'."

"Now, we need to get right to work if you are going to have time to make a good start today on the day's and week's assignments. For those of you whose folder says 'Listening Comprehension Center, 12:00,' you will start in the listening comprehension center and then move to either the reading or the writing centers. The rest of you may start in either the reading or writing center, and as this group and the other groups finish in the listening center, you will go to that center. Back here is a place for meeting and just relaxing. When you finish your daily assignments and you know you are making sufficient progress on your weekly assignments, you can come back here and play a game, put a puzzle together, read a magazine or a comic book, or just talk quietly with a friend. Ten minutes before the class is to finish, I will signal you to put up your materials; we will all meet back here to check your listening comprehension exercises together and evaluate the day's activities."

Miss Yung and I then helped the students get started in the listening center (We appointed one child to be in charge of starting the tape and distributing the mimeographed comprehension sheets), and in the writing and reading centers. There was some confusion as several students tried to decide whether to go to the writing center or reading center first but, in a few minutes, most of the students had settled down. The four students who had not gotten their folders seemed at a loss as the other students began working. Miss Yung explained to them that they had work assigned in their folders and that they could start with a clean slate this week and achieve satisfactory grades in listening, reading, and writing by completing their assignments. Todd declared that he wasn't going to do anything and proceeded to sit in a chair in the back of the room. Jack and Jeff declared they wanted to play checkers, and Miss Yung informed them that they could play checkers when they had completed their assignments, but that at this moment their choice was to get their folders and begin working or do nothing. They chose to do nothing and sat at the back of the room talking and laughing. The other students complained that these four were not working, and Miss Yung calmly told them that if they chose to do nothing and continue to fail language arts in spite of being given a fresh chance, then that was their choice and they would have to live with it. She then went around helping and encouraging the working students and trying valiantly to ignore the horseplay at the back of the room. When Bill and Jeff went to their reading class at 12:30, Todd and Jack continued to do nothing, but they were evidently unhappy to see the others working diligently. Whenever they tried to move to one of the centers and interrupt the students who were working, Miss Yung told them firmly that their only choice was to do their assigned work or do nothing.

As the last group was completing their listening comprehension center exercises, Miss Yung signaled the students to put away their materials and meet her in the "relaxing corner." I helped her make sure that each center was put back in order, and the class then gathered together to check their listening comprehension sheet. Miss Yung reminded them that their grade of "satisfactory" for the day in listening was based solely on their attending to the activity while in the center and honestly checking their own sheet. After checking and collecting the sheets, Miss Yung collected the folders, complimented the students on their diligent work, and thanked them for their cooperation. As the students filed out, several were overheard to remark "Boy, she sure has changed. I guess Miss Tent must have given her some pointers." Several remarked that they sure were glad things had changed because their parents were mad that they were failing language arts. Todd commented that he didn't care what happened, he wasn't going to do anything for the old bag!

By Friday, Jeff and Bill had decided to complete their assigned listening comprehension exercise before they went to reading, and on Thursday they even completed the reading assignments Mr. Moore had sent back with them. Miss Yung patted them on the back as she recorded their satisfactory grades in listening and reading for those days. Jack looked as though he would like to join the others in getting some work done but was afraid of Todd's scorn. Miss Yung was worried about these two, as I was, but I assured her, "They weren't doing anything for you before you reorganized and at least now everyone else is working. Keep encouraging them and eventually they may give in— Jack especially. And I don't believe Todd will sit at the back all alone and fool around."

On Friday, Miss Yung gave each of the students who had satisfactorily completed the assignments a note to take home. In the note, she explained to the parents what a good job their student had done during that week and suggested that the parents allow their son or daughter some special privilege that weekend. These notes were only distributed to students who had satisfactorily completed their work, and they were a complete surprise to the students. Most seemed pleased by this thoughtful gesture. I'm sure those notes got home!

Since that first week, Miss Yung has set up the same arrangement for each of her classes. She thought the amount of paperwork would kill her the first several weeks but is now able to give the students a skeleton of their schedule and have them fill in the specific information. Each week she makes new listening comprehension exercises and adds some new creative writing activities to the writing center. Some very popular activities she leaves in the writing center for several weeks, and some she takes out and then puts back in a few weeks. During the class period Miss Yung is kept busy helping students score their reading comprehension exercises and edit their chosen writing activity. She demands the students be honest in checking their answers and assigns an immediate grade of "unsatisfactory" to any student who is not honest or who is disruptive at the center. Even Todd and Jack have begun to complete some assignments, although they have days when they don't do anything constructive.

I was in Miss Yung's class yesterday and suggested to her that she now think about doing some whole class and small group lessons again. "The students are now cooperating and working quite well independently, so now we need to think about some instruction with them." Miss Yung agreed that she hadn't really been doing any direct teaching and was worried about that. I promised to work with her to plan some adjustments in the schedule. We agreed, however, to leave those adjustments until we returned to school after our end-of-March spring break. For that break and some much-needed sun is where I am headed right now!

April

This month I have worked very closely with the English teachers. More accurately, I have worked with Miss Stern and her classes, and she has worked with the English teachers. Back in February, when I was so involved trying to salvage Miss Yung and her class, I met with the English teachers at Miss Stern's request. She wanted me to tell them about some of the teaching strategies we had used with her students and to encourage them to try some of these with their students. The meeting did not go particularly well. Miss Stern, obviously wanting the teachers to look to me for leadership, sat quietly as I demonstrated some of the teaching strategies we had used and talked about the students' reactions and improved learning and behavior. Most of the teachers listened politely, but the only request for demonstration teaching I got came from Mr. Bone. He teaches both English and French and was wondering if teaching strategies such as capsule vocabulary and Guided Listening Procedure would work with his French students. I had never thought about this before, but his intuition was right. It worked beautifully and with very little adaptation.

Capsule Vocab

For his first capsule vocabulary lesson, he introduced several French foods. He talked conversationally in French about the foods, showed pictures, and put word cards on the board on which were written the names of the foods. He then paired the students and gave them eight minutes to try to use, in French conversation, as many of the foods as possible. Next, he gave them ten minutes to use the words in an essay on French foods. He then read some of these essays to the class. The students enjoy these capsule vocabulary lessons which he does one day each week using a different category of words.

GLP

To watch Mr. Bone do his Guided Listening Procedures in French is a joy! He reads to the students an informative selection on some facet of French life, geography, or customs. As he reads the short selections, he tape records his reading. The students then list, in French, everything they can remember. Mr. Bone writes their remembrances on the board and, when their memories are exhausted, they relisten to the tape, raising their hand to stop the tape when corrections are necessitated. After making all corrections and determining main ideas, Mr. Bone gives his students a five-item true-false test over the material listened to. The entire lesson is conducted in French and the students listen attentively and participate more willingly than they usually do when asked to speak in French.

Sustained writing

Mr. Bone also used the Words on the Wall strategy to teach his students to read and spell essential French vocabulary, and last week he began having his students do five minutes of sustained writing at the beginning of each period. The students write in French anything they want to write. If they cannot think of anything to write, they write "Je n'ai rien écrire aujourd'hui. C'est dommage!" again and again until they think of something to write. Few students write this sentence for the entire five minutes. This sustained writing is not graded, but the students are required to do it. Mr. Bone writes as the students write, and often he reads what he has written to the students. Occasionally, students will volunteer to read what they have written. I have just explained to Mr. Bone how to do translation writing, and he plans to try this with his students. I never would have thought to suggest these strategies to foreign language teachers, but they seem made to order. The students are involved and active and become users of the language as they read, write, speak, and listen.

Unfortunately, Mr. Bone's French classes seemed to be the only classes benefiting from the meeting I conducted with the English teachers. Miss Stern was quite angry at the unwillingness of the other English teachers to try the strategies that worked so well in her classroom, and when Miss Stern is angry, something happens!

One day shortly after Spring break, she accosted me in the hall and demanded,

"Would you come in and teach my classes for a few weeks and let me go in and do demonstration teaching in the other English classes?" Somewhat taken aback, I agreed, if she thought this was the best way to convince the other teachers to try some different strategies. "I don't know if it is the best way or not, but I'm beginning to think it is the only way," she replied. "I will talk to each of the teachers today and set up a schedule. Then, starting next week, if you'll teach my classes, I'll teach theirs. I was teaching English at Upton Hill when many of them were in high school here. They won't refuse to let me come into their classes!"

Nor did they refuse, so she did teach their classes and I taught hers! I would never have thought of this particular plan of attack, but it certainly did work. All the English teachers respect (and perhaps fear) Miss Stern, and when they saw the lengths to which she was willing to go in order to demonstrate to them some strategies she believed in—and when these strategies were effective with their students—they gave up their natural resistance to change. All English classes now have ten minutes of USSR time every day, and many of the teachers are using some of the other strategies demonstrated and advocated by Miss Stern. Mr. Topps certainly was right when he decided to help me get a toe in Miss Stern's door!

I have also worked with the math teachers this month. I knew from comments I had overheard in the faculty lounge that the biggest problem teachers have with their general mathematics classes is in helping the students to understand and solve word problems. One evening I went over to the university library and searched through the periodical guide for some specifics on how to help students solve word problems. My search yielded many theoretical articles that explained some of the problems students have with word problems and several suggested procedures for having them solve word problems using a step-by-step procedure. As I was puzzling over how to get the math teachers interested and motivated to attend a workshop on helping students read word problems, I happened across an article by Sally Mathison in *The Arithmetic Teacher* (1969). Ms. Mathison suggests, in this article, a way of getting students motivated to solve word problems. I copied the article and the next day asked Mr. Gramm what kind of word problems his class was presently working on. He replied that they were working on fractions. I told him that I had just discovered a new way to get students motivated to solve word problems and that, if he would let me have his class for one period, I would like to try it out. He readily agreed!

I made up a set of cards following the instructions in the article. Since there were 27 students in that math class, I cut from newspapers and magazines 26 pictures. I used double-stick tape to attach the pictures to pieces of light-colored construction paper and numbered them. I then wrote on each sheet of construction paper a word problem that involved fractions and that related to the picture. I tried to make the problems of equal difficulty so that they would take about the same amount of time to solve. On the twenty-seventh sheet of construction paper, I wrote "FREE." My last task was to laminate the set of cards so that they could be used many times. Here are a few examples of the fraction problems:

1. Picture—Volkswagen Rabbit
   Problem: This spiffy little Rabbit sold for $6000 including tax, tags, and dealer prep. One-twentieth of the $6000 was for sales tax. One-third of this sales tax went to the state government. How much tax money did the state collect on the sale of the Rabbit?
2. Picture—Large pizza with all the trimmings

Math word problems

Problem: You are planning a pizza party for 20 people. You estimate that 1/2 of
the guests will each eat 1/4 of a large pizza, and the other half will
each eat 1/2 of a large pizza. How many pizzas should you order?

I began my lesson in Mr. Gramm's class by having the students number a sheet of paper from 1 to 27. I shuffled the cards and gave one to each person, explaining as I passed
out the cards that they would have two minutes to solve each card and then would pass
that card to the next person in the row. I showed them the free card and told them that if
and when they got that card, they had a free two minutes. I further explained that they
probably wouldn't get to all 27 cards and that I would stop them 10 minutes before the
end of the period. The student who had a particular card when I stopped them would be
responsible for giving the class the answer to that card as we check our answers. They
began to work immediately and worked against the clock as I called out "pass your card"
at two-minute intervals. The last person in each row brought his or her card to the first
person in the next row. Paul, who was the last person in the last row, got to run to Mary's
desk (first person, first row) every time cards were passed. He had a great time. Ten minutes before class was to end, I stopped their progress. There were actually moans and
cries of, "I didn't get the one about the pizza!" and "I was just about to get the free one!"

As the students were working, I took pictures of them with a camera I had borrowed
from Will. The next day I put the pictures and the set of fraction story problems on the
bulletin board in the office. I also put cards containing statements like "It really works—
ask Mr. Gramm!" and "The long-awaited solution to your story problem problems!" I
also posted a story problem which read:

Miss Tent is conducting a workshop exclusively for math teachers this
Wednesday afternoon (teacher planning day) from 1:00 until 4:00. If all
math teachers attend, what is the total number of teachers she will need to
prepare materials for? If each of these math teachers teach 150 students
each day, how many students will be reached by this workshop? What
percentage of the workshop participants will be female? Under 40? Single?

The bulletin board with the colorful problems and pictures of involved students caught
their eye, and Mr. Gramm bragged about his class and the new strategy to anyone who
would listen. Consequently, eight math teachers plus Mr. Topps showed up for the workshop. I had prepared some humorous story problems for them to solve. I used the procedure Ms. Mathison had described in her article, just as I had done in Mr. Gramm's class.
The teachers, like the students, enjoyed the activity. I then took the opportunity of having
a captive audience to teach them about some of the specific difficulties students have in
reading word problems. I had them select a page in their math book that contained some
word problems. As they read a problem aloud, I noted the words and symbols the students would have to understand in order to solve the problem. When several problems
had been read, the board was filled with mathematical vocabulary and symbols. I then
demonstrated the structured overview strategy for helping students see the relationships
among mathematical terms. I also displayed for them some sample activities that their
students could complete individually or in pairs to help them increase the store of mathematical terms and symbols for which they had meanings. Most of these practical vocabulary activities I used came from a book by Richard Earle (1976) *Teaching Reading and
Mathematics*. After displaying the sample activity cards and sheets I had made, I showed
the teachers the book from which I had gotten the idea. I offered to let teachers borrow
my two copies of the book and told them the book was available from the International
Reading Association for a nominal fee.

FOR THE READER TO DO:

The same vocabulary activities constructed by Miss Tent and displayed to the teachers included such activities as *symbol solvers*—cards made by pairs of students that contained the symbol on one side and its translation on the other, crossword puzzles, matching activities, scrambled words, and multiple-meaning and context activities. Choose a mathematics textbook and decide which symbols and words students must understand in order to complete a particular lesson or unit in that text. Make some vocabulary activities that will help students master the meanings of these symbols and words.

Sharing these vocabulary activities took only about 15 minutes, so I followed this "listening time" immediately with a "doing time:" "Now, you didn't come here to listen to me talk," I admitted. "You came here to make some activities that will help motivate your students to solve word problems. The materials you will need—construction paper, markers, newspapers and magazines, scissors, and glue—are all on the back table. Let's get busy and see if you can each make a set of problems centered around the topic you are presently covering. You just participated in the same activity your students will and you have Ms. Mathlson's article with its explicit directions to guide you. I will help you make the cards." Within ten minutes, all teachers were busily involved cutting, pasting, writing with the colorful markers, and having a good time doing it.

FOR THE READER TO DO:

Make a set of story problems designed to teach a specific kind of word problem. If possible, use this set of problems with a class of students.

The teachers worked busily for almost an hour. We then took a break and enjoyed some coffee and cookies. Several teachers were impressed that I had taken time to make cookies for them, and I think this little personal, hospitable gesture helped them see me as a friend. As the teachers were coming back to work after their break, I interrupted them for just a few minutes to discuss the difficulty involved in solving word problems. I told them that most experts agreed that students who have difficulty solving word problems are helped by learning to follow a series of steps in solving these problems. I then turned on the overhead projector and displayed for them a transparency on which I had written a rather sophisticated word problem. Under the word problem I had written seven steps to follow in solving the problem. Together we followed the seven steps, making appropriate notes next to each step. When we had finished, I told them that if they wanted their students to follow a series of steps in solving word problems, they could use a transparency with only the steps on it and then, with an erasable grease pencil, write in the story problems at the top and the notations next to each step. In this way, they could use the same skeleton transparency again and again for different word problems. If they did this with their students on a regular basis, students would see the value of a step-by-step procedure and would begin automatically to use it as they tried to solve problems. I then gave each of them a skeleton transparency I had made using the machine in the office.

FOR THE READER TO DO:

Here is the skeleton transparency Miss Tent made and gave to her teachers. Using this transparency, select an appropriate word problem and lead a group of students through the seven steps to its solution:

The Problem
    Step 1. Read to get an overview.
    Step 2. What facts are given?
    Step 3. What is the question?
    Step 4. What mathematic operations must I use?
    Step 5. In what order should I do the above operations?
    Step 6. What is a sensible estimate of the answer?
    Step 7. Solve the problem. Compare the answer to the estimate.

The teachers got back to work to complete their set of story problems. Their expressed sentiments and my observations through their classroom doors during the following week demonstrated beyond a doubt that the story problems, transparency skeletons, and even the vocabulary activities were being used! I must remember to thank Will for his help, since it was he who, when I was trying to figure out what to do to motivate the math teachers to give up part of their work day to come to the workshop, reminded me that a picture is indeed worth a thousand words and loaned me his camera. I think I ought to take him to the theatre this weekend to show my appreciation!

May

I can hardly believe that this year is over—or just about over. Next week we have all the senior activities and graduation. After that comes postschool days for the teachers, the report I have to make to the school board, and then finally some time to make my own plans for this busy summer and fall.

This month has been one of taking stock, finishing up, and laying some groundwork for next year. In preparation for the report I had to make to the school board, I sat down and reread this journal which I have been keeping all year. I was rather surprised to realize how many teachers I had worked with and to discover that I had helped teachers in all the content areas except science, business education, and vocational education. Wanting to get a toe in the doors of these content areas (since I will definitely be coming back next year) and wanting also to be able to report to the school board that I had worked with teachers in *all* academic content areas, I decided to try to make a special effort to work with at least one teacher in each of these areas. I had talked with several of the science teachers before and, for the most part, they didn't feel that their students had difficulty reading the assigned text. In courses that were required of all students, the instructors used a special text-lab manual which required very minimal reading skills. They also paired their students for laboratory work and tried to pair an able reader with a poorer reader to further minimize the effect of poor reading skills on the learning of their subject matter.

Not sure what I could do to help the science teachers, I asked Bunny Burner if I could observe some of his classes so that I might look for some ways I could help the science teachers. He agreed, and I spent a morning in physical science, biology, and chemistry. The physical science and biology classes were using the simplified text-lab manual, and they did indeed seem to be functioning quite well in these materials. I did notice, however, that Bunny did a lot of talking and demonstrating to the students, and I made a note to try to get science teachers to use Directed Listening Activities and Guided Listening Procedures as ways of improving their students' listening comprehension.

The chemistry section contained mostly college-bound students, and they could indeed read their textbooks. I noted, however, that they didn't use the textbook very effectively. They appeared to begin at the beginning of a chapter and just keep reading until they got to the end. I realized that, given the importance of charts, graphs, tables, and other illustrative material, these students could read more efficiently if they used a specific study strategy and got in the habit of always looking first at the illustrative material in order to predict what information was going to be covered in the chapter. I suggested to Bunny that I would like to teach a Directed Reading-Thinking Activity to his students and that I would like to try to get the students to use a study procedure, such as PQ4R, when reading dense technical material like that contained in their chemistry texts. I explained to Bunny what a Directed Reading-Thinking Activity was and that I had observed Mr. Moore using it very effectively as a way to improve students' comprehension of what they read. While he was interested in and willing to try a Directed Reading-Thinking Activity, he was dubious about PQ4R. "I tried during my first year of teaching," he explained, "to get the students to use SQ3R, and it just didn't work. They just didn't use it. I think PQ4R sounds like the same kind of thing. I don't believe the students will actually use it."

"Well, then, this is precisely the time to try it," I argued. The year is almost over and, while many teachers don't want to try anything new at the end of the year, I have always thought that was the perfect time to try something new. If it works, great! You can start right off with it next year. If it doesn't, you haven't lost much since the students with whom the new strategy or organization didn't work quickly finish the year, and you don't have to live with or try to live down for the remainder of the year a good idea that just didn't work!"

DR/TA   My logic won him over and he agreed to work with me on both DR-TA and PQ4R. Wanting to be absolutely sure I was doing the DR-TA correctly, I checked with Mr. Moore. Together, he and I wrote down the steps so that I would be sure to go step-by-step and so that I would have a list of the steps to give teachers after I had demonstrated the strategy. When I did the lesson with Mr. Burner's chemistry class, I found them somewhat hesitant at first to make predictions. I waited them out, however, and after encouraging them a few predictions were volunteered. As the students read portions of their textbooks and saw that many of the predictions were confirmed, they became more willing to make predictions. Mr. Burner has since done several DR-TAs with the class and reports that they are much more willing now to make predictions and like to see their predictions verified.

FOR THE READER TO DO:

Find a group of students and teach three Directed Reading-Thinking Activities to them. Expect to have to encourage and wait them out the first and maybe the second time you use this procedure. Explain why this strategy helps even good readers to improve their comprehension. Here are the steps Mr. Moore and Miss Tent wrote down. Follow these steps carefully.

1. Students are asked to read the title of the selection silently, to read all headings (if any) silently, and to examine pictures, charts, and illustrations (if any).
2. Students are then asked to volunteer guesses or predictions as to what the se-

lection will say or be about. (Books should be closed during predictions—use bookmarks.)

3. The teacher records each prediction on a chart or on the chalkboard, putting the name of the student who made the prediction in parentheses after the prediction.

4. When there are no more predictions being made, the teacher asks the students to read from the beginning of the selection to some stopping point which the teacher decides. When a student reaches the stopping point, he or she is expected to close the selection or book with the bookmark and look up at the teacher until everyone finishes.

5. When everyone reaches the stopping point, the group examines each prediction in light of what they have read. Taking the predictions one at a time, the students are asked to say whether or not each was a good prediction.

6. When a student expresses the opinion that a prediction was or was not a good one, he or she must read a part of the text that supports or refutes the prediction. The text itself is the only source of verification or refutation of predictions. Some predictions will be verified and marked as such by the teacher; some predictions will be refuted and erased by the teacher; still other predictions will remain possible but unproven, and will be marked with a question mark by the teacher.

7. Based on what they have already read, students are then asked to volunteer new predictions about what the rest of the selections will say or be about.

8. Beginning with step 3 (above), continue the reading, verification, refutation process. For some selections you may choose to have only one stopping point for evaluating old predictions and making new ones. For other selections you may choose to have several stopping points throughout the selection.[1]

PQ4R

I approached the PQ4R lessons with a scientific attitude. I told students that many of them would soon be finishing high school and going on to college and that knowing how to study a textbook was an important prerequisite for getting through college successfully. I told them that during that week we would perform an experiment to see if using a specific study technique helped them learn more in the same amount of time and to see if what they learned was retained one week later. I called the first part of the experiment "just reading." On the first four days of the week, the students were assigned to read two chapters. On Friday, the students took a test over the material contained in these chapters. Students then exchanged papers and graded the texts. We then computed an average number of items correct for the class on the test of the "just reading" chapter. Out of 50 items, the average number correct was 30.8.

The following week, I led the class through the Preview, Question, Reflect, Read, Recite and Review steps as outlined by Thomas and Robinson (1977). Following closely the suggestions made by Thomas and Robinson, I began by telling the students they had five minutes during which they were to find out as much as they could about what was going to be said in the chapter. I set my timer for five minutes and watched the students frantically try to read as much as possible. Some started with the first word and read as much as they could. Others read the first and last paragaph and looked at the visuals and headings. When the timer signaled the five minutes were up, I had students close their books

[1]Adapted from Russel G. Stauffer, *Directing Reading Maturity as a Cognitive Process* (New York: Harper & Row, 1969).

and write as much as they could remember. Some students were still writing when I stopped them and asked them to show their papers to one another. The students quickly realized that some students had learned much more in five minutes than others had. I then explained to students the differences I had observed in the way they had utilized the five minutes they were given. For the most part, students who had previewed the chapter had learned more in five minutes than students who had just started reading. Next to *preview* on the chart we were making, I wrote: Take five minutes. Read headings and first and last paragraph. Look at all visuals. How much did you learn?

For the *question* step, I helped the students to turn the headings in their textbooks into questions. They then read and reflected on the portion of the text covered by that heading. As each portion of the text was finished, I required students to close their texts (keeping the page with a finger in the book) and recite what they had learned. They were to answer the question raised by the transformed heading and try to recall as much else as they could. If they couldn't remember what they had read, they read that section again. In this way, we read the entire chapter completing the question, read, reflect, and recite steps section by section. Finally, we reached the review stage. Although our time was now quite short, I encouraged students to take a few minutes and reread the first and last paragraphs, look once more at the visuals, and go through each section, thinking of the question raised by the heading and trying to recall as much information as they could.

The reading of one chapter using the PQ4R study method occupied us on Monday and Tuesday. On Wednesday, I had the class help me complete the chart we were making by writing alongside the steps just what they were to do in each step.

FOR THE READER TO DO:

Here is the chart begun by Miss Tent and Mr. Burner's chemistry students. Complete the chart as you think Miss Tent and the students may have completed it:

PQ4R

PREVIEW—Take five minutes. Read headings and first and last paragraphs. Look at all the visuals. How much did you learn?

QUESTION—

READ and REFLECT—

RECITE—

REVIEW—

Following the steps and working together as we had on the first chapter, we then went through another chapter. This time the students were much more effective in their use of the strategy. The first chapter had taught them what was expected of them.

On Friday, the students completed a 50-item test similar to the test they had completed the week before. Again, they exchanged papers and corrected them. This time the average number of correct answers was 35.7. This was a full 5 points better than the students had averaged by just reading the chapters in their usual manner. We recorded this information on a graph we were keeping.

On Monday of the following week, students took a long-term retention test concerning the material they had "just read." This test indicated that students had forgotten almost 40 percent of the material. Their average score on this 50-item test was 18.4. On the following Monday, the students took the long-term test on the material we had read using the PQ4R technique, and although there was some forgetting, the drop—from 35.7 to 29.6—was not nearly so great as that from 30.8 to 18.4.

Mr. Burner then admitted to the class he had been skeptical about whether or not students would actually use a study technique as they were completing their reading assignments, but that the "scientific experiment" they had conducted certainly proved to him as a scientist that the method was effective in helping students learn more and retain more of what they learned. He then read to the class some of the evidence from the other experiments with PQ4R cited by Thomas and Robinson.

"I am only sorry," commiserated Mr. Burner, "that I didn't start you using this study strategy right off at the beginning of the year. I believe that, if I led you through the steps several times and then continually encouraged you and reminded you to use this study strategy, you would have learned a lot more chemistry and also be better prepared to do well in college. This experiment has taught this 'old dog a new trick.' I hope you will use it in your future study. I certainly intend to make sure that next year's chemistry students use it until it becomes automatic with them."

My other two "end-of-year/try-something-new" strategies also worked quite well. I helped Mrs. Hammer teach a Guided Listening Procedure and a Directed Listening Activity to her industrial arts students, and I showed Miss Quick how using a *Words on the Wall* strategy could help her students review their shorthand symbols. In both classrooms, I convinced the teachers that they had nothing to lose by trying out something new at the end of the year. If it worked, fine; they had a good strategy for next year. If it flopped—well, the year was almost over anyway. At least they had tried, and the students with whom they had flopped would soon be off on their summer way. I must remember this end-of-year strategy for next year!

The School Board Meeting

Miss Tent sat fidgeting with her notes as she watched Reed Moore make his presentation to the assembled school board members and interested public and press. "He is so confident," she thought. "I would be too if I had the kind of objective data he is presenting." The remedial students with whom Mr. Moore had worked all year had, indeed, made remarkable progress, and she could tell that the school board members were impressed with the facts and figures he was reporting to them. She wondered for the hundredth time if she had made the right decision in deciding to go with a slide-tape anecdotal presentation of what she and the other teachers had accomplished that year. At first she had tried to get Miss Werth, Miss Stern, Mr. Burner, and the other teachers she had worked most closely with to make short presentations to the board explaining how she had helped them adjust their instruction to the varied reading abilities in their classes. She could tell, however, that the teachers, while wanting to support her, were very hesitant to stand up and speak out in front of the board, reporters, and citizens. "I'll come," was Mr. Burner's reply "but I won't stand up there and give a report. You never know what those board members will ask you." Miss Stern said that she was not afraid of the board but that they had heard her so many times they had quit listening to her. Miss Werth apologized, "I'd just be scared to death. I want to help you because you have helped me so much, but I just can't get up in front of all those people."

It was Mr. Topp's suggestion that she use some of the slides she had been taking all year and, at the last minute, she decided to tape record several of the teachers talking about what they had done differently this year and how the students had reacted. At Will's suggestion, she also taped some of the students. The combined slide-tape presentation was the basis of her report to the board tonight.

Mr. Topps winked confidently at her as he finished his introduction of her to the board and the audience. He then helped her to set up the screen and turned off all the lights. "At least," she consoled herself, "people will only be able to hear my knees knocking—they won't be able to see them!" Speaking rapidly, she gave a brief overview of her year's goals and program to the board. Relieved when that part was over, she turned on the slide projector and the tape recorder.

The first slides were taken in Miss Werth's home economics class. Miss Werth was shown doing Directed Listening Activities, Guided Listening Procedures, and translation writing lessons with her students. Slides of the Words on the Wall for both the foods preparation and sewing units were also shown. As the slides were shown, Miss Werth's taped voice explained why she had used these strategies with her students and how she thought they had helped. "Many of my students," she explained, "are failure oriented. They lack basic reading and writing skills, and they also lack the intrinsic motivation necessary to overcome these deficiencies. By adjusting my reading and writing demands so that they can succeed, and by using translation writing and the Words on the Wall strategy as ways to improve their reading and writing abilities, I have helped them to become more competent and more confident. I have also observed a subsequent increase in their motivation."

The slides taken in Miss Stern's room showed Miss Stern teaching a Guided Reading Procedure, a capsule vocabulary lesson, and a vocabulary meanings through context lesson. Several of her students read aloud on tape the essays they had composed using the words from the capsule on religion. A final slide showed Miss Stern and her entire class engaged in their daily USSR time. Several students' taped voices gave their reaction to daily USSR time. Even R. R. Rowe chuckled when Billy's taped voice said "Lots of teachers, they say you gotta read. It's real important to read, but you never see them read, and they never give you no time to read what you wanna read. Miss Stern, she say 'reading is so important and none us has enough time to read so we gonna take time out of class every day to practice our reading.' Then Miss Stern, she reads a book while we read our books. Lots of times she tells us what she is reading. I borrow books from Mr. Moore's class where we have USSR time too. I read 16 books this year, and I never read any books before this year. That's amazing!"

Next came the slides taken in Mrs. Epock's class. Slides of several structured overviews were shown while students explained the terms and the relationships between various terms. Another slide showed the information from a Guided Listening Procedure with the main ideas circled. Following a slide of the flow chart "How a bill becomes law," were slides of the students acting out the "becoming a law" process. Finally, there were several slides that showed the students who could read the text using the text while the other students worked with Mrs. Epock on a translation writing lesson. A student who had failed U.S./state history the previous year explained, "I worked hard in history class this year because I knew I had a chance of passing it. I didn't like it at first when Mrs. Epock put me in the group of kids who couldn't read the book. But I knew she was right. I couldn't read that book. Mrs. Epock made us work, but she was fair. She read all the items on the test to us and I passed history. It was even fun when we acted stuff out and when we had to listen to remember everything. I was one of the best listeners in the class."

Next came slides of the students in various math classes working on the special word problem sets Miss Tent had helped the teachers make during the math faculty workshop. Other slides taken in the math classroom showed Miss Mathers leading her students through the steps in solving a word problem using a skeleton transparency and also slides of the students working in pairs with cards on which a word or symbol was written on one side and the meaning or translation on the other side. Miss Mathers explained that she had never thought of math as presenting reading problems for students, but that their mathematics achievement had drastically improved since she started helping them systematically attack word problems and emphasizing meaning vocabulary.

The PQ4R chart made by Miss Tent with Mr. Burner's class, and several slides of his students being led through the PQ4R steps, were the slides Miss Tent included to emphasize reading in the sciences. Mr. Burner's taped voice explained how he intended to start off the year immediately next year by leading his students through the PQ4R steps until they became second nature to them.

The final slides showed Mrs. Hammer's class engaged in a Guided Listening Procedure, Miss Quick's shorthand class reviewing the symbols using the Words on the Wall strategy, and Ms. Ball and Coach Wynn with their bookshelves of sports books in the gymnasium. Will's taped voice was heard interviewing some of his football players about their newly discovered interest in books.

At the conclusion of this slide-tape presentation, Miss Tent thanked the board for their attention and then waited, anxiously, to see what questions they would have. To her embarrassment, R. R. Rowe announced that while he was impressed by most of her presentation, he questioned the objectivity of the remarks made by Coach Wynn! Mr. Snyder stated that while he was glad to see the students were learning, he was still concerned about standards. "How do they get into high school not being able to read and never having read a book is my question," he harangued.

R. R. informed him that they had been through all that a hundred times before and that they were working to upgrade the curriculum at all levels but that, in the meantime, there were students who can't read and "we just have to do something about it." R. R. then announced that several of the members present had another important event to attend that evening and that he would entertain a motion for adjournment. The board quickly adjourned and, as Miss Tent was heading for the ladies room, she was whisked into a meeting room where most of the Upton Hill faculty were gathered to share in a surprise shower for her and Will!

Unit Three
Middle/Junior High
School Reading

9 A Middle/Junior High School Reading Program

THE MIDDLE/JUNIOR high school student is an "in-betweener." He or she is neither child nor adult. It is sometimes difficult for adults to know how to deal with these in-betweeners. They are trying to figure out where they fit into the world; who they are; what they want; and why they want it. It is a time of change, a period of confused physical and emotional feelings. They can be loving, hostile, moody, or ridiculously silly.

Middle schoolers vary greatly in their reading abilities, ranging from beginning readers to high school-level reading. Because of this, it is imperative that the reading/language arts program be personalized and integrated. The teacher personalizes instruction through the use of large and small groups as well as individual work. There is variety in instructional techniques as well as in materials and activities. The teacher makes judgments about the type of instruction different students need based on a diagnosis of their reading abilities. The integrated aspect of the instruction allows students to apply their language skills in a variety of situations. In Chapters 10 and 11, Mrs. Wright describes one way to personalize and integrate the reading/language arts program.

An Integrated Language Arts Program

Mrs. Wright integrates reading instruction with instruction in the other language arts. The language arts areas she teaches are reading, writing, listening, and speaking. None of these exists in a vacuum; therefore, they cannot be taught as isolated subjects. The middle school/junior high language arts program should not be an English class that focuses on teaching parts of speech and the literary classics. Although students should, indeed, be encouraged to

173

read selections from our vast literary heritage, there does seem to be a need and a place for the inclusion of some of the literature which has been written specifically for them.

The writers in the field of adolescent fiction are prolific; therefore, there is more and better literature for young adults available than ever before. For a language arts program to be meaningful and useful, it is imperative that the teacher make every effort to use this growing, vibrant body of literature and to teach some of the same skills that would be taught with the readings in a more traditional curriculum. The literature is pertinent because it addresses itself to the real, everyday concerns of adolescents, such as drugs, divorce, "going all the way," death, the generation gap, belonging, and the myriad other problems which beset the adolescent.

The classroom teacher who is truly concerned that the students learn to read, write, and speak well will employ whatever means or materials are needed to accomplish the goal. Niensted (1977) described one such program. She had had no formal training in the teaching of reading prior to working with the classroom described in the article. She was an English teacher who was merely trying to teach a group of "unmotivated" students. These students were unable to read the eleventh grade texts which had been assigned to them. Through a program which integrated the study of reading, writing, listening, and speaking, she not only taught them, but she also restored to them the self-respect of which they had been deprived by years of failure.

This is not an easy task, but surely such success as Niensted described should not be considered a phenomenon. There can be little doubt that a dedicated teacher — willing to work hard and to learn from mistakes, journals, and other classes, and workshops — could replicate the same success. If this is not true, then what hope can there be for these students? And if the academically unmotivated can be more effectively taught through the integration of the language arts areas, then what implications must there surely be for the average and the above-average student? It is the contention of this author that there is not really a dichotomy between remedial and developmental instructional techniques. Good teaching identifies where students are instructionally, and defines their strengths and weaknesses. These are then worked with, regardless of whether the student is at, above, or below grade-level placement in terms of achievement.

Development of a student's skill in speaking can be transferred to writing if the teacher is willing to transcribe the student's thoughts in order to help him or her analyze the constructions. Additionally, the student's own words written down can serve as interesting reading material for the student. Students' skills in speaking can be improved by giving them time to speak about those things that interest them or that they have read. *Expecting* them to do well in the language arts is a necessity. Part of that expectation includes providing time for all of the language arts to be developed during the class period.

The more associations we have for information, the more easily it is remembered and retrieved. The same is true for the interdependency of the language arts. It would be highly unusual to have a student who is proficient in writing, but who does not read well. Whereas some students may be better writers than speakers, at least the potential exists to develop those speaking skills to the same level as their writing skills. Growth in one or more of the language arts areas can encourage growth in others. The sensitive teacher need only provide opportunity, instruction, support, and encouragement.

Most middle school students have been taught with basal readers, few of which make many provisions for the integration of the language arts. Basal readers are a series of books that follow a developmental skill sequence. They normally begin with readiness materials for use in kindergarten and/or first grade and continue through sixth or eighth grade. They are multiauthored books that become progressively more difficult.

Basals can run the gamut from those that contain good stories and well-organized and developed skill sequences to some with dreary stories that don't even reinforce the skills the teacher is attempting to teach in the reading group or conference. They also can be as good or as poor as the teacher using them.

Mrs. Wright uses basals at her middle school level because she has multiple copies of selections available so that she can occasionally work with groups of students on a story. The basal reader selections for the middle school age student are primarily literature excerpts that she can pick and choose among. The use of basals is not incompatible with her emphasis on adolescents' literature in a personalized reading program. Very often, if the basal selection is a bowdlerized version of the original, she has the students locate the original source and involves them in some critical reading skills of comparing and contrasting aspects of the selections, such as use of figurative language, characterization, sentence length, and so on.

FOR READERS TO DO TOGETHER:

Locate a middle school level basal reader and identify a story that is excerpted from a work of literature. Next locate the original literature source and compare the two selections using the following criteria: readability level (see pg. 73 for a readability formula), descriptive language, characterization, and writing style. The readability formula will yield information about sentence length and word length. Discuss which selection is the better and why.

A Personalized Language Arts Program

Mrs. Wright uses various types of literature in her personalized program so that students will have the opportunity to experience various writing styles. This type of approach, while inherently more interesting for teacher and student alike, has some potential pitfalls as well. If the teacher has no idea what reading skills to teach or how to teach them — and if the teacher does not help students to develop a sense of responsibility for their own learning or is unwilling to develop materials needed for the classroom — then such an approach will be unlikely to succeed.

A simple, yet complete means for keeping track of students and materials is the crux of this approach. Without adequate record-keeping, the teacher has no idea what kinds of assignments to give to students in order to keep them working at instructional level. Even if the records of the students are kept up to date, there is no way for the teacher to monitor what materials exist and where there are surpluses and deficiencies. Consequently, the appropriate and needed materials will not be available to the students when required.

Mrs. Wright not only had students working in many different levels at the same time, but she also provided for the interests of the students by assigning interesting materials and letting them move around the room while working on those materials. She provided variety in the types of task they were asked to do by calling upon their skills and working on their deficiencies in other language arts areas.

Mrs. Wright's program could also be classed as a total language arts approach to teaching reading as well. Not only did she individualize instruction with literature, but she also provided activities in listening, speaking, writing, and art. This approach emphasizes the integrated nature of the language arts and uses the strengths in one area to build skills in others.

The same cautions apply to the total language arts approach to reading that apply to the individualized approach in using literature; the teacher must have a grasp of what reading is and how to teach it. Record-keeping *must* be complete enough to ensure progress, yet not so complex that it impedes progress. Students should always know what is expected of them and what the expected results of their work are to be. It is unreasonable to assume that students will infer what their particular strengths and weaknesses are; the teacher should regularly share that information with the students in oral and/or written form.

Mrs. Wright may well have used a form like the one below. She would have each student's form in a separate file folder, stored alphabetically by class section, so that she could have ready access to it during the conference. Students would always have access to their files so that they could review her comments at will.

Name: *Phillip*

Name of reading selection: *Ch. 5, My Side of the Mountain*
Pg. *37-43*

Oral reading: *fluent, expressive - you made me feel I was there.*

Silent Reading rate: *216 wpm*

Comprehension: *Good recall of details a sequence; let's work some more on main ideas - okay?*

Meaning vocabulary: *"spring beauties" has another meaning than the one you're used to! How about checking!*

Comments: *I can tell you're enjoying this book more, now. Are you really going to try some of the recipes?!?*

Mrs. Wright can have these duplicated by the gross so that she can fill one out each time she meets with a student, either in a group or individually. During the reading conference, however, she would take notes on 5 × 8 inch file cards, one per student, and then would transfer that information later so that the student would have a more coherent picture of his or her evaluation of reading strengths and weaknesses. Similar forms would be available to evaluate the students in listening, writing, and speaking.

FOR READERS TO DO TOGETHER:

Form three groups within the class. One group will devise an evaluation form that Mrs. Wright might use for listening, another group will develop the form for speaking, and the third will devise a reporting form for writing. Critique each group's efforts and revise the forms accordingly. Duplicate the final copy of each for all class members.

Mrs. Wright used many devices within her classroom that utilized the total language arts approach without their being patently obvious. The graffiti board certainly incorporated the use of many areas of the language arts as students wrote, discussed, listened, and read one another's writings. The class newspaper was yet another way of incorporating various aspects of the language arts in an instructional, meaningful, and interesting fashion.

Another approach used by Mrs. Wright is one that has a considerable acceptance among primary grade teachers, and which has great applicability for readers in the intermediate grades, and through adulthood. The language experience approach draws upon the language and thinking of the student to provide reading material at the appropriate level. The interest in the material is inherent, since the student is responsible for the words that he or she is reading. There is some element of personalization, even if a group is reading a story created by one of its own members. Additionally, other language arts skills are called upon to produce the written story that the student or students will read. Of course, Mrs. Wright uses a more sophisticated version of this approach than does her mother-in-law who teaches first grade. Mrs. Wright uses the story as a *starting* point and creates activities to develop reasoning, writing, speaking, and reading. She finds that working with a group of students using the same high interest story dictated by one of them, is an effective way of teaching the skills that will enable them to begin reading and understanding the writings of others.

Teachers also have an abundance of kits and programmed materials available to them. The students select a reading, according to some previously designated criteria, and after completing it, take a written test on the material. Less often, there is a reading conference with the teacher for the purpose of discussing what has been read. Students even score their own written tests and keep their own records. These can be enormous time-savers for the teacher, to be sure, but they can also result in merely drilling on isolated skills from which can ensue a sense of insecurity concerning the student's actual placement and achievement on a skills continuum. Also, these materials use the same format throughout a particular program in order to simplify instructions for the student. However, this simplification can also result in boredom with the materials, if they are overused.

Intelligent use of basals, adolescents' literature, the language experience approach, or kits of books or skills can yield a great deal of information about the reading strengths of students, and knowing the strengths of students provides clues to their weaknesses. Of course, that is the point of any approach to teaching reading. The teacher needs to know the students, personally and academically. Simply to maintain that the student doesn't care, or that he or she is lazy, is not enough; it is not even enough to realize that he or she doesn't understand what is read. The real teacher is one who knows why the student doesn't do certain things — or is unable to do so — and is prepared to deal with each situation without placing blame or abrogating the responsibility which he or she assumed when assigned a class of students. Allington's (1975) article stresses the necessity for differentiating instruction at the middle school level in order to provide the essential bridge from a skills-oriented curriculum to a content-oriented one. In this article he discusses instructional strategies that prove useful in aiding students through the transition.

Assessment is, of course, crucial to a personalized program, and articles such as the one by Clary (1976) provide help in assessment for the classroom teacher. The content area teacher, or the language arts teacher, often deals with such large numbers of students at the middle school level that it is essential to use as many group measures (such as the cloze) as possible. The informal reading inventory should include samples of reading and word lists from the various content area books in order for a relatively accurate estimate of instructional reading level to be reached.

After the assessment of students, the teacher needs to know which skills the various available resources deal with. This is another type of assessment. By examining, categorizing, and organizing materials, the teacher is ready to identify those which will be of greatest benefit to individual students.

FOR THE READER TO DO:

Read the article by Linda Mixon Clary in the November 1976 issue of the *Journal of Reading.* After reading the article, follow her directions to create an informal reading test using a textbook written for the middle school student. Administer the test to a group of students at a local school. Score the tests and give a copy of the results to the classroom teacher. Revise your test incorporating what you learned during the administration and scoring. Make copies for each member of your class.

It has been said many times that without the will to read it doesn't matter if the skill is there. Those students who will not read are no further ahead than those who cannot. But why do the former have no desire to read?

FOR READERS TO DO TOGETHER:

In groups of five or six, think back to and discuss your remembrances of reading in the elementary school. Were you grouped? What group were you in? How did you feel about going to reading groups? Did you enjoy reading aloud? Why or why not? Did you do workbook pages and ditto sheets? How did you feel about them? Why were they used? Was there a regular time in the school day for independent, free choice reading? Were your teachers excited about reading? How do you know? Did your teacher read to you? How often? Was it a waste of time? What books do you remember reading or having read to you in school? Do you think your teachers enjoyed reading? Why?

Perhaps from your discussion you will begin to notice some patterns emerging. Surprisingly enough, schools with the best resources and most attractive environments are not necessarily the schools with students who are voracious readers. The factor of teacher enthusiasm and encouragement plays a far larger role in determining whether or not students are readers.

If you are not now a person who enjoys reading, perhaps you can begin to understand the reasons. Reading in school is often geared to group instruction rather than to individual tastes. Much of the emphasis is placed on skills, with very little time given to the practice of those skills in reading materials. Most of the practice is external to reading through workbooks, games, and worksheets. It is nearly certain that students will read better and derive a greater enjoyment from reading if two things are done daily. There must be time for the teacher to read to the students, and there must be time allowed for students to make free-choice reading selections and then read those materials. Both of these activities show students that the school values reading and allows time for the practice of skills related to reading.

Hunt (1971) refers to this independent reading time as USSR — Uninterrupted Sustained Silent Reading. He maintains that USSR can be used in any classroom K–12, and that, indeed, it should be. There are guidelines for middle and secondary teachers who may, by the very nature of the school schedule and curriculum, have to make adjustments. One Ohio high school which recently participated in a "sustained silent reading month" throughout the entire school district voted to continue the program because of the positive attitudes and changes noted in students. If students never participate in the glorious experience of losing themselves in another time or place, then why should we expect them to become "readers" when they have free time or are no longer in school.

Mrs. Wright subscribes to these principles and allows time in her classroom not only for a daily reading time, but also for writing, since she values that development as well. In addition, she tries to make the library an integral part of her students' school lives by having an attractive classroom library (to which the students have contributed many of the books), as well as by requiring them to visit the school library to work on special projects.

A Reading-to-Learn Language Arts Program

One key to being able to research is familiarity with the library, and not just the familiarity that comes with dropping in once a week to check out books. Children should see the library as the central part of the school and what the school stands for. Children often enjoy weekly trips to the library while in the primary grades, and even in the intermediate ones. The library can appear to be a bewildering maze of stacks, numerals, letters all arranged in some unfathomable way. Many students simply go to the same shelves continually, for they know what is there, and that is easier than trying to locate other types of books.

Language arts classes at the middle school level provide the perfect entrée to library use. Perhaps a period every two weeks or so could be spent at the library with the teacher instructing students in some of the library skills they do not have, such as alphabetization, knowing what the parts of a book are and how to use them to greatest advantage, the use of the card catalog, introduction to various reference materials and the most efficient use of these materials, using periodicals to locate information, using indexing services to locate information in periodicals, and being able to use the Dewey Decimal and/or Library of Congress System. Other pertinent study and research skills are to be able to locate information both in and out of libraries, to organize that material into some meaningful sequence, to select and evaluate the material, and finally, to retain the information garnered. Both organization and selection/evaluation are the keys to retention and are therefore the most difficult to teach.

Organization of material requires skills in note-taking and outlining. Students should be given practice in taking notes both from oral and written references. After those notes are taken, help students put them into outline form. Students often learn best with modeling, so begin with short selections that you read to them or that they read for themselves. Ask the class to tell you what the main points were, and then write those on the chalkboard or on a transparency for overhead projection. After the major points have been reached by consensus and the sequence agreed upon, ask the students to give you more information that helps to clarify or expand upon the main points. Write these underneath the main points. There should not be any enumerating or lettering of points at this stage. After all of these have been clarified, help the students identify categories that each of the major points fit into. Label these with Roman numerals I, II, and so forth. The major points that fit under the categories can be labeled A, B, and so on, and the subpoints are 1, 2, and so forth. If other details have been given, they can be labeled with a, b, c, as far as need be.

Students should now compare and contrast their class effort at outlining with the outline you prepared in advance of the lesson. There may well be differences between them, but this is a good way to lead into a discussion of emphasis and organization. After doing two or three of these whole class lessons with either listening or reading and taking notes, have the class work in small groups to come up with individual notes that they convert into a single outline. Students learn note-taking as well as outlining skills from this type of activity.

FOR THE READER TO DO:

Do a lesson like the one described above with a group of students. Be sure to explain to the teacher what you are trying to do and leave him or her with enough information to do future lessons. Discuss your successes and failures with the others in your class.

One can also teach students to skim and scan, two important reading skills in research. Skimming is rapid reading in order to get the gist of the author's ideas; the main points can be identified. In scanning, the reader looks for specific information such as names, dates, phrases, or other such details. After scanning, the reader would not know what the main idea of the selection was.

FOR THE READERS TO DO TOGETHER:

Divide the class into an even number of small groups of four or five. Even number groups must develop a skimming lesson plan for a page in this text book. Odd number groups must develop a scanning lesson for a page in this text. Write out the plan and then exchange with another group (skimming changes with scanning). Evaluate the lesson given to you. Would it help students learn to skim or scan better?

Teaching students to evaluate what they have read is also difficult, for many of us still find this hard to do. Students can be taught to look at the author's qualifications, to look for corroboration of statements ("Can they be verified?"), to check the copyright date as a way of ascertaining whether the most recent information is being reported, and to evaluate the author's language in order to detect instances of bias rather than objectivity.

Once students have been taught to locate information, to select pertinent information, to organize information, and *then* to evaluate it, the bulk of the work is done for the retention of that information. It has been said that comprehension is organization. Having worked through the material so many times, the student has many associations for the material. The more associations one has, the more likely it is that one will remember it.

Teaching a Reading Lesson

Every well-planned reading lesson should have the following aspects as part of that lesson: vocabulary introduction, review, guided reading, comprehension, and enrichment activities. There should also be daily sustained silent reading time to enable students to choose materials at their independent levels and to read materials that are of special interest to them.

After the new words are taught, the teacher may, in the "review" segment of the reading lesson, relate other words previously learned with those that are new and may also emphasize other areas that have been previously taught and that may need some refreshing before proceeding with the day's lesson. The teacher may recall for the students that they were identifying main ideas through the use of story titles, chapter headings, bold faced words, and italicized words. A brief exercise using those skills could be introduced here in order to give the students practice with the teacher's supervision and instruction. After the teacher feels that the students have demonstrated a grasp of the concepts, he or she will begin the next section of the reading lesson.

The next part of the lesson is the reading of the text. Reading will either be silent or oral, depending upon the teacher's purpose for having students read.

FOR THE READER TO DO:

List the reasons for having students read orally. List the reasons for having students read silently. What does the teacher learn? What do the students learn?

The teacher should rarely, if ever, have students read silently without some advance organizer. The teacher may say, "While you're reading, be looking for and thinking about the answers to questions like these. . . ." Or, a partial plot summary may be given to create interest in the story prior to reading it. This type of guided silent reading is given for reading to be done away from the reading group or before the reading conference in an individualized program. These organizers enable students to read using a frame of reference.

Another type of guided silent reading is that used during the reading group or reading conference. The teacher may ask students to refer to their texts in order to locate specific literal-level information, or they may be asked to read in order to corroborate the tone detected in a passage, or they may be asked to read and interpret sections in light of new information. The teacher must plan just as carefully for the guided silent reading segment of the reading lesson as for any other; however, it also requires the teacher to be flexible and alert to the strengths and weaknesses in the reading group or conference, so that spontaneous questions and guidance can be employed to maximize student understanding of the reading material.

The purposes for oral reading vary as well. If the teacher wants to emphasize some information, he or she may ask a student to locate and read aloud the sentences which elucidate a point. One of the major strengths of guided oral reading is the emphasis placed on location skills. The teacher may say, "In the next two pages, find the three reasons Jaimie was unable to go camping." The students then use skimming or scanning skills to locate the reasons. The oral reading part is simply a way for the teacher to check the accuracy of the students' location skills.

Oral reading should never be used punitively, nor should it be used when it might embarrass a student. Nor should oral reading be held "round-robin" style, with one student after another taking a turn to read a paragraph or so. You knew immediately, when you were a student, whether or not you were a good reader. The good readers got to read long paragraphs, while the students with reading difficulties read one short paragraph. Also, most of us "tuned out" until it was time for us to read; you simply counted ahead and found your place and settled back to daydream until time to "tune back in" to the reading. No one, not even the person reading, benefits from oral reading conducted in this way.

The major reason for most oral reading in the classroom is for diagnostic purposes. While the student is reading, the teacher can be attending to the student's intonation, phrasing, punctuation recognition, pauses, hesitations, reversals, omissions, substitutions, additions, sight word knowledge, and decoding skills. If the teacher keeps a card for each student on which comments pertaining to oral reading performance can be written, then the teacher has a running, dated commentary about those strengths and weaknesses which he or she needs to know in order to instruct the students effectively and to grade them fairly. On this same card, the teacher can add comments relative to the student's understanding of the material whenever questions are asked and answered. Information on the cards should be regularly shared with the students, for it is hardly possible for the student to improve his or her reading performance if he or she does not know in what areas improvement needs to be made. Likewise, the students' anxieties decrease when they know that they will have ready access to the information contained on the cards. These cards, in addition, are very effective ways to help build students' self-concepts, since they can be used to show even the slowest students that they have indeed, with instruction, made progress.

After reading the story, the teacher can lead the students in a discussion and/or ask the students to answer questions. The questions can be asked and/or answered orally or in written form. There should be a balance of literal-level questions and interpretive- and applicative-level ones. That is, the students should not be expected to answer only those questions that are the easiest for the teacher to grade, for these lower-order questions do not require the kind of analysis and synthesis which demonstrates a real grasp of the material being read. Admittedly, discussion questions such as "Why do you think he did that?" and "Have you ever been confronted with such a decision? What did you do to resolve the problem?" take up a great deal of class time, but it can be time far better spent as far as real learning is concerned than questions such as "What color was the wagon?"

Finally, of course, each lesson should include some type of extension or enrichment activity, preferably a choice of them so that students can make some decisions based upon their own interests. These activities may involve writing a different ending to the story or the addition of another chapter to the story. The assignment might ask the student to become one of the characters and write a diary concerning feelings experienced during the course of the story. There are innumerable writing assignments that not only help to strengthen the student's writing skills by providing practice, but they also require a grasp of the story in order to complete them well.

The enrichment activities may be designed to develop the oral language skills of speaking and listening. As an example, a student may choose to give a one-minute commercial designed to entice others to read the same story. Or the students may have a "readers' theatre" during which sections of the story are delivered with appropriate props and sound effects designed to enhance the production.

The teacher may want to integrate several of the areas by having students read the story, discuss the main points and characters, put them in outline form, and then turn the story into a play that they can practice and present to their peers. There are so many skills involved in such a production that the teacher can meet several objectives at once.

FOR THE READER TO DO:

Select a short story or a chapter from a book appropriate for middle-school-age students. Write a lesson plan for that story which includes the components of a Directed Reading Activity.

Teaching Meaning Vocabulary

Mrs. Wright knew the importance of teaching meaning vocabulary to her students. In order for words to become part of the students' permanent vocabulary of understood words, she introduced such activities as the development of the "living dictionary" described on page 208, word gatherings (page 212), making a thesaurus (see page 218), and working on the school newspaper. Other opportunities for students to use and read words in new contexts came from the graffiti board described throughout the model chapters, the language study unit done in October, and the reading slogan contest held near the end of the year.

Internalizing the meaning of new words — or new meanings for words already known — is not a simple matter of enough repetitions so that the student can parrot back definitions. As a case in point, think back to those days when you were in junior or senior high school and you had vocabulary study. In many cases this may have consisted of taking the vocabulary test in the middle of the *Reader's Digest*, making a list of those words and their definitions which had been missed on the test, and then writing those words and their definitions several times, either in isolation or in contrived sentences. The theory was that if you used a word 20 times, it was yours! Interestingly enough, this author can still remember some of those words today; however, their definitions escape me, and I have little desire to rediscover their meanings. This is the reaction of a person who has had a life-long love affair with words! Just imagine the reaction of a student who has no interest in words and their meanings or origins.

The real key to teaching meaning vocabulary is to give students a vested interest in those words — such as with the various activities conducted in Mrs. Wright's room — and to provide as many associations as possible for those words. Clearly, the more language arts areas involved in the development of meaning vocabulary the better. With the firm belief that words cannot be studied in isolation, that all words must be anchored in the context of other words — for example, the sentences, paragraphs, and chapters of a text — vocabulary development begins to take form as a viable, integral part of the curriculum, rather than as a way to spend part of Friday afternoon's class because there is nothing better to do.

The word lists that proliferate probably have little usefulness for the serious study of meaning vocabulary. Spache and Spache (1977) suggest that one of the best — in the sense of most meaningful — sources for vocabulary study probably comes from the students' texts and other materials used in teaching them. These words, at least, are ones the student needs to know in order to survive a particular course, whereas, purchasing a supply of dittos with word lists, sampling the dictionary, using the *Reader's Digest* vocabulary tests, or copying words from a list of commonly occurring words may have little or no influence on the students' development of meaning vocabulary. When was the last time you used the word *truculent* or had to distinguish between *sensual* and *sensuous*? Isolated word study can lead to *lacunae*, because one feels that one should remember those words or definitions. Sometimes one can even remember the context in which the words were presented (e.g., warm, muggy afternoon; teacher wore a red dress; you remember the dandruff on Janie Clark's new sweater), but the words themselves escape you.

Teaching a Language Arts Block

Mrs. Wright teaches the language arts, in an integrated time block. This is not unusual in today's middle and secondary schools. Sometimes the block will include both social studies and language arts. The wise teacher integrates as many skills as possible in the block. In this way, teaching is more efficient and learning is better accomplished since the students use their skills in a related and applied fashion.

Learning centers in the middle school classroom are still rare, but they are gaining in popularity. They are no longer the exclusive domain of the elementary teacher. Beach (1977) has written an excellent book to help secondary and middle school teachers begin to use centers in their classrooms. For Mrs. Wright there is no choice. She knows what a wide range of abilities she has in her classroom. She knows too that group instruction for the entire class at once will only result in frustration for the students who don't learn upon first introduction and frustration for her as she tries to reteach the information.

Personalizing her language arts/reading program enabled Mrs. Wright to work with individuals, small groups, and even, when appropriate, the entire class. Students at the centers busily engage in activities that strengthen their skills, freeing Mrs. Wright to work with groups and individuals. Her approach is only one of the many possible ones. Aulls (1978) describes other alternatives for individualizing instruction. Other plans are described in Smith and Barrett (1974) and Duffy (1974).

Mrs. Wright could turn to sources such as Hafner (1974), Aulls (1978), Smith and Barrett (1974), or Burmeister (1978) for practical suggestions on materials and activities to use with students in the middle school. She might also belong to professional organizations and receive their publications and attend their meetings, in order to garner more ideas. She might also continue to take courses in the teaching of reading and the language arts. All of these would come together to help her form a room organization and classroom structure unique to her and her group of students. Nor would she ever have it down pat, for each group of students would be different in some ways, and new materials and methods would constantly be tried.

Mrs. Wright's chapters may not include some of the elements of reading instruction that are described elsewhere in this book. That does not mean that she does not use these strategies, for in the interest of space we have limited the focus of each of the chapters. Let us assure you that Mrs. Wright would use whatever techniques were useful in a particular situation. In other words, assume that she is employing many of the strategies Connie Tent has previously described whenever they are appropriate.

Mrs. Wright's classroom is described in the following two chapters. Open the door and walk right in. She's expecting you.

10 A Year of Middle/Junior High School Reading and Language Arts (September-December)

The Radio Program

RITA WRIGHT WAS sitting at her cluttered desk when Mr. Topps rapped gently on the door. She glanced up and was surprised to see stress lines on his usually calm face. She gestured to an empty seat and watched him sink wearily into it.

"What's the problem?" she asked. "Is the school board finally on to your bohemian style of administration?" Her little joke raised the faintest of smiles.

"Actually, I've come to ask a favor on rather short notice. Do you remember the faculty meeting two weeks ago when Mr. Badger spoke and asked that some of us appear on his radio program, 'Badger's Bailiwick,' to discuss our reading/language arts curriculum?"

"Oh, yes—wasn't he wondering why we weren't teaching 'the basics' and how we could 'possibly expect today's children to live in tomorrow's world'?"

"Right. Well, the staff agreed that Miss Stern should represent the reading/language arts department since she is the chairperson. She and I have worked together for two weeks to prepare for the short talk and the question-answer period. The program is only two days away, and I have just learned that Miss Stern is not going to be able to do it! The doctor has ordered her to bed for at least five days with this flu that's going around. Rita, I know that you don't like to toot your own horn, but I really like the activities you have going on in your class. Will you be on the program with me? I know that Badger will allow us to move the emphasis from the entire reading/language arts curriculum to a focus on what is happening in the middle school. And, since you are the middle school representative on that curriculum committee, you are the logical person."

Rita dreaded even the thought of such an ordeal. She had heard the program a few times and had winced at Mr. Badger's acidulous journalistic style. But

186

she agreed. Did she really have a choice? Mr. Topps had been so supportive of her program. She and Mr. Topps began to make plans.

Two days later, Mrs. Wright sat nervously at the table on the set of "Badger's Bailiwick" with Mr. Topps and Mr. Badger. On the way to the station that afternoon, Mr. Topps had tried to reassure her that their presentation would go smoothly and that they were performing a great public service for the community. She was not convinced. "It's only half an hour," he kept saying. But she knew just how long half an hour could seem.

Mr. Badger had greeted them in the reception area of the station, and chatting amiably, had led them to the studio from which they would broadcast. Rita began to relax as Mr. Badger explained the sequence of the program.

"Now, I don't want you to be so tense, Mrs. White. Just look at Topps here; he's been on radio so often that some folks out there think he has his own show!"

Rita forced a smile as she reminded him that her name was Wright, not White.

"Right, right—Wright. Hey, that's a good one! Now just relax Mrs. White. Remember that I will introduce you two and the topic of the program, then you will talk about the . . . the . . . the . . . the, what's this? Can't read my own writing . . . oh, yes, the reading/language arts program at Upton Hill. Then I'll ask an easy question or two, just to get things going, and then we'll go to the telephone to answer questions which are called in. Okay? That won't be too bad, now will it?"

Mr. Badger paused but a moment for breath before he began again. "Okay. Ready to go? Remember, I'm just here to clarify points and get information. I won't intrude upon your presentation unless I think it necessary—y'know, my reputation as a bully is completely undeserved . . . just doing my job . . . never interfere when the program is going well. Only thing you have to worry about . . . well, let's not say worry about . . . let's say be aware of . . . is that we're live. That means every word, sigh, grunt, belly rumble . . . everything . . . goes out over the air. But, relax—enjoy!"

Rita felt a distinct discomfort in the pit of her stomach. Her quick glance to Mr. Topps was rewarded with a thumbs-up gesture and a smirk in the direction of the departing Badger.

"Hey. Don't worry . . . just be as clear and concise as you were at our rehearsals and everything will be fine. Badger is a bit hyper, but we'll make it!"

Badger returned and almost immediately the lights indicating that the program was "on the air" came on and Mr. Badger began his welcome. As soon as he was finished, he pointed a finger at Mr. Topps who launched into an explanation of Upton Hill's reading and language arts department. After a brief description of the different components of the school's reading/language arts program, Topps explained that the middle school component embodied the major principles of a student-centered approach to improving the language arts. He turned to Mrs. Wright and signaled her to take over.

Rita began in a wavering voice. "The middle school reading/language arts staff consists of three and a half teachers to teach the roughly 430 students we have in grades six through eight. That means that I have a daily class load of 120 students. These students are assigned to one of my four daily groups for instruction. Since each class period is 90 minutes long, I have two groups in the morning and two in the afternoon." Rita paused for breath and went on in a much stronger voice.

"We at Upton Hill have made a commitment to teach all of the language arts. Language arts include speaking, listening, reading, and writing, and so we have tried to establish a curriculum that will produce a balance of all these areas. Since my classroom is the one with which I am most familiar, I will try to describe it for you. Students in my classes soon learn that reading for enjoyment is a high priority, because we take class time everyday for sustained silent reading of materials of their choice. I have the room set up with learning stations, or areas, created around a different theme every month. For example, this month all of the activities are developed around 'Saturday Night at the Movies.'

The whole room is a learning center comprising four different stations: listening, speaking, reading, and writing. Each student has a folder in which all assignments are listed. All folders are turned in to me weekly. In this way I am able to check on student progress. During class time, while students are completing individual folder work or small group work in centers, I work with 'skill groupings' on specific language skills. These skill groups cover many areas including handwriting, spelling, listening, usage, meaning vocabulary, and comprehension. Basically, however, the students follow a personalized reading plan. They choose their own reading material and work along as quickly as they can. Many of the students enjoy getting together to read and discuss a story much as some local book groups do. Each of the group members reads the same story, following assignments that their elected chairperson chooses.

"All in all, I feel that we at Upton Hill are meeting our responsibilities toward your children quite well. We are teaching the 'basics' and more, for, in order to survive in today's world, students need more than just the basics."

Mr. Topps clasped his hands together over his head giving her a silent cheer of approval. This accolade was interrupted by Mr. Badger's question to Mrs. Wright.

"Did I hear you correctly, Mrs. White? I cannot believe that you said that you are teaching *reading* to these young adults. Surely, they learned how to read in our fine elementary schools. Or did they? And if they didn't, why not?"

Rita and Mr. Topps smiled at one another, for this was one of those questions that they had anticipated might be asked, and they were prepared to answer the question. Mr. Topps began the answer as they had planned.

"Well, now, I wouldn't think of condemning elementary school teaching, for, as you know, I have been an elementary school principal. Some of our students, when they reach us, have not learned the basic skills in reading, that is true. Those students didn't learn for a variety of reasons. It might be that the student didn't learn to read well because of poor teaching, or it might be that the family moved so often that the child had no sequential reading program, or it might be that reading was such a low priority in a child's home that even with good teaching it was difficult to convince the student of the need for reading, or . . . or . . . or. . . . There are numerous reasons, but going into reasons does not help the situation. What does help is to try in yet another way to give these students the reading instruction they need in order to function within our society."

At this point Rita interjected, "And most of our middle school students *have* learned the basic reading skills. What they need is further instruction in reference and study skills. The reading program I have in my classroom includes these skills in addition to a literature program."

Mr. Badger interrupted at this point. "We must really get to the phone calls. Good afternoon, 'Badger's Bailiwick.' What is your question, please?"

"Hello? Hello? I . . . uh . . . I . . . uh wanna know how come my kid is doin' so much readin' at school? When I was in school, we took our readin' home and did homework."

"Your question is really two questions, I think," said Rita. "Please correct me if I am wrong. First you want to know about our USSR program, and then you want to know how we handle homework."

"Wait a minute. I don't know what Russia has to do with anything, but, yeah, that las' part's right."

Rita smiled at Mr. Topps, for they had encountered this same reaction before. "Sir, USSR stands for a technique called Uninterrupted Silent Sustained Reading (Hunt, 1971). My students think USSR stands for 'U Select Something to Read,' as that is what it goes by in my room. At Merritt Elementary, Mr. Topps' former school, it was called SQUIRT (Sustained Quiet Reading time), but regardless of what we call it, we are doing essentially the same thing. Each participating teacher sets aside a period of time each day for silent reading in the classroom. The students and the teachers read at the same time, silently, anything each chooses to read. By setting this model for reading and allowing time to practice their reading skills, we are providing them with the incentive and skills necessary to develop a reading habit."

"Let me respond, please, to the second question, Mrs. Wright. In any school as large as Upton Hill or even as small as Merritt Elementary, there are bound to be many differences among the teaching staff. One of these differences relates to the assignment of homework. Many of our teachers at Upton Hill do give the kind of homework you refer to, but some of the others only give homework when they feel that an assignment can only be completed at home or if the work needs long-term thinking and/or writing. For these teachers, homework is meant to be an extension of classroom activities, not busywork to occupy free time."

"Thank you, and let's go to our next caller. Hello. You're on 'Badger's Bailiwick.' What is your question, please?" asked Mr. Badger.

"Hello? Am I on? I wondered just how much is being done with writing in this curriculum? You speak of a writing station, but what about themes and book reports? I always felt that the old curriculum allowed ample opportunity for speaking and writing and reading. The students read a piece of literature; they wrote a theme about it (or maybe a book report); and then they spoke before the class to inform others."

"I guess," began Rita, "that the change is as great for me as it is for the students. Many English teachers agree that they are what they are because they love literature. It is sometimes distressing, to one who loves literature, to hear adolescents' viewpoints and interpretations. Granted, some of the literature we have given students at this age is inappropriate. And for this reason, they are unable to empathize with characters and situations. But even using the more appropriate literature that we have now—adolescents' literature—I still disagree with the premise that all students should read the same material at the same time. For this reason, I have set up a personalized reading program. Sometimes an individual or a group will make a whole class presentation. Most of these kids are interested in their own books and ideas; they don't want to sit through boring presentations. Some of them, however, will sign up for presentations on a voluntary basis. That's fine, but I truly hate to take valuable class time for long oral book reports. We have many other ways of showing understanding of books read; we also do many different activities emphasizing the analysis of the books they have read. But the kind of book report I had to do in school — no, I guess we don't.''

"Before we go to our next caller, Mrs. White, may I ask a simple little question? How will these students be able to express themselves in written form unless you teach more grammar? These 'skill groups,' whatever they are, don't sound to me as if they will do the trick."

"Most parents tell us they want us to teach more grammar; in fact, what they really mean is that they think we should be teaching students standard usage. Grammar is simply a description of how words are formed and how they can be combined into language. Usage refers to the conventions of language use. I have never taught a student with poor grammar; that is, one who would say 'car garage in is the' for the sentence 'The car is in the garage.' I have, however, taught myriad students who have difficulty learning another level of language usage, that is, standard English. The skill groupings are formed after careful analysis of the students' own writings, so that the groups address themselves to specifics that each student needs. By far, the best ways to teach the conventions of language use is through the students' own work, for they can see a direct application of the instruction in the context of their own ideas. They don't need to try to make the transfer to their own writing, which is what must happen if the instruction is built around workbook exercises or someone else's writing."

"I see. Let's go to our phone again for one last question. Hello. You're on 'Badger's Bailiwick.'"

"Hello, Mr. Topps and Mrs. Wright. I've been listening with great interest to this program because I have a daughter in Mrs. Wright's class. We've been worried about Yolanda for some time, because she has had a reading problem since second grade. Yolanda has, understandably, not really enjoyed school, and so I was astonished when I overheard her telling a girlfriend last night that she loves her language arts class! She even picks up a book to read after dinner when we all have our family quiet time. Until recently, Yolanda spent her time working jigsaw puzzles or knitting. I just want to say that I am delighted with whatever methods you are using."

"How very nice of you to call," said Mrs. Wright. "Your call does permit me to mention one more significant bit of information. At a recent Right-to-Read meeting I attended, an important point was made. In order for students to experience the greatest amount of success with reading, two things need to happen daily: reading to them and allowing them time to read silently in materials of their own choosing. If your child's teacher does not have a USSR program and/or does not read to students, isn't it nice to know that at home, without any special training or equipment and only a minimum of time, you can do these two things? Please come to visit our program at Upton Hill. Just call the office to arrange a date and time. We'll be glad to show you what we are doing!"

"Thank you, listeners. And be sure to tune in next week to hear how you can make your own dog food, right here on 'Badgers Bailiwick.'"

Monthly Logs

September   I hope this journal will be what Mr. Topps wants from me. I'd feel much better submitting lesson plans. I understand his rationale for wanting the journals; he wants the essence, not just the outline, of what happens in each classroom. To know that good instruction is taking place, it is important to be able to see the successes and failures. Since he cannot visit each classroom as often as he would like, these written visits will help him stay informed. I agree with the theory, but will it actually happen? Will I be able to report my failures? Can I see my classroom objectively enough? Or is that part of his plan also—to train us to begin to look more objectively at what we are doing?

In my journal, I am going to describe the activities of only one of my classes. To describe the activities of each of the four would be too time-consuming and repetitious. The following are the students from the class I have chosen:

Walter	Chad	Don
Sharon	Patricia	James
Harry	Phillip	Anne
Deborah	Mavis	Geraldine
Elizabeth	Tammy	Lynda
Yolanda	Michael	Dennis
Joseph	Brett	Frank
Robert	Charlie	Carmela
Renée	Carl	Carla
Stuart	Clarence	Bruce
Geoffrey		

From my observation of the class thus far, I can tell that it is going to be an interesting year.

USSR   One thing that especially pleases me is the introduction of USSR into our school. All of the teachers have been invited to participate, and most of the language arts teachers are doing so, but the other subject area teachers are much slower to adopt it. I have USSR with my students every class period as soon as it is time to begin the block. They enter the room, get a book, and sit quietly reading until they hear the timer ring.

In rereading what I have just written, it sounds so easy, so simple, but it wasn't the first day! I told the students what I expected of them and showed them where to find interesting books in the room. I even helped some of them to locate books for the next day's class. The second day was a disaster! Most of the kids, upon arriving, and with a reminder from me, pulled out books and sat down to read in some comfortable location in the room. Mickey and Dennis, however, arrived a minute late and came crashing into the room, laughing and joking, with books balanced on their heads. Since they were startled that everything was so quiet and that everyone in the room was staring at them, all of the books on their heads came tumbling down amid the laughter of my entire class—well, almost the entire class—I was *not* amused!

"Oops! Sorry, Miz Wright. We forgot that you tol' us to do this today, and me and Mick, here, we couldn't get our clothes back on after gym class, you know how that is with your clothes sticking to you, and so we was a little late," explained Dennis for the two of them.

"No problem, Dennis and Mickey, but do try to remember that this class begins *on time* with USSR *every day.* If you can't arrive on time, please sit on the bench outside the office until the class is ready to begin . . . (at this point, the timer sounded) . . . begin our activities. Okay, put your books away for today. Tomorrow we'll try again."

Well, *that* problem appeared to be resolved, for a while anyway. I began the timer for only seven minutes of silent reading initially, for I know that even that short time may seem like an eternity to some of these students. After they are easily able to sustain for seven minutes, I will move the timer ahead one more minute. It is crucial to the success of USSR that students are not required to read for too long. Another factor that must be constantly kept in mind is that the teacher, too, must read while the students are reading in order to set a model. Mr. Topps even drops by periodically during USSR to read and to provide a male model for reading. I placed this chart on the wall so that all students would be informed of the rules for USSR.

U-Select Something to Read (USSR)
1. Choose a book that you will read quietly.
2. Everyone in the room will be reading at the same time, even Mrs. Wright and any visitors we have.
3. The timer will be set for the number of minutes for which we can continue to read.
4. When the timer rings, you may read for a little longer if you want to.
5. No one will ask you what you are reading, but if you want to tell about it you may.
6. Only when we are ready to read for a longer period, will the timer be set for one minute more.

FOR READERS TO DO TOGETHER:

Initiate a USSR program in your class. Form a committee of students to fill a box with reading materials just for this class. Include adolescents' literature, professional journals, supplementary texts in teaching reading at the middle/secondary school, and xeroxed articles of professional interest. Begin with seven minutes every class period and extend the time to as many minutes as can be spared from class time.

The only real difficulty that I have encountered with the classes abiding by the rules was one day when the school board members were visiting various classes to meet with students and talk to teachers. As luck would have it, R. R. Rowe, the loquacious school board president, came to my room just as the kids had gotten their books and I had set the timer. When he walked in, I glanced at him in dismay and shoved a book into his hands, put a finger to my lips, and pointed to the chart on the wall. After his initial sputtering he settled down, whether reading or not, I don't know. But at least he didn't disrupt the class. Fortunately, he seemed to understand when I made my explanation to him at the end of our nine minutes of reading. However, he *was* a bit put out that I would continue with our USSR time when he was there, rather than postponing it until later. I hope that he brings it up to Mr. Topps, for I know I have a supporter there!

And I may be needing that support soon, for at a yard sale this summer I discovered a gallon of chalkboard paint that I simply could not resist buying, much to the amusement of my husband. "Now what are you going to do?" he inquired. "Let's hope that it doesn't involve me!"

Graffiti board

Actually, for once, I really didn't want to involve him. I had had an idea for a graffiti board at school while I was pregnant with Willy, and this can of paint was going to make it come true. In order for the board to be effective, I felt that I had to discuss with my students the idea of having a place where they could write their thoughts, sayings, and philosophical wonderings. So, last week, I brought the can out of my closet, heaved it onto my desk, and explained my plan to the class. With their help we could convert a rather tired section of the wall into an exciting learning opportunity. They responded most enthusiastically! Charlie, Rob, and Jim all came up to my desk requesting brushes immediately.

"Hey! Wait a minute. We can't really take school time for this, but anybody who would like to come to school this Saturday afternoon to paint this section of the wall is welcome. I'll have colas and chips for those who show up. Bring your own paint shirts and wear old clothes. Now who would like to take charge of organizing workcrews, getting supplies, and generally keeping track of what is happening?"

There seemed to be no doubt in the minds of all present that "Phillip the Fastidious" would be the one to take charge of the details. Phillip is an organizer, sometimes to the point of being prissy. His myriad lists of "things to do" have evidently caused him to be the butt of jokes for years; nevertheless, his thoroughness was welcomed by me. Phillip began immediately to divide the afternoon into time blocks and each time block into tasks. This was circulated for the others to sign and the worst was over. (I thought! That Saturday was another story!)

The following Monday, our virgin graffiti board stood waiting. No one wanted to make the first mark. I was at a loss to decide what must be done. I realized that they had worked so hard and were so proud of their work that they didn't want to defile it. So, as soon as the last student left, I wrote a question on the board:

> Why bother going to school? All it does is make you lose sleep and take up time you could use to do other things. If I had a choice, I'm not sure that I would come back to school. What good is it going to do me?

The next day I was tingling with excitement when the students, having finished silent reading, began moving around the room to finish up work. All of a sudden there was a gasp from the graffiti corner, and the students started piling up around the board to see what had been written. I pretended not to notice. "Hey, you guys! Who wrote that?" challenged Gerry. When no one answered, someone else (Joey, I think) said, "Well, I don't know, but it sure is right. Going to school keeps me from practicing ball. How am I ever gonna get to be a pro if I hafta hang around here for years?"

"Me, too. I wanna be a nightclub comic and get lots of money. School ain't where it's at, baby!" interjected Dennis.

"But," Rob inserted, "how can you do all of those things if you can't even read the contract you'll be signing? You learn lots of stuff in school that will make *everything* better someday."

"Yeah, someday," said Geoff, "but what about now?"

"Yes, what about now? I see that what I wrote stirred some feelings, but instead of talking and interrupting one another, why don't you write your thoughts on the board and give others a chance to read and respond?" Now the only problem with the board is that it is always so full that it's hard to find a bare spot to write on! The board is erased every couple of days unless a request is made to leave something on longer. A committee of students has taken it upon themselves to screen discussion questions to be written on the graffiti board so that not too much prurient material appears there! There has still been little of the spontaneous writing I had hoped to stimulate—most of it directly relates to the topic at hand. Oh, well, if the restroom walls are any indication, they should be writing spontaneously any day now.

FOR THE READER TO DO:

Make up at least three other controversial topics on questions which Mrs. Wright could have written on the graffiti board to get students started writing. Duplicate these and share them with your classmates. What suggestions for change do your classmates have for you?

I have just reread Herb Kohl's *36 Children* (1967) and made a recommitment to really observe my students and really listen to what they are saying. So, right after silent reading every day, when students are forming their work groups and plans for the day, I sit back and watch or wander around the room and observe the interactions. Already I can see various cliques forming—residual from last year? I don't know. I have quite an interesting crew to deal with. Liz seems to be the leader of her pack, and I use "pack" with full knowledge of the word. She, Tammy, Debi, Lynda, and Anne always eat lunch together and are constantly discussing boys, clothes, make-up, and dating. Anne is the real puzzle. I can understand such an overweight girl wanting to be part of this group, but what is the advantage to Liz and company? I must keep alert to this situation.

I also have a Mutt and Jeff combination that is interesting to watch. The tiniest girl in the class (Pat is all of 4 feet 11 inches) and the tallest (Sharon, not an inch under 5 feet 8 inches) have a strong friendship that seems to be based on mutual respect rather than envy or domination. Yolanda frequently eats and reads with them, to the enjoyment of all. These three are generally liked by most of the students, and they enjoy the nonsexist company of boys in the room. They are particularly close to Jim, Rob, Harry, Stuart, and Charlie. Jim is a real leader in this group and loyal to his friends, especially Harry. These are all good students who try (most of the time) to do their work well. Sometimes, however, other things interfere with that. Rob, for instance, sometimes gets so hung up on the fact that he is black that he shuts out his friends and me. He and Charlie, who came to this town just last year from his reservation in Minnesota, at these times will sit and discuss all that they have in common. Stuart, however, is welcomed in nearly any group he chooses to join. Although he has a physical handicap, he has not let it deter him from participating in school and life to the fullest. I think it is his remarkably cheerful disposition that draws others to him.

Of course, Mickey, Joey, Brett, Dennis, and Don have an uneasy alliance that shifts with the phases of the moon, it would seem. These are the ones my college professors would call the "discipline problems"; I suppose they are or could be, but I'm pretty easygoing, and if I keep them occupied, we usually make it through the 90-minute period without too many problems!

There are some extremely strong female personalities in this class. I wonder if this is just an isolated phenomenon or if the liberation movement has begun to affect girls of middle school age? Mavis, Renée, Gerry, and Carla all have career goals and all question the "whys" of nearly everything we do. They are not really a group in the sense that some of the other formations are, for each one is too independent to sacrifice herself to others' needs. I suspect that most of the students are not even aware that Carl and Carla are twins; they neither look nor act alike. It's as if they are the positive and negative forms of the same person—Carla so vibrant and Carl such a nebbish.

Many others have no alliances at all. Because her mother works the third shift, Carmela misses too much school. She doesn't really fit in. Chad doesn't particularly like school and so makes no effort to make friends. Walter, who stutters, is so self-conscious that even the attentions of well-meaning students like Harry don't seem to move him out of his shell. Clarence and Bruce leave the class to attend Mr. Moore's reading class so they, too, are not here enough to cement relationships. Geoff is just a loner. He enjoys his own company and, while he doesn't resist being drawn into a group, he does try to avoid situations that might lead to that. I did an experiment recently. I asked students to write down for homework the names of all the students in their language arts class. They were honor bound not to call on other people's memories or a school list. I told them that I wouldn't grade the homework, but that I just wondered how many of their classmates they could remember once they were away from school. Only three students could remember Frank's name; five more said that they thought there was someone else, but they couldn't remember *her* name!

My "Libbers," as I call them, are up in arms as this month draws to a close. Mavis, Gerry, Carla, and Renée have handed me a petition that requests that the school board strike sexist language from our texts, from spoken or written statements of school policy, and even from the language of the teachers! Several of the teachers are quite upset, particularly Kurt Mudgeon, whom the girls seem to have fastened upon as their main target. Everytime he makes a simple statement, such as, "Every one of you must do his own work on this test," the girls attack. They *are* gutsy, I'll say that for them. Kurt asked, in desperation, if I would talk with them (only he said *to* them) and see if this could be resolved. I agreed and began the first leg of my "shuttle diplomacy."

"Would you girls like to have someone sit down and talk with you about your sexist language concerns?" I probed one day.

"Actually," began Mavis, "there's nothing to talk about. We know that the system discriminates against women and other minorities. We feel that the unfair portrayal of sex roles and the sexist language in our texts is just another manifestation of the prejudice we women have been subjected to for thousands of years!"

An impassioned speech. "Well, it's hardly fair to attack the teachers' language is it? After all, we're the 'victims' of this same society. What would you have us say, if not, 'To each, his own'?"

"Oh, Ms. Wright," burst in Carla, "you should understand. You're a woman who's been discriminated against, too. Why can't you just say, 'To each, their own,' or 'Each one must do their own work'?"

"I'll deal with that discrimination statement later, but you're all good students. You know that you need subject-verb agreement. That's why you cannot have 'their' replacing 'his.' Long before any of these issues arose, the masculine pronouns were used to indicate mankind, not just men."

"You see," chimed in Renée, "you see what you just said—'*man*kind.'" Even the word 'woman' has the word 'man' in it."

"Well, we won't go into etymologies at this point, though I think it might be a good idea, but you *do* realize, I hope, that you are not going to get away with lack of subject-verb agreement in this class. Why don't you read this article (Hultgren and Arthur, 1978) and let me know tomorrow what you think of it. Okay?"

"Okay."

"Yeah."

"All right," they chorused as they left me to my cold lunch. "I wonder what the 'morrow will bring," I remember thinking.

I could hear them coming all the way down the hallway the next day. The other teachers' reactions had been pouring in all morning. "Good afternoon, what did you think?"

Gerry began with, "Ms. Wright, we think every teacher in this building should do shimself a favor and adopt these new pronouns."

"I agree," said Mavis. "Each of us could do shis work without any more concern about the matter."

"That's right," put in Carla. "If each of us thought carefully, for just a short time, heesh could learn these with no trouble."

I couldn't really break it to the girls, but I *know* that the other teachers will not be using *heesh, shis, shim*, and their compound forms. However, I will.

October   I began the month by removing September's station material and putting in October's. What a job that was, but the students did seem to enjoy the variety of activities that were planned around the theme "Saturday Night at the Movies." There were direction cards and posters in each of the four stations, and students were expected to complete at least two different activities in each one of them. Below is a list of those activities:

listening

watch movies
analyze the sound track for sound
   effects
listen to record of movie soundtrack
how does music promote plot
sound effects and onomatopoeia
separate the music from the lyrics
listen to orchestral version
listen to poetry reading of lyrics

writing

outline the basic points of the plot
read movie reviews—observe established criteria
identify characteristics of a review
write a movie review
write scenario from a book
put a character in another situation,
   reaction
film title synopses
write denouement
character analyses
write obituary for a character, author
critically analyze first and last ten minutes of film—how is attention
   gotten and held

speaking

do an oral movie review
à la Shalit
dramatize a scene
issue discussions

reading

movie mags—compare and contrast
   stories
research: character, times, place,
   situation

debate issues
analyze the speech of various
   characters

read/react to movie reviews
compare book/play to movie
read biographies of stars
read something from bibliography of
   related literature

Webbing   I arrived at all of these activities by using a process called "literature webbing" (Charlotte Huck's term). One of the sessions I attended at a children's literature conference led us through the process, and I then further refined my skills by referring to a publication of the Ohio State University Reading and Language Arts department (*The W.E.B.* * *Wonderfully Exciting Books*). Webbing is similar to outlining, but without the rigid structure. It is organized brainstorming. One can "web" a book for activities to do during and after reading, or web a concept for questions to ask, or web a genre for related materials and activities. Webbing is versatile and fun. A web for an adolescents' novel from one of these issues (1978) appears on pp. 198-199.

FOR READERS TO DO TOGETHER:

Mrs. Wright's stations for October are all developed around the theme "Monsters We Have Known and Loved." Form groups of five or six and "web" that theme to help her develop station activities for speaking, listening, reading, and writing. Compare what you came up with to what Mrs. Wright did in her classroom as explained in this chapter. Duplicate your webs for each of your classmates.

The other day, Jim, my outspoken rebel, came forward and wanted to know why I treated them "like kids." In answer to my question of what did he mean, he replied that several of them had been talking, and they were insulted with the names of the four stations that I had set up in the room. He hastened to add that the activities were fine, but he and the others just could not understand why, as middle school students, they had to go to an area called the "listening station." Evidently it evoked memories of elementary school. I told Jim that I would bring up the problem to the entire class and see if that were, indeed, the consensus.

At the end of every class period, I bring all the students back together to share their work and successes (or failures) with the group. We also deal with any procedural matters that need attention. That day I told the group that someone had approached me with a concern about the names of the stations. It was immediately evident that it did bother them. I promised to try to come up with some new names. Geoffrey requested that we have an art area, too, because it can be just as expressive as speaking or writing. Walter, for one of the few times so far this year, spoke out in front of the whole group, in spite of his stuttering. "That's a real good idea, Mrs. Wright, I'd like to do that!"

So, new names! My odyssey led me to contact my college Greek teacher who enjoyed neologisms so much. We met for coffee, and in a very short time he came up with names for all five of the stations. My discussion with him led me to plan an etymology unit for the students so that they could better understand each of the station signs I worked during

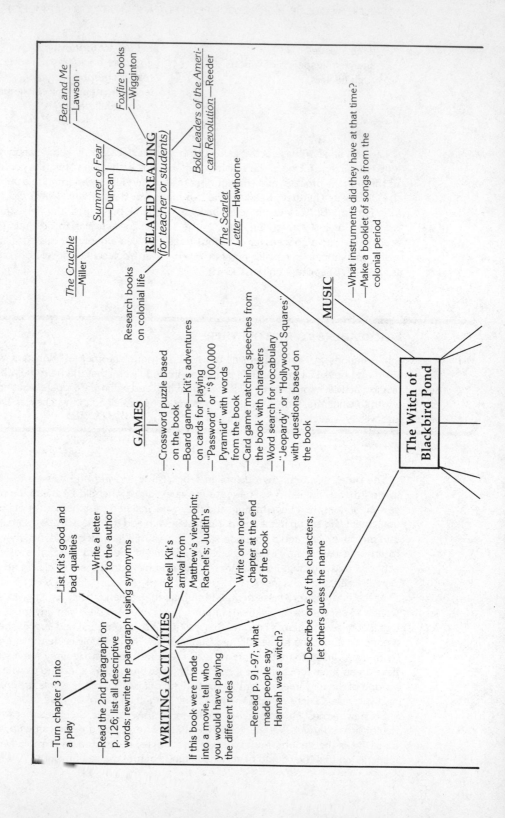

The Witch of Blackbird Pond

RELATED READING
(for teacher or students)
- *Ben and Me*—Lawson
- *Summer of Fear*—Duncan
- *Foxfire* books—Wigginton
- *Bold Leaders of the American Revolution*—Reeder
- *The Crucible*—Miller
- Research books on colonial life
- *The Scarlet Letter*—Hawthorne

MUSIC
—What instruments did they have at that time?
—Make a booklet of songs from the colonial period

GAMES
—Crossword puzzle based on the book
—Board game—Kit's adventures on cards for playing
—"Password" or "$100,000 Pyramid" with words from the book
—Card game matching speeches from the book with characters
—Word search for vocabulary
—"Jeopardy" or "Hollywood Squares" with questions based on the book

WRITING ACTIVITIES
—Turn chapter 3 into a play
—List Kit's good and bad qualities
—Write a letter to the author
—Read the 2nd paragraph on p. 126; list all descriptive words; rewrite the paragraph using synonyms
—Retell Kit's arrival from Matthew's viewpoint; Rachel's; Judith's
—If this book were made into a movie, tell who you would have playing the different roles
—Write one more chapter at the end of the book
—Reread p. 91-97; what made people say Hannah was a witch?
—Describe one of the characters; let others guess the name

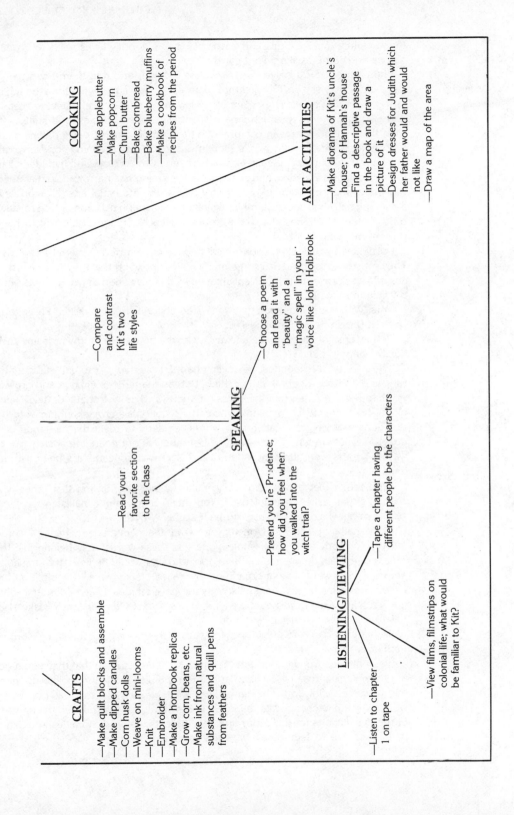

COOKING

—Make applebutter
—Make popcorn
—Churn butter
—Bake cornbread
—Bake blueberry muffins
—Make a cookbook of recipes from the period

ART ACTIVITIES

—Make diorama of Kit's uncle's house; of Hannah's house
—Find a descriptive passage in the book and draw a picture of it
—Design dresses for Judith which her father would and would not like
—Draw a map of the area

—Compare and contrast Kit's two life styles

SPEAKING

—Choose a poem and read it with "beauty" and a "magic spell" in your voice like John Holbrook

—Read your favorite section to the class

—Pretend you're Prudence; how did you feel when you walked into the witch trial?

LISTENING/VIEWING

—Tape a chapter having different people be the characters

—Listen to chapter 1 on tape

—View films, filmstrips on colonial life; what would be familiar to Kit?

CRAFTS

—Make quilt blocks and assemble
—Make dipped candles
—Corn husk dolls
—Weave on mini-looms
—Knit
—Embroider
—Make a hornbook replica
—Grow corn, beans, etc.
—Make ink from natural substances and quill pens from feathers

the weekend, making signs and lesson plans. On Monday I was ready to unveil the new names and some exciting word games.

Meaning
vocab

Right after USSR, I called the entire class together and told them I was going to suspend or, as they say on TV, "preempt" part of their individual work time today. I began by telling them that about 70 percent of our language comes from Greek or Latin sources and that that is why so much time is spent with roots, prefixes, and suffixes. Knowing what those elements mean can give one the etymological or basic meanings of words. Over time, however, many words adopt more specialized meanings or even totally different ones. For example, the Greek word for "art" was *techne*, and included all of the art forms: sculpting, painting, and so forth. That meaning has narrowed so that our modern-day conception of technology is mainly that of the industrial arts. "Pastor" and "mansion" originally had much humbler definitions of "shepherd" and "place to stay." "Silly," on the other hand, has changed from its original definition of blessed or happy to its present meaning of foolish.

I could tell by their expressions that it had never occurred to them that words change. They must view language as some great adult imposition that they must learn the vagaries of! I was probably as much enlightened by this revelation as my students had been by my little introduction.

"Mrs. Wright, do you mean that words can change? Really?" asked Phillip, his tidy, organized mind upset by the possibility.

"If they are going to change anyway, then why bother learning words and their definitions?" Gerry probed.

"Well, Gerry," I responded, "it doesn't happen overnight. You can still count on 'silly' meaning 'foolish' for some time, I think. But language does change and grow. None of you can recall a time when there was no such word as 'astronaut' or 'television' or 'airplane,' but there are lots of people who can. So not only are we changing words to fit new situations, but we are creating new words regularly to meet the demands of our language—which, in turn, must meet the demands of our changing society. We didn't always have the word 'hotdog,' either; it just seems so because it's been with us for so long."

"You mean that people can really make up new words and that other people use them?" Stuart asked incredulously. "You mean that I might make up new words, and others might like them and use *my* new words? Wow!"

"As a matter of fact, Stuart, one of my former teachers made up the new words for our stations. Nobody else in the whole world has these words; they belong just to us. But others might like them and use them, too, and that would be fine. But for just now, they are ours. New words that are made up are called 'neologisms.' (I wrote it on the board, broken down into prefix-root-suffix.) Anyone have an idea what 'neo' might mean?"

"Well, I know the word 'neon' is a kind of gas, so does it mean 'gas'?" asked Harry, who has always been fascinated by words.

"Very good, Harry. 'Neon' is from the same Greek word, but the same word they both come from means 'new.' "

We continued working through the parts of 'neologism' so that they could determine the etymological meaning. Then Pat got out the dictionary and looked up 'neologism" and read the definition to the class. They were pleased that this was *not* one of those words which had changed its meaning. In the same way I introduced the names of each of the five stations for the room and the students, using dictionaries and lists of word parts, were able to determine what each area name meant.

FOR THE READER TO DO:

Mrs. Wright and her professor renamed each station with the following words. Determine the etymological meaning for each of them, and then translate those into the five station areas she has: art, listening, speaking, reading, writing.

lexicorium   loquorium   technicorium   graphologicorium
audiologicorium

A logical outgrowth of all of this word activity has been that a group of students has decided to spend some of their class and home time putting together a book of words with their histories and changes. I showed them a section of the library that has quite a few useful sources for this and asked why they wanted to do it when these were available to them. Sharon, Yolanda, and Pat replied that they wanted a book with words they had found and were especially interested in. Of course, I encouraged them and offered to find some literature books that "play" with words, too, since that might be interesting to them as well (Gwynne, 1970; Juster, 1961; Goodspeed, n.d.).

With the increasing interest in words, the graffiti board is beginning to come into its own. More and more students are writing spontaneous comments, and I can tell that last month's movie theme is not yet dead, for I discovered the following among the graffiti recently:

> MOVIE TITLES AND SUMMARIES
> *Georgie Girl:* heartwarming story of a transsexual's life after shis operation.
> *Ben Hur:* another story of a transsexual—tragic tale.
> *Camelot:* fun story of a used camel lot where Abdul has many adventures.
> *The Exorcist:* tells of the life of a famous physical fitness idol.

On and on and on they went—some pretty good and some dreadful. But at least they are thinking, creating, and writing!

Everything is running so smoothly now that I look back to the first of September and shudder. For the most part, the students continue in active learning situations for the entire time they are with me in class. Everyone comes in and gets a book to read for silent reading time. I've nearly completed *Roots* (Haley, 1976) by reading it only here at school. Rob would like to borrow it when I finish, because he thinks it is an important work that he should know since he has been investigating his own roots. We are reading for 15 min-

Classroom management

utes, and everyone is sustaining well at that level. After reading, students get their work folders out of a box. Each class has a different box. By keeping each of my four sections in separate boxes, each with a different color code, sorting out folders and assignments is not such a problem. This class has a blue box, and on each folder there is a blue circle with a numeral indicating that person's alphabetical-numerical order on the class list. Renée Zenn, therefore, can always find her folder at the back of the box with a "31" written in the blue circle. In the folder are assignments for the students to complete and then some choices for alternative learning activities. If all of these are completed by the end of the week, then the student must write in the other learning options which heesh has chosen for the remaining class time.

Within each station I have also color-coded the materials. Purple dots indicate that the materials are difficult (above grade level); orange dots mean that the materials are appropriate for that grade level; and, yellow dots mean that the materials are easier ones to handle. In this way, students can select materials that they can use instructionally, and I can assign them materials, too. I try to make sure that the dots are not too conspicuous, for I don't want students to reject materials that others know are easy (or hard) in order to avoid embarrassment.

It is imperative that there be a variety of multilevel, multisensory material available for the students to use. Allowing them some choice in the work they do gives them the opportunity to make decisions, and they need that experience if they are ever going to be independent learners. Renée, with her career goal of becoming a medical doctor firmly in mind, is quite capable of making learning decisions for herself. She tends to think of language arts as a waste of her time; she'd rather spend all day in laboratory courses. Jim and Pat are both able to and indeed do direct many of their own learning experiences. Clarence and Bruce, on the other hand, have such low reading levels that they still need much basic skill work. Along with this lack of readiness for middle school work is the lack of responsibility that some of the others manifest. I must closely supervise and direct their learning experiences and give them limited choices. Just yesterday I was looking over Bruce's folder with him and explaining to him his choices.

"Bruce, these three activities should be completed this morning. Tell me, please, which one you want to work on first, second, and third. Also, by the end of the week you must complete at least one activity from this group. Which one would you like to try?"

By giving Bruce some choices, I am aiding him in the development of his own independent learning style; by restricting those choices through teacher-judgment, I am helping to focus his learning on needed materials and skills. Students like Renée meet with me for 30 seconds to show me the study plan they have devised for themselves for the five-day study period. I look it over and make suggestions for change—deletions, substitutions, or additions—or approve it as is. To avoid getting 120 folders all turned in to me on Fridays, I have to put each class on a five-day cycle. This class picks up its folders and begins planning its five days on Wednesday; on the next Tuesday, the folders are turned in to me for evaluating. Other classes have different five-day cycles, so that I go home with only 30 folders a night. After evaluating what students have completed, I write a brief note to each of them and place it right where they will find it upon opening the folder. The. notes might say anything from

LIZ: Really glad that you were able to complete this; you must feel very proud of yourself!

to

GERRY: Something bothering you? I know that you can write more imaginatively than this. Maybe the topic just wasn't right for you to deal with at this time. Eager to see what you have for me next!

Wednesdays are my days! No folders are turned in to me, and I can use that after-school time to catch up on whatever I am presently behind in. I also use that time to work on station materials for the next month's theme. I find that by doing it bit by bit, it doesn't overwhelm me and I can set up my stations more easily. Many of the materials that I have in my stations, and some of the ones that are around in the room, are self-checking regardless of the unit. I believe in self-checking for three reasons: students get immediate responses to their work so they can make whatever adjustments are necessary in their learning; the more the students check their work, the less time I have to spend doing it; and self-checking fits in well with my idea of fostering independence in students. With self-checking, students can see right away if they need to recycle themselves into different learning options; with this information at hand, progress is obvious to the student as well as to me. With the students doing a lot of self-checking, I can then evaluate their work rather than merely grade it. With a checking table equipped with colored markers, the students have fewer opportunities for cheating.

I use coding systems so that students can have ready access to materials. I teach them these codes, what they mean, and why, so that they will know why I assign them to do certain activities. My theory has always been that unless students know why they are learning information, that information will not necessarily be assimilated. Once a reason has been established, then the mind set for dealing with it is established.

Reading levels

The secret to any successful personalized program lies in keeping kids working at their own instructional level, rather than at frustration or independent levels. The students who tend to cause classroom problems have been, in my experience, those who are either bored or frustrated with their work. The middle group of students are rarely the troublemakers, since they are, for the most part, working at instructional level. My first priority each year is to find the instructional reading level of each of my students. I also obtain three separate writing samples from each, so that I have some idea of writing proficiency.

To determine instructional reading level, I spend the first three days of school checking the oral reading of students, one at a time. While students are working together on small group projects, reading quietly or writing, or working at stations, I call each student back, one at a time, to where I am sitting in a quiet corner of the room, somewhat removed from the rest of the class and its distractions. I called Liz to come to me and handed her a seventh-grade book opened to a page in the middle. I asked her to read aloud a couple of paragraphs, and as she read, I made notes on a file card with her name on it and the date. That first day, as Liz and her classmates read or tried to read the seventh-grade basal, I made notes as to fluency, vocabulary knowledge, punctuation recognition, reading habits, and so forth. That evening I sorted my cards into three piles: seventh-grade basal too hard, just right, too easy. Next day when I went in, I called each of those for whom the book had been too hard back to me and had them read from the middle of the book of the next-lower grade level. I continued to make notes on my cards.

For the students for whom the book had been too easy, I asked them to read from the next-higher grade-level reader, always, of course, making my notes. For those students for whom the book had been just right on the first day, I retested with another page near the middle of the book to see if my judgment had been correct. Some of them had read the book so easily that I tried them in a higher-level book just to see what would happen. I continued to test the students who had found the book easy or hard on the third day; the just-right students were not tested again at this point.

I was able to refine my estimates of oral reading level fairly well within this three-day period, because the group had become much smaller by the third day. Here is a list of how some of the students performed on this informal test. I must hasten to add that it is important to note that at this point I am not trying to check comprehension of material read; simply for expediency, I am getting an oral reading score. The asterisk indicates the level, on this basis, that I judge them to be ready for:

LIZ: 7th grade, too hard
   *6th grade, just right
   5th grade, too easy

YOLANDA: *7th grade, just right
     8th grade, too hard
PAT: 8th grade, too easy
  *Above 8th grade

CHAD: 6th grade, too hard   MICKEY: *8th grade, just right
        *5th grade, just right   7th grade, too easy
        4th grade, too easy

HARRY: 6th grade, too easy   CLARENCE: 6th grade, too hard
        7th grade, too easy   5th grade, too hard
        8th grade, too easy   *4th grade, just right

GERRY: 7th grade, too easy
        *8th grade, just right

DENNIS: 7th grade, too hard
        *6th grade, just right
        5th grade, too easy

After I have tentatively established oral reading grade levels for each student, I give each student a book at that grade level and ask shim to read a selection from it silently and then answer ten questions. If they answer five or fewer correctly, I am concerned that it is too hard. If they get 6 to 8 right, it's probably okay. If they can answer 9 or 10, it may be too easy for them. I ask them, too, to jot down beginning and ending times for each story read, so that I can get an estimate of silent reading speed. While I have the class involved in doing this, I am busy with my note cards jotting down any information about students which will help me in teaching them. For example, I noticed that both Clarence and Bruce were mouthing the words and pointing to them with their fingers while they were reading. Chad was squirming around in his seat. Sharon kept rubbing her eyes. At this point I am not attempting to evaluate the reasons for the behaviors I note; I am simply listing the behaviors. There is sufficient time to find out, by further observation and testing, whether, for example, Sharon was rubbing her eyes because she needs glasses. Likewise, the story I gave Chad might have been too hard for him, which could be the reason that he was exhibiting a sign of nervousness. That too will be checked, but without my lists of observations I wouldn't know what to check.

One final form of information about each student which I gathered in a formal way was from an interest inventory. I asked each student to complete the inventory and then looked them over to see in what direction I could go with each student. The inventory had questions such as, "After school I . . . ," "After school I would like to . . . ," "If I were going to travel to the moon, the three personal items I would take with me are . . . ," and so on. Each of these requires a minimum of writing for the student, so that those with poor expression skills are not penalized.

FOR THE READER TO DO:

Finish Mrs. Wright's inventory. Construct another 17 to 22 questions/statements and duplicate them for class distribution. Revise your inventory after class evaluation and administer it to a junior high or middle school student. Does your form need further revision? Write an evaluation of this entire process and the results you found upon administration of the instrument.

I wish I could say that the entire file folder system of personalizing instruction just naturally followed after I had acquired a rather accurate profile of each student's reading level. Unfortunately, this is not true. Some of them are now, and were upon entering this class, independent learners. Many are not. However, with a gradual increase in student responsibility and a gradual decrease in teacher directives, more of the students are capable now of picking up their folders and getting right to the work that must be done. There are still a few for whom I must make specific short term assignments so that they can see what they have accomplished before going on to the next task. By the end of this very long month of October, I feel that I have aided many of the students in accepting the responsibility for their own learning. I feel proud of them and, I must admit, of myself!

USSW

Oh, I almost forgot to mention another strategy which I am trying as a means of integrating writing and the desire to write into my program. I was looking through my professional journals one evening, searching for some technique that might be useful for my students, when I happened upon an article outlining the importance of sustained writing in the classroom (Allington, 1975). This idea appealed to me because I had already seen an improved interest in reading that I attribute to USSR. I adapted the idea and made a chart to hang in the classroom so that the students would be able to refer to the rules for USSW. This is the chart that is hanging on the wall by my closet door:

USSW (Uninterrupted Silent Sustained Writing)
1. Get out your writing notebook for the last few minutes of the period on Tuesday and Thursday.
2. Everyone is to write silently during the time for which the timer is set.
3. It doesn't matter what you write. You may copy anything, write letters, or make up anything you want.
4. No one will read what you wrote unless you want.
5. You may read what you wrote to the group if you want.
6. The timer will be advanced by only one minute at a time when the whole group is ready to write longer.

I set the timer for five minutes the first time we had USSW and found that that amount of time was almost too long! We'll stay at five minutes for several weeks and see then if the time can be increased to six minutes.

Learning stations

The kids have really enjoyed the various activities in the stations built around the theme "Monsters We Have Known and Loved." When I introduced the month's activities to them, I began by asking the students to form small groups of five or six and to write the definition for the word *monster* and then to think of as many monsters as they could. I set the timer for five minutes and let them go to it. At the end of the time allotted, each group let one of their members report both the definition and list of monsters. After all had been given, we compared and contrasted definitions and lists. At this point I took my copy of the Oxford English Dictionary from the shelf and asked Harry to look up the word for us. They were amazed to find more than two full columns devoted to the meanings and various literary references for the word. But even more amazing to them was the original definition—"something extraordinary or unnatural; a prodigy, a marvel."

In looking over their various lists of monsters, we discovered that we often apply the term "monster" when we do not know what something is, or when it is out of our realm of experience. One really good example of this is the poor, maligned Loch Ness Monster, Nessie. If, indeed, there is anything in Loch Ness that is of the proportions reported, then surely the thing is not a monster in our modern sense. No one, to my knowledge, has ever suffered harm from it, therefore, the idea of calling Nessie a monster is probably erroneous. With this introduction, the students were quite eager to get into the various stations and see what sorts of activities there were for them to do.

Some of the activities in the technicorium were to develop a drawing, painting, or sculpture of a monster and name shim. (These were then placed in the graphologicorium for other students to write about.) Another activity was to make a "magazine monster." Students were to cut pictures out of magazines that were related in some way and then assemble them into a form to be named. Liz did an absolutely great one with make-up containers, powder puffs, and similar items. She assembled them into a rather provocative shape and named her "Ceci Cupp." We had a lot of illustrations of monsters that were done after listening to songs about monsters.

The graphologicorium has posters challenging students to write "Why we are afraid of monsters," to develop a catalog of monsters they know, and to complete a dictionary of scary terms. There are ditto sheets with monster crossword puzzles. Different famous monsters are listed on file cards, and the directions for use ask students to write a defense of that character. Other file cards have story starters so that students can write their own monster stories.

Some of the activities in the audiologicorium directed students to view old monster films on TV and evaluate them critically, or to view the TV program "In Search of . . ." when it was investigating "monsters." There were several monster stories on tape for them to listen to, both classics and student-created ones from the graphologicorium. Not only could they listen to sounds on records and identify them, but they also had the opportunity to create tapes of other sounds for their fellow students to identify. Of course, classical music gives us many pieces which have scary or supernatural elements, and listening to selections such as "Night on Bald Mountain" or "Danse Macabre" led students to the writing or art stations to create other forms for what they had heard.

The loquorium invited a lot of student participation, too. Students could choose to create an oral monster story with a group that would be taped and put into the listening area. Or, if preferred, an individual story could be created on tape. There were several debate packets that included directions for students to divide up and discuss—using debating rules—the existence of monsters or the merits/demerits of a particular monster. Some activity cards directed students to take the part of a particular monster and try to defend shimself and shis actions. I had gotten copies of pictures of famous monsters through the ages and displayed them in this station. The students were to describe the characteristics of each one, based solely on appearance. There were many activities for student discussion on rituals and the powerful effect that ritual has. The next logical step was to create sample rituals to keep away homework or to make everyday a Saturday. One other activity that nearly everyone read, I know, but that was ignored by the class was to have a Monster Day when each was to come dressed as a monster and let others try to guess who (what?) heesh was. I guess they are just too self-conscious at this age to try something of that sort.

The fifth station, the lexicorium, had volumes of monster stories and short stories, as well as biographies of famous people who created them. With the help of Penny Sills, Mr. Topps' secretary, I had the stories created by students transcribed and placed in the reading area. There were reference books on witchcraft and black magic so that the students could see the origins of some superstitions. There were posters with symbols and explanations of the symbols. I had a stack of old (and, I'm told, valuable!) Classic Comics which I placed in the lexicorium for students to read. "Frankenstein" in that version was much more easily read by some of the slower students. I also had books with classical myths in them, for some of our greatest monsters come from the Latin and Greek stories.

I finally feel that the graffiti board is here to stay. When I entered the room this morning, I discovered that new graffiti had been added:

> *Frankenstein:* along with gold and myrrh, one of the gifts given to the baby Jesus
> *Werewolf:* advertisement seen in furrier shop
> *Mummy:* nickname for mother
> *Monster:* French word for Mr.

November

What with meeting with groups of students for skill groups, directing student work at various stations, meeting with reading groups, and having students forming their own reading groups, this can be a very busy classroom! I learned long ago that the best way to bring order out of chaos is to have a good system established and explained to the pupils, and then to work with them in developing a set of classroom rules which they help to monitor. So, during that first week of school in September, each class develops its rules, which I then post on the wall. To keep each set of rules separate from other classes, I use color-coded poster board. I, of course, insist on some input, but basically the students identify what they expect of their peers. I find that cooperation of individuals and groups is much better if the students have helped identify appropriate behavior; they tend to monitor "their rules" even more conscientiously than I would. That done, I am able to concentrate my energies on teaching methods and materials.

Book box stations

I had a busy weekend creating book box stations for my room. With every corner of the room (and then some) taken up by the five stations—and with an area for me to meet with individuals and groups of students —I found that the only place left for a station was on top of the bookshelves. Unfortunately, they are narrow and don't lend themselves well to the activities that I would like to have students doing during and after reading. So, I took several different books home with me on Friday, ones I knew the students enjoyed reading. For each book, I created a series of activities to be done, popped them into a box with the book itself, and covered the box with self-adhesive plastic in a pattern that was somehow reflective of the content of the book. I had eleven different activities to do with *How to Eat Fried Worms* (Rockwell, 1973), some of which I will list here:

> *Card 1* Put the tape into the tape recorder and turn to page 1 in the book, *How to Eat Fried Worms*. The first four chapters of the book are on tape. When you reach the end of page 21, rewind the tape, turn off the tape recorder, and return the tape and book to the box.
>
> *Card 2* Finish reading the story *How to Eat Fried Worms* by Thomas Rockwell. Don't try to eat anything while you read this book—you might get sick!
>
> *Card 7* Using the recipe titles on pages 74—75 of the book, make up a recipe book telling how to make those special worm dishes. Make a title for your recipe book, and put your name on it. Place the book you have made into the classroom library.
>
> *Card 9* Make up your own special recipe and enter it in the annual Ver de Terre Recipe Contest at California State Polytechnic University. Be sure to try it first to make sure that it is a good recipe.

Card 10 Read the enclosed newspaper article which tells about this year's prize-winning worm recipe in the contest sponsored by California State Polytechnic University. Dig up 16 earthworms and make the recipe so that everyone in the class can have a little to try. Isn't that good?

Other cards had students writing to Thomas Rockwell about his book, creating stories about the rubber worms I had purchased in a bait shop, reading a worm recipe book created by students at another school, and unscrambling sentences to form a logical sequence (based on a book paragraph). I made four different box stations this weekend, and I'm going to make more next weekend. At this rate, I will soon have all of my best books transferred into stations, neatly stacked in their boxes, and making more room in my ever overflowing bookshelves.

FOR THE READER TO DO:

Choose an adolescents' literature book and develop a box station with a minimum of seven different activities that could be done with, about, or after the book. Have a balance of listening, reading, writing, and speaking activities. Share your boxes with other students in your class, perhaps by having a class period during which the various book stations could be examined.

Living dictionary

I believe that I have settled a problem that has bothered me for as long as I have been teaching. Each student is expected to keep a loose-leaf notebook for new words that heesh is learning. I wanted them to keep them in alphabetical order, just as in a dictionary, but as soon as there were a few words on the page, they were hopelessly out of order. I puzzled for a long time as to how these words could be kept in alphabetical order without requiring constant rewriting. Finally, it hit me! A "living dictionary"! What each student needed was a shower curtain ring and a stack of 3 by 5 inch index cards with holes punched in the upper right hand corner of each card and the identification(s), etymology, part of speech, and so forth, beneath it on the lines. I ask them to use as their first definition the meaning of the word in the context in which they first encountered it. They also write an original sentence to show that they have the word as part of their meaning vocabularies. Subsequent multiple meanings are listed later as they are found. Most of the students (wish I could say all) enjoy this kind of word hunt and are delighted when they find another meaning for a word in their "living dictionaries."

Basals

I use basals as one type of reading material. At this level, the basals are less skill oriented and more literature based, which is what I emphasize. However, the real advantage to the basals available for middle school is that I have bunches of them! If I want eight students to read the same selection, they can without sharing books. We certainly don't sit down and go through the books page by page, but each student receives assignments in the basals a couple of times a week. We skip around in the books, omitting stories of marginal interest. Often, a story in the basal is an excerpt from a longer work, and I point that out to the students. Sometimes I am able to make the full text available to them.

In addition, I use adolescents' literature that has appeal for middle school students. I have little signs over different sections of my bookshelves that indicate where students can find mysteries, romantic novels, myths, science, science fiction, magazines, biography, fables, animal stories, supernatural stories, books on other people and cultures, fantasies, and others. We also have a shelf we call "Look here first" on which I place any new books that we have gotten, any which I have finished reading to the class, or any that I just don't have a category for. Even Bruce can find the section that says "Magazines" and the one that says "Cars and Hogs." He may not be able to read the books there, but he surely tries! Our major problem with the shelving of books is that they are invariably returned to the wrong section, and it is sometimes weeks before this is noticed. I have asked the students to see if they can come up with some sort of system to keep the books in order, at least enough so that they can be used.

FOR THE READER TO DO:

Begin making an annotated bibliography of books that could be used with middle school students that would fit the categories Mrs. Wright has established. Duplicate your bibliography for distribution.

I have felt much closer to my students this month as a result of the theme activities they have been doing at the various stations. Everything has been developed around "Who Am I? Who Are You?" There are lots of books to help students identify with and react to this theme. They cast their horoscopes, analyze handwriting (they were amazed that the scientific analysis of handwriting is called graphology, similar to the station name), read palms, and write anonymous biographies in which others must identify the protagonist. They can write of bad and good experiences that have made them what they are today, make sculptures and self-portraits, or make dioramas of their homes or rooms. Some students even staged a mock TV program, "This Is Your Life." They can trace their family trees, rename themselves with a name they like better than their own and then justify the change, do collages that describe themselves to others, make a list of ten songs that would describe them to others, and write or find poems about themselves and the way they see life. They may write stories about people in the class; describe themselves from their own viewpoint, parent's viewpoint, sibling's viewpoint, or from a friend's viewpoint; and many other such tasks. They have gotten quite involved with this theme, which is not too surprising, for what is more fascinating, to any of us, than ourselves!

FOR THE READER TO DO:

What other activities could Mrs. Wright have students do with "Whom Am I? Who Are You?"? Does she have a balance of activities for each of her five stations? Make a list of adolescents' literature that could be used to help develop student's identities and self-concepts. Would you bring any resource people in to the class for this unit? Who?

In order to get them even more ego involved, I told them that next month's theme, short month though it is, will be "Breaker, Breaker" and is going to deal with CB radios. I asked them to help me web activities that we could do for that theme and they enjoyed doing this. I think they did a pretty good job. I will look it over and see if there are any areas I would like to add, and then I will complete the activities, cards, posters, and so forth, so that, come December, I'll be ready!

The graffiti board now indicates that ecology jokes are "in." I suppose when something is so deadly serious, we all take refuge in comic relief in order to bear what must be born. I nearly cried, I was laughing so hard, when I read, "Save a tree—eat a beaver"! But my husband Al's favorite was this one, which he suggested we ought to investigate! "Save water—shower with a friend"!

December   Mercy sakes, Good Buddy! Here we be comin' up on that ol' Santa time, and we be doin' real fine! 10–4? Slowly, but surely, I'm learning the CB lingo. What started out as a learning experience for them has become one for me. I must say, it was an excellent idea to have the students plan the types of activities that were to go into the stations. I added only a few ideas to their original plans and removed some because they were impractical (such as setting up a base station in the room). The topic certainly has encouraged a lot of listening, speaking, reading, and writing activity.

A WEB of POSSIBILITIES for "BREAKER, BREAKER"

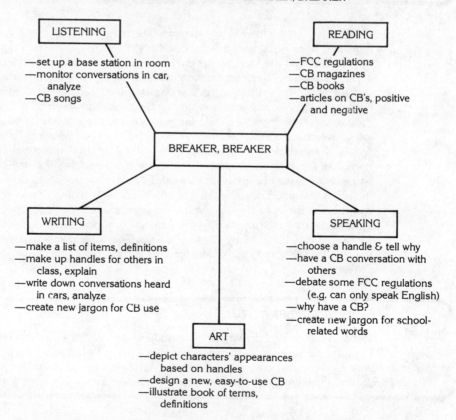

LISTENING
—set up a base station in room
—monitor conversations in car, analyze
—CB songs

READING
—FCC regulations
—CB magazines
—CB books
—articles on CB's, positive and negative

BREAKER, BREAKER

WRITING
—make a list of items, definitions
—make up handles for others in class, explain
—write down conversations heard in cars, analyze
—create new jargon for CB use

SPEAKING
—choose a handle & tell why
—have a CB conversation with others
—debate some FCC regulations (e.g. can only speak English)
—why have a CB?
—create new jargon for school-related words

ART
—depict characters' appearances based on handles
—design a new, easy-to-use CB
—illustrate book of terms, definitions

Overused words   The more that I read of the students' writing done in the graphologicorium, the more convinced I am that we must do some work with synonyms! If I read one more time that it was a "good day" or a "good time" or a "good thing," I will probably scream. There is a serious paucity of language in some of these students. What *could* be well written turns out to be a cliché or uninteresting. I have tried proofreading their writing with them and identifying some alternatives for them, but this has had little impact. So a new strategy is needed!

I initiated the strategy by announcing that as soon as USSR was over we would have a group activity. That certainly piqued their interest, and I could see that I had done serious damage to the concentration of that day's silent reading time. When the timer rang, I set up the overhead projector and put on a transparency that the kids could read quickly and silently:

> We went to town. We saw some nice things there.
> We had a good time. It was fun.

"What," I asked them, "do you think about these few sentences? Are they well written? Are they expressive? Are they descriptive? Tell me what you think. Yes, Don?"

"Did you write that, Mrs Wright? Or did somebody else do it?"

"Well, Don, I did write it, but that isn't really the question. What do you think of it?"

"Oh, Mrs. Wright, I think it's great. Like, you see, you don't have any mistakes with punctuation, and you didn't say, there in that last sentence, like, you know, 'It were fun' or nothing like that. I think you did a good job!"

"Thank you for your support, Don, but I really wasn't looking for approval of my writing. All of the things you have said are true—there are no errors—but would you like to read more? Is it written in such a way that you are eager to find out more about this trip to town?"

"Gosh, Mrs. Wright," began Harry, "I don't want to hurt your feelings, but, well, I got kind of bored reading even that little bit. I was glad there wasn't more!"

"And why do you think that was?"

Several of the kids began talking at the same time, but I pointed to the chart on the wall with discussion rules which directed them to speak one at a time and listen to others.

"All right," I said, "one at a time. Yes, Carla?"

"I agree with Harry. The reason I think it is not interesting is that the sentences are so short. There's not enough in each to keep my attention."

Mavis, at my direction, started a list on another sheet of acetate on the overhead of the different ideas that came forth.

"And," put in Pat, "there aren't any words that tell *about* the things seen or *why* they had a good time, uh, descriptors, right?"

Mavis wrote that down, and I called on Jim.

"I guess that one thing I don't like about those sentences is that it's too easy to read. I mean, I know all of those words, and I have known them for a real long time. I think that different words would make it more interesting."

"Which words do you mean, Jim?" I asked, trying to direct the discussion in this way. "If any of the rest of you agree with Jim, tell Mavis which words to write down."

The list they came up with had *went, saw, nice, things, good,* and *fun* in it. Fantastic, I thought, now to begin the lesson.

"These words which you have listed are very common words. They are so common in fact that they often are overused. I am very guilty of using the word "thing" when I can't think of a really appropriate word for a sentence. I always think that I'll go back and change it later, but many times I do not. Remember the word gatherings we had when we were writing *haiku* poems? We all sat down and thought of autumn words in order to write poems with the nature emphasis that *haiku* requires. We're now going to have a word gathering with different ways to say *nice*. Ready to write, Mavis?" I handed her another sheet of acetate, and she wrote NICE at the top, as the students began fast and furiously calling out synonyms for nice. When they were finished, their list looked like this:

NICE

lovely	charming	pretty
enchanting	kind	friendly
amiable	tasteful	pleasant
civil	agreeable	

We continued with word gatherings for each of the words they had identified from my sentences, and each one was written on the acetate and projected for all to see. A committee composed of Chad, Anne, Clarence, and Joey were given responsibility for listing these words on charts that we could hang so that everyone could refer to them when writing.

FOR READERS TO DO TOGETHER:

In small groups, do word gatherings for the other words identified by Mrs. Wright's students. Discuss ways these could be made available to students other than charts hanging in the classroom.

Junque

Last summer I attended a seminar on personalizing reading at the middle school level. We made a lot of our own materials out of scraps and "junque" (one professor told us that there is "junk" and there is "junque"; knowing the difference and being able to use it can make or break a personalized program). Dr. Scott Baldwin from the University of Miami gave us some very practical ideas that he had used in his own junior high English classroom. Following his directions, I brought boxes of stuff from home: single copies of texts, comic books, sample workbooks from salespeople, worksheets, magazines of interest to adolescents, and so forth.

He directed us to sort all of these materials into categories; for example, I put all of the comic books in one stack, all the car magazines in another, kits to assemble in another, and so on. Then, using round, sticky circles in various colors, I coded each of my stacks with an alphabet letter. All the comic books now bore the letter A with a numeral, 1 through 15, to indicate the 15 different comic books I had. I similarly coded each of my other categories.

The next step was a lot harder. We had to devise a 5 by 8 inch index card of activities for each of these materials. I was beginning to regret having been such an eager beaver! Dr. Baldwin helped each of us to look at particular materials to determine how each material could be best used. For some of the comic books, I devised word-hunt activities to deal with essential vocabulary. For others, I was able to make puzzles, evolve comprehension activities, and create "real life" work such as filling out forms to order materials.

FOR READERS TO DO TOGETHER:

Divide your class into five or six groups. Each group is to choose a different material (such as comic book, newspaper clipping mounted on cardboard, commercial game, etc.) and devise a series of activities that could be used with that particular material. Create a list of your ten best ideas.

Each index card was then coded with the same letter-number code that appeared on the front of the material and filed in a file box. As a further coding, I have written the letter-number codes in one of three colors on the white index cards. Yellow means "cinchy"; orange stands for "not too bad"; and purple is for "genius only." I started to color code the materials, too, but then I realized that it would be terribly obvious to everyone what level a particular student might be working on, so I just coded the cards. That way, when they are looking through the file box to choose materials to use, only they and I know how difficult it might be. Inside the back flap of each student folder is a graph that looks like this one. Upon completion of a particular activity, the kids record it. A quick glance helps them identify those they have not yet done and so their next assignment selection is facilitated.

	Dec. 3	Dec. 4	Dec. 5	Dec. 8	Dec. 9	Dec. 10	Dec. 12	Dec. 15	Dec. 17	Dec. 18		
YELLOW	A2	A7	C6	L5	G4				M1			
ORANGE		A8			C10			M7				
PURPLE						F5	F6			M10		

I introduced the shelf of materials and the accompanying file box this month, having (finally!) completed what I started out to do. Thus far, it is one of the more popular areas in the room. The students are told that they must plan to do three different file box activities a week, but if they wish to do more, they may. Both good and poor readers like comic books, the difference is that the good reader reads the stories while the poor readers gather their information from the pictures. Comic books are very hard reading—filled with unpronounceable protagonists and antagonists, place names, and specialized vocabulary. Much of the vocabulary is scientific or pseudoscientific, resulting in difficult concepts, as well. If only the opponents of comic books in classrooms would use a readability formula on one, they would soon realize what a challenge comic books can be.

If it weren't for the well-established routine in the room, chaos would prevail. Even so, it is hectic with so many different things going on at once in this 90-minute block. When the students enter the room, they pick up their folders (which are colorcoded for each of my four classes) and remove the books from them. (They keep their books for USSR in their folders.) When they are seated with their books, I sit down with my book. The timer is set, and we all begin to read. I find that starting the class with USSR really quiets the students and sets the tone for the work they'll be doing the rest of the period.

When the timer rings, students place their books back into their folders and check the schedules they have prepared for the week to see what they will be doing. On Friday, I post a list of the reading groups that I will be seeing each day of the next week, and the students enter the necessary information into a chart. Here is Mavis' chart for this week:

Time	Monday	Tuesday	Wednesday	Thursday	Friday
12:30	USSR	USSR	USSR	USSR	USSR
12:40	Reading group	Loquorium	Reading group	Audiologi-corium	Folder work
1:00	USSW	USSW	USSW	USSW	USSW
1:10	Folder work	Individual reading project	Folder work	Audiologi-corium	Dictionary update Etymology book
1:30	Individual reading project	Writing skills group	10-minute conference with Ms. Wright Individual reading	Reading skills group	Technicorium
1:50	Whole group	Whole group	Whole group	Whole group	Whole group

At the beginning of the school year, I prepared the students' schedules for them. Then, I taught them how to plan their time to meet all the class requirements, and now they do all the paper work! They do bring it to me for a quick check on Friday so that I can make sure they've left out nothing vital. Mavis was able to fill in the times for her reading group with me and her skills group sessions by looking at the chart I had posted the Friday before. She also fills in the other sections based on the assignments she must complete from her folder and the learning stations. She has also signed up to meet with me for a conference about her work in all the language arts areas—reading, writing, listening, and speaking.

Obviously there is not enough of me to go around, so not every student has a conference with me every week. But then, it is not really necessary anyway since I meet with them so frequently in small groups; one "biggy" every once in a while does it. The times for USSW and USSR are, of course, the same for the week, since all students participate at the same time in those. Mavis has some personal entries on her chart as well, for she wanted to take time on Friday to update her "living dictionary" with the week's words and also to work on the book begun earlier in the fall on words and their etymologies. She is also doing an individual reading project that is helping me as much as her. She is reading books on science from our classroom library, writing a paragraph summation, entering bibliographic data on the top of a file card, and then, using the Raygor readability formula (see p. 73), she is determining the reading level for the book and writing it in the upper right hand corner of the card. All the cards are being filed in a box near the bookshelves so that anyone who wants to check on the reading level and synopsis of any of the books completed can do so. The worst thing is that there are so few books listed in the filebox right now, and all of them are science books. I'm hoping that Mavis's enthusiasm for her project will extend to some of the other students (and therefore topics) soon.

Everyday when Mavis arrives, she checks her schedule to see what she will be doing with her time that day. All schedules are written in pencil so that adjustments can be neatly made, for who hasn't over- or underestimated the amount of time necessary to complete work?

December 20 has finally arrived, and now I can go off to a few frantic days at home during which time I *will not* think of school (too often), nor will I prepare materials (too much), nor worry about the kids (too frequently)! Last seen on the graffiti board was: Fiddling is a violin act.

11 A Year of Middle/Junior High School Reading and Language Arts (January–May)

I believe that most of the students are as glad to be back to school as I am. After all the parties and visits and dinners and giftgiving comes a lull during which boredom sets in. I found, despite my resolve to the contrary, that I was indeed thinking of my students and planning activities for them to do this month.

I spent an inordinate amount of time worrying over the performance of Bruce and Clarence. These two, my poorest readers and writers have been going to Reed Moore's Reading Center since early fall. Maybe I expected too much, but I felt so discouraged with their progress. So, over the vacation I called Reed and asked if I could meet with him the first week after vacation.

I went to Reed's room the Thursday after we returned to school. I am ashamed to admit that this is the first time I have been to his room this year. The boys have seemed so eager to go and willing to try to do in my room what Reed had suggested to them, that I haven't felt any pressing need to talk formally with him. But the more I thought of the two of them over vacation, the more I realized that I needed help. Reed and I had a long talk. I told him that I was very concerned about Bruce and Clarence and wondered what I could do to make the reading experience a more pleasant and profitable one for them.

Reed surprised me by his opening remarks. "I am really delighted with Clarence's performance, Rita. He's doing so well! He's the best reader I have in that class."

"You're kidding! This record shows that he has a fifth-grade level of functioning. And he is your *best*? I don't know how you do it. I'm afraid I would be horribly frustrated in your job."

"I think things are beginning to come together for Clarence this year. Look at this. In the fall he was reading on a fourth-grade level. Now, only a few months later, he's at fifth-grade level. That's not frustrating for me! It's very, very satisfying. Clarence has just the right combination of factors going for him right now. It's a new experience for him to be the best reader in the class. I've been giving him and some of the others more independence, too, and that is a new experience for him. He has always been in classes where

216

both he, and his teachers, considered him a dummy, and consequently he performed that way. He is now experiencing success and a sense of achievement. Here he knows success and a supportive environment, and he then goes back to your room where he also encounters success in his reading and a supportive environment. That kid can't help but make progress! You should feel very good about what you are doing for him—I do!"

"Thanks, Reed, but surely you're not going to tell me the same thing about Bruce. I know that he is not improving, either academically or behaviorally."

"Well, you're right, Rita, Bruce is a different kid. But even though he may not appear to have changed much, can't you see a difference in him from fall?"

"Yes, I guess you're right. Last fall I had the feeling that he was going to your room mainly because Clarence was, but lately *he's* been the one to notice the clock and tell Clarence when they should go. He's even tried to go early a few times. In my room, though, I can count on him to be the one who will disrupt the station work if anyone will. He actively resists going to the reading area, even though I have tried to keep it as attractive and varied as possible."

"You know, I'm really glad you initiated this discussion because I have been meaning to talk to all of Bruce's teachers about the results of my observations and testing. Bruce needs, as you can see from my records, more listening and oral language development activities. Is there any way that you could weight his work in your class so that he is engaged in *those* activities more than in writing and reading? I'm not suggesting that you should avoid any reading or writing activities with him, but just trim them down and fill in with oral language development."

I nodded my agreement to that, and after some more discussion of specific activities that I could have the boys doing, I left ready to do some planning.

FOR READERS TO DO TOGETHER:

In groups of five or six, discuss what Mrs. Wright can do with Bruce and Clarence in her classroom.

The graffiti board may have to go. I told the kids that they had a one-week grace period, and if at the end of that time changes have not occurred, then it will be no more. Last fall when I introduced the board to the kids, I told them that we had to keep it "clean." Since then, of course, there have been many obscenities and near-obscenities that I have quietly erased and tried to ignore. I felt that preaching at the kids wouldn't do it, and that if I could just be tolerant and quietly erase, eventually they would tire of trying to shock me. But the last one was not only obscene but also hurtful, and that I will not tolerate! Liz's mother's morals have been a source of speculation and gossip in this school for years but, at least to my knowledge, no one has ever taunted Liz about it. When I discovered the graffiti put there, I erased it and vowed to talk it out with the kids. The next day I told them that if there were any more objectionable comments put up on the board, I would have it painted over to match the room and it would no longer be written on. The choice is theirs; they are to police the writings. I hope they will be successful, for the board has been a real source of pleasure for me and for most of the students. They frequently gather around it to read, reflect on, and chuckle about the latest writings. So far the only effect seems to be that nobody wants to write anything; they may be wondering what my definition of obscene is. Goodness knows, that is a real enough issue today. Maybe we need to have a discussion about that.

Quotes books

Some of the graffiti has been quotes the students have encountered in their reading. Renée was the one who began that, I believe, with a Gide quote. Since I found it an interesting one, I asked Renée why she had put it on the board. She told me that all her life people had been criticizing her for her ideas and attitudes, trying to make her conform to their ideas. Renée, my little rebel, couldn't accept that. When she came across that quote, she said she felt that the author had said what she had not been able to articulate. One person cannot do everything, but still there are things that one can do. At least in her little corner of the world, she is doing what she can. Others started following her lead, and when quotes or poems affected them, they shared them with others on the graffiti board. I wrote each one down, too, in my planning book so that I could use them in writing and discussion stations where appropriate. However, with the possibility of the board's disappearing from use, I had to come up with another way of saving those quotes and encouraging more.

I made a ditto of all the quotes to date and left enough space before each for the students to write a category. Then, with the group, we looked at the first five quotes (I purposely put the harder ones first so that students could do the easier ones independently), and together we discussed what the main ideas were. We came up with "love," "friendship," "self-reliance," and "individuality" ("love," of course, had two quotes!). I told them to finish categorizing the rest of the quotes and then we would let a committee decide the categories for each quote. The result of all this is a book of quotations similar to Bartlett's famous one. After the group had finished with their task, I showed them *Bartlett's Quotations* (Morley 1963) and asked them to help me make a similar book for the class. We made it loose-leaf so that additional pages could be added as more quotes are found. Since the book has been put together, we have had an incredible number of quotations submitted to the committee. As added incentive, there is a line after each quote that indicates who found it and where; the students enjoy seeing their names in a book.

FOR THE READER TO DO:

Start a book of quotations with a class of middle school or junior high school students. Parallel the sequence that Mrs. Wright followed. The whole process should take two or three weeks in order to allow students time to find quotes that they particularly like. Bring the book to class and share it with your classmates for suggestions for improvement.

Class thesaurus

Necessity has prompted the beginning of another book. The few charts made from our word gatherings to find synonyms for overused words have grown to 21 and counting. There is just not enough room to hang more in here, and the ones that are up distract from the other materials in the room. Sometimes kids have trouble finding the chart they need. So a group of students and I sat down with another loose-leaf notebook and began our classroom thesaurus. We simply transferred the charts onto sheets of notebook paper, arranged them alphabetically by the word at the top of the sheet (*e.g.*, "nice," "fun," etc.), and put them into the notebook. Now the students just pick up the book and turn to the appropriate page when they are writing and find themselves overusing certain words. At the back of the book is a page that asks students to suggest other words for word gatherings and eventual inclusion into the thesaurus. As those are done, a line is drawn through that word in the back so that they can see that their book is indeed growing in response to their expressed needs. The students found, while using their thesaurus, that they had to add synonyms to the lists because the context in which they needed to use a word did not have a synonym listed. When that happened, the student would go to one of the committee members or to me, and we would come up with a synonym and add it to the thesaurus. In this way the thesaurus grew both in width and breadth.

FOR THE READER TO DO:

Go to a middle or junior high school classroom and do a word gathering with students on other ways to say *said*, *like*, *came*, *big*, and *beautiful*. Arrange their word gatherings into a thesaurus and help them add to it periodically. Show them how to use a thesaurus and then ask them to write a paragraph for you trying to avoid using hackneyed words by using synonyms for them.

The "Boob Tube" has been this month's theme around which all the station activities have been built. Long ago I realized that no matter what sociologists, psychologists, or teachers say about the detrimental effects of television, students will watch it. And so, in my classes, I have always tried to capitalize on this viewing. The kids and I webbed activities for this month's theme on the last day of school in December so that I could work on the materials over the vacation. The web of activities appears on p. 220.

I have tried to guide Clarence and Bruce into activities that would facilitate the work Mr. Moore is doing with them. So almost all of Bruce's assignments take place in the audio-logicorium and the loquorium. I hope this extra emphasis will help Bruce make the kind of progress he is capable of, whatever it may be. They have really enjoyed the reading activities I have had them doing this month. As a matter of fact, so have I. I think that at last I am beginning to see some progress. Both of the strategies operate on the principles of modelling and memorization. Both also require the use of a tape recorder, which was a bit of a sticky wicket since all of mine were always in use in the room. Good ol' Mr. Topps came through with one he had been "saving for an emergency," and it is now reserved exclusively for the use of the students in all of my classes who are not reading well.

Imitative reading

The first technique is called imitative reading (Huey, 1908/1968; Chomsky, 1976). I drafted Al's aid in taping stories that the two boys were working on in their reading in this room. They both enjoy the stories in the *Breakthrough* series (Allyn and Bacon) as well as the *Sprint* books from Scholastic. They are interesting to kids this age and are written on a very easy reading level. After Al taped the first stories for each of them, I got them together and explained what they were going to be doing. Each was to listen to his story on the tape and follow the print along for as many repetitions as were needed to be able to read the story to me without hearing the tape. After that story was mastered, they would be given another. Because they were reading two different stories, they did have to establish tape recorder time between them.

Clarence listened to his story eight times, he told me. After the eighth time, he signed up for a conference with me and read the entire story with only three word recognition errors. When I asked him questions about the story, he laughed and said that I could ask him *anything* because he knew every word of that story! As an additional check, I isolated some of the words from the story that he had had some difficulty with in the past, and he knew them. He was impressed with himself, and, of course, I was ecstatic for him. He couldn't wait to get started on his next story. Bruce, on the other hand . . . After listening twice to his story, Bruce told me that he was ready to read to me. I didn't argue, even though I was certain that he wasn't. We met that day; it was a disaster! He missed words

A Web of Possibilities for The "Boob Tube"

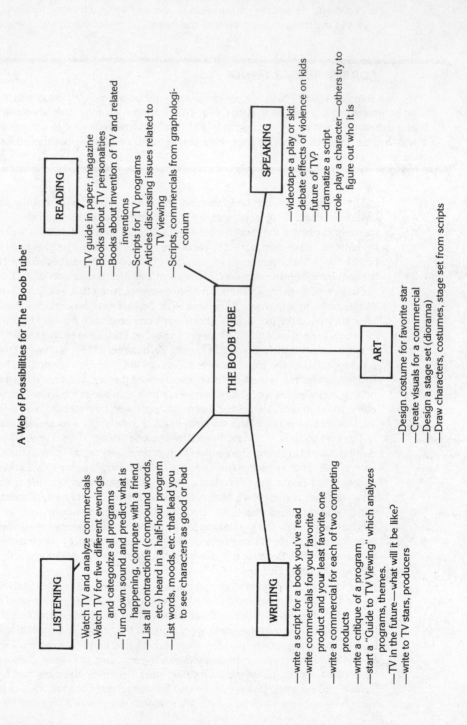

READING
—TV guide in paper, magazine
—Books about TV personalities
—Books about invention of TV and related inventions
—Scripts for TV programs
—Articles discussing issues related to TV viewing
—Scripts, commercials from graphologi-corium

SPEAKING
—videotape a play or skit
—debate effects of violence on kids
—future of TV?
—dramatize a script
—role play a character—others try to figure out who it is

ART
—Design costume for favorite star
—Create visuals for a commercial
—Design a stage set (diorama)
—Draw characters, costumes, stage set from scripts

LISTENING
—Watch TV and analyze commercials
—Watch TV for five different evenings and categorize all programs
—Turn down sound and predict what is happening, compare with a friend
—List all contractions (compound words, etc.) heard in a half-hour program
—List words, moods, etc. that lead you to see characters as good or bad

WRITING
—write a script for a book you've read
—write commercials for your favorite product and your least favorite one
—write a commercial for each of two competing products
—write a critique of a program
—start a "Guide to TV Viewing" which analyzes programs, themes.
—TV in the future—what will it be like?
—write to TV stars, producers

THE BOOB TUBE

and became so nervous that he began to miss even ones I knew he could read. It was a short session. I went back to the tape recorder with him and explained again that he could learn to read this story well if he would only sit there and make sure that his eyes followed the lines of print as he listened to the tape. I encouraged him to read quietly along with the tape, keeping up with it, however, rather than getting stuck on specific words.

Again he listened two times, and again he bombed during the conference. This time when we went back to the tape recorder, I marked a page in his book, about one-third of the way through the story, and told him to listen to that much of the story at least four times and then to come see me again. It seems to have worked. I just don't think Bruce was ready to handle an entire story at once. So now we mutually pick stopping-places at two or three points in the story and that is what he practices on. When he has mastered that portion, he does the next section and so on. He can't seem to believe that he is learning to read this way, but he knows something is happening and so keeps plugging away.

Repeated readings

After the boys were feeling some measure of success with imitative reading, I introduced another method that pits them against themselves and the clock. I gave each of them a blank tape and asked them to tape record a story they had just finished with in imitative reading. On a sheet of paper they were to write the name of the story and the starting time (for when they taped) with minutes and seconds. They then read the story and recorded their finishing time, substracting to see how long it took them to read the story. Next, they listened to the tape and followed along the text and kept track of errors made. The number of errors made was then listed beside the time. They went through the entire sequence four times and then had to come see me with their time and errors sheet. In both boys' cases, the number of errors made and the time to read the story decreased with each successive reading. They were impressed; figures don't lie! Bruce wanted to compare his time and errors with Clarence's, but I explained that that was impossible since they had been reading different stories. The effectiveness of this method will be destroyed if it turns into a competition between these two. Now, they do repeated readings (Dahl 1974; Dahl and Samuels 1975) right after they have been approved on their reading from the imitative reading practice. It gives them a break from the listening as well as another way to practice their reading.

There weren't a lot of graffiti this month, but there were a few choice ones. My favorite was written by Gerry:

Man was created before women—
Every masterpiece has its rough draft!

FOR READERS TO DO TOGETHER:

In groups of five or six, web next month's theme, "Tomorrowland." Mrs. Wright wants to include science as well as science fiction in her stations developed around this theme. Find some adolescents' literature books that could be used in the lexicorium and duplicate this list.

February

Connie Tent was in last month to observe my room and check with me on my organizational and record-keeping devices. She stayed for a very long time and took quite a few notes. Now, I'm not an insecure person—normally—but I was curious as to the nature of her comments and reactions. I arranged to have lunch with her a couple of days later and asked if she had some suggestions for me.

"Oh, Rita," Connie began, "that's not why I came to your classroom. Another teacher was having problems and asked me to help her. I merely came to your room to get some pointers and to observe the process your kids go through."

I knew exactly who she meant! "I've heard, of course, as everyone has, that Lee can't get control of her class and, as a result, there is little instruction going on. When she first came here last fall, I offered to share materials and ideas with her, but she was so aloof that I gave up. Really not too professional of me, was it?" I confessed.

"Oh, I don't know," Connie reassured me, "there's only so much that one person can do. She admitted to me that she is awed by your classroom and by you. Lee just can't imagine how you do what you do."

"I hope you told her that I should be a little better organizer since, after all, I have had a few more years of teaching experience. Connie, if there's anything I can do to help you or her, I would be more than willing to do so—you know that."

Well, in this short time that Connie has been working with Lee, the transformation has been incredible. Lee has become one of Connie's staunchest supporters; no one now dares to criticize the notion of having a content-area reading specialist at Upton Hill. Connie has certainly improved her credibility with the whole staff as a result of her success with Lee Yung. The "teacher underground," which knew of Lee's problems, now also knows of her successes. And these successes have been attributed to the genius of Miss Constance B. Tent! Some of the staff felt that she was just a theoretician who would fall apart if she actually had to implement her ideas; now they know differently. Many of the former resistors are beginning to use some of the strategies she taught us at the faculty meeting before school began last fall. I have great hope right now that Upton Hill is, indeed, on its way up, even though "going up" is not always easy. I'm proud to be a part of this school.

Language experience

I have been trying to provide Bruce with experiences of the sort suggested by Reed Moore, and so I began going through some old file folders at home to see if there might be anything of use there. In so doing, I came across a handout I had received at a seminar conducted by Tony Manzo on improving language and comprehension by use of language experience stories. [See Appendix B]. Language experience is a technique that my mother-in-law, who teaches at Merritt Elementary, uses with her first-graders. Lately, she has been doing the same thing with my Willy, who is five. Because language experience is based on the language and thinking of children, it is an excellent way to teach initial reading to them; their own words and ideas, the things they are most interested in, are what they learn from. The technique, however, is not limited to young children, but can be used effectively with beginning readers of all ages. Manzo's handout, in fact, is an adult language experience story as are the activities related to it.

I could see the parallel with what Freda was doing with Willy at home and what Manzo was doing with an adult in Missouri; both required that a story, using the person's own language, be given to someone to be written down. Both had a series of related, developmental, sequential activities to be done with or to the story. Both emphasized the integrated curriculum idea of working simultaneously with reading and other language arts areas. From Manzo's explanation, I knew that I needed to get an individual story from Bruce, and then duplicate a copy for everyone in the group with him. This temporary group consisted of several others who could benefit from some language extension activities. The activities were comprehension checks, a reasoning guide, language improvement, improving mood, and reorganization and rewriting. I added a section on word study to deal with the word identification skills that I wanted to focus on.

Well, in spite of my preparation, I blew it! It looked so easy that I didn't anticipate that anything could go wrong. I called Bruce in to a corner with me, and with a ditto in the typewriter, asked him to tell me a story so that I could type it out. He looked at me blankly for a minute, and then he said, "I don't know no stories."

"But this doesn't have to be a story you know. We're going to make up a new one!" I broke in confidently.

"What you mean, 'we'? I thought you said that I had to do it. Can I type?"

"No, Bruce," I was trying to be patient. "I will type and you will tell me what to type. Now, let's think of a story, okay?"

Nothing. I have rarely ever heard just nothing!

I tried again. "Okay. Then think of a story someone has told you, and we'll type that."

"I told you I don't know no stories."

"Come now, Bruce, surely someone has told you a story sometime. Think about it." My nerves were getting frayed.

"Oh, yeah! I know this one about this travelin' salesman, see, and he goes to this farm. And, let's see, there's this girl, you know, the farmer's daughter."

I stopped typing at that point. My jubilant mood was destroyed by the lascivious smile I saw on his face, and I knew that I had better not continue this story.

"I'll tell you what, Bruce. I have some other things to do, but we'll continue this later today or maybe tomorrow. Thanks a lot, and keep thinking of some stories you've heard that aren't just jokes, all right?" With an uncontainable sigh of relief, I watched him go back to his seat. That evening I called up Freda and asked her what I did wrong.

We discussed Bruce and the others, their various levels of functioning, and their strengths and weaknesses. She suggested that I do a group story with them after using a stimulus for thinking and speaking. She told me to think about what these kids (all boys) were most interested in and then try to give them that experience. The result should be that they would create enough language together to make a group story. She thought, too, that having the typewriter there for their first efforts might inhibit them. Instead I should write the story on the board or on chart paper so that all could see, since such a device would not be so distracting.

Al and I happen to share one of the interests of boys of middle school age, and he was willing to come over to school the next day to help me out with the lesson. At the prearranged time, Bruce, Joey, Clarence, Brett, Chad, and Dennis went out into the school parking lot with me, wondering all the while what I had dragged them outside for. Right on schedule, Al came roaring up on his "hog" and pulled up beside us with a flourish. He kept the bike idling for a few moments, shut it down, took off his helmet, and tucked it under his arm.

"Hi, guys." Al sat high on the bike. The boys all greeted him excitedly, having met Al on a few other occasions.

"Wow! What a nice hog. I never seen a bike like this before," Joey chattered.

"Golly! Bet this one has a lot of torque, huh, Mr. Wright?" said Chad.

"Not too bad," said Al. "Enough for me, anyway."

"I'd rather have a four stroke than a two stroke any day," said Bruce. "Wouldn't you, Mr. Wright?"

Al looked over at Bruce and said, "You know, Bruce, some of the new two strokes have a lot more torque than some of the four strokes. My wife has a two stroke Japanese bike."

Finally the boys noticed me again—with wonder and (could it be?) admiration!

"You do?"

"I never seen you ride it, Mrs. Wright."

"Why don't you bring it to school?"

"Well, it would be a little tricky to bring all my stuff to school on my bike," I replied.

"Not if you brought this one! Just look at them saddle bags!" exclaimed Clarence.

They began a minute inspection of Al's hog from the windshield to his leather jacket to the black and white paint job. It was obvious that they approved.

"Did you know that this bike has a reverse gear? With one this big it's a necessity, or you could never get it turned around. Let me show you." To their delight, Al demonstrated the reverse gear.

The kids were impressed.

"What's your top end, Mr. Wright?" Brett wondered.

"Oh, about 110 mph, I guess. Stripped, it can go up to 120."

Dennis reached over and stroked the engine casing, "Ever had it that high?"

"Well," Al grinned, "since I'm a member of the Ton-Up Club, I guess you could say I have."

Bruce and the others looked puzzled, so Al explained that the Ton-Up Club is an unofficial club in which you can claim membership if you've gone over a hundred miles an hour.

"How 'bout you, Mrs. Wright? You belong to the Ton-Up Club, too?" asked Chad.

I told them that of course I belonged, but I must admit that I didn't tell them that you could be a member if you have been on the back of a bike that has gone over a hundred!

Al and I both began to talk with the boys about why we enjoy our bikes. There's an indescribable thrill in speeding along with the wind in your face and the sun warm on your cheeks. The sound of the engine and the feeling of the power you sit on all add to the excitement.

It was difficult to get the boys back into the building, but I knew that I wouldn't have any difficulty this time with the language-experience story that we would write in class that day. Using Manzo's lesson as a guide, I developed activities to extend the story beyond merely reading it and learning the words in it; we spent four days with the same story. Right after that I asked each of them to make up a story about owning a bike—what it would look like, where they would go, why they wanted it. These individual stories were much shorter, but still usable for the various activities Manzo recommends. I think I'll be able to continue a pattern of this type for a while with whole group stories and then individual ones with the same theme, if I can keep them interesting.

FOR THE READER TO DO:

What are some other interests of junior high or middle school age students—girls or boys—that could be used to stimulate language-experience stories. Share your list with others in your class. Be able to justify your choices.

FOR READERS TO DO TOGETHER:

In groups of five or six, write the story that you think the boys in Mrs. Wright's room would have dictated. Create the activities that she could use with that story as the base. See Appendix B for a sample story and exercises. Duplicate your group effort and give copies to everyone in your class.

Bruce now is seen poring over the various "hog" magazines that I have added to the reading materials. I also found a set of high interest-low vocabulary books in the library that deal with motorcycles and racing cars. These, too, are carefully perused.

Student conference

Another lesson, that was a lot more easily done, was an individual conference with Pat. She was beginning the book *Summer of the Swans* (Byars, 1970). Before she began the reading, we discussed vocabulary words such as "retarded" that she would need, and we looked at some examples of figurative language, such as "crown jewel," that might cause trouble. Then she told me how many pages she was going to read before our next conference later that week. I skimmed over the book to review it. During our discussion of "retarded," I had filled Pat in on who was in the story (main characters) and what Sara was concerned about, how she felt about her retarded brother.

Later that week we met again, and I asked her to read the first page of the second chapter to herself in order to answer the following questions: Why was Charlie concerned? Give one reason why he might have shut his eyes. Why was Charlie unwilling to trust Sara? Pat answered all the questions well.

She read the next page aloud so that I could check her oral reading fluency and expressiveness. I made notes, underlining the word "illusion" that she had had trouble with. I would teach it later. After the reading we did "ping pong questioning"; that is, I would ask a question and then Pat would. We alternated questioning until neither of us could think of any more good questions. I find that ping pong questioning gives me a great deal of information about a student's comprehension, since I can evaluate shis level of understanding by the questions asked as well as by the responses to my wrong answers. Finally, I asked her to "free recall" what she had read from the first 34 pages of the book. She capsulized the main ideas, but there were also loads of details, some of them unnecessary, that she got in, too. I made a note on my card to help her identify essential parts for retelling at our next session.

During the skills session, I worked with her on some of the words she had had difficulty with in her oral reading, such as "illusion," and we did a quick game in which she identified the root words in words from her story that contained prefixes and suffixes. She is keeping a book of prefixes and suffixes so that she can learn their many meanings. I wished her the best of luck with that one!

I told her that I had been trying to think of something she could do after completing the book that would be useful to her and to others. Unless she had some other project in mind that we could discuss, I wanted her to make a notecard summary of the book which we could file under the heading "Kid's Problems" in the filebox for our classroom library. She was to feel free to make notecard summaries on any other books she had read that might also fit the heading.

Having made sure that she had a good start on her book, I told her that she did not need to sign up for another conference until she was finished with it, unless she were having problems. Total conference time: 12 minutes!

We're doing well with sustained silent writing (USSW) right now. Last Thursday, the students wrote for 15 minutes without interruption. They keep all of these writings in their notebooks, and some of these notebooks are very fat ones. It is really impressive to see the volume of unassigned writing that has been done. I've been using the time, in part, to catch up on my letter writing, but I have also been writing an adolescents' literature book during this time. I find the 15-minute limit very frustrating, because I just get started and it is time to quit. I take a few minutes each day to share with the students what I have written. When I told them I was trying to write a book, they were impressed and thrilled to know an author! I assured them that they did not know an author (at least a published one) yet, but that I enjoyed trying to create a continuing story. True to my expectations, after this there was a spate of book writers in the class, all of whom were more than eager to share what they had written with anyone who would listen.

Oh, I guess I forgot to mention it, but the graffiti board is here to stay. The kids told me that they would watch out for the stuff written there and prosecute offenders. Thus far they have, and I'm delighted; otherwise, we would never have had my favorites this month:

> SOCRATES: "To be is to do."
> GOETHE: "To do is to be."
> SINATRA : "Do be do be do be do."

March

Throughout this year there have been shifting allegiances, strange alliances, and many revelations of various personality facets. With 32 of us living together in this room, one cannot help but observe the activities of the other 31. I have some grave concerns about how some of these students of mine are going to turn out. Carmela misses so much school to stay home and take care of her younger brothers and sisters while her mother works that I wonder what hope there is for her to break this pattern. How will she ever be able to acquire enough training to get the kind of job that will allow her daughter to come to school regularly?

And Brett. So indulged by his parents and so unliked by the other students that he attempts to buy their friendships. I overheard his party plans one day. He had invited most of the kids in the class and was promising them the best time they would ever have in their lives. I might even go myself, if invited, I thought. Brett could use some support like that. Well, the next thing I heard was Brett asking kids if they liked dark or light rum in their colas; he needed to know before he and his dad purchased the party supplies! I was a bit shocked, though I shouldn't have been. I'm well aware of nationwide statistics on adolescent alcoholism. That afternoon I went in to see Mr. Topps and asked him what I should do. I didn't feel that it was something I could ignore. Mr. Topps agreed with me and suggested that he might call Brett's parents and tell them that he had heard that such a party was being planned. In this way he would not be revealing me as the source, and Brett would not consider me a traitor. But it was necessary that Brett's parents know that the school was aware of the situation. From the remarks I heard on the Monday after the great party (I was *not* invited—but, would you believe, *Al* was!), the rum and cola did not materialize. It was strictly pizza and pop. I guess I will never know if the plans had been squelched or if they had just been part of Brett's ploy to get people to come to his house.

Liz's group has remained the most cohesive this year. She is undisputed leader of the four other girls. Tammy and Lynda will do anything Liz will do, and they will not do anything that Liz will not do. Trying to get them to be individuals this year has been a waste of my time so far. The other girls are the ones I'm more concerned about. Debi could be doing average work, but she is barely passing. I took her aside one day and asked her why she didn't try harder, since I knew she was capable of better work. She confided to me that she doesn't want to be left out of Liz's group, and if you are smarter than Liz or have a boyfriend cuter than Mickey (who goes with Liz), you're out. It's as simple (and complex) as that. Debi doesn't feel that she can make it alone, or that some of the other girls in the class would welcome her into their groups. It's true that she could never be in with my "Libbers," but I suspect that Sharon, Pat, and Yolanda could become friends with her fairly easily.

Anne, poor chubby thing, is so badly used by Liz and the others that I can't believe she puts up with it. I finally realized why they took Anne in with them. They needed someone to do their dirty work (such as calling up boys to ask how much they liked one of the girls, pulling dirty tricks on other kids, and carrying notes from one to another), and Anne, for the few crumbs they grant her, is willing to do anything. She is Liz's slave. And I cannot get her to improve her image of herself and begin to have a little more self-esteem. I wonder if she'd like *The Cat Ate My Gymsuit* (Danziger, 1974)? I'll suggest it to her even though it doesn't fit the "theme of the month."

Learning stations

"Yesterdayland" is the theme for the month, and the kids and I have been having a lot of fun at the various stations built around the idea of looking at life as it used to be. Actually, it's a bit of a hodgepodge because there is a good bit of "yesterday" to look at! But it is fun. The reading station has, surprisingly, been one of the most popular this month for all but two people in the class. Liz would not care if all the reading material fell through the floor to the basement. Brett is being contrary—if the others like it, he won't.

In the reading station I have included reprints of old *McGuffey Readers* and a box of old newspapers (dated in the 1880s) that my parents found in an outbuilding they were tearing down. The kids just cannot imagine how anyone ever learned to read with those books. They look at the illustrations and compare clothing and life styles. From those and the newspapers, I have been able to get them to look at outdated history books which refer to the Indian as the "noble savage," to blacks as "colored people," and predict that someday we might go to the moon. They love it. It's coming through to them slowly that what we are reading and thinking and feeling now will one day seem outmoded to our descendants. They also like looking at Macaulay's books, *City* (1974), *Cathedral* (1973), and *Pyramid* (1975). They find it fascinating to think that one could actually build a pyramid, given the proper resources, by following the directions given.

There are many Newbery Award winning books which take a look at different periods in history, and so I brought those into the class, too. Another favorite is *The Best of Life*, a fine look at America and the world through the years.

The audiologicorium contains old 78-rpm records for the kids to listen (and dance?) to, as well as tape-recorded reminiscences of older people in our community. But the all-time favorite are my records of old radio programs; the kids are begging for more! I guess TV hasn't completely extinguished their imaginations.

At the writing area they are encouraged to read excerpts from famous diaries and then to begin keeping one themselves. There are, of course, many story starters that transport them to another era and expect them to respond. One of my favorites is the archaeology box which has different things buried deep in the sand in the box. The students dig in, find something, match the number written on it with the numeral in the book beside the box, and read the directions written there. An example of one set of directions which went with a styrofoam cup are:

> You are an archaeologist living in the thirty-fourth century. You have found this object from the twentieth century and are trying to determine what it might be or have been used for. It never occurs to you that it might be a drinking cup, for in the thirty-fourth century man no longer drinks water. When the water supply in the world was exhausted in the twenty-second century, scientists found other ways to supply man's need for moisture. What could this object be, if not a cup?

The technicorium had various art prints of people through the ages, books with Brady photos from the Civil War, directions for making stone sculptures and coil pots, and other such stuff.

There are various debate topics in the speaking station, as well as chances to role play famous personalities from the past, and directions for conducting interviews with community oldsters who might be able to remember what things were like before television, airplanes, rockets, color and talking movies, and other such modernizations that we take so much for granted. They also have opportunities to look at art prints and decide what can be told about the culture and times from these pictures.

All in all, it's been an interesting month. We almost lost the graffiti board again when the following ditty appeared. But, the students assured me that if I found it obscene the obscenity was only in *my* mind. Looking at it objectively, I would have to agree!

Ree ree ree
Kick 'em in the knee.
Rass rass rass
Kick 'em in the other knee.

April

ANNOUNCEMENT

Reading Slogan Contest

Write a slogan to encourage reading and win ten dollars. In addition, your slogan will be made into a bumper sticker with *your name* on it! Any student in grades 6–12 may enter. All slogans must be original. In case of duplications, slogans with the earliest date received will have top choice. Send your slogan to Miss Tent by April 16. There will be three winners. The winners will be announced on April 30.

First Prize: Your slogan made into bumper stickers and a cash prize of $10.00.

Second Prize: Your slogan put on a banner and hung in the office and a cash prize of $5.00.

Third Prize: Your slogan put on a banner and hung in the office and a cash prize of $3.00.

When my kids saw this poster in our room they couldn't believe it. Money and fame all at once! Almost all of them made a resolve to win the grand prize. I think Connie really outdid herself this time. This may be the greatest thing to happen to this school since football games! There were scraps of paper all over the school as the students wrote and then discarded slogan ideas. Connie, Mr. Topps, R. R. Rowe, and Miss Stern were to select the winning slogans. In order to prevent the possibility of someone being chosen because shis name was recognized and respected, Penny Sills opened all envelopes, wrote the same numeral on the top and bottom portions of the official entry form, and then tore off the bottom part with the student's name and filed it in an envelope. Only Penny has access to this file, and therefore no one will be able to cry "unfair practice."

The excitement around the school was incredible as the deadline approached. Some of the students wanted me to intercede for them with the committee, but I told them that even the committee members didn't know who had written what. The day the winners were to be announced, it was impossible for anyone to get any work done. The kids would start to settle down and then someone would bring up the contest again. What a day! At about 2 P.M., after a whole day of this, I was ready to submit my own slogan, "Down with reading slogan contests!"

There was an assembly at the end of the school day during which the committee members were to announce the winning slogans and their authors. We all filed expectantly into the auditorium wondering if anyone in the middle school section really had a chance, but hopeful all the same. We sat attentively as Mr. Topps read the winning slogans to a hushed crowd.

"Third prize goes to the author of this slogan: 'A book a week is what I seek!' And the winner is . . . Francis McGillicuddy in the tenth grade." Yay-yay-yay," the crowd roared.

"The prize-winning slogan in second place is: 'Some of my best friends are books!' And the winner of that prize is Jim Bean in the middle school."

We went bananas! We all screamed and yelled and cheered and clapped Jim on the back. What a day! I was so excited that I didn't even hear the winning slogan that was to be made into bumper stickers. I had to check with Connie the next day. Some girl in the twelfth grade had won with a philosophical statement about reading and your mind. I can't even remember it, but I will use the bumper sticker when they are given away next month.

Of course, Jim's triumph had to go into our classroom newspaper which is distributed throughout the entire school. I'm afraid that we didn't maintain impartiality, as we really should when dealing with news items. Jim's story took up as much space as the other two winners combined.

FOR READERS TO DO TOGETHER:

What would your entry for the reading slogan contest have been? Using a form like the one described by Mrs. Wright, have each member of the class submit a slogan. Have a committee of students duplicate a list of all the slogans submitted and then let each member of the class vote for shis three favorite slogans. Announce what the top three slogans are for your class. What other incentives could you use to get students to participate in such a contest?

Class newspaper

The newspaper has been an excellent experience for my students this spring. It began in the writing station as part of our theme this month, "Meet the Press." All of the station activities are built around newspapers, news and other magazines, and radio and television news. I wanted the students to acquire a feeling for the various types of journalism which are required by the different methods of reporting the news. We also looked at the elements that must be included in a news report in order to inform the public.

Some of the discussions in the speaking station became pretty lively as students discussed confidentiality and the public's right to know, as well as other issues in journalism. They also enjoyed the role playing of different journalistic styles of interviewing and reporting. (I suggested that they might want to listen to "Badger's Bailiwick" for another type!).

Political cartoons and their analyses are probably the most used articles in the art station, and of course the reading station is full of various newspapers, magazines, and books about writing for a newspaper and how printing is done. But the most surprising response came from the writing station. About a week after the stations were in place, Pat and Sharon, who have aspirations of being writers, approached me with a suggestion. They wanted to modify one of the activities in that station and expand it into a regular part of the classroom rather than restricting it to this particular theme. The activity to which they were referring was an add-on bulletin board. Anyone who had any news (clean, of course) about anyone else could write it on a piece of paper and tack it to the board for others to read, similar to what was done before actual newspapers existed.

"Couldn't we have a real kind of newspaper, Mrs. Wright?" asked Sharon. "Pat and I would be willing to start it and be the editors and make sure the articles got in and stuff like that."

"I don't think you have any idea how much work that could be," I cautioned. "Running a newspaper involves much more than just writing articles. They have to be edited, typed for reproduction, and then run-off and collated and distributed. And how are you going to get all the paper and stencils and things of that sort? You know I've cautioned all of you about paper use since Mr. Topps told us we might run out of paper before the end of the year."

Pat spoke up, "Well, we thought maybe we could sell the copies to the whole school during lunch time once a week. Do you think people would buy them?"

I thought for a moment and said, "They might. That is, if it contains more than just middle school news. If you can include topics of interest to the whole school and keep down the 'Johnny loves Susie' stuff, it just might sell. Let's sit down and talk about the different sections your paper will have. And, by the way, what are you going to call it?"

The girls were delighted. It so happened that they had already mentioned the idea to most of the other students in the class—I was the last to know what my little bulletin board had started! They had lots of people lined up for sales and distribution, for reporting and article writing, for continuing columns, for typing and editing, and for advertisements. They had indeed done their groundwork well. And that was how the *Upton Hill Times* came into being. It is incredible to me how hard these kids work, both in class and out of it to put the paper "to bed" every week. They have not yet, in three weeks, missed an issue deadline. I'm so proud of them. And the money they make! I really had some concerns as to whether or not the senior high students would buy a paper put out by "kids," but they certainly seem to be buying! I guess there was a need for this paper, and my students were in the right place at the right time.

We have agreed to spend the entire profit from the paper on a pizza party at my house when school is out for the summer. The kids are not entirely profligate, however, for they are also stocking a supply of paper and stencils and other materials they can use next year to start the paper from the beginning of the school year.

FOR THE READER TO DO:

Can you anticipate some of the difficulties that Mrs. Wright's students would have with the production and marketing of a weekly newspaper? What could you do to circumvent them? Make a list of all the continuing columns that could be in the paper. What sorts of editorials would have interest for students at this level?

PIRL

Reading to make inferences is very difficult even for some of my best students. As a result, I'm always on the lookout for articles and workshop sessions dealing with ways to teach comprehension skills to students. At one workshop, I received a handout on a technique called PIRL (Planned Inferential Reading Lesson) which sounded reasonable. I got permission from Mr. Topps to cut pages out of discarded basal readers. These were put through the thermofax machine and made into dittos which I duplicated. I tried to choose characterization passages mainly, because they lend themselves so well to making inferences. Then I followed the steps outlined in the handout below:

PIRL

(Planned Inferential Reading Lesson)

In a Planned Inferential Reading Lesson, students must decide which statements about a selection are literally stated in the text and which are not literally stated but can be inferred from what is stated. For the inferred statements, students find the parts of the selection which lead them to make the inference. When students show some facility with distinguishing literal from inferential statements and are able to support the inferential statements with literal statements from the text, they are then led to determine which inferential statements are true (supportable) and which are not true (unsupportable).

Steps:

1. Prepare for the lesson by reading the selection and listing several true statements. Some of these statements should be literally stated in the text. Others should require the students to make inferences. For the first several lessons these statements should probably be made for one page of text at a time. As the students gain facility, increase the material covered to 2–4 pages. Eventually, statements should be made up which cover an entire story.

2. Have the students read the statements. Tell them that all the statements are true and that they will read the page(s) to decide which statements are written "right on the page" and which they have to "figure out." (You may want students to guess before reading which statements are literal and which are inferential.)

3. Have students read the page(s) and decide which statements are written right on the page (literal). (Pairs of pupils working together help insure that all can read the material.)

4. For those statements which students believe are literal, have them read orally the sentence or sentences in which the statement is made.

5. For the statements you have to figure out (inferential), have students find statements in the text that lead to these inferences. Have them try to verbalize what else (besides what is stated on the page) one would have to know in order to figure out the inference (prior knowledge).

6. When the students have demonstrated fairly consistently the ability to distinguish literal from inferential statements and are able to support inferential statements with literal information from the text, they are ready to begin to distinguish true (supportable) inferences from untrue (unsupportable) inferences. The teacher prepares for these lessons by reading the selection and listing several statements, some of which are true inferences and others of which are not.

7. Students read the prepared statements before reading the text. They are told that their task is to read the text to determine which of the statements are true according to what is stated in the text.

8. Students read the selection, decide which statements are support-

able inferences, and support these inferences with statements from the text and prior knowledge.

I did the first lesson with Jim, Harry, Rob, Renée, Yolanda, Pat, Geoffrey, and Mavis. It went beautifully. They followed the directions well and worked through the exercise with very little difficulty. And they enjoyed it, too. I did several more with this group, and then told them that I would allow them to go through the exercise themselves. They were to select a group leader who would meet with me to choose the statements for the list of true statements. That leader would then take the group through the exercise. I observed, without seeming to, the next lesson that was done. I was quite impressed with Yolanda's ability to lead the group through the activity. I felt confident that they could work on PIRLs for the rest of the year, in that group, or in another, with little direct assistance from me.

Encouraged by this success, I decided to tackle the same exercise with students for whom it would not be such an easy task. Walter, Anne, Liz, Dennis, Brett, Joey, and Chad were my next targets. By then I knew the steps so well that I could have repeated them in my sleep, but it just didn't work. They were distracted and couldn't stay on task. They had arguments over whether or not something was literally true or not. If the statements were: "Mr. Jones avoided going home in the evenings," some of them would argue that it was "really true" (meaning 'literally true') because he had so many children and their own dads had said the same thing many times. We worked and worked on finding the words that would prove their contentions, but so many of them were such poor readers that it was a struggle. I knew that the technique was a good one, so it was a matter of finding out how I could present it to students like these.

That night, I thought and thought about what it meant. I recalled times when these students had difficulty with instructions in class because they had "thought" I said something other than what I had said. Then it struck me. These students first needed work with listening for inferences.

PILL

And so, PILL (Planned Inferential Listening Lesson) was designed. I dragged out the records of old-time radio programs and listened to one of the shows called "The Shadow." First I just listened for the story. The second time, I listened to the program and made notes on literal and inferential true statements. I wrote these out and planned my lesson just as I had planned the PIRL ones, except that this time the emphasis was to be on listening comprehension.

I planned and taught eight lessons from those records. After they could listen for inferences, they were ready to read for them. Then I transcribed the second half of the radio program *The Green Hornet*. I listed the true statements from each half on separate sheets and took both lessons to class with me. We did the first half as usual. The students listened to find out if statements were literally or inferentially true. After that short lesson was completed, I told them that we were going to do the second half a little differently. I again gave them the list of true statements, but this time they were to read the transcribed page that I had made from the record. Because they were already familiar with the plot, the reading part was much easier for them. In addition, I had taught them the few words that I thought they all might have trouble with. We got through it all right. They enjoyed it and seemed to understand the transfer we had made from listening to reading for inferences.

In a moment of madness, I scribbled what I think is the best of the graffiti this month:

God grant me patience—
And I want it right now!

FOR READERS TO DO TOGETHER:

Mrs. Wright is using careers and career alternatives as her unit theme for next month. Describe the activities that will be included in each of her learning stations.

May

This has seemed like the longest and shortest of months! Short because it is my last month with one of the brightest and most creative groups I have ever taught; however, the first week was especially long! I took a three-day leave of absence the first week of May to attend the annual International Reading Association Convention. And I was on the program! What an experience! I was a nervous wreck, but I loved it. I have become such a ham. I think I can trace that back to my brief career in radio last fall. I've not been the same since.

Although there are only three and a half weeks of school for me this month, I feel as if I have put in seven weeks already. It's a strange phenomenon that one tries to cram in all of the things not yet accomplished as time runs out—and the shorter the time, the more cramming must be done. We worked with careers this month in our learning stations using the theme "What's My Line?" Each station provided many opportunities for students to explore career alternatives and to think ahead to the future as they plan the courses they will be taking for the next several years. In conjunction with our theme, I

Career day

asked Mr. Topps if we could have a career day at school and invite people who are successful in various occupations to meet with students, describe their jobs, and answer questions.

Two of the guidance counselors—Kay Rears and Guy Dance—and I contacted 50 people in different jobs and asked them to participate. The response from both middle school and high school students was overwhelming. The school board members, who were invited to attend, were quite impressed with the number of participating occupations and with the number of students who chose to spend part of their free time in the gym where the different people had set up their tables and chairs. Students were permitted to visit a different person (occupation) every 20 minutes. A master list of those attending the career day, and the times each would have sessions, was made available to all students. In that way the students could explore their particular interests. I think that even Mr. Topps, who had been so supportive throughout the whole thing, was amazed at how well the day went. He told me that as a result of this success he hopes to make this a regular feature of the school year. With earlier planning and more people involved, he feels that the program could be expanded. Many of the people who were here were the parents of students in this school; Carmela was so delighted when her mother came to school (missing some of her precious hours of sleep) to talk about jobs at the local shoe factory and the special training and skills needed to do her job. The day really stimulated a lot of discussion and writing among my students.

USSW

The students have been bringing their USSW notebooks up to me lately to share some of the things they are especially proud of. I had asked them to go through their notebooks and throw out those writings that they know they will not rewrite and to reorganize those which they have edited and rewritten so that we could make bound copies of some of their best writings. Many of them, however, don't trust their own perceptions; they want me to choose the best ones. I can't seem to convince them of the fact that something I like isn't necessarily the best. So we now have a review board consisting of eight people. Students who would like feedback as to which writing others consider to be their best submit their writings to this board. At least three members of the board will react to them with a numerical ranking from 1 to 5, with 5 being the highest.

Everyone benefits from this. The review board members are getting experience reading and evaluating writing. The student who submits the writings is getting reactions which heesh is free to take or not. Many of them have already bound together volumes of writings which they have proudly contributed to our classroom library so that their names will live in perpetuity.

Having finally finished my adolescents' novel, I submitted a few chapters to the review board and waited for their responses. They categorically refused to endorse it for binding for the classroom library. With their comments (no numerical rankings given), which were very positive, was a list of addresses of publishers for me to try sending my book to. I was pleased, but fortunately, realistic; it's a *nice* story, but not a great one. I guess I'll have to bind it secretly and place the book on the shelves next year.

There will be lots of other books on the shelves next year, too. Lee Yung and I were having lunch together one day last month, and she mentioned that her students were somewhat envious of mine because of their thriving newspaper. She said that she had talked them out of their original plan to come out with a rival newspaper, but only with the promise that she would approach me and see if my newspaper group would work with them on some sort of project so that they could have a pizza party at the end of school, too.

"Well, Lee, what do you suggest? I think it should be something useful and related to the language arts; the prime purpose should not be to raise money, but that could be a side benefit."

"Some of the kids thought that we could sell something, like at an auction," she replied.

I thought back to the last auction that Al and I had attended. The work was incredible, and it really wasn't language arts or reading related. But they were fun. And I had gotten that huge box of old books for only . . .

Book fair

"Lee, I've got it! We'll have a book fair! That would be a service project and a money-maker too. It'll keep the kids busy for weeks!"

The students were intrigued. They wanted to know if it would be like a regular fair, with rides and food and acts. We discussed the impracticality and the unrelatedness of most of those activities, but what they were asking did trigger an idea. Most so-called book fairs I have attended have racks and racks of books, with little categorization and very little to entice one into buying the books. I saw no reason why some extra effort and an eye for details couldn't improve upon these. We got all 63 students together in my room, and Lee and I asked for suggestions. I put the words "Book Fair" on the chalkboard and asked the kids to web with me. (Lee's kids, having never done this before, were intrigued and caught on very quickly.) I reminded them that anything suggested had to be directly related to books and the promotion of those books.

FOR READERS TO DO TOGETHER:

Draw a picture of the web that Miss Yung and Mrs. Wright's students devised. How many different activities did you come up with? Would there be problems implementing any of your suggestions? Plan a schedule and timetable for the completion of this activity.

After the webbing was completed, we began to make a timetable to follow and a list of tasks to be completed. We also arranged the time for our next entire-group meeting. Chairpersons volunteered to head up each group and to have a progress report at the next meeting which was only one week away. The director of the First Annual Upton Hill Book Fair was chosen by the group. I knew that Rob was sufficiently conscientious to oversee the program and would not be hesitant to come to me if there were any problems.

The second meeting of this group was called to order by Rob. He asked for reports from each chairperson. One by one they indicated that each committee had been hard at work and the project was moving ahead well. The publicity committee showed us a newspaper and radio release that they had prepared to inform the public. The book fair was to be held during school hours, but we were inviting interested adults to drop by the school from 10 A.M. to 6 P.M. on the day of the fair. We wanted to make the books available to teachers and others who might not be able to come during school hours. They had a glowing report written for both the local newspaper and for the school paper which would come out simultaneously ("cause we don't want to scoop anybody," Pat explained). They were hard at work on a series of posters to be displayed around town and all over the school.

The book selection committee told us that they had established nine categories of books and a miscellaneous category in which they put anything that did not fit into the other nine. They had contacted a company that would send books on consignment for a book fair, and any not sold would be sent back to the company. Not only would we receive a percentage of the total amount of money earned, but we would also receive a certain number of books for our room libraries for every so many books sold. The books had been ordered and were expected to arrive a week before the fair so that we could sort them out.

The entertainment committee announced that they would need help. Their group had decided that they would set up ten different tables in the gym, decorated so as to reflect the main idea of that category. They needed decorators and people to work in the booths. They also wanted to have traveling skits that would set up and perform (with a minimum of props) little shows during the entire day. There was to be a puppet booth where various books could be featured. Of course, the skits and any other activities had to relate to books we would have for sale. They only had a month to work on everything. On the day of the fair, costumes, some still in need of a few stitches, were brought to school and finished up. Of course, at this point, our entire class time was donated to the cause. The paperbacks had arrived a little late (the day before), and we were frantically sorting them into their preassigned categories. Lee and I seemed to be everywhere and nowhere on that day. I will never know how I survived, but 6:15 arrived, and the last customer was ushered out the door. We boxed up the remaining books (since we didn't have to send them back for a week) and placed them in the office. Throughout the next week, whenever anyone had free time, heesh would go to the office to sell books. In that way we sold 38 more books and had fewer to pack up to ship out. The book fair was enormously successful—both financially and from the standpoint of morale—but what a lot of work! Worth it? Oh, yes! Do it again? Are you kidding?

P.S. I had finished this journal and had gone home yesterday. The students have been gone for two days now, and I too will be leaving for the summer in just a few more minutes, but I came back to the school to pick up some materials and to turn this journal in to the office. I heard someone in my room, so I crept up and peeked in the room, and there was Dusty, our janitor, standing by the graffiti board, writing something. I backed out and down the hall and then pretended, with many loud noises, that I was approaching the room for the first time. Dusty greeted me as he swept through the doorway and down the hall. I was so curious. I went up to the previously bare board and saw what he had written: "I have scoured the restrooms to find some graffiti for this board!"

Presentation at the International Reading Association

Rita Wright stood hesitantly looking around the huge airport baggage terminal trying to spot a sky cap who could help with her enormous load of luggage. Not everyone arrived here with five pieces, all of them large. Finally, she settled back into the cab en route to her hotel and began to relax and then tense up again. She had relaxed because she had managed to get through the huge airport with no loss of luggage; she was becoming tense because she realized that what she had just accomplished was the easy part. It was Tuesday evening; on Thursday morning, Rita would be making a presentation to scores of reading teachers from all over the world.

She arrived at the hotel and checked into the room she was to share with her college roommate who had lived in another state for many years. She looked forward to the reunion and, she had to admit, to a rather late supper! Over dinner she and Lottie English shared reminiscences and laughed over never-to-be-forgotten girlhood experiences. Finally they got around to discussing the current conference.

"Well, Rita, I don't envy you. I can remember those huge rooms they use for the various sessions — some are just packed while others are embarrassingly empty. You just never know. How did you know how much to prepare?"

"I prepared handouts for 150 people and made a sign which I will put outside the door that announces that my session is filled. That should do it! I know how frustrating it is not to get a handout because there are too many people in the session, some of whom only come at the last moment to help themselves to any handouts that are available."

"And other than that? How are you feeling?" Lottie inquired.

"As you well know, I'm a nervous wreck! If it weren't for Al's cool head and clear thinking, I would probably have tried to get on the wrong plane. What if 150 people do show up, Lottie? I know I'll never be able to handle so large a crowd, especially with what I have in mind."

"Oh no, Rita! You aren't planning to go creative with your presentation are you? Tell me you've just planned to stand up there and talk throughout the session. That's right, isn't it?"

The look of dismay on Rita's face told Lottie all she needed to know.

"Okay. Tell me about it. I'll help in any way I can — except, I *won't* talk, and I don't want any acknowledgement. This is your show, and I'm just your dumb English teacher friend who's helping out. Oh, Rita, *why* can't you just *talk* to them?"

"Well, you know me. I've never been terribly good at standing and talking in front of groups. Besides, it would seem pompous to stand in front of a group and *lecture* to them about how to personalize a reading/language arts program. Much better, I thought, to set up learning stations, just as I do with the students in my room. Mr. Topps—you remember I told you about him—thought it was by far the most honest approach and has helped me prepare materials and displays. I had a lot of support from other teachers and our content area reading specialist. And with your help . . . ?"

"Well, I hate grumpy roommates. Besides, I was coming anyway. You may as well take advantage of my remarkable organizational skills."

Back in their room, Rita and Lottie began unloading the four pieces of luggage which did not contain clothing and toiletries. Rita had packed them as they would be used, so that all of the materials for each station were together. She explained each station to Lottie and indicated what each of them would do. Late that night they fell into their beds and in moments were asleep, eager for the sessions they would attend the next day and eager to see the room which was assigned for Rita's presentation.

Thursday dawned bright and clear. Another very hot day but the room in which Rita's presentation would take place was air-conditioned to the point of being chilly. She wished for a lot of participants simply to make the room a little warmer. An hour and a half is a long time to be both scared and cold. A half hour before the scheduled session time, people began drifting into the meeting room. Every five minutes Rita would count them as she made her way around the room, setting up the stations for the session. She politely, but firmly, asked people not to go to the stations and/or take the handouts yet. That would come in due time.

One woman said, "You mean all of this is just for this session? We get copies of all that stuff?"

Reassured that this was true, the woman, placing materials on her recently vacated seat, left the room hurriedly. She came back in a few minutes with a smug smile on her face that was explained when 15 others came in and sat with the woman who pointed to the stations and clearly gesticulated what was on her mind.

Rita always hated to go to sessions that began late, so right on time, even as others were still streaming in the door and sitting on the floor, Rita began by introducing herself, telling them where she was from, and how many years she had taught. She also told them that she would talk *at* them for 15 minutes only, then they would be able to spend five minutes at each of the stations set up on the room's perimeters, and that finally they would get back together for the remaining time for questions. She told them that a timer would be set to go off every five minutes and that they were then welcome to spend another five minutes where they were or could go around the room counterclockwise to the next station. She told them that she must insist that they follow this procedure, for there were too many people in the room to be wandering around indiscriminately.

Rita began the formal part of her presentation after the "housekeeping" details were out of the way. "My classroom was set up so that students could progress at a rate which was congruent with each one's learning style. One of the major thrusts this year was to try to help my students become independent learners. I am pleased to say that by the end of this year most of them were. They can be responsible for completing their various tasks with a minimal amount of nagging on my part. Actually, with the room regulations that the students themselves established, I do far less nagging than they do to one another.

"I guess that I would attribute the main success of my program to three factors: everyday, without fail, we have a sustained silent reading period that all of us participate in. In order for USSR to work, it is necessary that I set a model for my students by reading too. Our principal even comes in periodically so that the students see him reading as well. A second factor that I consider of paramount importance is sustained silent writing. Twice a week the students take out their writing notebooks and silently write for a period of time. I too, of course, write at the same time. Once a month, each of us looks in the writing notebook to find some piece we care enough about to want to edit. This editing is done during the regular working time, for the USSW time is kept for writing only. In one of the stations, you'll see samples of writing from several students that show monthly progress in writing skills. I didn't just choose my *best* students, either, for I always become a little angry when people try to fool me with work that they claim is 'typical' and then I find out that it *was* typical — but for geniuses! So some of the writing you'll see will obviously be from average and below average students, but I couldn't resist bringing some work from my 'genius' group too." Rita paused for breath before launching into her third and final factor.

"Students in my classes work almost entirely at instructional level. Not always, because I don't think that students should be deprived of experiences with independent level materials. However, I do avoid frustration level work, for it only causes student unrest and a sense of failure for teacher and student alike. How I achieve this is part of what I'll be showing and explaining to you today.

"Diagnosis is the heart of any successful program, as are appropriate assignments based on that diagnosis. I got an oral reading measure of each student by having him or her read from a grade level book and then decided whether or not that book was too hard, too easy, or just right. On the basis of that initial diagnosis, the students read to me again the next day in a harder or easier book so that I could refine my diagnosis. This went on for as many days as was necessary in order to get an oral reading level for each student. Then I asked each student a series of questions developed around a reading passage in the book that his or her oral reading indicated might be appropriate. If the student was unable to comprehend in that level book, then an easier book was selected for instructional level reading. An interest inventory completed my initial diagnosis.

"I tried different grouping methods throughout the year for my students. I did this in part so that there would not be any stigma attached to being in any specific group, but I also did it in order to vary the classroom routine. Sometimes I would work with students grouped by ability. At other times I would randomly group students so that the brighter ones could teach the less capable ones both directly and by example. If poorer students never have clear examples of logical thinking and reasoning modeled for them, how can they possibly be expected to manifest clear thinking themselves? We had interest groupings too, with student readings and assignments developed around themes rather than around a specific story.

"Students did a lot of their own checking, and then I did the evaluation. There is a difference! As much as possible, I made materials self-checking so that I was spared that interminable job. In my evaluation, I looked over their papers (which they had marked at a grading table) and wrote comments on them that indicated how well I thought they were doing. All of their work was kept in a folder which each student was responsible for turning in once a week. I taught the students, when checking their own work, to write a C for 'correct' in front of the right responses and to leave unmarked the others that needed redoing. I try to put the emphasis on what students have done well, rather than on those things that need improvement."

Rita went on to explain her classroom organization and other management devices she used. She then set the timer and told them to form groups of no more than 15 people. Each group was to stay together as they progressed from station to station. They were permitted to go back to other stations, but they could not go forward to any stations they had not yet seen, except as a group. Rita concluded her remarks and asked them to begin their progress from station to station, as she and Lottie would also do; Rita was reassured to see Lottie, hands clasped over her head in a sign of victory, silently cheering the "first act."

Each of the stations had explanatory material in it, so that Rita and Lottie were not really required to circulate at all, but Rita felt that some of the participants might have questions or concerns which they wouldn't want to bring up in a large group.

The first station that Rita came to was the one on work folders. Participants there were listening to the four-minute tape she had prepared and were looking at sample folders she had brought, each with its schedule and record-keeping chart. The only question here was, "How *do* you do it every week?" She smiled and shrugged and said, "I have a high level of energy, besides that, the students eventually take a lot of responsibility for filling in their schedules." She passed on to the next station.

The next station she went to had charts with rules for USSW and USSR and samples of students writing notebooks. She had thought of bringing some of the books read in her class this year but had settled instead for a listing of 100 or so titles read by some of the students during the course of the year at USSR time. The time charts the students were so proud of were there too.

Rita was making her slow but steady progress around the room and its stations when she was attracted to a commotion at a station several away from her. She walked quickly over and asked the people standing there if she could be of any help. The station sign said, "Classroom Books."

"Oh, Mrs. Wright! These are just darling! What a cute idea to have the children make their own dictionaries, thesauri, and books of quotations!"

Mrs. Wright had an instinctive mistrust of anyone who gushed.

"Thank you, I'll tell the class. What you see there represents a great deal of work and preparation. None of them started out as a book, you see. Your group just came from the "Pictures" station, and there you saw our graffiti board. That's where the quotes originated. And in another picture you saw charts hung all over the room; those charts, from our 'word gathering,' grew into the thesaurus. The dictionaries were also a necessity as each student's group of words grew to an unmanageable number."

"Wouldn't it have been easier on you just to have announced to the class that they would produce a thesaurus than to go through all the time-consuming work of those word gatherings and making the charts for them?" a young man asked.

"Actually, I think it would have been harder. You see, these books grew out of necessity and out of their own ideas, bit by bit. To have begun the quote book simply to have a quote book, rather than to preserve some of the excellent graffiti they were finding and producing, would, I feel, have been contrary to the spirit in my classroom. It's also a lot harder to explain to students what you mean if they have not themselves been involved daily."

Mrs. Wright left the group and went back to the station she had left in such a hurry. Finding no questions there, she moved on to the school newspaper station. Here she had placed copies of each of the issues to date and a handout on how it had gotten started, lists of the various committees who worked on some aspect, and how it was distributed. Several teachers were remarking on the quality of the writing.

"Don't you sort these out so that some of this stuff doesn't get in?" asked one horrified teacher.

"Oh, no, I don't have time for that. I'm a busy lady. The job of editing is done by the two editors, Pat and Sharon. Occasionally they will request help, but if I took over, then it wouldn't be their newspaper, would it? You should see some of the stuff they rejected. You'll notice that the errors in the paper are typographical; they are very careful about punctuation and usage. Or were you referring to content?"

At the woman's nod, Rita just shrugged her shoulders and said, "They all buy it."

She wandered over to "File Box Activities." Again there was a handout with directions and her file box of activities to go with some of the materials she had brought. There were chuckles, exclamations of surprise at some of the excellent ideas she had created to go with comic books and car magazines, and groans of appreciation for the hours of work it represented.

"How did you ever do it?" asked one man.

"After my initial group, I just kept doing a few a night. After a couple of months, it was amazing what I had. It's not impossible that way, for each one only takes a few minutes. I could never have disciplined myself to sit down and do the whole thing in one awful weekend."

Moving to the next station, "Book Boxes," Rita noticed with chagrin that some stations had 25 and others only 2 or 3 people. She saw several teachers going from station to station only picking up handouts and never bothering to look at what the stations involved. That angered her, for she realized that many of these same teachers would be furious with their students for not observing the rules and following the directions. Oh, well, she wasn't here to teach manners to a group of fellow school teachers. The group at the book box station greeted her with enthusiasm, though. The ideas were unique and interesting. They gave her many kudos.

The next group was listening to a tape about the process of using the modified language experience approach with middle school students. They were looking through some of the group and individual stories and follow-up activities she had brought along. She had charted on big sheets of poster board all of the monthly theme webs that the class and/or she had created during the year. Another handout explained the process of webbing and how she had involved the students.

The last of the stations was a photo collection of various activities in her classroom. She had pictures of all of her stations for the entire year, many different pictures of the graffiti board, the book fair, newspaper production and distribution, and pictures of reading groups working alone, with a monitor, or with her. A brief sentence under each picture identified it.

Rita ascended the small stage just as the final bell rang announcing to one and all that it was time to get back to their seats for a final wrap-up. All of this took longer than Rita had anticipated, so that there were, in actuality, only a few minutes left of her allotted time.

"Are there any questions in the brief time we have left?" she asked.

"Uh, yes, Mrs. Wright. It would appear that a great many of these activities are student initiated or at least in response to students 'needs,' whatever that may be. Now, tell us truly, your classroom isn't really like this is it? There's no way it could be!"

"Right. Many of these are student initiated or in response to the needs of my students," Rita began, trying not to show her anger. "But, I must correct you. This display does truly reflect my classroom. As to whether or not anyone could teach as I do, I just don't know. But what I do know is that it is the only way *I* can teach."

"How do substitute teachers fare in your class, Mrs. Wright?" asked a matronly looking lady in the front.

"Well, I'll tell you, I'm not exactly sure, never having been there at the time." There were chuckles of appreciation around the room. She continued, "But I do know from the notes that have been left on my desk and from talking with the principal that if the substitute is willing to let them tell *him* or *her* what they know they must do, things go along rather well. As soon as she or he tries to ignore them and their offers of help, the class starts to deteriorate. It arouses a rather primitive instinct in them to 'get the teacher.' "

"Mrs. Wright, I speak for several of us here in this row, and we want to know what the kids at home are using this week at school? It appears that you brought all your materials with you!"

Laughter greeted this comment and Rita said, "Oh, no. I only brought the less dog-eared copies of my materials. Besides, with the newspaper coming out later this week, many of them are gainfully occupied."

Time was up. Rita and Lottie wearily began the packing of Rita's classroom back into the boxes and made plans to enjoy the rest of the conference until they left for home on Saturday evening. Now that it was over, Rita was pleased that she had come and had made a presentation, but she truly doubted that she would agree to do it again for at least a few years. However, in the back of her mind the ghost of a question was forming: "Let's see—what *could* I do next year?"

Unit Four
Remedial Reading in the Middle/Secondary School

12 Remedial Reading

ANYONE WHO IS familiar with today's middle and high schools is aware that illiteracy and lack of discipline are severe problems for many teachers and students. Whether rightly or wrongly, social forces have encouraged students to stay in school longer and have discouraged teachers from retaining students for any reason. These forces have resulted in many students attending middle and high schools today who 25 years ago would have dropped out, been pushed out, or been retained in the lower grades for one or more years. Unfortunately, increasing the likelihood that these students will stay in school and be promoted has not in any way guaranteed they will learn to read and write or that they will learn to behave in acceptable ways toward teachers and peers.

Parents, teachers, administrators, school board members, and legislators have become increasingly concerned with the problems of literacy and discipline in today's middle and secondary schools. Many states have decided to require all students to pass a high school competency test before receiving a high school diploma. Some states are emphasizing reading instruction in the primary grades in an attempt to prevent later reading failure. Some states are attempting, by a variety of means, to end so-called "social promotion." While these actions may increase pressure on both students and teachers for more and better efforts, it should be obvious to all that testing and failing students have been part of education for a long time and have never before guaranteed that students will succeed at learning. Neither will prevention of reading or writing problems do much for those students who are already in the middle or high school and who are illiterate.

If neither promoting students, retaining students, encouraging students to stay in school, testing students, or preventing future students from having reading problems will solve the reading, writing, or behavior problems of today's middle or secondary students, effective remedial programs are called for. This chapter will discuss the major issues and outline the basic principles of middle and secondary school remedial reading instruction. Chapters 13 and 14 will show how the principles laid down in this chapter might be applied in an actual middle/secondary remedial reading class.

Selecting Students For Remedial Reading Instruction

Unless all students are to receive reading instruction, some process of selecting students for special reading must be developed. When resources limit the number who can receive special help, it is hardly an educational decision to determine who most "needs" or "deserves" that help. Such a decision is really a political one. This section of the chapter will discuss three philosophies of selection with respect to the educational consequences of each. Whether or not one philosophy tends to select students who most need or deserve remedial reading instruction must be left to the interpretation of the reader's ethical, moral, and legal beliefs.

The "Right to Read" Philosophy of Selection

In the early 1970s, the phrase "right to read" became an important term in American education. The phrase represented the commitment of the federal government to the eradication of functional illiteracy in this country. In practice this meant that schools and nonschool agencies were funded to reach as many people as possible who could not read at the sixth-grade level and bring them up to that level. Once clients reached this functional literacy, they were to be graduated from the program to make room for others who lacked that basic level of ability.

This practice was based on the philosophy that every American is born with the inalienable right to learn to read at a basic level. Being able to read "at grade level" or "well enough to attend college" were not the standards applied. The right to read simply meant the right to achieve functional literacy in reading.

If one were to practice the right to read philosophy in selecting students for middle/secondary remedial reading instruction, one would simply select the poorest readers in the school. Selecting these students then becomes a problem of developing testing and interview procedures adequate to ensure that the poorest readers in the school are discovered and placed in the program.

Methods for Selecting the Poorest Readers

Teacher referrals.   This method has the advantage of selecting the students who are actually experiencing the most difficulty in school regardless of test performance. Unfortunately, many teachers are unreliable judges of which students are having the most difficulty. Some teachers are prone to refer students who are discipline problems, whether or not these students are poor readers.

Standardized achievement tests. This method is often used because the test scores already exist and can be used without additional testing. The scores are notoriously inaccurate, however, because a chance or "guess" score on an achievement test designed for use with older students is several grade levels above where some of the poorest readers actually read. As a result, poor readers who guess well may not be included in the remedial program. All test authorities know that these tests are not dependable enough to be used to make placement decisions for individual students, yet they continue to be used by some schools for that purpose.

Criterion-referenced skills tests. These tests determine the degree of mastery a student has attained in each of a set of supposed reading skills tested in isolation. Once poor readers have been identified by some other means, they may have value to specify which skills certain students need to be taught. They should never be used to identify poor readers, because they are skills tests, not reading tests. Some students can read but don't know the skills; others know the skills but can't read. This occurs because of our inability to know what "real" reading skills are. Any list of reading skills is someone's best guess.

Informal tests. Tests made within a school for the specific purpose of selecting the poorest readers in that school have the advantage of being based on the particular materials and expectations of that school. Their principle disadvantage is their testing error; they have not been rigorously developed or standardized.

It should be obvious that economy of time and money requires that any method of selecting a school's poorest readers must be quick and inexpensive, but it would be foolish to use a method that was not reasonably accurate as well. It is recommended that teacher referrals be used in combination with two or more scores obtained from either standardized or informal tests for selecting students for a remedial reading program based on the "right to read" philosophy. (For an example of how this recommendation might actually be applied, see pages 287-288.)

The "Upward Bound" Philosophy of Selection

"Upward Bound" has been a lesser known cycle of federal funding which has had as its purpose the improvement of students' basic skills so that they might be able to take advantage of higher education. The population to be served by these grants has generally been quite different from that served by right to read funds. The attempt has been made to reach those students who are sufficiently behind in basic skills so that they risk failure if they enter higher education, yet are sufficiently grounded in both achievement and intellect to make them good candidates for success in higher education if they receive remedial instruction.

If one were to practice the upward bound philosophy in selecting students for middle or secondary school remedial reading instruction, one would select those students with academic problems but who were not so far behind that they would be bad risks for postsecondary education after remedial instruction. In practice, this generally means that any student who is reading below grade level is eligible as long as that student is no more than two or three years below grade level. Selecting these students then becomes a problem of developing test and interview procedures adequate to ensure that average to poor readers, with ambitions to continue their education beyond high school, are selected and placed in the program.

Methods for Selecting the Most Promising Poor Readers

Self-referrals. Students who seek special help are most likely to benefit from it. Moreover, seeking such help suggests that the person is ambitious enough to succeed in higher education without superior abilities in the basic skills. Of course, the student cannot be expected to be a good judge of his or her reading in comparison with grade-level or with the abilities of the other students in the school.

Teacher referrals, standardized achievement tests, and informal tests. Each of these methods for student selection has the same advantages and disadvantages as does selecting students by the right to read philosophy, with the added problem that in trying to identify students within a range of ability and ambition, testing errors and errors in human judgment are even more likely to occur. It is recommended that a system of self-referral, teacher referral, and the use of two or more scores on standardized or informal tests be used in combination for selecting students for a remedial reading program based on the upward bound philosophy.

The "Reading Potential" Philosophy of Selection

Over the years in education, a number of reading clinicians have argued that if a person were reading at potential, it would only be frustrating to everyone concerned to attempt to raise that person's reading level by remedial instruction. The more famous of these clinicians have developed competing formulas for estimating how close to potential a particular individual is reading. These formulas either use IQ, or the mental age from IQ tests, as the principal means of estimating reading potential or the maximum level at which the person can be expected to read.

If one were to practice the reading potential philosophy in selecting students for secondary remedial reading instruction, one would select those students reading furthest below their potentials. In practice, this generally means that the most recent IQ score that students have on their permanent records is used in conjunction with the most recent reading score they have on their permanent records in a reading potential formula to estimate at which percentage of potential each student is reading. Students who are reading most below potential are selected for remedial instruction.

Methods for Selecting Students Reading Most Below Potential

Reading potential formulas. Whatever intuitive appeal the reading potential philosophy may have, there is no reasonable means for determining what percentage of potential a student has achieved in reading. The use of these formulas is based on the following assumptions:

1. That there is a high correlation between reading ability and IQ or mental age;
2. That it is possible to read at potential;
3. That a group-administered, pencil-and-paper, intelligence test is powerful enough that an individual's score can be used to make placement decisions about him or her;
4. That a group-administered, standardized achievement test gives reading scores that are dependable enough that an individual's scores can be used to make placement decisions about him or her;
5. That reading scores from a standardized achievement test are interpretable as estimates of the level of materials students can read; and,
6. That the formula used correctly represents the relationship between intelligence and reading expectancy.

Because each one of these assumptions is either seriously questionable or has been refuted, it is difficult to see how any knowledgeable person could counsel the use of reading potential formulas to place students in remedial reading programs.

Educational Implications of the Three Philosophies of Selection

Each of the three philosophies, purely applied, will result in remedial reading classes with a distinct make-up, and each will leave some students unserved who can profit from such instruction. Combining philosophies in an eclectic manner will result in still different students being selected or rejected.

The right to read philosophy will generally result in classes with the school's poorest readers. In some schools this will mean a preponderance of students reading at or below third-grade level. One justification for selecting such students for remedial instruction is that if no such instruction is given, they are at a loss to help themselves. They cannot find materials of interest in either school or public libraries and their expectation of failure and frustration makes them reluctant to seek help outside the school.

On the other hand, such students cannot be expected to make significant progress unless two factors are present: (1) a remedial teacher trained in teaching the severely disabled reader in small-group situations and (2) a long-range commitment of more than one year of remedial instruction for these students. Any student who improved 1½ years in reading for each year of instruction would improve 6 years in reading over a four-year period of remediation.

The upward bound philosophy will generally result in classes with capable and motivated students in them. In most schools, this will mean a preponderance of students reading one or two years behind grade level. The most successful program for these students will probably emphasize meaning vocabulary and study and reference skills along with independent reading in tradebooks selected by the students themselves. The goal of the program would be to make more successful students out of persons who can already read at or above a level of functional literacy. The likelihood of success is high. Unfortunately, it will be difficult to explain to parents and teachers why remedial reading instruction is being given to students with minor problems and no help is being given to students who are totally unable to cope with their content-area subjects.

The reading potential philosophy will generally result in classes with a broad range of reading levels and problems. Students with below-average IQs will seldom be included in such classes because it will be difficult for them to score low enough on a standardized achievement test to be classified as reading "below potential." Students with IQs in the average range will tend to be included if they read several years behind grade level, and even students with very high IQs who read at grade level may also be eligible. Reading levels from beginning first-grade level to grade level and everywhere in between are likely. Students who would be eligible for a learning-disabilities class because of their reading would, in every case, probably be eligible for the remedial reading program, because a discrepancy between measured mental ability and measured achievement is a major criterion on which the diagnosis of learning disabilities is based.

FOR THE READER TO DO:

Consider these nine hypothetical students (assume they are all in the tenth grade):

Student	Reading Score on Standardized Achievement Test	Mental Age from Group IQ Test
1	3.1*	12.4†
2	3.5	9.2
3	4.2	10.0
4	5.1	12.3
5	6.0	15.8
6	6.9	13.9
7	7.8	16.8
8	8.5	16.5
9	9.6	13.7

*Third grade, first month.
†Twelve and four-tenths years.

1. Select three students by the right to read philosophy.
2. Select three students by the upward bound philosophy.
3. Select three students by the reading potential philosophy. Use Harris' (1960) formula:

$$\text{Percentage of potential at which a person is reading} = \frac{\text{Standardized reading score}}{\text{Mental age} - 5.2}$$

Organizing For Remedial Reading

Before beginning the diagnosis and remediation of reading difficulties for older remedial readers, several decisions concerning scheduling, size and frequency of classes, materials, and classroom organization have to be made. These decisions will be made somewhat differently depending on the philosophy of selection used to determine which students are to be given priority for admission to the program.

Scheduling, Size, and Frequency of Middle/Secondary Remedial Classes

If it can be assumed that older remedial students, regardless of philosophy of selection used, are having at least some difficulty coping with the reading requirements of their content-area subjects, then it does not make much sense to increase their course loads by adding a reading course. On the other hand, if reading is taken in such a way that the completion of subject-area requirements is postponed or delayed, the students' progress toward eventual graduation is slowed, thus increasing the discouragement for already frustrated students. As a result, taking a reading course may indirectly contribute to a student's dropping out of school, rather than preventing it. Even though school politics may provide obstacles to it, the best interests of the remedial student can only be served by allowing reading to be taken as a credit course, in lieu of a subject-area requirement or elective.

Once this is admitted, the question arises as to which courses it may be substituted for. Two approaches may be taken. The first approach would be to substitute reading for those courses it most resembles in goals, methods, and materials. Taking this approach would almost always result in English credit being given for reading, although reading could conceivably be improved using appropriate material from any content subject. A reading course that emphasized the reading of tradebooks and the improvement of writing would parallel the recommended English curriculum of English education authorities. The second approach would be to substitute reading for those courses that require the most reading and consequently those in which the students are probably doing poorest in anyway. Ekwall (1976), who takes such an approach, has suggested that remedial students take reading in lieu of social studies or science if these subjects rely heavily on textbook or other written materials.

In either case, reading must be substituted in toto for the subject-area course. The authors continue to be amazed that some schools pull a remedial student from a content-area class two or three times a week, leaving him or her in the regular class the other two or three days. How can a student, who is already struggling in a course, be expected to survive in it if he or she is forced to miss 40 or even 60 percent of the classes? And remedial instruction in reading for only one class period per day must be given five days a week if any appreciable progress is to be expected for the majority of students.

Scheduling may also be a problem once it is determined which subjects reading may be taken in lieu of. If any attempt is made to equalize class size across the different periods of the school day, either some students must have their entire schedules rearranged or some students who are eligible for the program must be excluded simply because of scheduling. If the remedial classes are to be of varying size, the largest classes should be in the morning when discipline is generally better and learning is most likely to occur. The smallest classes

For remedial programs in which a right to read philosophy of selection is used, the classes should be considerably smaller than classes in which the upward bound philosophy of selection is used. From personal experience, the authors do not see how an unaided teacher can succeed with more than 15 severely disabled students at a time, and many would find that number excessive.

When the upward bound philosophy is used, classes of up to 20 would be reasonable, provided that sufficient instructional materials were available. In either case, at least 45 minutes is required for effective classes. Those middle schools that schedule a 30-minute period for special reading do not realize that they make any individualization of instruction almost impossible. If remedial instruction is to be successful, it must have some individualization built into it.

Remedial Materials

Those of us who are so-called reading authorities are often wary of cookbook approaches to the teaching of reading. We are fond of saying, "Why, you can teach reading with a phonebook if you know what you're doing." While it is certainly true that the teacher is much more important than the materials and that "materials don't teach, teachers do," it is unreasonable to expect remedial reading teachers to construct all their own materials. A teacher will have more time to plan instruction and carry it out if he or she is not required to spend hours each week duplicating previous efforts and "reinventing the wheel." Moreover, it would be a rare teacher who could duplicate the quality of some of the high-interest/low-vocabulary materials being produced especially for older remedial readers.

Of course, a reliance on materials requires that the teacher know enough about how reading is learned and improved to evaluate their quality and potential contribution to the remedial program. The teacher must always place students in materials based on diagnostic information of what instructional needs those students have. The authors have seen remedial programs that were flashy and appeared on first glance to be individualized — no two students working on the same thing. A closer look revealed, however, that each student was merely being rotated through several kits and other commercial programs, working on first-grade level phonics on Monday, third-grade level structural analysis on Tuesday, comprehension of short paragraphs at second-grade level on Wednesday, map and graph skills on Thursday, and round-robin oral reading in a play of unknown difficulty on Friday. These programs are "materials poor," having no continuity of instruction and having little long-term success because the students are not receiving assistance in their specific areas of need. If incidental instruction were going to succeed for these students, it is likely that it would have done so before they arrived at the middle or secondary level.

Materials, then, are a crucial part of any successful remedial program in reading at the middle/secondary level. Such materials fall into four classes:

1. *Teaching aids:* includes filmstrips, transparencies, charts, sentence strips, flashcards, word wheels, and any other material the teacher manipulates while working with one or more students on specific reading or reference/study skills.

2. *Self-teaching materials:* includes word-identification workbooks and kits, reference/study-skill workbooks and kits, machine-delivered programs, comprehension kits, vocabulary workbooks and kits, and any other material which the students can use with only occasional assistance.

3. *Instructional-level materials at appropriate interest level:* includes all collections of short reading selections, whether narrative or expository, that are appropriate for remedial students with respect to both difficulty and interest. These materials correspond to elementary basal readers in that students may be placed at their instructional levels and given comprehension-oriented instruction in small-group settings. Unfortunately, few publishers have produced any materials directly for this purpose. Any set of graded materials can be used, of course, but the teacher must plan each lesson if there is no teacher's guide.

4. *Trade books:* a trade book is any book that is written solely to be read for enjoyment and/or information. They include novels, collections of short stories, biographies, plays, how-to books, and nonfiction. They do not include textbooks. Many publishers now produce high-interest/low-vocabulary books. These are also classifiable as trade books.

All four types of materials serve useful functions in the remedial reading class. Teaching aids help the teacher teach more effectively. Self-teaching materials should only be used to provide practice, since they really do not teach. They are necessary, however, in order for students to practice skills while other students are receiving instruction in new skills. Instructional-level materials are the most important part of the remedial program, since maximum improvement in reading for most remedial students comes from being taught directly by the teacher in materials at their instructional level. Trade books are almost as important because reading for enjoyment in easy materials is the only way most remedial students can develop the automatic use of reading skills and develop the habit of regular reading.

Organizing a Classroom for Remedial Reading

The remedial reading room should be organized to accomplish three goals:

1. To make it possible for small-group instruction, independent reading, and individual activities to occur simultaneously without students in one activity distracting students in another;

2. To reduce the similarity between the reading classroom and the classrooms where the student is having difficulty; and

3. To reduce the stigma that automatically becomes associated with any remedial program.

Even when the upward bound philosophy of selection is used, any middle or high school remedial reading program will have some students who are discouraged with school. When the reading potential philosophy is used, this tendency increases, and when the right to read philosophy is used, most of the students will be very discouraged. If a remedial reading program is to succeed with these discouraged students, the classroom itself must be a pleasant, positive place.

In the experience of the authors, many severely disabled readers, and even some mildly disabled readers, really do not believe they can improve significantly in reading, that reading can ever by enjoyable, or that schoolwork can be anything but frustrating for them. Classroom organization is one way the remedial reading teacher can break the habit of failure for some students.

The poor readers who are used to attending class where whole-group instruction is administered, and who are used to spending those classes in hopes of not being called on, find themselves less able to be aggressively passive in small-group instruction at their level or in independent work geared for their individual needs and abilities. Moreover, they soon discover that, unlike in whole-group situations, they are able to take risks and make mistakes without everyone in the class being aware of them. Such alternate classroom organizations do not insure learning, but they may prevent the student from bringing a pattern of failure-oriented behavior into the remedial class.

More subtly, alternate classroom organizations may contribute to reducing the stigma of remedial programs, especially if an alternate classroom organization is combined with various gimmicks like having some top students come to the reading room for independent reading projects for elective credit, having occasional activities in which a well-known athlete or other celebrity visits the reading room, or awarding records and posters to students on a random basis simply because they are enrolled in the program rather than as rewards for work. When students who are ineligible for the program begin to express an interest in it, the stigma has obviously been reduced.

Diagnosis of Reading Difficulties in the Middle/High School

In the diagnosis of reading difficulties at any level, there are two general approaches to methodology: standardized-test diagnosis and informal diagnosis. Standardized-test diagnosis relies on commercially produced norm-referenced or criterion-referenced tests,[1] whether administered to groups or individuals.

---

[1] All tests yield scores like 3.2, 45%, 72, 5, etc. How one interprets a test score depends on whether it is norm- or criterion-referenced. A norm-referenced test yields scores that are interpreted by seeing how a particular score compares with the scores obtained from a norm-group of persons; a criterion-referenced test yields scores that are interpreted by seeing how a particular score compares with a criterion score of acceptable performance. A criterion-referenced test can be developed, given to one person, scored, and interpreted. A norm-referenced test must be given to a group of persons to establish norms before the test can be given to one person, scored, and interpreted.

Informal diagnosis relies on teacher-made tests and teacher observation of student reading behavior.

Standardized-Test Diagnosis

Standardized-test diagnosis makes use of one or more commercial, standardized, diagnostic reading tests. While these commercial tests have the advantages of already being constructed, of having been more-or-less rigorously developed, and of having standardized administration and interpretation procedures, the authors do not recommend their use with older remedial readers for three major reasons:

1. *They were developed primarily for use with elementary-aged pupils.* Passages to be read are generally of a length, style, mode of discourse, and interest which are inappropriate for older students. Moreover, they emphasize oral reading and word identification abilities when improving reading comprehension must be the priority if students in middle/secondary school are to survive in their classes and on graduation competency tests.

2. *Their construction generally does not reflect recent advances in understanding the reading process.* These tests to not differentiate between oral reading errors which maintain the meaning of the passage and those which do not. Often, word identification abilities are tested using nonsense syllables in isolation. These practices and others like them are not supported by recent opinion and research into the reading process (Goodman, 1965; Cunningham, 1975–1976; Spiegel, 1978).

3. *Measures of comprehension used by these tests usually are not reading dependent.* For example, Allington, Chodos, Domaracki, and Truex (1977) found that their group of third-graders averaged 32 percent of the questions correct on the *Diagnostic Reading Scales* (Spache, 1973) without even reading the passages. And the questions were not multiple-choice questions. The least that one should expect from a comprehension test is that the reader should have to read the passages in order to score well on the test.

Informal Diagnosis

Informal diagnosis consists of three subtypes: tests constructed by the teacher using prescribed test-construction procedures but made with materials or items available in the classroom; tests both constructed and designed by the teacher; and diagnosis by observation.

Teacher-made tests following established procedures. The principal example of this kind of teacher-made test is an informal reading inventory (IRI). Betts (1946) outlines procedures by which one can select passages from the actual materials to be used in instruction, have students read these passages, apply specific criteria to evaluate the students' performance in these passages, and determine from this procedure which, if any, of the passages are appropriate in difficulty for the student. Betts's criteria were:

	Word Identification Accuracy in Contextual Reading		Reading Comprehension Accuracy After Silent Reading
Independent level (Free reading level)	99%	and	90%
Instructional level	95%	and	75%
Frustration level	<90%	or	<50%

Cunningham (1977) has argued that procedures for constructing informal reading inventories should be determined by the methods used to teach the materials in which the student is to be placed. If students will not be asked to read orally in material, for example, they should not be asked to read orally to indicate which passages are most appropriate for placement.

Whether Betts's criteria or others which reflect teaching practices are used, an informal reading inventory can be used very effectively with older remedial readers because it is constructed from passages selected from the actual materials to be used with the students.

The cloze procedure (Taylor, 1953) is another example of how teachers may construct tests from their own materials using established test-construction procedures. As in informal reading inventories, representative passages are selected from available books. In this case, however, a cloze test is constructed from each passage by retyping the passage in the following manner: every fifth word is deleted and replaced by a blank of uniform length. This test is then administered to groups of students by giving them the cloze tests and asking them to write in each blank their best guess for what word they believe was originally there. The scores are interpreted in much the same way IRI scores are interpreted, but with different criteria being used (Bormuth, 1968):

Percentage of Exact Replacements on the Cloze Test

Independent level	58–100%
Instructional level	44–57%
Frustration level	0–43%

A third example of teacher-made tests following established procedures is miscue analysis[2] (Goodman and Burke, 1972). While much more discussion is necessary than is possible here, miscue analysis is a procedure in which teachers use a series of passages of various difficulties to obtain an appropriate sam-

[2]If Goodman and Burke's *Reading Miscue Inventory* (Macmillan, 1972) is used, miscue analysis would become a commercial, standardized, criterion-referenced test.

ple of the student's oral reading. All miscues (deviations from what the passage leads you to expect) which the student made in this sample of oral reading are qualitatively analyzed. This analysis is conducted by asking a series of questions about each miscue. These are the four questions from a simplified miscue analysis:

1. Did the miscue look like the original wording?
2. Did the miscue leave the syntax of the passage essentially the same?
3. Did the miscue leave the meaning of the passage essentially the same?
4. Did the reader successfully correct the miscue?

Miscue analysis is based on contemporary opinion on and research into the reading process. This fact has led Cooper and Petrosky (1976) to say that it "makes anything else currently available seem medieval." We feel that it is a valuable tool for teachers who are knowledgable in its use to diagnose students who have them stumped, but that it is too time consuming and narrow to be given to every student.

Any other test which teachers construct by using test-construction procedures established elsewhere would fit under this general rubric. Of course, the test will be only as good as the original test-construction procedures and the way they are applied.

FOR READERS TO DO TOGETHER:

Get together in groups. Have alternate groups make one level of an IRI or one cloze passage using graded high-interest/low-vocabulary materials. These should be duplicated, shared, and discussed with the whole group. Everyone should know how to construct both types of tests.

Teacher-designed tests.   Almost every remedial reading teacher has a few tasks or tests that he or she designed to test some aspect of reading performance. These tests often give information that cannot be readily obtained from either a commercial test or a teacher-made test using established procedures. They are inexpensive to construct, and teachers usually believe in them. The problem with them, of course, is that it is very difficult to create valid, reliable, and interpretable tests.

Diagnosis by observation.   Every test gives scores which have some error in them. This is true for both standardized and informal tests. Such error is due to students scoring worse on the test than they should because they do not understand the format of the test, because they do not feel well at the time of testing, or because they are anxious or nervous. Error also results when students score better on the test than they should because they cheat, or because they feel better than usual at the time of testing, or because the test allows them to take advantage of some special interest or knowledge they have. For this reason, any one test score must be considered only an estimate of the student's true score on that test (the score the student would have gotten had there been no error).

This fact has led most testing experts to recommend that no curriculum decisions be made for a student based on a single test score.

There are only two ways to eliminate error from test scores: (1) administer the test to a large group of students and look at the average score for the group as a whole or (2) administer parallel forms of the test to each student many times and look at the average score for each student across all testings. This average score tends to be error free because for every instance in which a student scored better than he or she should have, there should have been an instance in which a student scored worse than he or she should have. With a sufficiently large number of testings, these instances of error should cancel each other out. Unfortunately, this system of averaging scores does not seem very practical for diagnostic purposes. An average score for a group of students gives no help in making diagnostic decisions for one student. An average score for one student is impractical to obtain because it requires that each student be given parallel forms of the same test over and over again for weeks or months. The solution to this dilemma is for the teacher to give several standardized or informal tests to a student to get estimates of reading strengths and weaknesses and then to monitor the student on a daily basis using some system of diagnosis by observation. Diagnosis by observation has error like any other testing or data-collection procedure, but because observation is taking place every day, the cumulative effect of the observations tends to be error free. If a teacher knows how to observe students systematically and reliably while reading, he or she can supplement and substantiate standardized and informal test results with a great deal of easily obtainable data. In fact, the best teachers have always carefully observed their students' performance to determine which students were doing well and which ones were not. The following checklist is just one possible system of diagnosis by observation in reading:

Signs of Frustration
Finger pointing while reading   _____
Lip movement while reading   _____
Frowning while reading   _____
Squinting while reading   _____
Squirming or fidgeting while reading   _____
Crying before, during, or after reading   _____
Refusing to continue reading   _____
Tensing up before, during, or after reading   _____
Aggression before, during, or after reading   _____
Being easily distractable while reading   _____
Avoiding reading   _____
Making errors while reading orally which make no sense in
  the context   _____

Signs of Ease
Reading silently   _____
Smiling while reading   _____
Stillness while reading   _____
Page turning at an appropriate rate while reading   _____
Eye movements while reading   _____
Relaxation before, during, and after reading   _____

Being difficult to distract while reading   _____
Sharing books with others or with the teacher   _____
Making errors while reading orally which make sense in
   the context (including translating the author's words into
   the reader's dialect)   _____

A reader who consistently exhibits signs of ease while reading trade books or instructional-level material or while completing activities directed by the teacher or in self-teaching materials should continue with that same kind of exercise in increasingly difficult material as long as no signs of frustration are exhibited. The purpose of diagnosis by observation is to place the student at a level of some challenge without any frustration — instructional level. Because diagnosis by observation is based directly on student behavior during the learning situation, it should take precedence over test data from either standardized or other informal measures. If a reader exhibits signs of frustration during an activity, that material or activity is too difficult regardless of what score the student obtained on a test. If a reader exhibits signs of ease during an activity, the teacher should feel free to experiment with slightly more challenging material or activities regardless of what score the student obtained on a test. At the heart of the matter is this principle: A teacher should observe every student as often as possible with the question, "Do the activities and materials I have given to this student seem appropriate and effective?"

Interpreting Diagnostic Information

Remedial reading instruction has several goals, but first among them is that the student will increase the level of difficulty of material in which he or she can read silently with comprehension. To the extent that it is possible to measure a student's instructional level in a series of graded passages, the main goal of remedial instruction for that student at any one point is to raise his or her reading level to the next highest level. If Jane reads at third-grade level in the series of books used to estimate her instructional level, the immediate goal of the remedial reading teacher is to have her read at fourth-grade level in that series. When she is able to read at fourth-grade level, the immediate goal becomes one of having her read at fifth-grade level.

If one accepts that the purpose of remedial reading instruction is to increase the student's instructional reading level to the next highest level, then two questions must be answered by the diagnostic information obtained: (1) "What is the student's current instructional level?" and (2) "What is keeping the instructional level from already being at the next highest level?"

A tentative answer to the first question can only be obtained from a test with graded passages. A standardized test often only tells how well a student did on the test compared with other students in the norm population. If Joe scores 4.5 on a norm-referenced test, this score means that the students in the norm group who were in the fifth month of fourth grade averaged the same score Joe got on the test. There is no guarantee however that the average student in the fifth month of fourth grade could read at the middle of fourth-grade level.

The teacher can use a test such as the *Botel Reading Inventory* (Botel, 1978) or the *Classroom Reading Inventory* (Silvaroli, 1976) to estimate the current instructional level or a teacher-made test such as an informal reading inventory or a graded series of cloze tests may be used. An informal reading inventory rigorously made by the teacher from the actual materials to be used in remediation would have the best chance of placing the student accurately. Answering the second question, "What is keeping the instructional level from already being at the next highest level?", can be answered by interpreting either standardized or informal tests. The procedure for determining what needs to be done to raise the current instructional level to a higher one depends on one's beliefs about the components of reading, the nature of the reading process, and how reading is learned. Such beliefs are inherent, albeit implicitly, in the manual of every standardized test. Likewise, they are implicit in the established procedures used to construct teacher-made tests. It is impossible here to outline all the different ways to use diagnostic information to infer what is keeping a student's reading level where it is. (For one way of proceeding in answering this question, see pages 312–319). In each case, however, diagnostic data obtained from a student is interpreted in the light of conscious or unconscious beliefs about reading to infer the cause of the student's low reading level. Remediation then attempts to remove this cause or diminish its influence so that the student can become a better reader.

Remediation of Reading Difficulties in the Middle/High School

Providing remedial instruction to anyone, at any age, is difficult because the fact that one has been identified as needing special help indicates that previous instruction has not been as successful as someone important to the student (teacher, administrator, parent, peer, or self) believes it should have been. This difficulty is markedly increased when providing remedial reading instruction to older students. In most cases, the fact that they are identified as needing special help indicates not only a lack of success with previous instruction, but often with previous remedial instruction as well. Teaching students who have experienced little success in reading, even with special help, challenges the teacher's knowledge of diagnosis and remediation, but even more it challenges the teacher's knowledge of how to encourage and motivate students. There is no room in a middle or secondary remedial reading class for any teacher who thinks less of people because they do not read well.

The successful remedial reading teacher in a middle or high school must have:

1. The ability to use standardized tests, informal tests, and observation to diagnose how well students read, their strengths and weaknesses in reading, and what about their reading is keeping them from reading better.
2. A knowledge of remedial reading techniques and how to apply them.
3. The belief that the students can all learn to read better and that they all deserve to read better.

Because 1 has been covered and 3 is assumed to be the belief of anyone who would dare collect a pay check to help remedial readers, this section will be concerned with 2, remedial reading techniques and how to apply them.

Remedial Reading Techniques

The techniques which follow are not *all* the strategies one could use with older remedial readers. Rather, they are techniques the authors have used successfully with middle and secondary remedial readers or techniques which research strongly supports or the authors have witnessed being used successfully with middle and secondary remedial readers. In the experience of the authors, older students are more often in need of improvement in comprehension than in word identification. However, because the other chapters in this book are so heavily weighted toward improving comprehension, this chapter will attempt a thorough overview of the major beginning reading and word identification techniques. The sections on reading and listening comprehension will refer mostly to techniques described in this book and discussed elsewhere in the book and will merely explain how best to use them with older remedial readers needing comprehension improvement.

Techniques to Teach Beginning Reading

Anyone who is in middle or high school who has not learned to read beyond a beginning level is likely to be pretty confused about what reading is and how it is accomplished. This confusion has resulted from years of frustration and failure and from having several methods or parts of methods being tried by various teachers. It is essential that whatever method is now tried with these students be one that allows for quick success and that proceeds systematically. It is also necessary that this method be one that teaches the students what reading is while it teaches reading itself. Methods that teach sounds in isolation or words in isolation may work for some beginning readers in first grade, but they will seldom succeed with confused beginning readers in middle or secondary school. Instead, the following techniques are recommended:

Language-Experience Approach (LEA) as a remedial technique. No method works for all students and LEA is no exception, but in our experience it is the only hope for some older beginning readers. If they do not know about the relationship between speech and writing, they learn it while learning to read. If they do not know left-to-right, top-to-bottom progression, they learn it while learning to read. They do not have to read from babyish preprimers; they read their own language which should have intrinsic interest for them. They do not have to postpone success; they can read during the first lesson. It requires no special materials to teach, and may be taught to individuals or groups. If taught systematically for a sufficient period of time — and if students are not required to sound out words — LEA can be used to teach students to read for whom every other method has failed. (For further information on Language Experience as a remedial reading technique, see pages 300–301 and 346–350).

Linguistic readers. Several publishing companies have basal readers that follow a so-called linguistic method. A "pure" or synthetic phonics method teaches letter sounds in isolation and then teaches students to blend these sounds together to make words. The linguistic readers teach students letter sounds and blending inductively, but very systematically. Groups of words that differ in only one sound serve as the basis for a series of stories until a number of sounds has been learned. Because these sounds are never isolated, they are always blended for the student. When a student inducts a sound, like /p/ for example, the student does not learn that "*p* says puh," but rather learns the contribution that /p/ makes to a word when it is blended with the rest of the word.

VAKT and VAK.   Grace Fernald (1943) developed two techniques for teaching sight words which made success possible for students who had not learned to read by other approaches. The student was asked to choose a word to be learned. This word was written by the teacher in crayon on an index card in large letters. The student would use an index finger to trace the word repeatedly while saying it. When the student felt able to, he or she would turn the index card over and try to write the word from memory. Any error or hesitation required that the word be traced/said again. This technique has come to be called VAKT (visual-auditory-kinesthetic-tactile). Once a body of sight words has been learned, the student begins to write language-experience stories, trying to use words which have been learned. Any new words that are needed for the student's story are taught by VAKT.

A less drastic technique, which Fernald used when VAKT no longer seemed necessary, was similar to VAKT but did not use tracing. The student was asked to choose a word to be learned. This word was written by the teacher on an index card. The student would look at the word and say it, then close his or her eyes or look away and try to "see" it. This process would be repeated several times. When the student felt able to, he or she would turn the index card over and try to write the word from memory. Any error or hesitation required that the word be studied again. This technique has come to be called VAK (visual-auditory-kinesthetic). As in VAKT, language-experience stories are written by the student using the words learned. (For exact procedures to use in integrating VAK with LEA, see page 306.)

For any middle or secondary student who cannot read comfortably at a second-grade level, we recommend that the teacher provide remedial instruction that starts at the beginning using one of the three beginning-reading techniques described above. The order in which we described them is the order in which we would try them. A diagnosis of the reader's strengths and weaknesses may give an indication of which technique is most likely to succeed. Regardless of which technique is used with a student or small group of students who are beginning readers, it must be taught intensively, systematically, and at a pace that gives the student a feeling of progress without being in the least frustrating. Be certain of one thing: Beginning readers in the middle/high school can still learn to read.

Techniques to Improve Word Identification

Techniques to Improve Word Sight Identification

Controlled-vocabulary method.   This method requires commercial materials in which the number of new words introduced at each level is tightly controlled and restricted primarily to words which occur most frequently in English writing. These high-frequency words are repeated so often in the materials that the students are expected to learn them merely by reading the stories as part of a Directed Reading Activity (see pages 304–305 and 320). This method is employed at the beginning levels of most basal reading series used in elementary schools. Several publishing companies are marketing remedial materials for secondary students that have controlled vocabulary in the lower-level books.

Catalog cards. A highly motivating technique which is relatively easy to manage with groups of students is that of catalog cards. Students are given magazines and/or catalogs and scissors, paste, and large index cards or shirt cardboards. They look through these magazines or catalogs until they find two pictures of objects they like. They cut these pictures out and paste them one each to a card or cardboard, leaving space under the picture. The teacher moves around among the students. When a student has a picture mounted, the teacher asks the student what the object in the picture is called. Whatever the student calls the object is printed on the other side of the card in large, clear letters. Under the picture, the teacher writes a sentence which the student dictates using the word which is the name of the object. The word is underlined in this sentence. The student is told to study these cards until he or she can read the word by itself without looking on the side of the card with the picture and the sentence. Each day the student makes two new catalog cards and is responsible for knowing all catalog words to date. Students making good progress can begin making three, four, then more catalog cards per day. Students who are unable to learn the words from just studying the cards can have extra help from the teacher or a tutor in studying the words by VAK or VAKT to supplement the pictures and sentences.

Learning high-frequency sight words on flash cards using VAKT. (see above)

Learning high-frequency sight words on flash cards using VAK. (see above)

Techniques to Improve Use of Context Clues

The blankety-blank oral reading strategy. When students are reading orally, they should never be told a word by teacher or peers. Older remedial students are notoriously dependent on others to help them with decoding. The authors have worked with middle and secondary remedial readers who would make no effort at using any of their decoding skills because they seem to have learned that if they pause someone will either tell them the word or cue them how to decode it ("what would make sense here?" or "what letter does it start with?"). Rather, teachers should encourage these students to rely more on the best aid to decoding unknown words, context clues. The strategy is simple. The student is told that no one will help him or her with any of the words. The student will just have to manage without help. If there is a word the student is unable to identify, the student should say "blank" and keep reading. The student is encouraged to reread any part of the selection at any time when the skipped word is figured out. If this strategy is tried for one lesson only, a noticeable improvement in the students' rate and fluency of oral reading will occur. (*Caution:* If a student consistently says "blank" more than 5 times per 100 words, the material is almost certainly too difficult for that student and little improvement can result.)

Modified cloze as a teaching technique.   This group technique is especially effective in getting students to become aware of the value of context clues as aids to word identification. In the first stage, the teacher writes sentences on the board, leaving out of each sentence a word which the context makes clear, and replacing that word with a blank. The sentences should be constructed so that the students can easily guess the missing word. When the correct word is guessed, the student who made the correct guess is asked to explain in detail how he or she knew what the word was. ("What other words in the sentence helped you?" "What did you know already before you read the sentence that helped you?" etc.) It is this analysis-discussion phase that really teaches the process of context clue use. When the teacher is satisfied that the students are really able to be introspective about using context clues, then the sentences should become more challenging. Finally students should be given passages with an occasional word left out and asked to read these passages, supplying the missing words with the least possible interruption of the flow. Only the difficult items are discussed afterwards.

Techniques to Improve Use of Phonics

Using initial consonant sound plus context to decode.   Most middle and secondary remedial readers have had phonics instruction. Most know their initial, single-consonant sounds (*s, t, v,* etc.), although some may not know initial digraphs (*sh, ch,* etc.) or blends (*br, tw,* etc.). It is remarkable then how many older remedial readers fail to use the sounds they know when decoding unknown words in contextual reading. Many students who do make use of phonics sounds when decoding unknown words seem totally to ignore context by coming up with pronunciations that are phonetically approximate but that make absolutely no sense in the context of the passage. A simple way to teach students to use both phonics and context while reading is to use modified cloze passages in the following manner.

Use a passage that is easy for the students to read. Use a dark pen or crayon to darken out everything but the initial consonant, digraph, or blend of about 1 word in every 20. Pick words that are somewhat constrained by the context. After carefully instructing the students how to do it, have them read the passage silently, then orally. You will know that they have gotten the idea when they read the word without skipping a beat even though the only clues they have are the initial sound, word length, and context clues. (*Caution:* This simple procedure is rendered almost completely ineffective if the students are required to write in the end of the word. It focuses their attention on spelling rather than reading, on the end of the word rather than the beginning, and slows their rate so that the integration of context and phonics is slow and laborious rather than fluent and automatic.)

Inductive phonics lessons.   Using initial consonant sound plus context to decode unknown words is certainly the strategy the authors recommend for teaching middle and secondary remedial readers to make use of the phonics most have learned but do not apply. In most cases, however, the instruction just described above must be supplemented with instruction in the initial consonants the students still do not know. Students who do not make use of their phonics when reading almost always have some blends or digraphs they do not know. For those sounds which the students still need to learn, inductive lessons should be taught. An inductive phonics lesson follows these steps:

1. The teacher determines by a standardized phonics survey, an informal phonics test, or by observation which initial sounds the student does not know. These sounds should be taught in this order: (1) single consonants; (2) consonant digraphs (*sh, th, wh, ph,* etc.); (3) two-letter consonant blends (*bl, br, cl, cr, fl, st,* etc.); and (4) three-letter consonant blends (*str, spl,* etc.). They should be taught one at a time until learned, but review of those previously learned should occur regularly.

2. Once the initial consonant sound to be taught in a particular lesson has been selected, the teacher needs to have several words which are sight words for the student and which begin with that sound as represented by that letter(s). If the student knows few, if any, appropriate sight words, some should be taught prior to the inductive phonics lesson.

3. These words are written in list form. The teacher points to these words in a random order, and the student pronounces them in rapid fashion several times. At a point, the teacher tells the student to continue pronouncing the words as before but that, instead of merely pointing to the words, the teacher will underline the initial letter(s) in each word. Because each word begins with the same sound represented by the same letter(s), the students should begin to notice that they are saying the same sound at the beginning of each word and that the words are all spelled alike at the beginning. Following this insight, the students should begin to make a link in their minds between the sound and the letter(s) presented. Because this link is made in their minds and not by isolating the sound with the voice, there is no need for sound blending training.

Using a compare-contrast strategy to identify one-syllable words.   Although initial consonant sound plus context is a highly effective decoding strategy for readers who know their initial consonant sounds and who can use context and these sounds together while reading, there will always be words in reading material that cannot be decoded using these clues alone. In the sentence, "I want to buy my father a c_____ for his birthday," the context and initial sound limit what word goes in the blank, but many possibilities remain. Certainly a number of the more probable possibilities should be taught as sight words in one of the ways described above. However, a good knowledge of sight words and the ability to use initial consonant plus context to decode words which are not sight words are not sufficient for all the decoding needs of remedial readers. Unfortunately, a strict phonics method, given the amount of sound blending training required plus the incredible complexity of the English vowel system, would take a very long time to teach to these students, when in fact it would only be needed for those words that were not sight words and that could not be decoded using initial consonant plus context.

A simpler but equally effective system for teaching students to decode unknown words when the context is not sufficiently rich to give them away is the compare-contrast strategy (Cunningham, 1975–1976). It has the additional advantage of being a system which has not been used before with the students and which, consequently, they do not associate with failure or the primary grades. Students who know some high-frequency, one-syllable words and who know initial consonant sounds, including most blends and digraphs, are prepared to learn the compare-contrast strategy.

Pretest:

Have students pronounce the following 25 words. The starred words are high-frequency words. The other words are initial consonant, blend, or digraph substitutions into the high-frequency words. Students who correctly pronounce most of the starred words and who begin most of the unstarred words with the appropriate beginning sound but who do not correctly pronounce the unstarred words are students for whom the teaching strategy is likely to be optimally effective.

*and	crime
*cat	frown
*all	spy
*time	shook
*down	trade
*my	spent
*look	chin
*made	grand
*went	chime
*in	sly
brand	sent
flat	tin
hall	

Teaching Strategy:

1. Give each student six slips of paper. Have him or her print the following six words on the paper so they can be seen by the teacher.

   black, hold, kind, play, rain, run

   Display words from the following list. Have each student find his or her word which looks most like the presented word and at a signal from you (Ready, Set, Show!), let all students display their "lookalike" word. Students should respond to such questions as "Where are the two words alike?" "Where are they different?" Ask a volunteer to pronounce both words.

mind	crack	blind	blab	fold	lack
runt	pain	smack	hay	main	blast
slack	stack	gold	rind	bind	mold
tack	bay	bun	gain	gray	plain
raid	pray				

2. On the next day, add three words to the student's word store: *man, less, her*. They can now match their nine words to the following words.

clay	per	ban	lent	fan	bless	stain
pan	led	press	sun	sold	sack	

3. On the following day, add six more words to the student's store: *be, sit, stop, take, ten, will*. Students can now use their store of 15 words to match the following words.

flit	rut	scold	cop	crop	wit	span
bit	pop	top	train	lend	pack	hen
flake	plan	brain	spill	wig	bake	Ted
wake	Jill	stun	track	grain		

Evaluation:

Put the following ten words on the board. Have students copy the words and write next to each word the word from his or her store of 15 which looks most like the first word. Students should then individually read those words to the instructor.

rack	gay	slit	sin	snake
grill	tan	mast	sip	crop

4. Students should have their 15 words on slips of paper as previously described: *black, hold, kind, play, rain, run, man, less, her, be, sit, stop, take, ten, will*.

The teacher should put one of the words from the following list on the board. Students should copy the word from the board onto their papers and then try to think of which of their 15 words looks most like the word and write it under the presented word. Students should look through their store of 15 words only if they cannot first think of the word.

mad	rake	clack	ill	gun	grit	mop
van	lay	rub	pit	lake	tend	rust
fit	jack	cake	test	mask	pay	spun
hit	hop	fake	tent	dill	drain	flop
den	gill	herd	dress	slay	bran	kit
drake	pen	hill	clop	Bess	mat	sift
sake	Ben	kill	ray	clan	sway	plain
slop	mill	sill				

Evaluation:

Students should copy the following ten words from the board. They should write next to each word the word of their 15 which looks most like the first word. They should not refer to their 15 words to do this. Students should then individually read these words to the instructor.

spit	rug	grind	drill
tray	rail	mess	
snack	map	brake	

5. Proceed as in the previous lesson to write words on the board and have students think of a word they know which looks like the presented word. This time, however, they are *not* limited to the 15 words they have previously used. Rather, they may think of any of the words they know. Several students may think of several different words, and they should be encouraged to use several of these words to figure out the unknown word.

gland	chip	con	spat	scat	stall
clan	clam	jot	shot	clot	clog
bout	spout	worm	worth	spike	dike
free	spree	rim	trim	prim	brim
dim	disk	rid	Sid	lid	frog
crown	clown	strong	throng	spade	glade
grade	trade	rig	brig	sway	clay
spent	sent	rent	tent	lent	few
screw	shrew	lame	flame	fair	stair
ground	pink	rink	stink	blink	skin
slink	shell	well	spell	such	stray
gold	scold	hold	fold	yelp	face
lace	ace	blouse	trust	bust	rust
smart	raw	claw	flaw	twine	spine
blast	mend	bleat	cleat	frill	freight

Evaluation:
Students should copy the following ten words from the board. They should write next to each word a word that looks like the first word. Students should then individually read the words to the instructor.

spun	wing	fry	prove	dish
card	floor	flight	moon	dell

Posttest:
Have students pronounce the 15 unstarred words from the pretest. (These words were purposely excluded from the training.)

Using a compare-contrast strategy to identify polysyllabic words   (Cunningham, 1978).   While it seems abundantly clear that middle and secondary remedial readers need to be taught to deal successfully with polysyllabic words, the technique of syllabication training seems to be of very little or no benefit in achieving this goal. Canney and Schreiner (1976–1977), Cunningham, Rystrom and Cunningham (1980), and Marzano, Case, Debooy, and Prochoruk (1976) have conducted research, the results of which raise serious questions as to whether syllabication instruction is of any benefit whatsoever with respect to reading. A compare-contrast strategy for approaching polysyllabic word identification has shown promise (Cunningham, 1980) and is presented here as an alternative to traditional syllabication instruction.

Pretest:

Students for whom this compare-contrast strategy is appropriate and needed can be quickly determined by giving a simple word pronunciation test. For this test, two-syllable words which the reader is apt to have heard before but which the typical reader would not immediately recognize as sight words are suggested. The following 14 words could be used as a pretest:

problem	program
replace	moment
contain	copper
statement	convoy
provide	compound
thunder	broken
prepare	suppose

Assuming that a few of these words might be sight words for a reader, the criterion for mastery on this test is set fairly high. The student must correctly pronounce 12 of the 14 words in order to pass the pretest.

Step One:

Have each student begin a tangible word store by writing the following five words, one to an index card:

he	went	her	can	car

Tell students that you will show a two-syllable word, the parts of which are very similar to the words on the cards they have made. Their job is to find, for each two-syllable word, the two cards which match the parts of this word. (Students can write the two matching words, or a volunteer can display the two chosen words.) When the words are appropriately matched, have a student pronounce the two matching words and the polysyllabic words. Practice matching and pronouncing these words as quickly as possible. Words which might be used are:

charter	barber	garment	Herman
defer	banner	percent	barter
ferment	cancer	repent	decent
regent	canter	panther	farther
meter	German	serpent	recent
garter	merger	tangent	slander

Step Two:

Have the students make five more index cards for their tangible store:

in	at	then	it	is

Using all ten word cards, have the students match cards to these words:

bitter	bandit	center	Berlin
scatter	cretin	fitter	misspent
batten	ginger	winter	whisper

bitter	remit	margin	whisker
render	batter	hermit	splatter
bitten	charter	latter	matter

Step Three:
Add the five words:

| let | fish | sun | big |

and using the 15 cards, match these words:

market	clannish	trigger	letter
hunger	setter	regret	varnish
banish	catfish	digger	garnish
secret	blunder	punish	pigment
disband	Shetland		

Step Four:
Enlarge the tangible word store from 15 to 35 words. Do this gradually over several days' lessons. Since 35 cards is too many for students to be shuffling through to find the matching words, display the 35 words on a chart. When all 35 words are to be used, give each student a list of words that can be decoded from these 35 key words. Let the students form two teams and compete to see which team can read the most words on the list. The teams alternate turns, and each player may call out a number and read that word or pass to another team member. Keep the chart of 35 key words visible and available to the students for reference. You should notice, however, by this time that most students seem able to use the words stored in their heads.

The following 35 words were successfully used with a group of remedial readers. (They include the 15 words used in steps one–three.)

and	let	sun	big	fish	her
can	car	went	he	is	in
then	it	at	rain	Tom	go
on	care	us	ate	or	them
Bob	face	side	am	top	boy
dance	up	found	rose	but	

The following 200 words may be successfully decoded using this store of 35 words. The starred words have three or more syllables. Using the 35 words, have students match these words:

1. German	12. repent	23. scatter	34. setter
2. barber	13. panther	24. fitter	35. misspent
3. percent	14. serpent	25. bitten	36. banish
4. cancer	15. bitter	26. Berlin	37. disband
5. garter	16. ginger	27. hermit	38. hunger
6. garment	17. margin	28. blister	39. farther
7. merger	18. latter	29. punish	40. secret
8. meter	19. winter	30. market	41. decent
9. charter	20. batter	31. trigger	42. regret
10. banner	21. bandit	32. blunder	43. donor
11. Herman	22. center	33. catfish	44. donut

45. order
46. donate
47. orbit
48. homer
49. remain
50. organ
51. joker
52. motor
53. regain
54. bonus
55. rotate
56. combo
57. retain
58. sober
59. relate
60. voter
61. yo-yo
62. commit
63. prevent
64. command
65. debate
66. litter
67. grocer
68. blender
69. mainland
70. member
71. confide
72. clobber
73. misplace
74. decide
*75. remember
76. goblin
77. compare
78. landslide
*79. monogram
80. popper
*81. entertain
82. luster
83. embrace

84. probate
85. retrace
86. refrain
87. pinto
**88. entertainment
*89. employment
90. restate
91. robber
92. compose
93. disgrace
94. whisper
95. scarlet
96. splinter
97. slender
98. fritter
99. chosen
100. enclose
101. dispose
102. Sounder
103. ground
104. confound
105. decoy
106. founder
107. resound
108. unsound
*109. underground
110. flutter
*111. attendance
112. stopper
113. supper
114. mutter
115. shopper
*116. remembrance
*117. buttercup
118. rebound
119. shutter
*120. performance
121. stutter
122. chopper

123. clutter
*124. ignorance
125. sputter
126. entrance
127. cutter
128. instance
129. propose
*130. observance
131. gutter
*132. resistance
133. profound
134. employ
135. pittance
*136. repentance
*137. tupperware
138. repose
139. butter
140. disclose
141. boyish
142. tomboy
143. annoy
144. complain
145. comment
146. spoken
*147. November
*148. December
149. compare
150. refrain
151. matter
152. chatter
153. platter
154. sitter
155. recent
156. slander
157. whisker
158. splatter
159. letter
160. varnish
161. garnish

162. pigment
163. enjoy
*164. enjoyment
165. demand
166. deface
167. detain
168. hitter
169. border
170. porter
171. bandstand
172. grandstand
173. fender
174. tennis
175. tender
176. spender
177. Buster
178. locate
179. crocus
180. clover
181. focus
182. poker
183. Rover
184. permit
*185. persistent
*186. performer
187. open
*188. override
*189. understand
190. winner
191. dinner
192. thinner
193. dropper
194. cluster
195. fluster
196. pertain
197. manner
198. disdain
**199. independent
200. prefer

A final step in this compare-contrast decoding strategy is to help students develop the habit of using all the one-syllable words they have stored in their heads as key words for decoding two-syllable words in context. Students who have been lead through the previous four steps can usually see the value of figuring out an unfamiliar word by looking for similarities to words they already know. Having each student find a word in his or her reading book which has six or seven letters and which the student does not immediately recognize and letting the other students suggest words stored in their heads which will help decode the unfamiliar word is an effective strategy for leading students to use the words stored in their heads and for beginning to make the transfer to books and real reading. If the teacher wishes to select words for the students to use their cognitive word stores to decode, these words should be presented in the context of a sentence. This makes the activity more like real reading and gives the students practice in checking their pronunciation against a word which will make sense in the sentence. An additional aid to transfer is for the teacher to use the "What words do you know that look like this part?" question strategy when students ask the teacher to pronounce a word or otherwise indicate they are unfamiliar with a word.

Posttest:

The words used on the pretest were purposely excluded from these lessons so that they might be used again to evaluate the effectiveness of the lessons. Give the students the same 14 words used for a pretest and compare their results.

There are some word parts that occur only in polysyllabic words (*-tion*, *-ous*, for example). If students are to become independent decoders of polysyllabic words, they must be able to use the parts of polysyllabic words to compare to other polysyllabic words. A game called *Mystery Word Match* is effective in teaching students this advanced compare-contrast skill.

Pretest:

Have the students pronounce the following ten words. Students who can correctly pronounce nine of the ten words have mastered basic decoding skills. Other students should enjoy and profit from playing *Mystery Word Match*.

dismissal	advantage
repulsive	correction
unoriginal	political
imaginative	sacrifice
elective	productive

To play this game, the teacher divides the students into two groups. Each group takes a turn asking a question about the mystery word. Guessing the word after the first question is worth ten points. With each "no" answer, a point is subtracted. The team which guesses the word is awarded the number of points it is worth at that point. To play the game, the teacher draws lines to represent the number of letters in the mystery word. He or she then writes the clue words on the board and has the students pronounce the clue words several times after her. The meaning of these clue words can be discussed and the words can be used in sentences. The play is carried out by the students trying to find out which parts of the clue words are used in the mystery word. They ask, "Does the mystery word begin like _____?"; "end like _____?"; "have a middle like _____?" Here is an example for you to figure out.

TEACHER: "The mystery word has ten letters _ _ _ _ _ _ _ _ _ _."
                              (Draws ten lines on board.)
"Here are the clue words: absolute
                                        rebellion
                                        attention"
(Teacher writes each clue word on the board. Pronounces each. Students pronounce each, then define and use each in sentences.)

TEACHER: "Billy's team won the toss. They can go first. The mystery word is worth 10 points."

BILLY'S TEAM MEMBER: "Does the word begin like *attention*?"

TEACHER: "No, it does not. Joe's team for 9 points."

JOE'S TEAM MEMBER: "Does the word end like *attention*?"

TEACHER: "Yes it does." (Writes *tion* on last four lines: _ _ _ _ _ _ t i o n) "You may go again."

JOE'S TEAM MEMBER: "Does the word begin like *absolute*?"

TEACHER: "No, it does not. Billy's team, eight points."

BILLY'S TEAM MEMBER: "Does the word have a middle like *absolute*?"

TEACHER: "Good for you." (Writes *solu* on appropriate lines: _ _ s o l u t i o n) "You may go again."

BILLY'S TEAM MEMBER: "Does the word have a beginning like *rebellion*?"

TEACHER: "Yes, it does." (Writes last two letters in: r e s o l u t i o n) "The team may confer and name the word."

(Team confers and triumphantly pronounces *resolution*. Teacher records eight points for Billy's team. Game continues with next mystery word.)

This game is lots of fun, and the students are exposed to many polysyllabic words. While playing, they learn to use the clue words to figure out other words. This game is intended both to build a store of polysyllabic words to compare and contrast with other polysyllabic words and to give practice in the compare and contrast decoding skill. After playing the game for a sufficient amount of time, give the words used on the pretest as a posttest. They were excluded from the game for this purpose.

Use the following sets of mystery and clue words to play *Mystery Word Match*.

p a n t h e r	c a l c u l a t e	i n v o l v e m e n t
mother	incubate	revolver
pansy	calisthenics	excitement
	emulate	insurance
r a b b i t		
orbit	a r t i c l e s	i m p r e s s i o n
rabbi	artistic	depresses
	circles	impossible
c a n d y		persuasion
canter	S a t u r d a y	
Cindy	satisfy	d e t e r g e n t
	Thursday	agent
h a m b u r g e r	retained	detective
suburban		entertain
tiger	t r a n s p o r t a t i o n	
hamster	mutation	r e s o l u t i o n
	transfer	pollution
p a r a g r a p h	reporter	insolent
parachute		recipe
telegraph		

telescope
microscope
telephone

organize
organic
recognize

potato
poker
mistaken
tomato

popsicle
sensible
bicycle
popular

pineapple
dimple
pinesap
unappetizing

perfectly
happily
defective
performance

September
remember
separate
intemperate

motivate
renovate
activity
motion

partition
parliament
notify
instruction

revolution
convocation
pollution
renovate

committee
inductee
comfortable
permitting

politician
policy
mortician

professor
confessing
probation
assessor

exception
receptive
extra
nation

uncertain
understand
recertify
curtain

instruction
instigate
destructive
ammunition

telegram
program
testify
delegate

destination
dessert
articles
assassination

expedition
tradition
expedite
compilation

comical
compartment
critical

expressive
repulsive
experience
impressing

dictation
dictionary
prevention
potato

argument
regulate
statement
artistic

employment
deploying
embarrass
department

proportion
program
imported
ammunition

depression
extension
impressive
deliver

compartment
company
departing
government

invention
prevention
indent

photograph
telegraph
phoning
automobile

promotion
proposal
unmotivated
stimulation

removal
denial
reassess
immovable

contestant
constitution
pretested
informant

liberation
decoration
liberty

dialect
collect
diet
realize

inspector
respectful
inappropriate
equator

destruction
deliver
operation
instructor

centigram
telegram
centipede

conversation
overthrow
concert
sensation

ceremony
testimony
celebrate
direction

indigestion
incomplete
editor
suggestion

expectation
respectable
explorer
limitation

combustion
resolution
rebusses
communism

document
element
doctor
circulate

resistance
insisting
reform
inheritance

geometry
country
geography
remember

paradise
merchandise
paragraph

ministry
animal
middle
chemistry

popular
spectacular
popcorn

elevator
renovator
elephant

butterscotch
hopscotch
buttonhole
entertain

biblical
economical
bibbed
politics

disapproval
discovery
reapprove
removal

resistance
inheritance
assisting
realize

foundation
imitation
founder

insurance
assuring
interesting
distance

medication
medicine
vacation

independent
undependable
Pepsodent
inaccurate

Techniques to Improve Fluency of Word Identification

Repeated Readings (Dahl, 1974; Dahl and Samuels, 1975). A short passage of interest to the student which is also at the student's instructional level is used. The passage should be meaningful. The student is given the passage and told to read it silently so that he or she can read it orally with few errors and at a comfortable rate. After silent reading, the student reads the passage to the teacher who counts oral reading errors and times the reading. If the student makes more than 5 errors per 100 words, then the passage is too difficult to use and an easier one should be chosen. If no more than 5 errors per 100 words is made by the student, the teacher tells him or her the errors made and the time and suggests that the student practice the material silently again so that he or she can read it more fluently next time. This process is repeated until the student has read the passage three or four times with an increase in rate and fluency each time. Of course, while some students are practicing, another can be reading to the teacher, which makes it possible to use repeated readings with a small group of disabled readers. Also, each student can have a different passage, depending on his or her instructional level and interest.

Imitative method (Huey, 1908/1968; Chomsky, 1976). Short selections of three or four pages at most from the easiest high-interest/low-vocabulary material should be recorded on cassette tape in the most interesting and dramatic style possible. The student then listens to the taped passage while following along with the selection until the student can read the material fluently to the teacher. The student works independently for however many days or weeks are necessary for him or her to read the selection fluently. The passage really has not been memorized, since the student cannot quote the passage without "reading" the selection. Once a student has mastered a selection, he or she should be allowed and encouraged to read the selection for the class, parents, other classes, and so forth. In addition, the mastered passage can be used to aid in instruction in sight words, context clues, and phonics. A hole can be cut in an index card and placed over a word on a page in the selection. If the student recognizes the word, fine. If not, the card is removed to allow the student to read enough of the context to figure out what the word is. A discussion of the use of context can follow. The word missed can be taught as a sight word using one of the methods discussed.

Choral reading. Students are given a passage at instructional level or easier to read silently. After silent reading, the group reads the passage aloud, led by the teacher who reads fluently, expressively, and at a moderate pace. Occasionally the teacher lowers his or her voice to a whisper in order to hear how well the students are doing.

Improving Reading Comprehension

While there are certainly some older remedial readers for whom the beginning reading and word identification techniques described above are necessary, it is our experience that the majority of them need reading comprehension improvement more than they need word identification improvement. Perhaps this is due to the traditional emphasis on sight words, phonics, and oral reading for poor readers, or to the lack of practice in reading for most poor readers, or to the mistaken impression which many poor readers have that reading *is* word identification. At any event, providing students who need reading comprehension improvement with more word identification instruction will only result in small gains, if any. This section of the chapter will outline an approach to improving reading comprehension for these students.

It must surely be apparent how necessary for comprehension it is that a reader or listener be able to associate appropriate meaning with most of the concept words in a text being read or heard. Of course, this explains why knowing word meanings is so crucial in learning to read a foreign or classical language and why tests of meaning vocabulary correlate so highly with tests of reading comprehension. Knowing the meanings of the nouns, adjectives, verbs, and adverbs which represent the concepts of a passage is probably the single most important factor in reading or listening comprehension.

A good meaning vocabulary strategy is a good meaning vocabulary strategy. Third-graders reading at third-grade level, tenth-graders reading at college reading level, and even doctoral students reading at a postdoctoral reading level can all extend their meaning vocabularies. A successful technique for vocabulary instruction can be used with academically gifted students or with severely disabled readers as long as the words being taught are appropriate in each case and as long as the number of new words presented per lesson is consistent with the learning rates of the students involved. This means, of course, that the vocabulary techniques presented elsewhere in this book (particularly in Chapter 2) should be used with middle and secondary remedial readers who have problems with reading comprehension.

Because the remedial reading teacher is usually not limited to a content area or even to content-area-type material, the words selected to be taught as meaning vocabulary can be more relevant and interesting to students. In the article which first described the capsule vocabulary technique (Crist, 1975), the capsules of vocabulary which the students mastered were developed around topics of special interest and use to the students: food, sex, entertainment, sports, and so forth. The different words to describe food which are found on menus, for example, would be an excellent source of a vocabulary capsule for older remedial readers (words like *a la carte, soup de jour, entrée, hors d'oeuvres, appetizer*, and *cordial*). In addition to enlarging the students' meaning vocabularies for regular reading tasks, the instruction would also aid in preparing students for real-world, functional reading tasks of the type often tested on graduation competency tests.

The vocabulary techniques in this book are also very useful for preteaching vocabulary before students read a selection in a small-group reading lesson. Care should be taken in this case to teach all new meaning vocabulary as sight words by use of one of the techniques outlined in the word identification section above. VAK is especially appropriate and can be used simultaneously with whatever vocabulary technique is being used to introduce the new words. It is impossible to teach directly all the meaning vocabulary that remedial students should know, but these strategies allow the most obviously necessary words to be successfully taught. In addition, these techniques cue students in to the importance of vocabulary as well as improve their ability to use context clues so that they are more likely to learn new words from the independent reading.

Improving the Use of Grammatical Information in Reading

While the ability to use grammatical information is crucial to the reconstruction of meaning cued by a piece of discourse, it seems to be a very basic ability, at least for older remedial readers. In our experience, it is an unusual middle or high school student who does not make fairly consistent use of syntactic information. Given this sentence to read — "While traveling to Alaska, the man became so homesick that he took his portmanteau and jumped from the train" — many students call *portmanteau* a variety of other things, many of which make no sense within the sentence. It is unusual, however, for a older student to substitute a word which is not a noun. For the occasional older remedial reader who requires such instruction, the following techniques are recommended to improve the ability to make use of grammatical information while reading.

Cloze as a teaching technique with function words deleted.   A passage at the instructional level of the students, or easier, is used to construct a cloze passage. A function word which is a pronoun, a preposition, or a conjunction — and which is easy to guess from the context — is deleted from every sentence in the passage and replaced by a blank which is the same length for all words deleted. The passage should be put on an overhead transparency or duplicated so that students can readily see the passage. They should not write the words in (this is not a spelling lesson) and no mention should be made of what part of speech a word is or, in fact, that these words are called function words (this is not a grammar lesson). Instead, the group should supply all words which could fit in the blank and then vote on which one they believe was deleted, before being given the right answer. This group activity can be followed by an activity in which individual students silently read cloze passages with function words deleted so that they can answer one or more questions about the passage. Following this silent reading, they could be asked to read the passage orally, supplying the function word for each blank as automatically as possible from the context.

Reordering scrambled words to make sentences.   Beginning with short, simple sentences, students should be given the words and asked to put them together to make meaningful sentences. At first, the students may actually need to have the words written on index or flash cards so that they can manipulate the words physically. Later they can be given the list on the board and asked to rearrange them mentally into a sentence. In either case, the words must be in the meaning vocabularies of the students and must either be sight words or must be readily decodable by the students. This activity becomes more sophisticated as the sentences get longer and as the structure of the sentences becomes more complex. Better to be too easy than too hard.

Open-book activities to answer wh-transformation questions.   In order to make a wh-transformation question, one takes a sentence from a passage, deletes an important word or phrase from the sentence, replaces that word or phrase with the appropriate wh-word (who, what, which, where, when, why), and reorders the sentence to make a question. The following sentence will illustrate how wh-transformation questions are constructed:

SENTENCE: Lewis and Clark crossed the Missouri River in 1805.
QUESTIONS: Who crossed the Missouri River in 1805?
             What river did Lewis and Clark cross in 1805?
             When did Lewis and Clark cross the Missouri River?

If these types of questions are asked orally and intensively following reading and if the students are able to look for the information in the text, students can improve in the ability to use grammatical information as cues to comprehension. At first, short simple passages should be used. At a later time, longer, more difficult passages may be given.

Improving the Ability to Follow Cohesion Through Text

Like the ability to use grammatical information in reading, the ability to follow cohesion through text is a basic ability. It is primarily the ability to assign proper referents to pronouns and pronominal adjectives and adverbs. When students have problems following these elements of passage cohesion, it can be because the text is simply too difficult on all scores for that student. For the occasional older remedial student who really cannot comprehend across sentences, the following techniques are recommended to improve the ability to follow cohesion.

Reordering scrambled sentences to make paragraphs.   Beginning with short, simple paragraphs, students should be given the sentences and asked to put them together to make meaningful paragraphs. At first, the students may actually need to have the sentences written on sentence strips so that they can manipulate the sentences physically. Later they can be given the list on the board and asked to rearrange them mentally into a paragraph. This activity becomes more sophisticated as the paragraphs get longer and as the structure of the paragraphs becomes more complex. Again, the first activities should be very easy.

Determining the referent.   In a passage that is fairly easy for the students and that contains a number of pronouns and pronominal adjectives and adverbs, underline all of these pronominalizations. Duplicate or make an overhead transparency. Lead the students to define the referent for each *he, she, it, there, this, that*, and so forth. Ask each student to make a guess and explain why he or she thinks that guess is correct. Have the students vote and then give them the correct answer. Explain as completely as you can why the answer is correct.

Whole-Passage Techniques

As in the case of meaning vocabulary, a good reading comprehension instructional strategy is generally effective at all levels for all types of students. The

Directed Reading-Thinking Activity can be used quite effectively in teaching a short story in a college English class or in teaching a basal story from the primer in first grade. The difference, of course, is that students at each level should be properly placed in material at instructional level before any comprehension strategy is utilized.

At reading levels below sixth-grade level, students cannot be expected to follow the reasoning through material while reading that they could not follow while listening. If this principle is followed, students reading below sixth-grade level who can comprehend while reading at the same level that they can comprehend while listening will receive listening comprehension instruction:

> Directed Listening Activity
> Guided Listening Procedure
> Directed Listening-Thinking Activity
> Translation Writing
> Listening-to-Reading Transfer Lesson

The purpose of this instruction will be to raise the level at which the students can comprehend when listening so that their reading comprehension levels will later increase. The listening instruction will not automatically bring an increase in reading comprehension ability, but students who can listen better than they read will be better able to benefit from reading comprehension instruction. The material used for these lessons should be challenging to the students but, by no means, frustrating. Students' listening can also benefit from listening to easy, interesting material which does not require that one of the techniques mentioned above be used.

Students who read above fifth-grade level, students who read below sixth-grade level and who can comprehend better when listening than reading, and students who have benefited from listening comprehension instruction should receive instruction of the following types in instructional level material:

> Directed Reading Activity
> Guided Reading Procedure
> Directed Reading-Thinking Activity
> PQ4R
> Listening-to-Reading Transfer Lesson

In addition, these students should be allowed and encouraged to do as much easy, independent reading as possible. Sustained Silent Reading is a good way to get students in the habit of independent reading, especially if lots of high-interest/low-vocabulary materials are available for students to self-select.

It is unfortunately true that students rarely improve very much in reading comprehension from reading short selections and answering multiple-choice questions. What a shame it is that so many of the "comprehension" materials on the market for remedial readers rely so heavily on such a format. The remedial reading teacher can best improve the reading comprehension of older remedial students by using one of the reading comprehension techniques described elsewhere in this book with a small group of students who are reading in instructional level material. With a strong emphasis on meaning vocabulary and such small-group instruction, the reading comprehension levels of the students will improve.

Conclusion

This chapter has attempted to describe a set of techniques and principles for teaching middle/secondary remedial readers. The next two chapters will feature a fictitious teacher who attempts to apply some of these principles and techniques with a class of severely disabled middle/secondary readers.

13

A Year of Remedial Reading
(September–December)

Y OU HAVE READ in previous "Upton Hill" chapters about Reed Moore and his successful program of remedial reading instruction. In chapters 13 and 14 you will follow Reed as he envisions, implements, carries out, modifies, and evaluates a middle and secondary school remedial reading program. It is hoped that the narration in these two chapters will provide a starting point for a middle/secondary remedial reading teacher and provide understanding into the nature of the older remedial reader for the content-area teacher.

The Preschool Faculty Meeting

Reed Moore, the new special reading teacher, sat quietly and listened to the small talk going on around him. Mr. Topps and Mr. Battle were discussing the chances that Upton Hill's varsity football team would have a winning season. Mrs. Cash was describing her daughter to another new teacher whom Reed had not met. His mind wandered from one conversation to the other until it returned to the topic he had been thinking about for days: How was he going to screen the referrals he would get for the Reading Center?

Referral

He and Mr. Topps were in agreement that he should work with the poorest readers in the school. That had been decided the day they met in Mr. Topps's office with Ms. Erable, the reading supervisor. At first, she had insisted that Moore use intelligence-test scores, reading-test scores, and a reading-potential formula to select only those students for the program who were reading well below potential. Fresh from an M.Ed. program in reading/language arts education, Reed explained to her the many problems of reading-potential formulas. He underscored the high testing error involved in using a single reading-potential score to accept or reject a student. He informed her that those students often make the most progress who would have been rejected from special reading programs if selection were based on such formulas. Mr. Topps had supported him by saying; "And regardless of the research, it just doesn't make any sense to me that you would take students who can function somewhat in regular classes and give them special help, but leave others who cannot function at all in regular classes and not give them special help. This implies that regular teachers need help with students who are a little behind but do not need help with students who are far behind."

He and Mr. Topps had also agreed that teachers would be asked to refer students who seemed to be having severe difficulty reading their textbooks. The problem with a referral system, Mr. Topps pointed out, was that some teachers would refer only discipline problems or students who refused to do their assignments whether or not those students read poorly. Reed suggested that he screen the referrals in some way to select the actual students to be enrolled in the program, and Mr. Topps agreed to this plan. The problem was that the day of the preschool faculty meeting had come and he still had not determined how he would conduct that screening.

He had learned to administer individual, diagnostic, reading tests in his graduate reading courses, but the quickest one he knew took at least an hour per pupil to give, score, and interpret. Another one took over two hours! And he was to select 90 students from all those referred to him by the faculty.

The problem kept nagging at him until Topps tapped his pencil on the podium to get everyone's attention. "Teachers, it is the beginning of another year for all of us here at Upton Hill Middle/Secondary School. I look forward to this year with great anticipation. It's good to see those of you who return from last year, and we welcome those who are new to us. We try our best to teach both subjects and students here, even though that's not easy when each teacher sees so many students each day.

"At the end of this meeting I will introduce the new teachers and then there will be some time for you to get acquainted over coffee and donuts. At this time, however, I would like to move through our agenda as quickly as possible. As you remember, last year, for the first time, we had a special reading teacher at Upton Hill. She did a fine job and worked hard, but she resigned at the end of the year. Our new special reading teacher is Mr. Moore who comes to us from D. Utter Middle/Secondary School. He has taught English for 20 years, but this is his first year as a reading teacher. He had just completed his M.Ed. degree in reading/language arts education at State. Mr. Moore needs to talk with you for a few minutes about how you should refer students whom you think need special reading instruction."

Reed moved to the podium with a page of handwritten notes. His slender, athletic build and Marine posture made him look younger than his 45 years. He began, "Mr. Topps has explained to me how last year Mrs. Bennett took referrals from the English teachers and selected from among them on the basis of which students were reading most below their potential as measured by an IQ test. This year referrals will be accepted from all teachers in all subject areas. I will select students from those referred on the basis of how poorly they read, regardless of potential. Students with the greatest reading problems should get the special help. This system should help you with the students who are having the most difficulty surviving in your classes.

"Tomorrow morning you will find five referral forms in your mail box in the office. You may refer students at any time during the first two weeks of school, but the earlier the better. If you taught students last year whom you think should be referred, submit their names whether or not you teach them this year. Please put referrals in my box or send them to the Reading Center.

"Are there questions?"

Grading
Credit

"Yes," said Mrs. March. "I have one. Will the students be graded and will they receive credit for reading?"

"That will be the same as last year. Students will take reading instead of English, and they will get English credit for it."

"May I say something about that?" asked a man in the back whom Reed hadn't met. Everyone turned to hear him. "I'm Mr. Harden and I teach sophomore grammar and composition. Since you've taught English for so long, Mr. Moore, I'm sure you can understand and sympathize with what I have to say. Last year, Mrs. Bennett gave some As and Bs to sophomores who were reading at sixth-grade level! Those students had friends who were in my English classes receiving Cs and Ds. They didn't think it was fair, and I didn't think it was fair. I would like to suggest to you that it would be better to offer this reading class for no credit, and require those students who ought to be in it to take it. A student who doesn't pass high school English ought not to get credit for high school English."

Reed paused. He didn't agree with Mr. Harden, but he could see that several teachers were whispering to each other and nodding that they did agree. In some ways it was difficult to defend giving English credit for below-grade-level reading instruction. He began to respond, "Well, Mr. Harden . . ."

At that moment Mr. Topps stood up, "Let me bail you out here, Reed, since you weren't around last year when the credit and grading policies for special reading were decided upon. There are several reasons why we decided to give credit for special reading rather than have it be a noncredit course. We believed that students who needed special help in reading would be much more willing to take a reading course if they received credit. I might say that the parents of those students were also more agreeable when the reading course was for credit. And we believed that students would put forth more effort to improve their reading if the course were for credit.

"Moreover, if we did not give credit for the reading course we were creating other problems. For those students who took reading in addition to a regular course load, we would be requiring extra work from students who were already barely making it. Yet for those students who took one less credit course in order to take reading, we would be slowing their progress toward graduation. Often these students were already discouraged and ready to drop out of school. I believe that any reading course that is to succeed with the students who need it most must be a credit course.

"As to the reasons why we decided to give English credit for reading, they are less compelling. Reading is a tool subject. It can be taught using the content of any subject area. Students could be taught to improve their reading using only science materials or only history materials. In those instances, I believe science or history credit should be given for reading, since the students are learning more about those subjects as they improve their reading.

"In the case of our reading course here at Upton Hill, we decided to have a course in which the students did a lot of writing. Mrs. Bennett ordered a great many tradebooks for the reading center including junior novels and all types of adolescents' books. In addition, many of the high-interest/low-vocabulary reading materials used in our program are abridged versions of both traditional and contemporary fiction, nonfiction, and journalism. We are teaching reading in our special reading class, but the methods and materials we are using are quite compatible with those being recommended for English courses by English education experts.

"We give English credit for the reading course because it is essential that a special reading course be for credit, and our particular course resembles a good English course in its emphasis on writing and the use of library books and paperbacks. The fact that these tradebooks are easier to read than most books read by other students in high school English is only an indication that we are trying to instruct the students on their levels — certainly a defensible and worthwhile goal."

Miss Stern cleared her throat and began to speak. "Mr. Harden, I've taught English longer than you and Mr. Moore together. For most of those years I have been a strong supporter of standards and I still am, but the students we have to teach today are not like the students we used to teach. Twenty-five years ago students with reading problems dropped out, were pushed out, or were held back. They rarely reached high school. Back then, most of our students read well enough that with some effort they could meet our standards. Today we encourage all students to stay in school. As a result we have students who cannot read their textbooks regardless of how much they try."

Mr. Harden smiled. "Well, Mr. Topps, I guess we always get back to the elementary school. If they had done their job, we wouldn't have these problems." (Harden and everyone else in the room knew that Mr. Topps had been principal of Merritt Elementary School before coming to the Middle/High School two years earlier.)

Reed wondered how Mr. Topps would respond, but Miss Stern spoke again. "I don't think the elementary schools are doing any better today in teaching reading than they used to, but I don't think they are doing any worse. Our students who have reading problems would have had reading problems 25 years ago, too. They would be out looking for a job or on welfare, rather than in school where we still have a chance to teach them something. If we were to eliminate the students from Upton Hill who cannot read well enough to do independent work in their textbooks, we would have to reduce our faculty in half. Which half of you teachers want to give up your jobs? These students are here, some of us are here because of them, and we'd better be thankful that we have a special reading teacher to help us. Times have changed, Mr. Harden, and I've changed with them."

"Yes, but what about grades, Miss Stern?" Mr. Harden persisted, "Surely you don't think these students should get As and Bs for this below-level work!"

"I have mixed feelings about grades," Miss Stern confessed. "An A should represent excellence; I've always believed that. But I've never liked the idea of giving an A to the bright student who put forth little effort but still did well or a D to the slow student who put forth herculean efforts and barely slipped by. This kind of grading establishes an aristocracy based solely on intelligence. Laziness is often rewarded and effort punished. I feel that Mr. Moore should have the right to reward those students who exert themselves and make progress."

Mr. Harden and a few other teachers were obviously frustrated by Miss Stern's comments. If someone else had defended credit and grades above C for special reading they would merely have discounted it, but Miss Stern had been teaching English at Upton Hill for as long as anyone could remember. No one could accuse her of being a radical.

Mr. Topps returned to the podium. "This has been a lively discussion, but we must move on through our agenda. Please put your referrals in Reed's box as soon as possible. The students will receive English credit for special reading, and Reed is free to grade them as he sees fit as all you teachers are. We are glad to have someone of Reed's experience and training to work with our students who have reading problems."

The rest of the meeting passed Reed right by. Bus schedules were discussed as was ushering for football games. The new band uniforms had not arrived yet, and Mrs. March was distraught. Reed, however, spent his time doodling on his legal pad, thinking about the special reading program. "There certainly is some animosity toward the special reading class," he thought. "There is going to be some resentment of me and my students, and I guess I'll just have to get used to that."

His mind had just turned, once again, to the problem of screening the referrals he would get from the teachers when Mr. Topps adjourned the meeting by remarking, "Coffee and donuts are in the cafeteria. I'll wait until we're all down there before introducing the other new teachers."

Reed Moore, of course, had already been introduced!

Monthly Logs

September   Although this is my twenty-first year of teaching, September has seemed like that first September, 20 years ago. I have never taught reading before this year, nor have I ever had such a concentration of students with severe reading problems. In fact, I would probably still be teaching English at D. Utter High if it were not for my son Worth. A few years ago, my wife and I were called to the elementary school where he was completing the fifth grade and asked if we would agree to having him repeat fifth grade. We were shocked. His two older sisters had been excellent students. When we asked for the reason he should be retained, the reply was that he did not read well enough to succeed in middle school.

We had known that he was having to struggle along, but his grades had not been that bad and his teachers had always been cautiously optimistic during our conferences with them. I felt cheated. A teacher myself, how could I not have realized that Worth had been a poor reader who was falling farther and farther behind each year? I guess I had always held the belief that if you really try you can do it. I kept thinking that one day Worth would get interested in school, exert himself, and spurt to the head of the class. I was soon to discover how wrong I had been.

After we told Worth's principal and teacher that we needed a few days to think things over, we went home and made a frantic call to Dr. Lea, the director of the Reading Clinic at State. He had a waiting list, but when we explained that a decision to retain or not was in the balance, he agreed to have two of his graduate students test Worth the next afternoon.

The results were far worse than we feared. Worth could barely read at a second-grade level. Dr. Lea explained that he read one word at a time, very deliberately, and remembered little of what he read. He recommended against retention, arguing that if they could have done anything for him in the fifth grade, they would have done it. Rather, he recommended tutoring five days per week all summer and a special reading teacher at school during the following year. He wrote specific instructional recommendations for the tutor and teacher to follow and suggested that Worth be tested in the Reading Clinic again the next spring. By the next spring, he read fluently and confidently at the fourth-grade level. His progress was sufficient enough that when we read his textbook assignments to him at home every night, he could pass. Some years he had good special reading teachers, and some years he had poor ones, but in high school there were none at all. By that time he could read well enough to survive, but after high school graduation he went to work and refused to consider any more education.

During these years of tutoring, clinic testing, and special reading instruction for Worth, I became more and more interested in reading, and more and more committed to quality, remedial instruction for those students who are severely retarded in reading, especially in middle and high school. The more sensitive I became to reading problems, the more I discovered students with reading problems in my English classes. When I became convinced that many of my students could not read and appreciate the literature I loved so much, I tried to teach them to read. I used Dr. Lea for a free consultant and wore a path to his office. Finally, he advised me to take his introductory graduate course in reading, and the rest is history. I have survived my first month as a secondary reading teacher, including all the decisions which had to be made about screening, referrals, and room layout.

My years of experience as an English teacher are helping me deal with discipline and classroom organization, but I will have to develop from scratch most of what I teach and how I teach it. When Mr. Topps and I agreed that I should take the poorest readers in the school who were not enrolled in other special programs, we did so, realizing that all 90 of my students would probably read below sixth-grade level.

Screening referrals

One hundred and fifty-two students were referred to me by the faculty, and my first task was to select the 90 who would be enrolled in the program. With some help from Dr. Lea, I formulated a screening-diagnostic system. Originally Dr. Lea had suggested that I use a group-administered, standardized, diagnostic placement test. He had said, "It will give you a fairly accurate estimate of instructional and independent reading levels for most students. You can use that information for both screening and to plan initial instruction." But when he found out that I had three weeks to obtain and screen referrals and to organize my classroom, he changed his mind. "You have enough time to be more accurate than a single test can be. Use a couple of measures for screening so that you can really find the students who need the program. Once you have selected your students, then you should do some individual diagnosis to get the most accurate information possible. These students will have failed every year they have been in school; you need to start off with the most appropriate instruction possible for each student."

As the referrals began coming in, I called 10–15 students at a time to the Reading Center for screening. This process took a full 48-minute period for each group and consisted of two group tests. This screening was made necessary by the lack of any valid data on the reading abilities of these students. Some standardized-test scores did exist, but secondary-level achievement tests give notoriously inaccurate results for very poor readers.

**Limited
cloze**

Because I had referrals for students from every grade at Upton Hill, 6–12, I developed three levels of tests. I visited Merritt Elementary School and borrowed a science textbook and a social studies textbook for grades three and five. I also borrowed science and social studies books from one or our sixth-grade teachers at Upton Hill. Fortunately, they use series for which readability is controlled. I selected a passage from the middle of each of the six books. This passage was always the beginning of a new chapter and was at least 125 words long. In fact, I always stopped the passage at the end of the sentence which contained the 125th word.

After choosing these six 125-word passages, I typed six limited-cloze tests (Cunningham and Cunningham, 1978) on mimeograph stencils. Like traditional cloze, a limited-cloze test is a passage in which the fifth word and every successive fifth word have each been left out and replaced by a blank of uniform length. In this case 25 words were left out of each passage. Unlike regular cloze, however, in limited-cloze the deleted words are mixed in a random order and typed in columns at the top of the test. This change makes cloze more usable with poor readers. The job of the student is to put the words at the top in the appropriate blanks. A student's score on the limited-cloze is the percentage of blanks correctly filled. I ran off 150 copies of each test. Fifty of these tests I stored in the filing cabinet to use as a posttest at the end of the year.

FOR THE READER TO DO:

Choose a book. Construct a limited-cloze test exactly the way Reed did. Decide why each blank must be the same length. Decide what advantages limited-cloze has over regular cloze (where there are no words to choose from in filling the blanks.)

When the students came to my room for screening, I administered two tests to each student. Students in sixth or seventh grade completed the tests constructed from the third-grade science and social studies books. Students in eighth or ninth grade completed the tests constructed from the fifth-grade books. Students in tenth, eleventh, or twelfth grade completed the tests constructed from the sixth-grade books. If I were still teaching at D. Utter High, I would have used passages taken from higher-level books since students in that community score considerably higher on all reading achievement measures than do students from this community.

The students I selected for the program were the lowest of those referred. This system resulted in 91 students being enrolled in special reading. The next task was scheduling the students into the six sections. I did not want an age range of more than three grades in any one section of reading, and I did not want to take students from any other subject-area than English. As a result we had to change the schedules of 41 students! If there is a better way to do it I would gladly adopt it, but as far as I know, rescheduling is necessary if the students who most need the service of special reading are to receive it.

In all, it took three weeks to obtain the referrals, screen them, select the students to be included, and schedule them—including rescheduling some or all of their other classes. During this period, I was also organizing the furniture and instructional materials in the Reading Center.

**Classroom
arrangement**

It seemed crucial to me that my classroom be different in appearance and organization from a regular middle or high school classroom. Most of my students were doing quite poorly in their regular classes, and I did not want them to automatically associate an expectation of difficulty with special reading. I asked Mr. Topps to allow me to have only straight chairs, tables, and carrels in my room, removing those desks I have despised through all my years as a teacher. He had Dusty remove the desks and replace them with 20 straight, wooden chairs and 4 rectangular tables of various sizes. The only carrels in the school were needed in the foreign language lab, but Mr. Topps agreed to furnish lumber and other materials to build some for my room. He and I spent most of one Saturday building these carrels and setting them up in the Reading Center.

Mrs. Bennett had managed to obtain a used sofa and a large bookshelf last year, both of which I have kept. Mr. Topps found a second bookshelf for me, and he asked Mrs. Hammer to have her advanced shop students make two more, a task they have already completed. The room also had a closet, an old filing cabinet, and a teacher's desk and chair left over from last year which I am also using.

Deciding which materials I will use and how I will organize them has been difficult, and this difficulty has been compounded by Ms. Erable. She visited with me for two mornings during the first three weeks of September and in both cases strongly encouraged me to use the word-identification skills-oriented workbook series which she had ordered for Mrs. Bennett last year. When I mentioned how boring and babyish I thought the program was, she said that the purpose of a special reading program was to teach the reading skills. When I pointed out how little actual reading the students did in these workbooks, she said that one must learn the reading skills before being able to read. When I protested that the program was concerned solely with word identification, ignoring comprehension and critical reading, she said that comprehension was thinking and that you cannot teach thinking. "They either have it up here," she said pointing to her temple, "or they don't."

Finally I agreed to consider using the program with some students, she left, and I took two aspirins. It was obvious that she thought I had no ability to design a program for my students but needed to rely on some teacher-proof material. She obviously does not see her job as helping me do what I believe in doing, but rather as making me do what she believes I should be doing.

Fortunately, Mrs. Bennett did order a number of trade books. These include a number of junior novels and several series of adolescents' fiction. In addition, I found sets of high-interest/low-vocabulary books in the closet. One set of these books has the look of adult reading material, yet the stories in these books are written from first- to sixth-grade level depending on which books from the series you use. Another set of books is also adult in appearance and interest. The books are novels written at second-, third-, and fourth-grade level. Of course, these books have little literary merit to recommend them, but you must crawl before you can walk. When people are learning to talk, dance, play tennis, or juggle, we expect them to function at a low level at first; why not when reading fiction?

I have displayed all these books on the bookshelves or in the revolving paperback bookrack which the local bookstore donated to the center. As much as possible, I tried to place the books so that their front covers would show, since books so displayed are more popular with students than books shelved with only their spines showing. I purposely made no distinction in shelving between books with low or controlled readability and the others, in order to avoid giving the high/low books a bad name. The only ones which were not shelved with the other books were those held back to use instructionally in small-group lessons.

For individual, independent work I set up various kits and tape programs which Mrs. Bennett had used. I used five carrels, putting one kit or program per carrel. Miss Turner let me have another cassette tape recorder and two extension cords for this purpose.

FOR THE READER TO DO:

Draw a map of the Reading Center as you think Reed might have organized it. Assume that the room is 35 feet by 25 feet with windows along one wall and one door next to the corner on the opposite wall. Remember the furniture Reed has described:

sofa
20 straight chairs
4 rectangular tables of various sizes
5 carrels
teacher's desk and chair
closet
filing cabinet
large bookshelf
3 other bookshelves
paperback bookrack

Keep in mind possible discipline problems as well as Reed's belief that his classroom should be different in appearance and organization from a regular middle/secondary classroom.

Monday of the fourth week of September was the first day I actually held classes in the Reading Center, and by sixth period I was grateful for having had the first three weeks to prepare. That class begins at 12:15, which means that all 15 students have just finished lunch. The general consensus among them so far has been that they would like to nap through my entire class.

Two of my sixth-period students are eighth-graders, five are ninth-graders, and eight are tenth-graders. Two are girls, the rest are boys. When they came in for the first time last Monday, they all entered the room cautiously, acting almost as if they did not know each other. Everyone sat at the tables except for Seymour and Jeff who sat on the sofa. It turned out that they were the only students in sixth-period class who had been in Mrs. Bennett's special reading program last year. Obviously more comfortable with the idea of being in a special reading class than the others, Jeff quietly poked and kidded Seymour. Seymour would pull his long hair down over his eyes and pretend that he could not see Jeff.

Most of the other students sat and stared out the windows. They seemed to be avoiding my gaze and each others' as if they were embarrassed to be there. I thought of my poor son Worth and all he must have gone through to receive the extra reading help we obtained for him.

When the bell rang I moved to the door, made sure it was locked from the outside, and closed it. Everyone was seated. I moved to the chalkboard and wrote "Mr. Moore" in large manuscript letters. "I'm Mr. Moore," I said, "your English teacher. This English class has only half as many students as a regular English class which will allow me to get to know each of you better."

I called the roll. Everyone was there except Gene.

"In this English class we will specialize in improving your ability to read, write, and study. I will expect you to be here on time unless you have a legitimate excuse. When the bell rings I will shut and lock the door from the outside. If you're late, you must knock on the door and get my permission to enter.

"I expect you to work in my class and allow others to work as well. In return, I promise you that the work I'll ask you to do will be work you can successfully complete, and I also promise that you will all improve in your abilities to read, write, and study.

"In order to plan work for you that will help you I need to do some testing, but I will try to do no more testing than is necessary."

No one said anything, but I thought I detected an expression of hopelessness on some faces. I wondered how many of them had given up thinking that school could be anything but frustration for them. I was determined that they work and behave for me, and I was equally determined that they would make progress.

IRI

After Dr. Lea and I had decided that I would do individual testing with all students, I had constructed an Informal Reading Inventory using passages selected from graded materials at an older interest level. Using a set of high-interest/low-vocabulary books of short stories which I planned to use for small-group instruction, I selected a meaningful passage from the middle of each book, levels 1–6. These passages had to be at least 300 words long, and I made up 8 questions for each passage. To be sure my questions were "passage dependent", I asked them to my wife without letting her read the passages. Any questions she got right, I eliminated since one might be able to answer those questions correctly without having understood the passage.

To help me decide on what level to begin testing a student, I took a look at the results of the screening tests. For my sixth-period class these scores were as follows:

Scores on Limited-Cloze Tests Made from 5th-Grade Books			Scores on Limited-Cloze Tests Made from 6th-Grade Books		
	Science	Social Studies		Science	Social Studies
Bruce	44%	36%	Freddie	16%	16%
Clarence	56	52	Jeff	28	24
Eddie	44	44	John	36	36
Elsie	56	44	Marion	20	16
Gene	12	0	Otelia	24	20
Jake	52	48	Ricardo	4	36
Rufus	16	8	Seymour	28	28
			Willie	24	24

Because limited-cloze is a multiple-choice version of regular cloze, scores on limited-cloze tests tend to be higher than they would have been for regular cloze tests constructed from the same passages. If a student scores below 60 percent, it is probable that the passage from which the test was made is too difficult for that student to read without frustration.

FOR THE READER TO DO:

Examine the scores on the screening instruments for Reed's sixth-period class. The scores are reported as percentages; determine what the actual score was for each student on each test. Why did some students have scores on tests from a 5th-grade book and the others have scores on tests from a 6th-grade book? Since both passages were taken from books designed to be used with students in the same grade, why might the students tend to do better on the science passages?

With everyone settled after my opening remarks, I handed out a questionnaire which I instructed them to fill out in their best handwriting and spelling. I had constructed the questionnaire to give me some information about their interests and schedules, but the main purpose of the questionnaire was to find out how well they could write. I explained to them that I would be calling on them one at a time for testing while they were completing the questionnaire. When everyone began writing, I called the first student for the IRI.

Bruce walked over to my desk, looking at his shoes the whole way. He refused to look me in the eye. He threw his body into the chair beside my desk. "Bruce, I'm going to ask you to read some passages to yourself so that when you're finished you can answer several questions."

After looking at his scores on the screening tests, I handed him the passage from the third-grade-level high/low book. He read the passage rather quickly and handed it back to me. I asked him the 8 questions orally, and he answered 7 out of the 8. I next gave him the fourth-grade passage to read, and he answered 5 out of 8. From the fifth-grade passage he answered only 2 out of 8. Since the cut-off point I'm using is 75 percent (Betts, 1946), I recorded "level 3" by Bruce's name and asked him to return to his seat. Of course, I didn't tell him that he only seemed able to read at third-grade level. I also got to Clarence, Eddie, and Elsie, and all read as well as Bruce or a little better.

Monday night as I examined the questionnaires the students had completed, I was appalled. Their writing was incomprehensible. Elsie and John could spell pretty well, but everyone else had serious spelling problems, even on common words like "this" and "when." Legibility of handwriting was not a serious problem for anyone but Jake. Several of the students wrote primarily in standard English dialect, while the rest wrote in various other dialects. What amazed and shocked me was that regardless of legibility, spelling, or dialect, none of the students could write, not if writing means writing something comprehensible!

On Tuesday and Wednesday I finished giving the IRI while the other students completed some assigned activities designed to determine which study skills they could use. I knew from their performance on the questionnaire on Monday that they would be unable to write well enough or fast enough to take notes, but I wondered if they could use the parts of a textbook to help them find the answers to questions they were asked. I made an overhead transparency from a page in the index of the fifth-grade science book. I put this transparency on the overhead projector and pulled down the screen above the middle of the chalkboard. Beside the screen on the right side of the board I wrote several questions like, "On what page in this book would you find out how many moons Mars has?" All the students had to do was to guess what keywords to use and to find these keywords in the index. In several cases they also needed to be able to use subheadings under the main index entries.

From these three days of testing I learned that the students' writing abilities and textbook-reference skills were practically nonexistent. The IRI results provided me with an estimate of the instructional reading level for each student. I decided that I would not do any more testing at this time, even though there is certainly more to be learned about these students. It's just that so much of what I need to know about them concerns how well they will respond to certain kinds of instruction. The only way to find that out is actually to teach them and see how well they learn. Later I may do more testing, but it will only be with those students who do not seem to be gaining from my instruction.

I have quite a range of reading levels, but no one reads well. The results of the IRI are as follows:

Student	Level	Student	Level
Bruce	3	John	4
Clarence	4	Marion	2
Eddie	3	Otelia	2
Elsie	4	Ricardo	2
Freddie	2	Rufus	–
Gene	(not tested)	Seymour	3
Jake	4	Willie	2
Jeff	3		

It is incredible that these students read so poorly after so many years in school. Clarence seems to read better than any of the other students in my sixth-period class, yet even he is functionally illiterate. When I asked him to read from the sports page of the daily newspaper he stumbled through it. I didn't bother asking anyone else to try it.

The only student who hasn't been here every day is Gene, and I have yet to see him. The office sent a memo to me yesterday saying that he was in custody at juvenile court but might be released soon.

October   While I was an English teacher, I developed a philosophy of teaching that I have tried to implement in my new role as a special reading teacher. When I first started teaching, most teachers—especially at the middle and high school level—used whole-group instruction. All students were expected to be doing the same thing at the same time. All students were given the same textbook and the same assignments in that textbook. I moved away from this whole-group concept in my classroom early in my career. It was obvious to me that my students were so diverse in their interests and abilities that giving them all the same instruction was ludicrous.

In recent years, however, there has been a strong move to individualize at the secondary level. On the face of it, such a move seems valid, and I was one of the early supporters of individualization. Unfortunately, I soon found that the new "individualization" was no more compatible with my philosophy of teaching than whole-group instruction had been. The supervisors and consultants who pushed for increased individualization seemed to feel that a crime was being committed against students if they did anything together. One of our supervisors said that whenever she came into a classroom, she expected 35 different students to be doing 35 different things! Not only was such a definition of individualization impossible for teachers to implement, but it would have been disastrous had it been implementable. Students need structured interaction with teachers and each other. They must verbalize and communicate their understandings to see what they still need to learn. When I determined that what my supervisor meant by individualized instruction was students working in isolation on worksheets, I balked.

Classroom organization   My belief is that the best instruction consists of a combination of whole-group, small-group, and individual activities, and I have attempted to establish such a mixture in my special reading class. I started out the month by developing a system of folders which would give each student a schedule to follow. Students pick up their folders when they first come into class and deposit them upon leaving class. When I first put out the folders, a line formed, but the next day I spread them out in three different boxes, with each box divided into periods. I colored-coded the flap of each folder to designate the period so that students could easily see which folders belonged to their class and would only need to look among those to find the ones with their names on the flaps.

In each folder I put a sheet entitled "Five-Day Schedule." This sheet had lines at the top for the student's name and grade. Below that a line of numbers represented the periods of our school day, and the student's period was circled. The remainder of the sheet was divided into five boxes, each labeled with the day of the week. I write in each box what I have planned for the student to do that day. This folder system, with the five-day schedule sheets, was the key to my organization for instruction. Without such a system I would have been overwhelmed by the organizational problems of trying to design instruction to meet the diverse needs of 91 severely disabled readers.

SSR

Using the data I obtained during screening and initial diagnosis, I planned whole-group, small-group, and individual activities and tried to schedule them so that I could get maximum use of my time as a teacher. The first activity I planned was Sustained Silent Reading (SSR). I decided to do SSR at the beginning of class every period every day. SSR is a whole-group activity in which everyone reads including the teacher. Students select a book and read that book without interrupting or being interrupted for whatever length of time has been established by the teacher. I decided to begin every class with five minutes of SSR, adding a minute to that when the class seemed comfortable with five minutes. SSR is a valuable activity with any group of reading students, but it is especially so for students with reading problems, who rarely read unless assigned to do so. SSR tries to establish the habit of reading for relaxation and pleasure. The students are never tested over what they have read. They are only required to "appear to be reading" and not to interrupt anyone else who is reading. During October, I have found that SSR has a fringe benefit; after five minutes of quiet and relaxation, the students seem much more ready to get to work. (Otelia has already told me that it is her favorite time of the school day.) I wish I had done SSR in my English classes all those years. It always seemed to take several minutes for students to get settled down after talking and moving through the halls between classes. I put "SSR—5 minutes" at the top of all five boxes on every student's schedule sheet.

Circle activities

Next I decided that Friday would be the day for whole-group, language arts integration activities. Fridays have too often become throw-away days for some teachers, and I had no intention of that happening in my classes. On the other hand, I knew how difficult it was to keep students working on Friday, doing the same kinds of things they have done the other four days of the week. Some time has to be spent dealing with and preventing discipline problems, and some time should be spent dealing with issues of self-concept and allowing the students to be involved in planning and evaluating the special program. I used Glasser (1969) Classroom Meetings when I taught English and, I plan to use them this year. These meetings are an excellent way to cope with and prevent discipline problems, and they also allow the students to be involved in the operation of the class. Friday seemed like a good day for such meetings.

Also on Fridays, I thought we would occasionally do a play as a group, or have someone visit the class to talk to the students about some matter which concerned them. Coach Wynne has agreed to ask Tim Duncan, State's basketball star, to come to my classes on a Friday this fall. I grouped all of these activities under language arts integration in my own mind because they will often build on what the students have written and read during the week, and will always require the students to be active listeners. The main purpose of these activities is to encourage students to express themselves orally concerning some topic of interest.

When I explained what we would be doing on Fridays, I called these activities circle activities, because everything I planned to do on Friday would take place within a circle of chairs. I wrote "circle activity" in every student's Friday box right after "SSR– 5 minutes."

For the first circle activity, I planned a classroom meeting on the topic of television violence. In a classroom meeting, you lead a circle of students through a discussion by asking a series of questions. You do not give your opinion or comment on the opinions of the students. You ask questions which will stimulate discussion, encourage participation, and discourage interruptions or more than one person speaking at a time. For the second circle activity, we read aloud a play from a high-interest/low-vocabulary magazine I subscribe to. The third Friday, Mr. Cross came in and explained mouth-to-mouth resuscitation and other means of saving people in trouble. Marion tried to practice mouth-to-mouth on Elsie, but she kicked him in the knee! It's a good thing Red was there.

At that point in making out the five-day schedule sheets, I decided that SSR and circle activities would be the only regular whole-group activities I would have and I began planning small-group lessons. The first thing I considered in planning these groups was the estimate of instructional level I had obtained for each student on my IRI. I put the 14 sixth-period students into four instructional-level groups. These four groups were:

Beginning Readers	2nd-grade Level	3rd-grade Level	4th-grade Level
Rufus	Freddie	Bruce	Clarence
	Marion	Eddie	Elsie
	Otelia	Jeff	Jake
	Ricardo	Seymour	John
	Willie		

In the beginning I scheduled one small-group lesson per week for each of the four groups. I decided to meet with Bruce, Eddie, Jeff, and Seymour on Monday; Freddie, Marion, Otelia, Ricardo, and Willie on Tuesday; Rufus on Wednesday; and Clarence, Elsie, Jake, and John on Thursday. I put "small-group lesson" right under "SSR–5 minutes" in the proper box on each student's schedule sheet. Otelia and Elsie were disappointed that they were not in the same group, but I ignored their complaints.

The remainder of the students' work has to be individual activities, since I have no aide or student teacher to help. Perhaps later on in the year the students will require less supervision during independent work, and I can add a second group each of the first four days of the week. Ideally I think I should be teaching all the time after SSR.

Can't Stop Writing

The first type of independent activity I planned for the students was "Can't Stop Writing" (Allington, 1975). This activity is usually done with whole groups of students, but I modified it so that individuals could be scheduled during the time I was working with other students in small groups.

My students are such poor writers that I knew I must do something about it. Also I expected that improved writing would help reading, and improved reading would help writing. It upset me to think how many years these students had been given grammar instruction with the mistaken notion that teaching grammar improves the quality and correctness of student writing. Every year they spent struggling to put the correct word in the blanks in grammar book exercises or striving to circle the adverbs in a paragraph they copied from the grammar book put them further and further behind in the actual ability to write. One does not and cannot learn to write by memorizing rules for writing and definitions of parts of speech. In order to learn how to write one must practice until writing becomes a fluent activity.

Clarence told me English grammar was his best subject. He got As and Bs, and he couldn't write a letter to Santa Claus! Unfortunately, after years of instruction in grammar, many students are unable to write at all for fear of making a grammatical error. I call them "catatonic writers" because they have become immobile in writing. "Can't Stop Writing" is a technique that distracts students from thinking about grammar rules long enough that they begin to feel how language can flow on paper the way oral language flows in conversation.

FOR THE READER TO DO:

To see what Mr. Moore means by "catatonic writing," write a paragraph on the subject of "How to Teach Writing." Observe the following rules and directions:

Rules
1. Do not end a sentence with an adverb.
2. Every negative sentence must have double negation (not single or triple).
3. Use only the passive voice.
4. Capitalize all improper nouns; do not capitalize proper nouns.
5. Use a comma to separate the subject from the predicate. (*Exception:* This rule does not apply to sentences with intransitive verbs.)

Directions
Remember—it is the ideas that really matter.
Don't forget neatness, legibility, and spelling.
You may keep the rules in front of you as you write.
After you finish the paragraph, carefully check it for errors by using one rule or direction at a time.

When you have finished, decide if you know grammar rules which are similar to the ones in this exercise. When students write, do they have only five rules to apply? Do they have the rules right in front of them? Do they understand what the rules mean as well as you understood these made-up rules? Decide how you think many children learn to write correctly without formal grammar instruction?

"Can't Stop Writing," like any writing students are asked to do, should not be done cold. Students usually need some warm-up and stimulation for writing, and this is especially true for poor writers. The stimulation I use is the open-ended story. I find a story that has immediate action and sets up a problem for the character. It's best if the story is written in the first person. I record the first two or three paragraphs on a cassette tape and then direct the students to begin writing. The only rule is that "you can't stop writing." If a student cannot think of anything to write, he or she must write "My name is _____," over and over until he or she can think of something. The students leave the tape run-

FIVE-DAY SCHEDULE

Name: _John_

Grade: _10th_

Period: 1 2 3 4 5 ⑥ 7 8

Monday	SSR - 5 minutes "Can't Stop Writing" - 10 minutes Study Skills Kit - Level C
Tuesday	SSR - 5 minutes Comprehension Kit - Level D
Wednesday	SSR - 5 minutes "Can't Stop Writing" - 10 minutes Study Skills Kit - Level C
Thursday	SSR - 5 minutes Small - group lesson Comprehension Kit - Level D
Friday	SSR - 5 minutes Circle Activity

ning while they write. A bell rings on the tape after they have written five minutes; another bell rings at the end of ten minutes. Some students are assigned to write for five minutes, while others are assigned to write for ten minutes. When the time is up, each student counts the total number of words written and enters that number at the top of the story. The student tries to increase the total each time.

Other types of independent activities include a creative writing center which I developed in one of the carrels and the use of some of the kits and workbook programs which build passage comprehension, content-area reading, and reference and study skills. I entered these independent activities on the five-day schedule sheets so that all students are working independently while I am teaching small-group lessons. Following the small-group lessons, I walk around and help students individually.

After I planned the different whole-group, small-group, and individual activities and assigned each student to the activities by filling out a five-day schedule sheet and placing it in his folder, I was ready to implement the folder system.

Discipline   In sixth period I wanted to be especially careful of how I introduced the folders, because discipline was somewhat shaky ever since Gene started coming to class. The first day he walked into the class he was singing at the top of his lungs. When the bell rang I began to explain what Sustained Silent Reading is and that we would be doing it at the beginning of every class, every day. I used the examples of learning to play the guitar and of learning to ride a bicycle to show how important practice is. I explained that they had to act as if they were reading and not interrupt me or anyone else for any reason until the timer bell rang. During this explanation he grinned at me and the others and poked the students who were sitting close to him until both of them moved away from him. I tried to ignore him, but he only got worse.

Following my explanation of SSR, we did several trial runs in which each student walked in the room again from the hall as if the class were just beginning, selected a book from the bookrack or shelves, and sat down ready to begin. I started the timer and everyone began reading. Immediately I turned the timer so that the bell rang. The students then stood up and returned their books to the rack or shelf and returned to their seats. I have found that trial runs are important for students whenever you are trying to institute any new activity because the students learn the mechanics of behaving during the activity from the trial run. When the activity itself begins, they know what to expect and can concentrate on the learning part of the activity. Trial runs prevent discipline problems and enhance the chances of success of new teaching techniques.

This particular trial run went very well for all the students except Gene. When he went out in the hall to pretend class was just beginning, he left and did not return to class that day. I reported his absence to the office. The next day the students were prepared to come in, choose a book, and sit down so that when the bell rang we would have SSR for the first time. No one was enthusiastic about it, and a few students seemed to think it was a little babyish, but I had trained them in what to do and they all did it, even Gene. But, when the five minutes of time actually began, Gene wasn't even pretending to be reading. Within a minute he was out of his seat standing beside me. He pointed to a place on the page and said quite loudly, "What is this word?"

FOR THE READER TO DO:

Decide what you would do about Gene's interruption if you were Reed Moore.

I had had students like Gene before, and I knew how *not* to handle them. Ignoring them when they openly defy you is almost always fatal. They are demanding that you prove your leadership, and each time they are ignored they escalate the outrageousness of their behavior until the class is in turmoil. Shouting at them only makes them angry and makes you look foolish.

As he stood over me with a large grin on his face pointing to a word, I could feel the gaze of the other students. No one was reading. I felt myself growing angry and frustrated. Calmly I reached over and picked up the timer. I turned to Gene, "For SSR we read silently without any help. You must choose a book that you can read without help. If you want me to, I will help you find a book before tomorrow's class." I turned the timer back to five minutes, placed it on the table, and began reading again. The next time Gene interrupted, which was in about two minutes, I just picked the timer up and started it at five minutes again. I was prepared to follow this procedure until we completed 5 minutes of SSR if it took the entire class. I believe SSR is important, and I was determined that no student was going to prevent it from becoming a part of our special reading class. The third time I picked the timer up to start it again on five minutes, the entire class turned on Gene. Clarence said, "Sit down and shut up so I can finish reading." Others echoed these sentiments. Gene was so shocked that it was him against everyone else that he didn't interrupt again until the timer rang.

That same day I gave him the IRI during class. At first he refused to read for me. He had scored below even Rufus on the screening tasks, and I started him out on the first-grade-level passage. "I can read this easy stuff," he said.

"I don't believe you, Gene. You have to show me. Try to read it so I know what to do to help you read better."

Whispering to make sure no one else heard him, he began reading haltingly. Within a few sentences it was obvious to me how frustrated he was. Like Rufus, Gene was a non-reader.

Classroom organization You can understand, after these events, how nervous I was about putting out folders and having students begin working on more individualized activities. Of course, we began with a trial run after I explained the reason for the folders. Each student ran through his/her weekly schedule on this first day, and I went around asking questions to learn if students understood what to do and answering their questions about how to use kits and other independent materials. I had put Gene with Rufus so that I could work with them on Wednesday for a small-group lesson. Neither Gene nor Rufus was pleased about this arrangement, but I worked right through it without stopping for complaints about who was in which group. None of the boys wanted to be in the group with a girl, but I ignored that as well. The trial run went well and everyone seemed to understand what to do. They were to come into the room and pick up their folders, select a book to read, and sit down and chat until SSR began. Following SSR they were to place the book in their folders if they wanted to continue reading it the next day or return it to the shelves if they did not. They then were to move to the area of the room where their schedule sheet directed them and begin work. When the bell rang they were to put completed work on my desk in the box labeled "sixth-period" and put uncompleted work in their folders. They were to place their folders in a box on their way out the door.

The first Wednesday in October was the first day we operated sixth period with the folders. Most of the other classes had already begun using them, for I had staggered the days when each period would start so that I was not totally exhausted by the end of the day. Wednesday was the best day to begin with sixth period because that is the day each week that I work with Rufus and Gene for 20 minutes or so after SSR ends.

It was difficult to plan small-group lessons for Rufus and Gene because I had to teach them to read, rather than to teach them to read better. They could not read any material I had in the Reading Center, including the easiest high-interest/low-vocabulary short stories which were written down to first-grade readability. (The selection from those stories on the IRI had been too hard for both of them.) My first decision was to determine which method of beginning reading I would use with them, especially since every teacher they had ever had before had failed to teach them to read. As I pondered that decision, I remembered back to the two courses in diagnosis and remediation of reading difficulties I had with Dr. Lea. Dr. Lea taught us that the language-experience approach to teaching beginning reading was as good but no better than any other major approach for developmental students, but that language experience was the best way to teach beginning reading to remedial students. He taught us how to use a picture or an object to get the students to begin talking, and then he taught us to write down the exact words of the student (regardless of grammar or usage) but to spell all words the way the dictionary spells them. This student dictation becomes the material which is used to teach the student to read. He gave us several advantages for language experience as a remedial technique:

Language experience

1. Very little if any material exists for teaching beginning reading which is interesting to older students. Language experience is materials free, using the students' own language and experience as reading material.
2. It is very low in cost.
3. The student experiences real reading from the beginning.
4. It assumes very little readiness. Readiness concepts like left-to-right and top-to-bottom orientation are taught while the student learns to read, rather than before.
5. In most cases, it is different than what has already been tried and failed.

For these reasons I decided to use language experience with Rufus and Gene in our group work on Wednesday. That first Wednesday's lesson began with all three of us being a little nervous. Gene said he didn't want to work with Rufus, and I pretended not to hear that. When the three of us were seated at the table, I took the picture I had brought and laid it on the table. It was a picture of two cars that had collided in the middle of an intersection. I said, "I want you to look at this picture and see if you can figure out what happened right before the wreck. See if you can decide whose fault it was."

Discipline

Gene looked around to see if anyone was watching, but no one was. Marion, Otelia, Ricardo, and Freddie were doing "Can't Stop Writing" and everyone else was doing an assignment in a kit or workbook. "I don't want to do this. This is dumb."

"Whose fault was it, Rufus?"

"It . . ."

Gene interrupted. "It was that red Chevrolet's fault."

"Is that what you think, Rufus?"

"No, I think it was the other car, 'cause there's a stop sign there."

Gene grinned and twisted his head wildly around, "You're stupid!"

I wondered how many thousands of times Rufus had been called stupid. I looked Gene right in the eye and asked as softly as I could, "What are you doing?"

"Nothing."

"Why are you interrupting Rufus and calling him stupid?"

"Because he is stupid!" He laughed.

I continued calmly. "What are you doing when you interrupt him and call him stupid?"

"I don't know."

"What are you doing?"

"I don't know."

"What are you doing?"

"This is dumb. Why do you keep asking me that question?"

"I want to know if you know what you're doing."

"Yes, I know what I'm doing!"

"What's it getting you?"

"What do you mean?"

"What is it getting you?"

Gene was beginning to get uncomfortable. "Can't we go back and talk about this picture?"

"It's up to you," I said. "That's what we were trying to do when you put up the hassle." I sat and stared right into his face. I had had about enough of him. If he wanted to rejoin the lesson, he was going to have to make the first move. Poor Rufus sat looking at the floor waiting for something to happen.

Gene picked up the picture and looked at it intensely. He was trying to come up with something to save face. "I don't think the Mercedes ran the stop sign. I just think the other car was coming too fast."

"All right," I said, "now that you have both decided whose fault it was, I want you each to tell me what happened, and I'll write down exactly what you say. Rufus, you go first."

Rufus said, "The Mercedes run the stop sign and was hit in the side by the red Chevrolet."

I wrote down his exact words on the paper under the picture, but I spelled all the words the way the dictionary spells them. He said "duh side" but I wrote "the side." .

"Now, Gene, explain what you think happened."

Gene said, "Well, I think the red Chevrolet was coming so fast that the Mercedes didn't have time to get across the road without being hit." I wrote these words down under where I had written Rufus's contribution. Immediately I asked each student to read what he had said, and both did so. I stored the picture away until the next Wednesday when we would continue to work on beginning reading.

The following Wednesday, I took out the picture with their two statements written beneath it. As I moved my hand along under the sentences, I read their statements to them and then asked them to read them to me. After they both read their statements, I took out two small sentence strips and wrote the statements exactly as they appeared beneath the picture, including the same-size letters and same-length sentences. I asked both Gene and Rufus to match each sentence strip with its replica under the picture. Following these sentence-matching exercises, I took scissors and cut the sentence strips into words and had them match words. Gene had no problem with the task and was a little bored with it, but Rufus actually hesitated several times before correctly matching a word.

At first, students can match sentences and words when they cannot read the sentences or the words. In matching sentences and words, the students learn to pay attention to distinctive characteristics of words which make them alike or different. Dr. Lea taught us not to try to teach words to students until we were sure they could match them. At this stage Gene has no problem with the matching, but Rufus can use some additional practice.

The other small-group lessons have been much easier to plan and conduct because the students can read. In each case I am using one book from the series of high-interest/low-vocabulary books which I held back for this purpose. I use the second-grade-level book from that series with Freddie, Marion, Otelia, Ricardo, and Willie. I use the third-grade-level book with Bruce, Eddie, Jeff, and Seymour. I use the fourth-grade-level book with Clarence, Elsie, Jake, and John. (Because I had planned to use this series of books as a basal with my instructional level groups, I constructed my Informal Reading Inventory from the series. An IRI should be made from the material you plan to use for instruction if the groupings are to be at all accurate.)

DRA

The teacher's manual which accompanies the high/low series gives difficult vocabulary words that students need to know to comprehend each story and several comprehension questions. If I am teaching a Directed Reading Activity with the story, I introduce the vocabulary words before asking the students to read, and I put the questions on the board and go over them ahead of time so that they know the questions they are reading to find the answers for. Of course, the students always read silently before we do any oral reading, and we restrict oral reading to those parts of a story which the answers indicate the students did not understand.

By now I have taught four small-group lessons to each group, and these lessons have gone very well. Rufus and Gene have four stories they have dictated and can read to me with ease. They are still matching sentences and matching words following their reading because Rufus is so poor at it, but soon we must move on because Gene is getting bored. He is clearly ready to learn some sight words, and actually has picked up a few serendipitously during the lessons. The week between groups is obviously a problem for Rufus, but I don't know what I'm going to do about it.

The independent work is giving me some problems. "Can't Stop Writing" has gone the best of all of them, but just counting words isn't enough anymore. I'm going to have to do something else with their writing which allows them to share what they have written. I feel guilty about most of the work in kits and workbooks, although the students are cooperating in doing the assignments; I guess this is the kind of work they've always had to do, and they're used to it. The problem is that I see them going through motions but without their minds being really involved.

November

The first significant event in the Reading Center this month was the giving of grades. Remembering back to the fevered discussion we had about credit and grades for special reading in the preschool faculty meeting, I was somewhat apprehensive about the reactions of my students and of other students and teachers to the grades I would give. The system I worked out was rather subjective and operated this way:

Students making their best effort and who
    are making the most progress receive ....A
Students making a good effort and who
    are making good, steady progress receive ....B
Students making some effort or who
    are making some progress receive C
Students making little or no effort and who
    are making little or no progress receive ....D
For sixth-period the spread of grades was as follows:

As	Bs	Cs	Ds
Clarence	Eddie	Bruce	Willie
	Elsie	Gene	
	Freddie	Jake	
	Jeff	Marion	
	John	Otelia	
	Rufus	Ricardo	
	Seymour		

Although I have always hated giving grades, this first set of reading grades served to motivate an analysis of each of my students, and the work each is doing. I had not realized how well Clarence was really doing, or how poorly Willie was doing. Clarence had read several books by beginning them in SSR and then asked to take them home to finish them. He had asked me to read some of his recent "Can't Stop Writing" production. Every minute of class time was used wisely by him, and he had completed Level D of the Comprehension Kit and Level C of the Study Skills Kit. I did not tell him in advance what his grade was going to be, and I waited anxiously for sixth period on the day the cards were given out to see his reaction. He was the first student in the room, and he had his report card in his hand.

"Hey, Mr. Moore! You make a mistake on my grade?"

I could tell by his expression that he just had to know if he had really earned an A.

"There's no mistake, Clarence. You deserved it."

He put the card in his back pocket and never said anything else about it to me or to anyone else in the class. I am sure he had never made an A before in anything. If I had asked him to jump out of a tree that day I'm sure he would have done it!

Willie was another story. The day before the grade cards were to be given out, I asked Willie to stay after class a few minutes. "I'll give you a pass to be late to your last class," I told him as he sauntered over to my desk.

"What you want to see me for? I ain't been doing nothing."

"That's exactly what I want to see you about," I said. "You haven't been doing anything in my class. I've been working so hard trying to teach you all that I haven't been noticing how little work you've been doing. When I was deciding last night on the grades I would give, I couldn't find any completed work for you. I'm going to give you a D."

"Well, I put it in my folder. Somebody must have taken it out."

Discipline I ignored his excuse. "You're going to do some work for me this nine weeks, Willie."

I handed him a pass and he left the room. The next day though, he jumped on Rufus when Rufus walked into the Reading Center and pulled Rufus's grade card out of his back pocket. You could tell that Rufus was scared of him. He just stood and watched Willie open the card. I walked from my desk over to where they were. Willie looked at the card and then looked me straight in the face. He cursed, "You gave him a damn B!"

Calmly I said, "Give Rufus back his report card, and we'll go to the hall and talk about it."

I stared right at the bridge of his nose and took one step toward him. He threw the report card at Rufus and stormed into the hall. I guess he was hurt. Getting a D was nothing new to him, but getting a D when someone like Rufus who couldn't even read was getting a B—that was rough on him.

The tardy bell rang and the hall cleared except for Willie and me. I decided that pity would do Willie no good now. "You can't read a newspaper or fill in a job application or read the driver's license manual. If you will let me, I will teach you how to read and write better."

"I can already read better than Rufus."

"Yes, you can. But Rufus is working hard and he is improving, and you're not. If I graded you on how well you read, every one of you would flunk."

"Anyone else get a D?"

"You're the only one in sixth period."

"Maybe I ought to go to the counselor and try to drop this course."

"Suit yourself, but if you'd have done any work, I'd have given you a C. Starting today, you have a new nine weeks."

I heard the timer go off in the Reading Center, I opened the door and went in. I left the door open for Willie to follow; he did.

It seems that Clarence had taken my roll book and called the roll, and then set the timer for SSR. The timer going off had been the end of SSR. The students were all smiling when I rounded the bookcase. "We did SSR without you and Willie, Mr. Moore," said Otelia. "And when Gene punched Marion in the side, Clarence picked the timer up and started it again just like you do."

Clarence was looking at the floor and Gene was grinning from ear to ear. I smiled. "You folks don't need me for a teacher. Maybe we ought to let Clarence take over, and I'll just go home." Everyone but Willie laughed.

Surprisingly, there have been no repercussions about the grades from any other teachers or students that I have heard. I have tried to be fair in my grading system, and I have tried to build in a minimum grade of C for anyone making an effort and any progress. A and B are still reserved for those doing especially well.

We have added two minutes to SSR and now read for seven minutes at the beginning of each class. We added the sixth minute right after report cards went out, and we just added the seventh minute here at the end of the month.

More of the students in all classes are checking books out to take home after they begin them in SSR. This is especially true of the high-interest/low-vocabulary novels that I interspersed with the adolescents' fiction on the paperback rack and shelves. Elsie said her mother had read two of the books!

I have also done a little lateral thinking and am doing very well with the small-group lessons. I have taught Clarence, Elsie, Jake, and John how to do a Directed Reading-Thinking Activity [pages 163-164] without me being with them. I still meet with them on Thursday, and we complete a Directed Reading Activity together, but they also meet by themselves on Tuesday for their DR-TA.

The group is about halfway through with the fourth-grade-level, high-interest/low-vocabulary book of short stories from the series of books I reserved for small-group lessons. We do one story per lesson, in the order they come in the book. At the current rate of two stories a week, they will soon complete the book. My goal is that they will then have gained enough in ability to move into the fifth-grade-level book of the series.

DRA   When I meet with them on Thursday, we follow the steps of the Directed Reading Activity. We talk briefly about the topic of the story to be read; I attempt to pique some interest in it and build some background of general information for it. I introduce the words which are new or difficult. I write questions from the teacher's manual on the board before they read so they have purposes for reading. They know that when they finish reading, they need to be able to answer those questions.

After this discussion of interest and background, and after the introduction of vocabulary and purposes for reading, they read the story to themselves. While they are reading silently, I am free to move around the room to help students who are working on independent activities.

When they finish reading, they turn their books over so I can tell who is finished. Clarence always finishes first and John last. With all books turned over, I ask the questions I set as purposes. If any answer is not complete or if there is a dispute among them as to the correct answer, I have them return to the part of the story that deals with that question and someone reads the pertinent parts. This follow-up oral reading gives me information about their knowledge and pronunciation of words. The other day a story was so difficult that we read the entire story orally after they had read it silently.

FOR THE READER TO DO:

Decide why Reed does not have the students read orally first and silently second in those cases when rereading is necessary.

DR-TA

On the other hand, when Clarence's group meets on Tuesday, I cannot meet with them because I am meeting with Freddie, Marion, Otelia, Ricardo, and Willie, who are in the second-grade-level, high/low book. The Directed Reading-Thinking Activity seemed appropriate for them to do independently, and Clarence and Elsie are really keeping it going. I taught two DR-TAs to them on Thursday and then turned it over to them on Tuesday. Clarence will get the books off the shelf behind my desk and hand them out. Everyone turns to the next story that none of them has read. Clarence will say, "All right, let's read the title of the story to ourselves."

After a pause for everyone, including him, to read the title for the first time, Clarence says, "Let's look at the pictures."

In a few moments, everyone closes the books and holds the place with a pencil. Clarence sits down, and Elsie goes to the board. "What do you think the story is going to be about?" she asks.

When she gets a prediction, she writes down what was said and puts that student's name in parentheses after the prediction. She is allowed to make predictions, too. When there are no more predictions, she sits down and all four of them read to the bottom of the third page of the story. (If anyone tries to read ahead, another page has to be turned which gives it away!) When everyone has finished reading the three pages, Clarence goes down the list and asks about each prediction. He asks if it were proven, disproven, or neither. A student must read aloud some part that proves or disproves a statement or prediction. Proven predictions are starred and disproven ones are erased. Those that are neither proven nor disproven remain for the next round.

At this point the students predict what the rest of the story will say or be about, and Elsie writes these new predictions on the board. Then everyone reads the rest of the story and verifies or refutes each prediction as before. They enjoy being able to teach the lesson themselves, and they enjoy the predicting. I enjoy the fact that they are really improving their reading comprehension abilities.

It has been more difficult to arrange a second small-group lesson each week for the other three groups because they cannot manage the DR-TA on their own. I did create a second lesson for Bruce, Eddie, Jeff, and Seymour. They meet with me on Mondays for a Directed Reading Activity in the third-grade-level, high/low book, and that has been well. After Clarence's group got started so well on their Tuesday DR-TAs, I decided to do a Directed Reading Activity with Bruce's group on Tuesdays at the same time I am teaching Freddie, Marion, Otelia, Ricardo, and Willie. For this second lesson, I placed them in the second-grade-level book so that I wouldn't have to work with them so much. I write the questions which are to be their purposes for reading on the board just as I do for Freddie's group. Unlike Freddie's group, however, that's all the readiness I do. Both groups then read the story silently.

After silent reading, I work with Freddie's group, asking the questions and doing oral rereading when necessary. Bruce's group does no oral rereading in this easier material, but, instead, tries to write answers to the questions. Just this week, I have added a second lesson for Freddie's group on Wednesday after I work with Rufus and Gene. That seems

DRA

to be the day everyone works best on independent activities, and the first time, anyway, I was not interrupted too often. I have not arranged a second small-group lesson with Rufus and Gene as yet, but I have recently made progress on developing independent activities they can do.

FOR THE READER TO DO:

Using the format of the Five-Day Schedule Sheet, outline in detail what Reed is now doing each day in his sixth-period class.

Language experience

I can see some growth in Rufus and Gene, but progress is slow. It is a shame that I can only do one language-experience lesson with them each week. We follow this basic outline for each lesson:

1. I reread the story aloud that they dictated at the end of the previous week's lesson; then they each read it aloud. I always move my hand along under the words as I read them and as they read them. I make sure they are looking at the words as they read them.
2. We use sentence strips, and they match the sentences on these strips to the like sentence in the story.
3. I cut the sentence strips into words, and they match these words to the words in the story.
4. They select two words and I select two words from the words they have matched successfully. These four words I teach them as sight words. I tell them:
   a. "This word is _____. What is this word?" I make sure they are looking at the word as they say it.
   b. "Close your eyes and try to see the word."
   c. "Open your eyes and look at the word."
   d. "Close your eyes and try to see the word."
   e. "Open your eyes and write the word."
   After I have presented each of the four words in this way, I add the new words to the word bank. (Every Monday after SSR, I check Gene's word bank and reteach those words he misses. I do the same for Rufus on Thursday. This takes only a few minutes.)
5. Using a picture or interesting object, I get them to dictate another story to be used the following Wednesday.
6. If any time remains, we reread stories from previous weeks for review.

Independent activities

The independent activities that I now assign to Rufus and Gene are of three kinds: (1) sight-word drill; (2) context-clue exercises; and (3) Directed Listening Activities. For sight-word drill I either have them work together, testing each other on their word banks, or I have them work one at a time at the Language-Master with sight-word cards. The sight words they study there are concrete words selected from the Cunningham Secondary and Adult Basic Sight Word List [Appendix C]. Concrete words are easier to learn than more abstract words or function words like *of*, *it*, *too*, *is*, and *this*, and I want them to have as much success as possible. I do make sure they are learning a few function words during our language-experience lessons.

For the context-clue exercises, I use sentences that I make from words in their word banks or that they have learned at the Language-Master. I make eight sentences and leave an important word which can be represented by a magazine picture out of each one. I type these sentences on a sheet of paper and laminate the sheet. I also laminate the eight magazine pictures that complete the sentences. The pictures are also numbered, and the word is written on the back. All Rufus or Gene has to do is to read the sentence, decide which picture best completes it, and write the word for the picture in the blank in the sentence. When I have checked the answers, a tissue erases the answers which were marked in grease pencil. I plan to save all these exercises for use in future years.

DLA　　For Directed Listening Activities, I use the second-grade-level, high/low book used with Freddie's group. I make a cassette tape in which I introduce new words and set purposes for listening. I then read the story into the tape, making sure that the story does not require more than ten minutes of straight listening. Following the story, I ask several oral, true-false questions.

These questions are based on the purposes for listening set in the readiness step. I try to pick the most interesting stories. I do not know if these activities are really helping Rufus and Gene that much, but I have had to develop some exercises for them to complete independently so I can work with the other students.

As for the independent activities for the others, I am still not satisfied, but things have improved somewhat. I suppose I have over-used the Study Skills Kit and the Comprehension Kit, but the students can work independently at the appropriate level, and they are willing to do them. Even Willie is now completing Level A Study Skills exercises and Level B Comprehension exercises. They do not complete their assignments with great enthusiasm, but they do complete them.

In "Can't Stop Writing," rather than counting words, the students who are assigned to that activity at the same time read each others' stories after the writing and select the best one. I let a volunteer read the selected story at the end of SSR the following day. As long as the same person's story does not get chosen every day, I am going to continue this practice. I have modified five-day schedules again so all the people who write for five minutes are together and all those who write for ten minutes are together.

The last Friday in November, Tim Duncan visited my classes. He got everyone excited about State's upcoming basketball season. Everyone asked questions, even Elsie, who always pretends she knows it all. When he left, he asked, "Are all of these kids poor readers?" When I told him yes, he seemed amazed. "Really nice kids," he said.

It is a mystery to me why we seem to feel that anyone who reads poorly must be some kind of bizarre person. I remember feeling that way until Worth was threatened with retention in fifth grade. These last eight years, however, I have come to know many poor readers. As far as I can tell, the only thing they have in common is that they do not read well.

December　　One evening early in December, Mrs. Bennett called me at home. I had never met her, but, of course, I knew she had been Upton Hill's special reading teacher the year before. After introducing herself, she made a polite request. "Mr. Moore, may I come and spend a few hours with you in the Reading Center some day? I'm not involved in education right now, but I am considering working on my doctorate in reading education next year. I want to talk with Mr. Topps about it, and, while I'm in the building, I would like to see how the program we set up last year is going."

I was glad to respond positively since there were several questions I had wanted to ask about students she had taught and materials she had used with them. We agreed on a day that next week. I awaited her arrival on the following Tuesday, and she came in the room at the beginning of fourth period. She is a tall woman, about 30 years old. She greeted me in a very friendly manner. "It's so nice to meet you, Mr. Moore. Mr. Topps tells me your year is going well."

"Yes, I believe it is," I responded. "I appreciate the furniture and materials, especially the paperback books, I inherited from you."

At the beginning of the class, I introduced her and then we followed our regular Tuesday schedule. Mrs. Bennett read during SSR and then moved around the room observing and helping students who were working on independent activities while I handled my small-group lessons.

During fifth period I am off for lunch, and I asked her to eat with me. We got our trays and drinks and sat down at a table by ourselves. "What did you think of the fourth-period class?" I asked.

She seemed puzzled. "Is that the way you operate the class every day?"

I explained to her briefly how I group and how often I meet for small-group lessons. I also explained about the independent activities and about Friday's circle activities.

"No, that's not what I mean," she said. "I want to know if it is as relaxed every day, and if they work as hard as they did today? Frankly, Mr. Moore, I want to know if they were showing off for me."

I assured her that we had had visitors in the room before. Mr. Topps had been in several times and so had Connie Tent. Lee Yung and Miss Stern had each been in once or twice. "As far as I know," I replied, "what you saw was a typical Tuesday, which is a little better than a typical Monday and not quite as good as a typical Wednesday. I hope your question means that you think things went well."

"Well, I didn't really notice what skills you were teaching, but I must say I am impressed by how cooperative they are. They read at the beginning of class. They work together in small groups. They work independently without you having to stand over them. I guess men have an easier time with discipline."

That offended me slightly, so I said, "They'll do as well for you. Teach my sixth-period class for me, and I'll just walk around and observe like you did last period."

"Oh, Mr. Moore, I couldn't do that. I'd be afr . . . I wouldn't know what you do with them."

"Sure you will. I'll give you a handout to follow."

We finished lunch and went back to the Reading Center with 20 minutes to go before the beginning of sixth period. I showed her an outline of the steps to the DR-TA and explained to her that Clarence's group would complete that without her.

I gave her the teacher's manual for the high/low book of stories and explained to her how I introduce the new vocabulary and write the questions on the board to set purposes for reading. I told her that I leave Freddie's group while they read silently and help Bruce's group with any of the words or questions they do not understand as they attempt to write answers to the questions on the board. She liked the idea of Bruce's group getting a second small-group lesson each week by working more independently in this easier material.

I told her that Gene and Rufus would be working separately at the Language-Master and on context-clue exercises. "Don't be concerned with them," I said. "I'll watch them while you handle the three groups."

She was nervous, but I could tell that she really wanted to try it. After SSR, I introduced her and told everyone that she would be teaching the small-group lessons today. Only Jeff and Seymour had had her for a teacher last year.

Everything went smoothly. Willie reverted to his old habits and refused to do anything for her, but she kidded him along and brought him out of it. The only thing she did that bothered me was that when Freddie's group was rereading parts orally, she made every student sound out each word he or she did not read correctly. Otherwise she did well, I thought. She asked to do it again seventh period.

She stayed in the room until the end of school and then she said, "I cannot remember having had more fun. Thank you for letting me do some teaching."

At that point, I could not resist asking her, "I'm curious. Why did you leave your job here? You really seem to enjoy teaching."

She sat down in the wooden chair by my desk. For the first time that day she seemed really to relax. She smiled and took another look around the Reading Center. "Mr. Moore, I'm going to be honest with you in a way I haven't even been honest with myself. I told everyone that I was leaving last year for personal reasons and that I really regretted having to give up this program. The truth is: I could not handle the students. They would not do what I asked them to do, and they would not work unless I just dogged them. I decided I couldn't face another year like that one."

"Did you talk with Mr. Topps about it?" I asked.

"Yes, and he encouraged me. He said that I was used to teaching history to top students and that I would have a period of adjustment. He always complimented me on the furniture, materials, and general layout of the room. He called Ms. Erable several times to come and work with me. He even spent several hours observing me and making suggestions on how I might improve. I am afraid I was hopeless!"

I wondered to myself why Mr. Topps had not been able to help her. He had certainly helped me and several other of the new teachers this year. His suggestions were always so practical. I pressed her. "What did he suggest that you do differently?"

"He told me that I needed to stop teaching everyone in a whole group, and that everyone needed to read more from something interesting to them. He stressed the need to interest and motivate older remedial readers by showing them that reading can be comfortable, interesting, and informative."

"Did you try what he suggested?"

She paused a minute. "You know, for one thing, I wasn't certain that it was possible to do what he suggested. The students did not seem at all interested or motivated. I had been taught in my M.Ed. program that students must have basic reading skills before they can read. Some of my students could not even read at fifth-grade level. I felt that I had to spend all of my time teaching skills. Was that so wrong?"

"No," I responded, "I suppose not. Perhaps I don't do enough with skills. Students like Ricardo, Marion, and Freddie in my sixth-period class do have an awful time figuring out fairly easy words. I've been putting off that kind of instruction, however, because I agree with Mr. Topps. Convincing these students that reading is worth doing and that they can improve in reading seem to be the most crucial tasks for a remedial program.

"My job, after the holidays," I admitted, "will be to build on the motivation and cooperation you have seen today to get at the specific needs of the students. In the meantime, I believe most of them have improved their reading by reading material at appropriate levels for specific purposes.

"It may surprise you to know that, in the sixth-period class you taught today, there was not a single student at the beginning of the year who could read fifth-grade-level material."

She did seem shocked. "You mean the students I worked with in those three groups read that poorly? But they did so well. They could read and work independently."

"Well, they can only read material especially designed for them. Fortunately, we have a good deal of high-interest/low-vocabulary material being produced for older remedial readers. I believe that it is the most valuable material in the Reading Center. If I had to, I could make independent activities, but I have neither the time nor the talent to write material at their interest which they can read. And if they don't read, all the skills instruction in the world is a waste of their time and yours."

She sighed. "I wouldn't have believed it. And to think that I left those books in the closet to collect dust while I used that word identification skills-oriented workbook series which Ms. Erable ordered for me to use last year. By the way, what happened to those workbooks? I don't see them."

"After I took all the high/low material which you had stored there out of the closet, I replaced it with that series of workbooks. Ms. Erable and I had it out about those workbooks in September, and I have not used them at all."

We both laughed. She obviously knew how Ms. Erable could be. "Oh, Ms. Erable's all right. She did spend a lot of time helping me try to survive last year. Unfortunately, I followed her counsel entirely and Mr. Topps's not at all. I think one could combine your present program with mine last year and have it succeed. Don't you think so?"

I realized that I could have done more with that series of workbooks if I had not been so stubborn. "Yes, if I were to use the individual diagnostic test that comes with the series, and if I were to use only those parts that teach skills I believe in, I could incorporate more skills instruction in my class. Mrs. Bennett, you have taught me something today. My program is going well, but it can be improved."

She thanked me again for allowing her to teach for me. "Mr. Topps advised me this morning to be a remedial reading teacher again before trying for my doctorate. He said that I really ought to have been a successful reading teacher before trying to produce successful reading teachers. I wasn't going to follow his advice because I was scared to, but now I just may. If I do, would you help me set it up like yours except more in keeping with my belief in specific skills."

I agreed to do that and she left. Our conversation together has started a number of wheels turning in my own head about changes I need to make in my program. Her visit was very beneficial to me.

The next day in sixth-period class, I overheard Jeff telling Seymour that she must have learned something somewhere, since she could sure teach better now than she could last year. I smiled to myself, thinking how we had each learned something useful.

14 A Year of Remedial Reading (January–May)

January   Whew! Sitting down to write the journal for January is the first breather I have had since the holidays ended. I have spent almost every day this month, including weekends, working on the modifications I am making in the Reading Center's program. I may have neglected family and friends, but I can already see that the changes will bring an improvement. Over the holidays, I visited with Dr. Lea. After coffee and some of his delicious holiday cookies, we went upstairs to his study, and he asked how things were going in my new job.

"Well, Dr. Lea," I began, "I believe that we have a good program. My concern is that some students are not making the progress I would like."

Dr. Lea turned in his chair to face me. "Back before school started, when you and Mr. Topps made the courageous decision to take the poorest readers in the school, I lauded you. I still support you in that decision, but, having made it, you do need to lower your expectations somewhat. Perhaps you have been overly ambitious in the goals you've set for your students."

"No, Dr. Lea," I responded, "I don't believe that is the problem. You always taught us in your classes that no one is a perfect reader; that no one reads up to potential. My goal for each student has not been that the student will make a certain amount of progress, but that each student will make steady progress at a rate that seems satisfactory to that student. In other words, the student must be improving sufficiently for me to notice and for the student to avoid frustration and the fear of failure."

Dr. Lea smiled. "Since you almost use my exact words, I can't disagree with your means for formulating your expectations."

FOR READERS TO DO TOGETHER:

Discuss the problem of setting expectations for students in a middle/high school remedial reading program. Why is it necessary that the teacher have expectations? How should those expectations be modified throughout the year? Why had Dr. Lea not taught Reed to use an IQ test to predict how much progress a student should achieve in a certain period of time, making that prediction the expected progress for each student?

"Then you see my concern," I continued, "that several of my students are not making steady progress satisfactory to them or me. This is especially disconcerting since I have worked so hard to develop an atmosphere of discipline and cooperation in which everyone works on instructional level.

"My conversation with Mrs. Bennett a few weeks ago started me thinking that perhaps I need to develop more of a diagnostic-prescriptive, specific-skills program. Maybe I am not meeting the specific needs of the students with my global approach to raising reading levels."

"The problem, as I see it, Reed, is that your program is going so well, you can't credit lack of discipline or effort on the students' part for any lack of progress which occurs. If a student is not progressing, it must be because the program has some kind of theoretical problem rather than a problem with implementation."

"Why, that's it, Dr. Lea! The reason I have been worrying about my program in the Reading Center is that I know I have implemented it well. If there are any major problems, they are a result of my overall approach to improving reading ability. That is alarming because it means that more work on my part or more effort on my students' part will not ameliorate the situation. I have to change the basic approach to diagnosis and instruction that I believe in and follow. Yet my program is working so well for at least half of my students that I am afraid to shift to a more skills-oriented program. Now you know why I am here, disturbing you with my problems, when we both should be having a holiday. Do you think you can help me decide what to do?"

Dr. Lea concentrated a moment. "What you need to do, Reed, is to go see a young teacher at Merritt Elementary School named Ed Dunn. About three years ago, he developed a diagnostic system which is compatible with the program you have already established. I believe you will like it and will want to try it. Give him a call at home; I have his phone number downstairs."

In no time, I had talked to Ed on the phone, and he had asked me to come over. "I'm just taking it easy," he said. When I arrived at his apartment, it did not take long for me to describe my program to him. He seemed to have a good understanding of how classrooms operate, and he asked good questions. Before long, I felt that he understood and generally approved of my approach to remedial reading. When I told him my dilemma of whether or not to change to a skills-oriented, diagnostic-prescriptive approach, he was quick to offer advice. "I think you should stop looking at diagnosis and instruction from an either-or standpoint. When you are improving word identification abilities, I believe you need to be more diagnostic and prescriptive, but when you are improving reading or listening comprehension, I believe you need to be more global. Specific word identification skills can be tested and taught, but there is some doubt in the literature about the existence of specific comprehension skills. From the description of your program, I would conclude that you are doing very well with students who need reading comprehension improvement and with students who are beginning readers. However, I would be willing

Ceiling diagnosis

to bet that students with word identification and listening comprehension ceilings are the students who are not making the progress you, and they, expect."

"Ceilings? I don't understand what you mean."

"The diagnostic and instructional system I have developed," he explained, "is based on the notion that reading requires the integrated functioning of three global areas of ability: the ability to identify the words on the page, the ability to comprehend stories and informational material while listening to them being read, and the ability to process information from the page. In my system, the first diagnostic question to ask is 'Which of these three global areas of ability is keeping the student from reading better?' Another way of asking that same question is "Which of these three areas is acting as a ceiling on the student's reading ability?' Students with word identification ceilings are those students who comprehend better while listening than they can identify words, and who can comprehend while reading as well as they can identify words. If these students are taught to identify words more accurately and automatically, their ability to read with comprehension increases.

"Students with listening comprehension ceilings are those students who comprehend no better while listening than they do while reading, and who comprehend no better while listening than they identify words. They need listening comprehension instruction. Students with reading comprehension ceilings are those students who comprehend while listening and identify words better than they comprehend while reading. They need reading comprehension instruction."

His system made sense, but he was giving it to me too fast. "Hey, Ed, slow down a little. You're losing me. How about some examples of students who fit into these categories?"

"All right. I have a fifth grader this year named Warren who can listen with good comprehension to stories and informational material written at the seventh- or eighth-grade level. His silent-reading-comprehension level is in fourth-grade-level stories and books. If he reads orally from a fourth-grade book, he can get most of the words, and his mistakes or miscues make sense. However, if you give him the words from that fourth-grade-level passage out of context, he cannot read half of them. In fact, he identifies words in isolation about like an average second grader. He is only able to read as well as he can because he is such an excellent user of context clues. Unfortunately, his inability to identify words accurately and quickly is keeping his reading level low when he has every other requirement to be an excellent reader. Word identification instruction is what he has to have if he is ever to be a good reader."

"And you would say that this student has a word identification ceiling?" I asked.

"Yes," he replied, "and giving him listening or reading comprehension instruction might result in some small improvement in his ability, but poor word identification is the limit on his reading right now, and that limit must be raised if he is to improve."

"I see."

"I have another student who has been referred to every special program imaginable during her years in school. Beverly can identify words accurately and automatically in fifth-grade-level material, but she cannot comprehend at second-grade level. Her listening ability is almost as good as her word identification—about fourth-grade level if I remember."

I interrupted him. "You mean you have a student who can understand fourth-grade material when you read it to her and who can read fluently, orally, in fifth-grade material but who cannot read with comprehension in a second-grade-level book? I find that hard to believe."

"It's true."

"I don't understand how that is possible."

Ed Dunn walked from the sofa over to a bookshelf by the television and got a paperback novel Reed had heard of but not read. He came over and sat down by Reed. He randomly opened the book to a page near the middle. "Reed, I want you to read aloud for me from this page. After you get going, I will quickly cover the page with my hand. I want you to try to keep reading right through my hand."

"I'll do this, if you want me to, Ed, but I learned in my M.Ed. program about eye-voice span. I know that all good readers have their eyes four to six words ahead of their voice when they are reading orally."

"Then," he continued, "I'm sure you learned that comprehension without an eye-voice span is difficult if not impossible."

"Yes."

"The girl I was telling you about has a reading comprehension ceiling because she doesn't have an eye-voice span. She is always looking right at the word she is reading. Of course, this practice enables her to identify words very accurately while reading orally but it has destroyed her overall reading ability. She can comprehend while listening because it does not require an eye-voice span."

I thought a moment. "Aren't there machines that you can use to train students to improve their eye movements while reading? Why hasn't someone used one of these machines to improve her eye-voice span?"

"You're right, Reed, several companies sell machines that are supposed to improve eye movements while reading, but there is little research evidence that training eye movements improves reading ability. Eye movements seem to be symptomatic of good or poor reading, not causes of them. When a person becomes a better reader, eye movements will improve. The reverse is not necessarily the case."

"What are you doing for her?" I asked.

"In her case, additional word identification instruction would only increase her compulsion for accurate word calling. Additional listening comprehension improvement would also be worthless since she cannot now read as well as she can listen. My strategy has been to try to eliminate the factors that compel her to read so deliberately and analytically, and then to distract her from these habits.

"To eliminate contingencies in the reading situation that reinforce her word-by-word reading, I have enforced two principles: (1) She never reads orally, not even for diagnosis and (2) I only have her read material that is independent level for her, so that she will know almost every word and not have to decode them. If there are words I think she might have to decode, I teach them to her ahead of time as sight words.

"Once I have removed the need to be compulsive about word identification by having her read to herself in easy material, I enforce two more principles in order to distract her from her usual habits: (3) I always have her read for a specific purpose so that her mind is on gaining meaning while she reads and (4) I always time her when she reads to herself. We do not set goals or limits as to the time, but she is more aware of pacing herself when she reads."

I was impressed by how much Ed seemed to know about remediating reading problems. "That's fascinating. Are all reading comprehension ceilings a result of short eye-voice spans?"

"No one knows all the causes of reading comprehension ceilings, but not all are associated with short eye-voice spans. Some students seem to have failed to transfer the same types of comprehension activities they perform while listening to their reading. For these students, I use listening-to-reading-transfer lessons. A student is asked to listen to a story or passage for a specific purpose. That purpose might be to listen to determine what a good title for the story would be or to listen so that the student can arrange a list of important events in the order in which they occurred in the passage. Whatever purpose they listen to fulfill, they are then given another passage to read with the same purpose for reading. They are told that they should do the same thing while reading that they did while listening. For a student with a reading comprehension ceiling, this technique aids the transfer of listening ability to reading.

"Still other reading comprehension ceilings are caused by the inability of the reader to be able to segment the print on the page into phrases or syntactic units. When listening, pitch, juncture, and stress provide cues as to where these breaks occur. In reading, the reader must learn to predict where syntactic phrases begin and end without any aid except an occasional punctuation mark."

My head was swimming. "What about listening comprehension ceilings, can I have an example of that?"

"Sure, Reed. Last year I taught a boy named Francis who could identify words fluently in fifth-grade textbooks, but whose comprehension was very weak. I found out that he could only listen with comprehension at the same level he could read with comprehension, which was at third-grade level."

"But," I said, "I've read that a student like that is reading at potential. He is reading as well as he can be expected to, given his overall ability. How can you improve his reading?"

Ed continued. "We used to use listening comprehension level as a measure of potential, but that was before we discovered that listening comprehension ability can be improved in a relatively brief period of time."

"Does that mean improving listening improves reading?"

"No, but improving listening makes it possible for the student to benefit more from reading comprehension instruction than he or she would have before the listening ceiling was raised."

We spent another hour talking and asking each other questions. He agreed that he would help me install the Ceiling Diagnostic System in my classroom, and I have spent most of January doing exactly that. The first thing I had to do was to obtain a ceiling profile for each student, so that I could put them into ceiling groups. He said that any test that gives separate word identification, reading comprehension, and listening comprehension scores could be used to obtain the profile. He added, however, that his experience indicated that the profiles would be most accurate if I would use a Ceiling Informal Reading Inventory.

Ceiling IRI

He explained to me exactly how to construct a Ceiling IRI, and I madly took notes on my legal pad. I spent the first two weeks of this month making one from the high/low series of short story books I have been using for small-group lessons. Of course, I selected passages that we had not yet covered in any lessons.

FOR READERS TO DO TOGETHER:

Divide the class into six groups. Each group will make part (the tests for one level) of a Ceiling IRI. Duplicate what each group turns in, collate, and make sure that each class member receives a completed copy of the Ceiling IRI.

How to Construct a Ceiling IRI:
1. Select a series of graded books (reading levels 1–6) that are appropriate for instructional use with your students.

2. Select two representative passages of 300 words each from the middle third of each book in the series, reading levels 1–6. (These excerpts should be meaningful. One of the two passages will serve as the reading comprehension measure for that level; the other will serve as the listening comprehension measure for that level.)
3. From the reading comprehension passage at each level, select every tenth word and write these 30 words in random order on thick index cards, one per card. Place a thick blank index card between each two word cards. This deck of 30 words from the reading comprehension passage at each level will serve as the word identification measure for that level. Twenty-six words or 87 percent word identification is the criterion score for each level.
4. Prepare eight questions for each passage at each level. The questions should be asked in the order that the answers appear or are suggested in the text. You must be certain the questions are passage dependent, that is, the student should only be able to answer a question if he or she read and understood the passage. If a question is based on general knowledge, the student may know the answer to that question before reading the passage. For example, a question following a story which asked, "What did the cow eat?" would only be a good question if the correct answer was not "hay." Six questions or 75 percent comprehension is the criterion score for each passage at each level.
5. The six decks of 30 words each and the 12 passages with questions are the Ceiling IRI.

As soon as I had the Ceiling IRI constructed and duplicated, I decided to whom I would administer it. Ed had suggested that I only give it to those students who were not progressing satisfactorily. In the sixth period, because Rufus and Gene are beginning readers who seem to comprehend while listening much better than they can read, I did not test them. Ed said that beginning readers always have either a word identification or a listening comprehension ceiling, and that very few have a listening ceiling.

I did not test Clarence, Elsie, John, Seymour, Jeff, Rufus, or Gene. I did test the other eight sixth-period students since, in every case, I thought that they were not moving ahead as well as they might. Again I followed Ed's advice explicitly in the administration of the test. He said that I should start at the probable instructional level of each student and administer all levels of each test before administering another. That is, I found each student's word identification score first, listening comprehension score second, and reading comprehension score third.

The student's word identification score is the highest reading level at which the student can read 26 of 30 (or 87 percent) of the words in the deck before failing to do so on two levels in a row. When I was testing Bruce, for example, he missed eight words at level three, but only five from level four. Then he fell below 87 percent on both levels five and six. Level four was his word identification score.

The student's listening comprehension score is the highest level at which the student can achieve 75 percent comprehension after listening to the passage before failing to do so on two levels in a row. Bruce answered all the questions after the third-grade-level listening passage, but failed the 75 percent criterion on both the fourth- and fifth-level listening passages. Level three was his listening comprehension score.

The student's reading comprehension score is the highest reading level at which the student can achieve 75% comprehension after reading the passage silently before failing to do so on two levels in a row. Bruce answered six questions after reading the third-grade-level reading passage, but failed the 75% criterion on both the fourth- and fifth-level passages. Level three was his reading comprehension score.

As I gave the word identification test, I was careful to flash the words the way Ed told me to. He said that I should flip the blank card, then the word card in a quick, smooth action for each word. In this way, the student had about half a second to look at the word before looking at a blank card again. Then the student had about two seconds to actually say the word before another word was flashed. Using this system, students were tested for both accuracy and automaticity of word identification ability.

For both the reading and listening comprehension measures, I asked the questions orally, and the student answered them orally, if the student seemed not to understand a question, I would repeat it. I did not tell a student whether or not the answer was correct.

The only time I could administer the Ceiling IRI to these students was during independent activities, during lunch, and before and after school. A few students in each class volunteered to come at these times outside of class. I lost three pounds in one week of not eating lunch and decided it was not such a bad idea.

It took me over three weeks to construct, administer, and score the Ceiling IRI. During this time we operated the same five-day schedules that had been in effect before the holiday vacation. Trying to look at my program through Ed's eyes, I have concluded that, with the language-experience approach, sight-word practice, context-clue exercises, and listening comprehension improvement, I have been giving Gene and Rufus a balanced reading program with an emphasis on word identification which both Ed and Dr. Lea say beginning readers should have.

Clarence, Elsie, Jeff, John, and Seymour all seem to have the kinds of reading comprehension ceilings that can be raised by having small-group lessons on silent reading for purposes in instructional-level material, combined with free reading in books of their choice, further combined with independent activities in comprehension and study skills kits.

As for the others in sixth period, here is what their ceiling profiles look like:

Profiles Obtained from Ceiling Informal Reading Inventory

Name	Word Identification Level	Reading Comprehension Level	Listening Comprehension Level
Bruce	4	3	2
Eddie	6+	3	6+
Freddie	3	2	2
Jake	4	4	4
Marion	2	2	4
Otelia	3	3	3
Ricardo	4	2	3
Willie	2	2	3

The step-by-step method by which Ed told me to interpret the profiles in order to estimate each student's reading ceiling works as follows:

1. I first look at the student's word identification score. If that score is fifth grade or

above, I cross it out. (When word identification is fifth grade or above, it cannot be the ceiling.)

2. I then look at the student's reading comprehension score. If that score is sixth-grade level or above, I cross out the *listening comprehension score*. (When reading comprehension is sixth grade or above, listening comprehension cannot be the ceiling.)

3. The limiting factor or ceiling on the student's reading ability is the lowest score of those which remain after steps 1 and 2 have been completed. If there is a tie for the lowest score, and if listening comprehension is involved in that tie, listening comprehension is the ceiling. If there is a tie for the lowest score, and listening comprehension is not involved in that tie, word identification is the ceiling.

Ed explained to me that word identification cannot be the ceiling if it is fifth grade or above because any student who can identify words in fifth-grade-level material, accurately and automatically, has mastered basic sight vocabulary and decoding skills. Additional improvement in word identification ability should come in conjunction with meaning vocabulary building. Meaning vocabulary building is an integral part of reading comprehension improvement.

Listening comprehension cannot be the ceiling for students who comprehend while reading in sixth-grade material and higher because material written at about sixth-grade level and above becomes as easy or easier to comprehend when read as when listened to.

Based on the interpretation of the ceiling profiles, I have placed my 15 students in three ceiling groups. The students I did not test are placed in the ceiling category I feel they belong in based on their success and level of sophistication. These groups are:

1. Students with word identification ceilings:

   Gene   Rufus   Marion

2. Students with listening comprehension ceilings:

   Bruce   Jake   Freddie

3. Students with reading comprehension ceilings:

   Clarence   Jeff   Ricardo
   Eddie   John   Seymour
   Elsie

FOR THE READER TO DO:

Otelia and Willie have not been placed in the ceiling groups. Determine which group each belongs in, based on his or her Ceiling IRI profile.

In addition to using the profiles obtained from the Ceiling IRI to estimate reading ceilings, I also obtained a new estimate of instructional level for these students based on their performance in January. I set instructional level equal to the lowest of the three scores: word identification, reading comprehension, and listening comprehension.

For the students I did not test, I used my judgment of how comfortable they were with reading and of how much growth I had noticed since the beginning to determine whether or not to move them to the next higher level. I moved Clarence and Elsie to the fifth level, but left Jeff, John, Seymour, Rufus, and Gene at their same levels.

The second thing I had to do was to use this information to construct what I call a *Ceilings-X-Levels Grid*. I made one of these grids for each class so that I could see exactly where each student was with respect to instructional level and global area of need.

Ceilings-X-Levels Grid

Ceilings

Levels	Word Identification	Reading Comprehension	Listening Comprehension
1	Gene Rufus		
2	Marion Willie	Ricardo	Bruce Freddie
3		Eddie Jeff Seymour	Otelia
4		John	Jake
5		Clarence Elsie	

As January ends, I am using the grid for each class to plan small-group and individual activities. Once these activities are planned, each student will have a new five-day schedule sheet which will reflect the new organization. From the students' viewpoint, my program will not have changed appreciably. From my standpoint, I will have stronger theoretical underpinnings for what I do and when I do it.

February Unlike Archimedes, I have not leaped from the bathtub to run naked down the street shouting. But I do feel like writing *Eureka!* over and over again in my journal for this month. By following Dr. Lea's and Ed Dunn's leads, I have kept the parts of last semester's program which were most successful, and I have implemented new parts in keeping with the Ceiling Diagnosis and Remediation System. It is too soon to see much difference in the progress being made by the students, but the change in my perceptions of the Reading Center has been significant. When I think of the reading problem of a particular student now, I see it in context of overall strengths and weaknesses in the three global areas of reading. When I plan changes in small-group lessons or independent activities, I do so by consulting the Ceilings-X-Levels Grid in an attempt to better meet the needs and abilities of the students. Most of what I do instructionally each day makes sense to me, and I understand how my efforts fit into a theoretical approach to improving reading ability.

I do not regret for a minute the time and energy spent last fall building discipline, motivation, and a pleasant room atmosphere. I was learning about teaching reading to students with severe problems, and we laid a good foundation. I do not believe I was ready to establish such a sophisticated program as I have now when I was learning my materials, my students, and my new job. Next year, however, you can bet I will organize my instruction using the Ceilings-X-Levels Grid, right from the start.

DRA

The core of my organization is still the small-group lesson, and these lessons are still taught to students grouped by instructional level. The difference is that, within each small-group lesson, instruction is differentiated to some extent to address the ceiling of each individual in the group. The small-group lessons always follow the outline of the Directed Reading Activity as they did before. We talk about the topic of the story to be read to build interest and background of information. I introduce new vocabulary and write purposes for reading in the form of questions on the chalkboard, as usual. When presenting the new words to students with word identification ceilings, however, I make sure to teach the new words as sight words, as well as introduce their meanings. I use the same strategy I use when teaching sight words to Rufus and Gene, that is, I present the word, pronounce it, and require them to pronounce it; they close their eyes and try to image the word and then open their eyes to check the image against the word; the second time they open their eyes they must write the word first before checking the word. The added emphasis on word identification in the readiness step of the DRA is designed to help students who have a word identification ceiling and certainly will not hurt the others in that group.

After this discussion of interest and background, and after the introduction of vocabulary and purposes for reading, the students with word identification ceilings and reading comprehension ceilings read the story to themselves. The students with listening comprehension ceilings put on earphones which are connected by a listening center to a cassette tape recorder. While the others are reading the story, they listen to it on tape.

When everyone is finished reading or listening to the story, I ask them the questions I set for purposes. The small group then disbands and begins work in the assigned independent activities, except for the students with word identification ceilings. They remain behind for a short word identification lesson.

Word ID

To determine which skill to work on with students who have word identification ceilings, I use the Cunningham Word Identification Skills Checklist which Dr. Lea shared with me. Dr. Lea explained that the checklist is based on several principles:

1. Concrete words are easier to learn than nonconcrete words.
2. Words that occur most frequently in print are the most important words for students to learn.
3. Words that occur most frequently in print should be learned as sight words.
4. Consonants should be taught before vowels because they are easier to learn and because they are more important clues to word identification in context than vowels are.
5. Single consonants should be taught before digraphs (*th, sh, ch, ph,* etc.), and digraphs before blends (*bl, br, cl, cr, dr, pr, st, str, spr,* etc.), because of increasing complexity and decreasing utility.
6. One-syllable words should be taught before polysyllabic words.
7. A student has no need for vowel instruction who can recognize high-frequency words on sight and who can decode unknown words by using initial and final consonants, digraphs, and blends plus context clues.

I like the checklist for several reasons, but the main one is that it does not require me to teach all the rules about when a vowel has a particular sound ("when two vowels go walking, the first one does the talking and says its name"). These rules are very difficult for students to learn to apply and are not even true for many words.

The Cunningham Word Identification Skills Checklist

Phase One   Date Mastered

1. Recognizes on sight at least 20 concrete words.   _____
2. Recognizes the first 50 words from the Cunningham
   Secondary and Adult Basic Sight Word List.   _____
3. Reads sentences containing concrete words and Cunningham words.   _____
4. Associates sound with letter for all initial consonants. _____
5. Decodes words which are initial consonant substitutions on Cunningham words.   _____
6. Uses context plus initial consonant to decode words.   _____
7. Decodes words that have -s, -ed, or -ing endings on
   Cunningham words.   _____
8. Decodes words that are compounds of first 50 Cunningham words.   _____

Phase Two

9. Recognizes the first 100 Cunningham words.   _____
10. Associates sound with letter for all initial consonant
    digraphs.   _____
11. Decodes words that are initial consonant digraph sub-
    stitutions on Cunningham words.   _____
12. Uses context plus initial digraphs to decode words.   _____
13. Decodes words that have -er, -est endings on Cun-
    ningham words.   _____
14. Decodes words that are compounds of first 100 Cun-
    ningham words.   _____

Phase Three

15. Recognizes the first 150 Cunningham words.   _____
16. Associates sound with letter for all initial consonant
    blends.   _____
17. Decodes words that are initial blend substitutions on
    Cunningham words.   _____
18. Uses context plus initial blends to decode words.   _____
19. Decodes words that have un- and re- beginnings on
    Cunningham words.   _____
20. Decodes words that are compounds of first 150 Cun-
    ningham words.   _____

Phase Four

21. Recognizes the first 200 Cunningham words. _____
22. Associates sound with letter for all final consonants, digraphs, and blends. _____
23. Uses context plus initial and final sounds to decode words. _____
24. Decodes words that have -en, -ly, -less, -ness, -ful, and -able endings on Cunningham words. _____
25. Decodes words that are compounds of first 200 Cunningham words. _____

Phase Five

26. Recognizes all 300 Cunningham words. _____
27. Decodes any regular one-syllable word. _____
28. Decodes words that have pre-, mis-, a-, de-, pro-, in-, dis-, im- beginnings on Cunningham words. _____
29. Decodes compound words. _____

Phase Six

30. Decodes two-syllable words using a compare-contrast strategy. _____
31. Decodes polysyllabic words using a compare-contrast strategy. _____

For record-keeping purposes, I have a folder on file for each student in my classes. A copy of this word identification skills checklist is on file in the folder of each student who has a word identification ceiling. I determine whether or not a skill has been mastered in a variety of ways. For one, I use the individual diagnostic test that accompanies the word identification skills-oriented workbook series Mrs. Bennett worked with last year. This test provides a fair measure of consonant, digraph, and blend knowledge.

In the case of sight words, I use two copies of the Cunningham Secondary and Adult Basic Sight Word List [Appendix C]. The student reads the words from his or her copy while I mark the words as correct or incorrect on my copy. I only test the group of 50 words which the student needs to know in order to enter each successive phase of skills on the checklist.

In addition to these tests, I also use my own judgment. I either construct a brief test of a few items to administer to the student, or I ask him or her to read from a passage orally and I attend to how well the skill being tested is applied in that oral reading. Sometimes I compare how well students identify words when flashed with how well they identify them when given time to analyze them.

For all students with word identification ceilings, I use the checklist to decide which skill to teach next in the short word identification lesson that follows their small-group lesson, and to decide which pages to assign them for independent work in the word identification workbook series.

I have no checklist of skills for reading or listening comprehension because there is serious doubt about whether or not such skills exist or can be taught. My approach to improving comprehension is to have students listen or read silently for specific purposes in instructional-level material which is interesting to them. This instructional-level reading or listening is supplemented by easy reading or listening in independent-level material. The goal of this instruction is to enable the student to read or listen at higher and higher instructional and independent levels.

Based on the January testing, I have five small groups in sixth period, one for each level in the Ceilings-X-Levels Grid. These five groups meet for discussion in the following schedule:

Monday
12:15– 12:24—SSR (everyone)
12:25– 12:45—Small-group lesson with me (Eddie, Jeff, Seymour, and Otelia)
—Small-group lesson independently (John, Jake, Clarence, and Elsie)
—Independent activities (Gene, Rufus, Marion, Willie, Ricardo, Bruce, and Freddie)
12:46– 1:03—Independent activities (everyone)

Tuesday
12:15– 12:24—SSR (everyone)
12:25– 12:45—Small-group lesson with me (Marion, Willie, Ricardo, Bruce, and Freddie)
—Small-group lesson independently (John and Jake)
—Independent or free reading (Clarence and Elsie)
—Independent activities (Gene, Rufus, Eddie, Jeff, Seymour, and Otelia)
12:46– 1:03—Independent activities (everyone)

Wednesday
12:15– 12:24—SSR (everyone)
12:25– 12:45—Small-group lesson with me (Gene and Rufus)
—Small-group lesson independently (Eddie, Seymour, Jeff, and Otelia)
—Independent or free reading (Clarence and Elsie)
—Independent activities (Marion, Willie, Ricardo, Bruce, John, Jake, and Freddie)
12:46– 1:03—Independent activities (everyone)

Thursday
12:15– 12:24—SSR (everyone)
12:25– 12:45—Small-group lesson with me (Marion, Willie, Ricardo, Bruce, and Freddie)
—Small-group lesson independently (John, Jake, Clarence, and Elsie)
—Independent activities (Gene, Rufus, Eddie, Seymour, Jeff, and Otelia)
12:46– 1:03—Small-group lesson with me (Gene and Rufus)
—Independent activities (everyone else)

Friday
12:15– 12:24—SSR (everyone)
12:25– 1:03—Circle activity (everyone)

FOR READERS TO DO TOGETHER:

In order for Mr. Moore to implement the schedule he has just outlined for his sixth-period class, he had to prepare a new five-day schedule sheet for each student. Each reader should choose one of the 15 students and should construct a detailed five-day schedule sheet for that student. This sheet should contain the level of difficulty of material being used in the various instructional- and independent-level groupings as well as the independent activities. Because Mr. Moore has only mentioned a few independent activities he uses, the reader should use his or her knowledge of each student to select independent activities in materials or exercises with which he or she is familiar.

In sixth-period class, the only small-group lesson in which I have to make allowance for word identification ceilings is the second-grade-level group which contains both Marion and Willie. I meet with that group on Tuesdays and Thursdays since I want each group to meet twice a week, and they are just unable to work together without me being there to supervise. When the group disbands, Willie and Marion stay with me for their word identification skill lesson. I work with them on the same skill to make the lesson easier to plan and conduct. To determine which skill to cover, I select the skill closest to the beginning of the Cunningham checklist which neither student has mastered.

Unlike Gene and Rufus, Marion and Willie seem to have mastered basic sight words and initial consonant sounds before this year. Their chief problems have been final consonant sounds, ability to use consonants plus context, and ability to attack polysyllabic words. In their independent activities, I have assigned them exercises in word identification workbooks that concentrate on final consonants. In my lessons with them following the small-group work in the second-grade-level, high/low book, I have used modified cloze as a technique to teach them to use initial and final sounds plus context to identify unknown words. For these exercises, I take a selection from the first-grade-level, high/low book so that it is relatively easy for them to read. I cover the page in the book with an acetate sheet and fasten it with paperclips at the top and bottom so that it will not shift. I then use a grease pencil to mark out everything but the initial and final consonant sound of one important, one-syllable word per sentence. This leaves the initial sound, final sound, context, and word length as cues to what the word is. Students take turns trying to read a paragraph aloud without hesitating at the word with the middle deleted. It has been surprising how well this particular strategy has worked with them. It has forced them to use their phonics skills and context, because without the middle of the word they can neither identify it as a sight word nor can they decode it without attending to whether the word they produce makes sense in the sentence.

They have done so well on these lessons that I have begun working with them on decoding polysyllabic words. The strategy I am using for this purpose is different in several ways from the traditional one which teaches students to divide words into syllables, apply their knowledge of phonics on each syllable, and recombine the syllables to pronounce the whole word. I do not believe that such a system can successfully be taught to anyone, let alone poor readers. It is too complex and time consuming to use.

The compare-contrast strategy, however, teaches students to pay attention to the parts of words so that when they meet a long word they do not immediately recognize, they attempt to find known parts within the word. When they cannot segment the word into parts they know, they are taught to think of words they know that are like the new word which can help them identify it. Mystery Word Match [see Chapter 12, page 273] is a game we play to teach students to compare and contrast known polysyllabic words to unknown polysyllabic words.

I meet with Gene and Rufus twice a week since they cannot work together independently on their language-experience story. Their stories are now quite long, and they can read the stories from previous lessons with ease. They also have mastered the word identification skills in phase one of the Cunningham checklist, and I am currently teaching them initial consonant digraphs (*th, sh, ph, ch,* etc.) and how to substitute them into sight words they know to decode unknown words. For example, if you know the sight word *will*, the digraph *ch*, and if you have heard the word *chill* and can substitute initial sounds, you can decode the word *chill* even if you have never seen it before.

I meet with Eddie, Seymour, Jeff, and Otelia once each week for a Directed Reading Activity in the third-grade-level, high/low book. (Otelia listens to the story while the other three read it to themselves, so for her it is really a Directed Listening Activity.) On Wednesdays they also meet together independently and do a Directed Reading-Thinking Activity by themselves. Last semester they could not have followed the procedure without my help, but after seeing Clarence and Elsie leading their group through the DR-TA several times, Seymour and Jeff decided that they too could survey a story, make predictions, and verify those predictions without my presence. I acted as if I was not sure they could do it, which only made them more determined.

My four best readers in sixth period, Clarence, Elsie, John, and Jake, meet together twice a week, on Mondays and Thursdays, for a DR-TA which they teach themselves in the fourth-grade-level, high/low book. Then on Tuesdays, I have John and Jake read a story in the third-grade-level, high/low book and write answers to the questions.

On Tuesdays and Wednesdays, Clarence and Elsie are allowed to spend the whole period reading anything they like. I told them that they had to appear to be reading whenever I looked their way or they would lose this privilege. If they become tired of reading, they are allowed to work independently in either the Comprehension or Study Skills Kit.

For the independent activities, I have used the Ceilings-X-Levels Grid in an attempt to give assignments which are at the right level of difficulty and which focus on the area of need for that student. Students with word identification ceilings complete exercises which give instruction or practice in skills on the Cunningham checklist. I made very few of these exercises. Rather, I adapted sections of word identification workbooks and programs which Mrs. Bennett had used. Students with reading comprehension ceilings usually complete assignments at their reading levels in the Comprehension or Study Skills Kit. They also are often assigned to work on vocabulary and context clues exercises.

Students with listening comprehension ceilings either listen to taped stories or exercises, or they follow along in the book while they listen to a story, or they read in independent-level material. Occasionally I use a machine with them which has a record, filmstrip, and comprehension exercises for each lesson. This is a better listening than reading program in my opinion.

All students are still assigned to writing activities for independent work, and you should see the difference which quantity of writing has made for several of the students. They still have a lot of improvement to make in the correctness of the form of their writing, but at least they can express themselves on paper. A person who has nothing to say but who can write grammatically correct sentences still has nothing to say.

This has been an uneventful month which was a welcome change. I have no changes of consequence to report or incidents of special interest. The routine of my second-semester schedule has operated well and everyone has cooperated at least minimally. Rather than describing the month's events, I have decided to lead you through a typical week of March so that you can see exactly how I manage the program.

On Monday at 12:15 the tardy bell rings and I move to the door to close it. Everyone is in the room at the bell except for Gene and Bruce, who always run in the door as I pull it to. It is as if they are afraid they might spend an extra second in class and be somehow cheated out of some free time.

After closing the door, I get my book or magazine and sit down in one of the chairs. By the time I am seated, all the students have their folders and something to read. My rule is that anyone who does not have both folder and something to read by the time I sit down has to stay after class long enough to select something to read for the next day and place it in his or her folder.

I pick up the kitchen timer from the shelf, set it on nine minutes, and put it down with the face away from the group. We then read without interruption for nine minutes until the timer goes off. When SSR ends, each student reshelves the book if completed and selects another for the next day, placing it in his or her folder. If students have not completed their books, they may keep them in their folders or check them out by writing the name of the book and their name on a card. Then, students working in groups move to that part of the room, and students not working in groups move to the carrel or table where they are assigned for independent activities. Any student who is unable to consult the five-day schedule sheet to find and begin work is assigned a seat for the entire period, and I bring work to that desk. Needless to say, we have not had much of a problem with that kind of goldbricking. Freedom to move and responsibility are coupled.

Eddie, Jeff, Seymour, and Otelia come to the table by the board, and I join them. John, Jake, Clarence, and Elsie move to the table in the corner by the portable chalkboard. Everyone else begins work on an assigned activity at a designated carrel or table.

The only preparation I complete for the small-group lesson is to record the story on cassette tape for Otelia. Otherwise when I pass out the books it is the first time they or I have seen the story. Ideally, I would spend more time preparing each lesson, but with six classes each day it is impossible. I turn to the teacher's manual for the high/low series and write the hard words on the board. Sometimes I tell them what a word means, and sometimes I write it in a sentence and make them figure out what it means. Then I write the questions on the board that I want them to answer after they read the story. Otelia puts the earphones on and everyone else begins reading. I skim the story quickly, having read the synopsis from the teacher's manual. While they finish reading, I walk around to help those students working on independent activities.

I often use this time to test Rufus on some of the words he is studying at the Language-Master. Gene has a taped Directed Listening Activity on Monday, and I do not bother him. When Otelia is finished listening and the others are finished reading, I return to the group to answer the questions on the board. It is unusual for me to have to spend any time with John, Jake, Clarence, or Elsie, since they know exactly what to do about their lesson.

Checking student work

When the groups break up, the students go to the tables and carrels where assigned independent activities are found, and they work until the bell sounds. I use this time to check student work and record the completion of it in my grade book. I do not put a grade for an assignment completed, but rather put an S for satisfactory completion. If a student makes a mistake, it must be corrected. All work completed is completed satisfactorily, by definition. This system creates two problems which I have learned to handle. First of all, even the most conscientious student will cheat if the answers are too available. Programmed instruction where the answers are a page away is too much of a temptation and will not work (Kulhavy, 1977). Answers must be far enough away so that students have to leave their carrels and walk partway across the room to check their answers.

The second problem is that, in order to complete more work, a student will sometimes put just any answers to questions or exercises or vocabulary items, knowing that when the answers are checked they can be corrected and the work be satisfactory. To minimize this practice, I require the student to write a one-sentence explanation for each wrong answer. Since I require all work in ink, wrong answers cannot be erased. The student must correct wrong answers and must also explain them.

The key to successful independent work is to have the students at a level on which the work is not frustratingly difficult, but where the skills being taught are not known by the student. Moreover, the independent activities must have as much variety as possible, especially over several weeks.

On Tuesday, the class begins the same way except that after SSR, the groups are different. I follow the teacher's manual the same way in teaching the small-group lesson to Marion, Willie, Ricardo, Bruce, and Freddie as I did on Monday with Eddie's group, except that I stress teaching the hard words as sight words for Marion's and Willie's benefit.

While they are reading the story, I move to where John and Jake are working together on a third-grade-level story to see if they understand the questions I wrote on the portable chalkboard for them to answer and to see if there are any words they do not know. They usually need no help, so I can move to help the students working independently. Clarence and Elsie are busy reading, and I leave them alone. Eventually the time for small-group work is over and everyone finishes the period working on assigned independent activities while I check work and help with problems.

The groups on Wednesday are Gene and Rufus with me, Eddie's group doing a DR-TA independently, and Clarence and Elsie free-reading again. Gene and Rufus reread the story from the previous Thursday and pick words they want to learn to add to their word banks, which are now quite large. Then they reread some of the stories they dictated in past weeks. Usually I have selected a story which has several words beginning with a digraph or blend I am trying to teach them. Using typewriter correction fluid, I remove the rest of each of these words except for the initial sound I am trying to teach. Then I teach the sound and ask them to take turns reading the sentences, attempting to read without skipping a beat when part of a word is missing. Before long they can use the sound pretty well. For review, I use an old story with one or two words in each sentence clozed with only the beginning sound. The difference between the review exercise and the instructional one is that in the former I do not restrict myself to deleting ends of words beginning the same the way I do in the latter. While I work with Gene and Rufus in this manner, I am unable to get away to help others unless the situation is quite serious. Elsie helps anyone who gets stuck doing independent activities, and Clarence keeps an eye on Eddie's group and their DR-TA.

On Thursday, I work with Marion's and Willie's group the way I do on Tuesday, leaving them while they read to help with independent activities. When their group is over and I have taught my short word identification lesson with Marion and Willie, I spend the remainder of the period teaching a second weekly lesson to Gene and Rufus.

Friday, of course, is circle activity day. This past Friday, after SSR, we filled out a tax form for everyone who worked last year after school or during the summer. Several of the students admitted to me that they usually don't bother applying for their tax refunds because they don't know how. I signed every form as the assistant and mailed them for everyone. We figured that, in sixth period alone, they will receive over $800 in refunds because of that particular circle activity. They appreciated it.

April

There was no sixth-period class on the first Monday in April. Instead, my wife (Ophelia), Worth, and I each used our cars to transport the 14 students who were at school that day to see Gene at Memorial Hospital. During the last week or so of March I had noticed that Gene had asked me at the beginning of my lunch period if he could come into the Reading Center and stay while I was eating. He claimed that he wanted to read some of the magazines I kept in the room for SSR. At first, I was a little afraid to allow him in there without me, but he seemed so sincere. I was used to kidding him along to get him to do things, but he was so serious in this request that it disarmed me. After making him promise that he would not let anyone else in the room, I pulled the door behind me and locked it the way I always did when going to lunch. When I returned to the room at the beginning of sixth period, there was no evidence that Gene had done anything but what he promised me he would. Naturally, after such good stewardship, when he made the same request the next day, I again allowed him to stay in the room during my lunch period.

It was not until I received word that Gene was in the hospital and went to see him that I discovered the real reason for his new-found enthusiasm for reading during lunch. It seems that he had bought some barbiturates from the local drug pusher on credit and had been unable to come up with the money to pay him. This person came on Upton Hill's campus during lunch and waited outside the building to do business with anyone who came out to see him. None of the students will identify him, and Mr. Topps says that his presence, whoever he is, seems part of the price the school pays for allowing students the freedom to leave campus during lunch.

Gene was hiding in the Reading Center during lunch so that when the pusher sent someone in the building to tell Gene to come outside to see him about the money, that person would not be able to find him. It was a foolish tactic, but poor Gene did not know what to do. One afternoon the pusher and two other men found Gene in the street behind his house. They stabbed him in the arm and slashed his cheek. He lost so much blood that he had to be kept in the hospital for three days and was not allowed to come back to school for over a week. He seemed to really appreciate the visit from our reading class.

When we left, Elsie gave him an envelope with the $31 he had said he owed the pusher. They had taken up two dollars from everyone and everyone had contributed, although where Rufus had gotten two dollars I have no idea. They would not let me give more than two dollars, and Elsie herself had put in the extra dollar. "I have a good job after school and the punk don't have much going for him," she had said.

Gene is back at school now, wearing long sleeve shirts and a bright scar on his face. The incident has made us closer together as a class, and the students are now willing to express their opinions and concerns openly to me or each other about various matters. Because of my position in the school, I often can only listen without response to what is said, but I feel that sometimes it is enough for the students that they are comfortable enough to be candid around a middle-aged teacher.

It is most uncomfortable to me when I hear the students describing some of the events in their regular classes, over which I have no control and about which I cannot comment to them or to anyone. One day, for example, Otelia and Elsie were talking before the tardy bell about an incident which had just occurred in Otelia's biology class. Ricardo had apparently not been doing any work in the class and had been willing to accept the failing grades he was getting there. On this particular day, however, the regular teacher had been absent and a substitute teacher had been assigned to the class. This substitute had encountered some disciplinary problems with getting the students to fulfill the assignment she requested them to complete so she had everyone in the room read orally in round-robin fashion from the chapter in the textbook. Most of the students had problems with the special biological terms, and she supplied these without hesitation during the reading. When Ricardo read, however, he could barely read any of the words— even the simple ones. The substitute interpreted this to mean that Ricardo was showing off because the regular teacher was not there. She berated him, and when he refused to read it correctly, she sent him to the office for insubordination. If that substitute had only known that Ricardo reads at second-grade level and that the biology book was probably written at college level!

These events only make me more determined to teach these students everything I can and to continue teaching them right up to the bell on the last day. Even Clarence and Elsie, my best readers in sixth-period class, can only read on sixth-grade level. It is funny, but they seem like such good readers until I consider how poorly they would do against even the average readers in the school.

We now do SSR for ten minutes each day in sixth period, and almost everyone checks out a book on occasion to take home. Willie, about whom I was so worried last fall, received a B on the third grade report I gave this year and has read three of the high/low novels that are written at second-grade level. I have moved him into the third-grade-level reading group with Eddie, Jeff, and Otelia. I also moved Seymour into the fourth-grade-level group with John and Jake.

We still follow the same basic schedule as outlined and begun in February. I have made several changes in the materials being used with some groups, however. I have begun teaching Directed Reading Activities and Directed Reading-Thinking Activities to Gene and Rufus using the first-grade-level, high/low book, and they are amazed to find that they can actually read and enjoy a book. Some of the stories are about athletes whom they identify with and other stories are about youth-oriented concerns like dating, cars, and parttime employment. The DR-TA is especially effective in teaching them to use the skills learned from language experience to think and predict their way through these stories.

Literature response activities

For Marion's group and for Eddie's group I have selected high/low novels to teach the way I used to teach *Return of the Native* by Thomas Hardy to my high school English classes. For Marion's group I selected one of the novels written especially for older students who read at second-grade level. For Eddie's group I selected a Dickens novel which has been condensed and rewritten at third-grade level. I am sure that my name will be "Mudd" among some of my cohorts who teach English literature!

Reader's Theatre

For the lessons using the novels, we act out parts for ourselves or for the entire class. I have used two Fridays so far, allowing first Marion's group then Eddie's group to present their Reader's Theatre productions from their novels. Preparing these productions is as good a way as I know of to have the students really read the important sections of the novel. Reader's Theatre requires that the actual dialogue from the story or book be used, but with as little of the other writing included as possible. The group selects which conversations are crucial to the episode to be enacted and brackets them. The group eliminates all other writing except that which is absolutely necessary for the audience's comprehension. Parts are assigned to different group members, and one or more narrators are selected until everyone has a part. In some cases it may be necessary for a student to read more than one part. The group rehearses the resulting play to perfect intonation and timing, and then the final performance is presented. Even Bruce has become enthusiastic about these productions, and Jake has asked why his group cannot do Reader's Theatre with something they read.

Other activities the students complete as we study these novels include focusing on specific characters and tracing them throughout the book, retelling some scenes to make them better or funnier, and deciding on whether word choices are really the best in certain important scenes. Freddie thought "darn" was entirely too mild a word to use in a scene where a person's car was stolen. I have not focused on literary conventions or devices with these students the way I used to with my English classes, but the goal of all my activities was the same as those—to teach the students how better to understand and appreciate how a good story operates so that they will enjoy reading good stories.

Textbook reading

The remaining students, John, Jake, Seymour, Clarence, and Elsie, read well enough that I have begun stressing textbook reading and study skills with them in their group work. Until students can read at a solid, fourth-grade level, I see no need to attempt to teach them how to get information out of a textbook. Basic word identification and reading comprehension abilities are lacking if a fourth-grade reading level has not been achieved. Even at that level, regular high school texts are too frustratingly difficult to allow even the motivated students to learn from them. Fortunately, however, some publishing companies have produced social studies and science material written at sixth- to eigth-grade levels which contain content usually presented in high school social studies and science courses. I borrowed some of these books from the few teachers at Upton Hill who use them with their students who read below grade level. Even though they still find these books challenging, my best students can gain some information from these books, especially now that I am teaching them tricks of the studying trade.

Most of these five students have done independent work at appropriate levels in the Study Skills Kit and have learned some skills at using charts, headings, tables of content, and subject indices. In the group work I have tried to teach them a few new strategies, but mainly I have tried to get them in the habit of using the strategies they learned from the Study Skills Kit. Just because one has learned a skill does not mean that one can use it automatically or that one will use it in reading.

We began with the first chapter of the science series. On the first Monday in April they conducted a DR-TA independently the way they usually do while I worked with the third-grade-level group. Rather than using a story, they went as far as they could in this first chapter. They completed about two-thirds of it in the time allotted, and I freed them from their independent-activities assignments that day until they completed it. I knew that they had just begun to get into the chapter, but at least they were starting with the main points. For the rest of the week, they were assigned to answer the questions at the end of the chapter plus some more which I put on the portable board and left up for several days. In addition to each answer, they had to write the page and column in which they found that answer.

By the second Monday, a week later, they had completed these questions and some vocabulary exercises I gave them using the words at the end of the chapter. They knew the chapter well enough that we could begin to talk about how the ideas were presented. I wanted them to learn the actual structure of ideas used by the author, rather than the ideas themselves.

I put the following diagram on the board:

Heading # ___ : _____

_____

Heading Question(s): _____

_____

_____

Answer(s): _____

_____

_____

Important Words: _____

_____

_____

After getting Eddie's group started in their lesson on their novel, I moved over and led them through the first heading in the chapter they had been studying for a week. They had little trouble deciding what question the heading should be transformed into and little trouble deciding what could be discovered under the heading to answer the question. I returned to Eddie's group, leaving Elsie to lead the group through the second heading by filling in the diagram. I then told them to do the third heading at their desks, individually. When they completed the diagram, they were to compare the results and change theirs until they each had one they were happy with, whether or not it was like the others. They knew the material well enough that they could tell when they were correctly filling in a slot in the diagram and when they were not.

The third Monday, I passed out a group of mimeographed diagrams like I had put on the board before and assigned each one of the five students in the group to work individually, filling out the diagrams, one heading at a time, the first time they read the chapter. I wanted to see if filling in the diagram for each heading of the chapter in turn could serve to improve their comprehension as well as give them notes to study and review on the chapter.

The fourth Monday, they met together and compared their diagrams for each heading in the second chapter. I joined them off and on to discuss how good a tool they thought this diagram was. Most agreed that it helped them to read, understand, and remember what was being said. Clarence pointed out that he could do well on any open-book test on the chapter after filling in these diagrams, and could do well on any closed-book test which tested knowledge of concepts gained while reading and studying.

May

The first week in May, I attended the International Reading Association's national convention. It was the first time I had ever been to a national educational conference, and I really enjoyed and profited from it. Mr. Topps enabled me to obtain three days of professional leave and to use two more days of personal leave so that I could attend the entire conference, including a preconvention institute on Monday and Tuesday of convention week. I returned with many new ideas for specific materials and methods to use with students who have particular reading problems as well as ones to use with small groups of students that add variety and depth to the types of activities I already engage in. IRA's convention is really geared toward those of us who actually teach students to improve their reading, and it was, by and large, a practical conference. The most important aspect of the conference for me was that so much of it supported what I was already doing with my students. So, in addition to raising my competence as a reading teacher, it also raised my confidence.

While I was away for an entire week of classes, Mrs. Bennett acted as my substitute. It was Mr. Topps's idea. When we were discussing the possibility of my attending IRA, I was reluctant because I was afraid my students would miss out on a week's learning. When Mr. Topps mentioned Mrs. Bennett as a possibility, I recalled her visit to the Reading

Center in December and agreed that she would be the best person to have. When Mr. Topps asked her, she replied, "I will agree to teach Mr. Moore's classes for that week, since I am not able to attend IRA this year myself, if one condition is met."

"And what condition is that, Mrs. Bennett?" asked Mr. Topps. .

"That Mr. Moore agree to meet with me beforehand for a few hours so that I can follow his program as closely as possible. It is important to me that everything go smoothly, since I have reluctantly applied for the new reading position which will open next year at D. Utter High."

Of course, I agreed to meet with her, and I coached the students on the importance of cooperating with her. In the circle activity on Friday, the last class day before I left for IRA, we had a discussion about substitute teachers, and I allowed them to brag about how mean they had been on occasion.

After some of this, I frankly explained to them that Mrs. Bennett was not certain she wanted to return to teaching and that if they gave her a hard time the next week, it would be on their consciences if she never taught again. I showed them the similarity in lack of confidence between a reader who has failed and a teacher who has failed, and I could see that they got the point. I knew that such a pep talk to behave well would only give Mrs. Bennett a start, but I believed that she would maintain my routine well enough that such a start would be enough to insure a reasonable week for all concerned.

In prepping her, she was impressed by the changes I had wrought in the program by including the concept of reading ceiling in the diagnosis and remediation I used. She saw my current program as a nice compromise between ensuring real reading experiences for the students while dealing more directly with their specific strengths and weaknesses. As it turned out, she operated the program smoothly, and both she and the students felt that the week had been enjoyable and profitable. She did greet me on my return from IRA with a certain bombshell, however. I returned home from IRA so late on Friday night that I did not call her to see how things had gone, but I phoned her the first thing next morning. Her husband said she was still asleep—R & R after a week in the Reading Center—and that she would call me when she woke up. She called at noon!

"Everything went well enough that I am sure I want to teach reading next year," she began. "Oh, there were problems all right, but the program was operating smoothly enough that I could handle them without everything going awry. If I had to get after Gene, everyone else just went on working."

I was so relieved.

"In fact," she continued, "we got along so well that in the circle activity yesterday, the students confided in me what they thought of your class."

I gulped. "They did what . . . ?"

"All of them think the class is among their better ones. Even the ones who claimed to hate school said that you were fair and that you cared about them. They did admit that they were ready for the school year to end and that they felt they were in a rut. The instruction you have been giving them has had variety and they have learned from it, but, after so long, every day has become too predictable."

Mrs. Bennett sounded so much more confident and assertive than she had back in December. "Well, I was beginning to notice some 'senioritis' before I left, and it wasn't limited to the seniors." I responded. "But, since I am committed to teach them every minute I can, right up to the end, what do you suggest I do?"

Mrs. Bennett paused. "If this year's IRA convention was like the ones I have attended, you have brought home strategies, games, and sample lessons which sounded good at the time they were presented."

"Yes, that's true. I have a folder full of ideas and notes."

"Well, then, why not go through that folder and teach every one of those techniques or lessons once to each of your classes between now and the end of school. I'll bet that they will learn something and you will get to try out some ideas you just might use from the beginning of the term next year if they work well. The ones that don't work well, okay, you really haven't lost any face since it is so close to the end of the year and everyone is gearing down anyway."

"Why, Mrs. Bennett," I exclaimed, "that is a fine suggestion."

And that is exactly what I have done these last three weeks of May, except for my posttesting. I have taught a different strategy each day, and the students have loved it. It has made the last weeks fly rather than crawl, as they usually do, and I have learned that some of the ideas I got at IRA were duds and that others were quite successful. I have tried vocabulary strategies, strategies for improving study skills, strategies for teaching inferential comprehension, and strategies for building critical reading. No day has been like another, and we have all had a positive end of year. Even the testing was not such a boring task, since it did not come in the middle of several final, boring weeks of school. Perhaps that even accounts for how well the classes did on the tests.

Evaluation   For posttesting, I gave the same limited-cloze tests I had used in September for screening, and then I gave the placement IRI I had used in the beginning to place students in groups for Directed Reading Activities in high/low books. Here are the results:

Placement Informal Reading Inventory—Sixth-Period Results

Student	Level	Student	Level
Bruce	4	John	5
Clarence	7	Marion	3
Eddie	4	Otelia	4
Elsie	4	Ricardo	2
Freddie	3	Rufus	2
Gene	2	Seymour	4
Jake	5	Willie	3
Jeff	4		

Although, because of testing error, an individual's gain score from pre- to posttesting is not very reliable, average gain scores are quite reliable. My students in sixth period averaged a gain of almost a level and a half for the year's instruction. Considering how severely retarded in reading they were at the beginning, I consider that kind of progress remarkable.

On the limited-cloze tests I used in September for screening, no one scored 60 percent, or instructional level, on any of the passages. This time, four students scored 60 percent or higher on at least one of the two tests. These tests and my own daily experience have convinced me that all students have improved in reading. For some the progress has been remarkable: Clarence, Elsie, Gene, and Rufus; for some it has been small: Jake and Ricardo; but all have gained in achievement in reading and in attitude toward reading. I must say, I never taught an advanced literature course to college-bound students that rewarded me half as much as teaching basic reading and study skills to these students whose futures are still, at best, uncertain.

The Summer Seminar for Special Reading Teachers

Reed Moore was really making the most of his summer vacation. He played two sets of tennis every morning, read or reread novels and dealt with correspondence in the afternoon, and worked in the lawn and garden in the early evening. He felt that his first year as a middle and secondary school remedial reading teacher had been very successful, and he was rewarding himself. He had so immersed himself in the area of reading during the school year that he felt it only fair to his family and friends that they not have to hear another word about students with reading problems for at least two months. He had agreed to make only one exception to his moratorium on reading and that was to do a session for secondary remedial teachers at State's Summer Seminar for Special Reading Teachers. Dr. Lea was in charge of organizing the two-day conference and had asked Reed to do the session.

When the day arrived, Reed arrived at State early to find a parking place and to attend the first session of the day. He saw Mrs. Bennett at this session as well as several of the people with whom he had taken courses in his M.Ed. program in reading. He even spotted Ms. Erable across the room, but she apparently did not see him, and he made no effort to attract her attention.

Reed's presentation was the second session of the morning. Approximately 15 people were present. He wrote "Reed Moore" on the chalkboard and turned to introduce himself to the group. As the first words left his mouth, the door opened and Ms. Erable joined the group. Reed was sure that his surprise was showing, but he continued with his introduction, "After 20 years of teaching high school English, I earned my M.Ed. degree in reading here at State, and this past year I began the first of what I hope to be many years as a remedial reading teacher at Upton Hill Middle/Secondary School. While few of you have taught more years than I, many of you have probably had more experience in teaching remedial reading. As a result, I do not feel that I should tell you what you should do in your remedial reading classes. I do feel comfortable, however, describing our program in which we taught some severely disabled readers to read significantly better.

"I would like to give an overview of our program and then the remainder of the session will be question and answer." Reed took a drink of water from the glass on the table in front of him. "In the years between the first two world wars, the American military developed the concept of the *overall strategic objective*. This concept was based on the idea that, in any situation and at any time, there are several goals that are desirable to achieve, but that the greatest likelihood of success occurs when the most important of these several goals is made the single, uppermost goal. All forces are then employed and all decisions are then made in order that this overall strategic objective eventually be met.

"In reading, we can list several defensible goals for our students. For example, we want them to like to read, we want them to be able to read aloud fluently, and we want them to be able to make inferences, creative responses, and critical judgments about what they read. Many instructional and testing programs list literally hundreds of reading skills, each supposedly building toward one of many abilities that readers should have.

"In our program at Upton Hill, we have an overall strategic objective in reading — that every student will be able eventually to sit in one place and read

Overall strategic objective

silently with good comprehension in increasingly difficult fictional and text-book materials.

"Does that mean that we did not do any oral reading? No. Does it mean that we were not concerned with word identification or critical reading or interest in reading? No. But it does mean that these facets of reading were only engaged in to the extent that they moved a student closer to achieving the overall objective. Moreover, the objective suggested a major means by which it could be achieved. As soon as possible in a student's reading development, he or she was placed in material at instructional level and asked to read it silently to fulfill comprehension purposes. As soon as reading was fluent at a level, the student was placed in the next higher level of material and again asked to read silently to fulfill comprehension purposes until that level, too, was mastered.

"Diagnosis consisted of three parts: (1) determining the instructional level for each student in the actual material that student would be using to practice silent reading comprehension; (2) determining what global area of reading ability (word identification, reading comprehension, or listening comprehension) was keeping the student's instructional level down at that point; and (3) determining what specific skills in that global area of need to work on.

"We took the poorest readers in the school, regardless of potential, who were not in other special reading programs, and we improved their reading ability, on the average, one and a half levels for the year."

While explaining that many of these ideas were Ed Dunn's, Reed passed out copies of the Ceiling Informal Reading Inventory and the Ceilings-X-Levels Grid. He explained briefly how he used them and gave everyone permission to duplicate and use the materials in their own classrooms. He then asked if there were questions.

Several hands went up. He called on a man in the front row. "I have so many questions, I don't know where to begin," he said. Several heads nodded. The man continued, "I guess my first question ought to reflect my biggest concern as a high school remedial teacher — discipline. How did you discipline your students so that you could teach them?"

Discipline

Reed smiled. "Well, that was also my chief concern at the beginning of the year. My approach was to have just a few rules and to really stick by them. I established a routine as soon as possible so that students would always know what they were expected to be doing without even having to think about it. I made sure that every student was given assignments which were possible to complete successfully without frustration, and I kept them busy working when they were in my room. I would not continue teaching or any other activity unless the students were participating. Frankly, the thought never occurred to me that I might not know what was best for a student, and I guess I was always trying to sell that confidence to the students. My course was not just another class, as far as I was concerned; it was the difference between a chance in life or not for some of the students. Without being brutal, I always let them know that they needed help in reading, that I knew how to provide it, that I liked them and believed in them, and that anyone was stupid not to take full advantage of me and my course!"

Reed recognized a woman who had sat with a puzzled look on her face during his presentation. She stood to ask her question. "Your presentation was impressive, Mr. Moore, but I am concerned. I teach the basic track students in

Expectations

ninth- and tenth-grade English at my high school, and I am amazed that so many of them read so poorly. How do they get to high school not knowing how to read any better than they do? Doesn't that mean that they have some kind of problem, and isn't it too late to do anything about it by the time they get to us?"

Reed was not surprised at the question, having been asked it a number of times by friends and fellow teachers. "It may seem," he began, "that students who have been in school for nine or ten or more years and who only read at first- or second- or third-grade level must have some kind of special disability which prevents them from learning to read. In some cases, that is probably true. I believe, however, that most severely disabled readers in middle and high schools fell behind in reading early in school for any number of reasons and have been taught at frustration level ever since. It would be understandable if a student were taught for 20 years in material too difficult and did not gain a year in achievement in reading! Students cannot be expected to benefit from inadequate instruction in inappropriate materials. It is the students who do not profit from good instruction in materials at their instructional and interest levels who are candidates for having a special disability in reading. Even they can be taught using special methods. Obviously, you can see that I think older remedial readers can learn to read better. We saw some improvement in all our students at Upton Hill this year.

"Another part of your question refers to whether or not it is too late to help these students by the time they reach high school. I must admit becoming discouraged this past year when I thought of how far even my best students still had to go to be able to read at all well. Let me explain to you how I cured my own discouragement.

"The average student in our program this year, in September, read between second- and third-grade level, and gained one and a half years by the end of May. Now, you may say that this average student still only reads at a low fourth-grade level and still cannot function as a literate person. But, if we took students reading middle second-grade level at the beginning of ninth grade and gave them instruction so that they gained one and a half years per year of instruction, after four years they would read at middle eighth-grade level which is well enough to hold a job and even do some post–high school work.

"It is certainly too late to have a remedial course of six weeks or one semester or even one year and expect to improve the student to the point where no more remedial instruction is needed. But, given a long-range commitment to students or given adequate instruction in appropriate materials at the earliest possible grade, there is no reason why we have to give up on these students as readers."

A man in the back interrupted. "What was the average IQ of the students you worked with this year?"

Reed was always bothered by questions about students' IQs. "Please don't take offense, sir, but I don't know and I don't care! I will bet you, however, that it is either higher than it was last fall or that they can now do better with what they have."

Ms. Erable raised her hand and Reed said coolly, "You have a question, Ms. Erable?"

"Yes, Mr. Moore, I was wondering what kind of support you feel that you received for carrying out your program last year?"

"Well, I must give credit to Mr. Topps. No principal could have been more supportive than he was. And many of my colleagues were also of much assistance. In all fairness, no one acted as an obstacle; at worst, our program was merely ignored." He thought Ms. Erable was trying to smile at that last remark.

Other questions followed which were mostly concerned with scheduling, grades, and getting the program started. Reed answered all of them as completely and honestly as he could. When the session ended, several people remained for more individual questions. On her way out, Ms. Erable handed him a note that read:

Mr. Moore,
   If you would like to have better support from the central office than just being ignored, invite me to see you in September. I'd love to come.

Bett Erable

15
Preparing Students for a Graduation Competency Test in Reading

E ACH DECADE OF education has its own benchmarks. It is entirely possible that educational historians will refer to the seventies as the "Decade of the Competency Test." Beginning in a few states and quickly catching on in others, the passing of a test which measures basic literacy and computational skills in reading and mathematics is currently required for graduation in over half the states in the United States. This additional graduation requirement is usually hailed with shouts of "It's about time they did something!" by the general public and with shouts of "It's not a fair test of what we teach!" by secondary teachers. There is truth to the declarations of each group.

The requirement that all students pass a test of "survival" or functional literacy" skills has been, in most states, a reaction of the legislative body to the complaints of business and industry leaders that today's high school graduates cannot perform such "simple" tasks as filling out a job application and following a set of written directions.[1] Prospective employers want a high school diploma to "mean something." Legislators have, by requiring each student to pass a test, attempted to legislate that the diploma granted will indeed mean something.

Whereas it seems perfectly logical and reasonable to the public that high school graduates should possess these functional literacy skills "at a very minimum," teachers and other educators protest that these skills have never been part of the curriculum students were expected to master as part of their public education. In fact, if you look at curriculum guides written prior to 1975 from most states, you observe that there is no specific place in the elementary or sec-

---

[1] In some states, the competency test is not a functional reading test but a standardized reading achievement test. To prepare students to pass a standardized reading achievement test, general reading ability must be improved. Strategies such as those in the preceding remedial chapters should be implemented.

ondary curriculum where these "real-life" reading skills are taught. It appears that in most states, students were expected to "pick up" these functional skills as they went along. No direct teaching of these skills was included in the curriculum. The graduation competency test requirement calls attention to the fact that students learn mostly what they are taught, and many students did not just pick up the skills in question.

Presently, the responsibility for teaching these functional literacy skills falls to the secondary teachers. Many secondary teachers resent being saddled with this additional teaching burden and declare that these "basic" skills really ought to be taught to students in the elementary grades. Elementary grade teachers respond that they, too, already have a full curriculum and that filling out a job application and interpreting the warning on a household cleanser label are of much greater interest and relevance to secondary students than to elementary students. Elementary teachers also argue that teaching skills six years before students need them to pass a test will have little effect on most students' test performance.

Regardless of who is right, the argument over where these skills should be taught is academic. The students who must pass the test are in the secondary schools now, and secondary teachers must teach these students the needed skills. The question of where in the secondary curriculum these skills will be taught is a harder question. It is impossible to add so large a chunk of skills without taking something away from what has been taught. In many schools it is the English teacher who must assume this additional responsibility. Other schools set up a "survival" course as part of the social studies curriculum. In the secondary schools which have remedial reading teachers, these teachers assume some of the responsibility. Teachers of the mentally retarded and learning disabled must also adjust their program to meet the objectives of the competency testing program. Whoever receives the responsibility for teaching functional literacy skills must have information relating to four crucial questions: (1) What exactly are the functional reading skills being tested? (2) What kind of test must students pass? (3) How can I effectively and efficiently teach my students these skills? and (4) How can I prepare students to do their best on the test? The remainder of this chapter will present answers to these four dilemmas.

What Are Functional Literacy Skills?

Functional literacy skills are those skills needed by members of our technological society to "get along" on their jobs and in their personal life. There are many different lists of these skills and many different ways of categorizing them.

FOR THE READER TO DO:

Keep track over several days of all the things you must read as you carry out your daily living. (Don't overlook the obvious such as road signs and utility bills.) When you have a long list, divide the items on your list into five or six categories. Label these categories. You now have your own list of functional reading skills and categories.

Each state which has mandated a functional literacy test as a graduation requirement has its own list and categorization of the functional skills. This list is often available as a set of objectives or can be determined by examining the items included on the competency test. Whenever possible, the teacher charged with preparing students for the competency test should find out particular functional reading skills the students are expected to know and will be tested on so that instruction can be as "on target" as possible. Most tests, however, will include test items in the following categories:

1. Filling out forms and applications: Students are expected to demonstrate facility with all kinds of forms and applications including job applications, social security card applications, credit applications, library card applications, unemployment insurance applications, drivers license applications, voter registration forms, and income tax forms.

2. Following written directions: Included in this category are such tasks as reading recipes and directions for preparing packaged foods, reading care and washing instructions on garments and household goods, and following instructions for "easy-to-assemble" items.

3. Locating and using appropriate information sources: This category usually includes both the knowledge of which source to use to find certain information and how to use sources once they are identified. Reference materials such as telephone books, TV guides, and dictionaries are commonly included. This category also includes the ability to use the various sections of the newspaper, including classified ads, as sources of information. Train, plane, and bus schedules are another example of information sources. Often, to use these information sources accurately, the reader must read graphic material such as charts and graphs in addition to the written material.

4. Consumer information: This category includes the ability to read a label and decide what nutritional requirements a food product satisfies, as well as to decide which of several sizes or brands is the better buy. The ability to read and interpret guarantees, warrantees and advertisements is also included under the heading consumer information.

5. Personal and business mail: In addition to personal and business letters, other items such as notices, bills, and bank statements are often included under this category.

6. Pictorial representations: Interpretating the nonprint material of signs and maps is the major task of this category of functional reading skills.

What Kind of Test Must Students Pass?

Once the teacher has determined which specific functional literacy skills must be mastered by the students, the next step is to determine how these skills will be tested. In most states, a multiple-choice format is used. Students are shown a job application or a map or the label from a medicine bottle and are then asked to choose from four possibilities the best answer to a question. Questions about the job application are often of the "Which of the following information should go on line ten?" type. This means that the student shows he or she could fill out the application by deciding what goes where. Many students who might, indeed, be able to fill out the application will have difficulty with the strangeness of the test item. Other items ask students to show that they understand directions and know the meaning of specific vocabulary.

FOR THE READER TO DO:

Here are some sample competency test items. What is being tested in each item?

Item following a job application:
In which space will Bob write his place of birth?
   a. 2   *b.* 6   *c.* 11   *d.* 14

Item following cough medicine bottle label:
Four times daily means:
   a. every four hours
   b. once each day for four days
   c. four times during the day
   d. four times for four days

Item following a map:
To get to Boston from Lexington, you should take route
   a. 128   *b.* 95   *c.* 66   *d.* 2

Now choose some real-life reading material. Make up three multiple-choice questions to test comprehension of vocabulary and content.

Once the teacher has examined the format of the test items and the type of information required to answer test items (vocabulary, literal, interpretive, for example), material can easily be prepared which allows students to practice the test format as they master functional reading skills.

There are two other important variables which teachers must determine if they are going to have the maximum possible number of students prepared to pass the test. Is the test a timed test? and Is there a correction for guessing? Most graduation competency tests differ in these two important ways from standardized achievement tests to which students are accustomed. Most competency tests are not timed. This means that students should very meticulously work each item, and should reread and double check as often as necessary to assure that they have made no careless errors. Students who are used to timed achievement tests are apt to work the competency test as they would work an achievement test, and this difference alone could account for many failures.

The same is true for the "correction for guessing" factor. Because most competency tests are criterion referenced, there is often no percentage subtracted for incorrect answers. The teacher should determine if this is, indeed, the case; if so, students should be instructed to give their best answer for every answer. If there is no penalty for guessing, the answering of every item can improve a student's score tremendously. Having found out which functional literacy skills will be tested and how the test will measure these skills, the teacher is now ready to teach the students the needed skills and prepare them to take the test.

How Can I Teach the Skills?

There are in every high school two groups of students who are apt to have difficulty passing a test of functional reading skills. The smallest and hardest to help group includes those students whose instructional reading level is below fifth grade. These students do not just need instruction and practice in the particular kind of reading required by real-life materials, they need instruction in basic word identification and comprehension skills. The first step in preparing these students to pass the graduation competency test would be to set up and enroll them in an intensive remedial reading class. These students are in need of instruction such as that suggested in Chapters 3 and 4. Once they have reached an instructional reading level of at least fifth grade, they could benefit from a program of specific instruction in functional reading skills as described in the rest of this section.

The other group of students who may have difficulty in passing the test unless given specific insruction includes a majority of the students enrolled in most high schools. These students have instructional levels ranging from sixth-grade level to college level but have probably never had instruction or practice in filling out applications and reading and interpreting labels. Most of these students can quickly learn these skills and thus pass the test if provided with a short period of instruction and practice. The program outlined in the remainder of this section is intended to provide all students who read at sixth-grade level or above with instruction and practice in the functional reading skills and should result in a drastically reduced failure rate on the first administration of the test for this group of students.

The first step in preparing to teach the functional literacy skills is a special kind of scavenger hunt. Teacher and students gather from local business, industry, banks, post office, restaurants, and stores all the applications, directions, labels, signs, and maps they can carry. Using the information gained from an investigation of the skills to be tested and the format in which they will be tested, the teacher then uses the real-life reading materials collected to construct instructional and practice items for each category of items to be tested. For the applications category, for example, the teacher might make multiple copies of an application and then construct questions similar to those on the test. Led by the teacher, each student would fill out the application and then answer the multiple-choice questions. Vocabulary which is used again and again on applications would be discussed and perhaps listed on a chart of "application jargon." If many students were still experiencing difficulty with filling out an application and answering multiple-choice questions about that application, more applications would be done by the entire group under the direction of the teacher. When the teacher felt that most students were ready to tackle applications on their own, students would select an application and a set of questions from a box and independently answer the questions. The answers to the questions would then be checked with a key by the student or the teacher. When a student had successfully completed three sets of application questions on his or her own, the student and the teacher could feel confident in that student's ability to pass the "application filling out" part of the graduation competency test.

This same procedure of whole-class, teacher-led instruction followed by individual practice could be followed with each of the other categories of skills on any competency test. If the objectives for the test were in the six areas listed in this chapter, teachers and students would engage in practice and instruction in (1) filling out forms and applications; (2) following written directions; (3) locating and using appropriate information sources; (4) consumer information; (5) personal and business mail; and (6) pictorial representations. Of course the actual categories used by a teacher and the format of the questions used would be determined by the particular graduation competency test used in that teacher's state.

If each teacher were to have to construct his or her own materials to provide instruction and practice for students in all categories of skills, it would take a great deal of time. In this case, student help should be enlisted not only in gathering the real-life reading material, but also in creating the independent practice material to be used by the other students. For the category of following written directions, for example, the teacher might type the directions for two or three sets of directions and either duplicate these so that each student would have a copy or make a transparency. The teacher would then construct several questions using the appropriate test format. All students would be led through these several sets of directions together, the answers to the questions discussed, and a list of "following directions jargon" compiled. Next, each student would take a set of directions and write questions similar to the ones written by the teacher for that set of directions. The student would also make an answer key for the individual practice lesson. In addition to the excellent practice students would get in reading directions by having to construct questions about those directions, the class would now have approximately 30 individual practice lessons. Students could use each other's lessons to assure themselves and the teacher that they had mastered this functional literacy skill.

In some school districts teachers have worked together to create materials to be used by others. In a workshop conducted by Dr. Linda Gambrell of the University of Maryland, Dr. Gambrell told of some Maryland teachers who set up an assembly line and in one day produced practice material in each category of skills being tested by their test. Teachers formed teams of five or six, and each team created materials in one category. The information from the label or directions or other printed material was typed on a stencil. Vocabulary and literal and interpretive questions about that printed material were typed on another stencil. The answer key for those questions was typed on a third stencil. From the stencils, multiple copies of everything were made. They were then placed in color-keyed pocket folders, one folder for each teacher in the workshop. At the end of the day, teachers left with colorful practice packets for all the functional literacy skills.

FOR READERS TO DO TOGETHER:

Using the six categories of objectives outlined in this chapter and the multiple-choice test format, divide into six groups and construct practice packets for each category of skills. For each real-life reading material, construct three vocabulary questions, three literal questions, and three interpretive questions. If possible, type the printed material, questions, and answer keys on stencils, reproduce them, and provide everyone with packets ready for immediate use.

There are several crucial points to be noted about the preparation of students for the graduation competency test as outlined above. The first is that even good readers will probably need some instruction and practice with the specialized type of reading required by real-life reading tasks. The second is that in content and format, this instruction and practice should be modeled on the actual test to be given. Finally, since real-life reading materials have a specialized vocabulary, teachers must ensure that students understand the meanings for the specialized vocabulary they will encounter.

How Can I Prepare Them to Take the Test?

If you have provided students with a program of instruction and practice emphasizing those functional literacy skills to be tested and using the test format, students are well on their way to doing well on the test. Additionally, students should be instructed on how to take the test. The questions which relate to the printed material should be read before reading the printed material. If the test is timed, students should wear a watch and should move through the test items as quickly as possible. They should always guess at an answer if they can narrow down the possible answers, even if they are not sure which is the right answer among the remaining possibilities. If the test is not timed, students should take as much time as is necessary to check and recheck their answers. Better to spend an extra 15 minutes taking a test than an entire semester in a remedial reading class. If there is no correction for guessing on a test, students should answer every item. They will not be penalized for wrong answers and on a multiple-choice four-response item test they should average 25 percent right on the items they have no idea about.

Finally, the students and the teacher should approach the test with confidence and a positive attitude. You, the teacher, have provided students with the appropriate instruction and practice. The students have worked hard to master the skills, to learn the specialized vocabulary, and to understand the test format. With this preparation, almost all students who read at fifth-grade level or above should successfully pass the test the first time it is given.

APPENDIX A

A "cloze passage" is one in which words have been systematically deleted and replaced by blanks. Cloze passages may be used to determine a student's instructional reading level as *well* as to assess the *student's* ability to comprehend or *understand* a particular passage. This *procedure* has been used successfully *with* readers, fourth grade through *adult*.

To construct a cloze *passage*, choose a 300-word *selection*. Leave the first and *last* 25 words of the *selection* intact. Beginning with the *thirtieth* word in the passage, *delete* every fifth word and *replace* it with a blank until there are 50 blanks. *All* blanks should be of *uniform* length. Before administering the *cloze* test, one should direct *the* readers to complete each *blank* with the exact word *they* think has been deleted. *The* test should have no *time* limit, and students should *receive* no help. Tests should *then* be collected and scored, *marking* correct only those answers *which* match the original word (*misspellings* are correct if the *scorer* believes the correct word *was* intended, but synonyms are *to* be marked incorrect).

Students *who* correctly complete 44 to 57 *percent* of the blanks may *be* expected to adequately comprehend *that* material after some instruction. *The* passage may be said *to* be at their "instructional *level*." If a student is *unable* to successfully complete 44 *percent* of the blanks, the *material* is too difficult for *him* even with instruction and *he* should be tested in *easier* material. If a student *correctly* completes more than 57 *percent* of the blanks, he *may* be expected to read *the* passage without instruction. The *teacher* may want to test *him* in more difficult material *to* find an instructional level.

APPENDIX B
Improving Language and Comprehension Through the Language Experience Story

Manzo's Language Shaping Paradigm (LSP)*

Purpose: The primary purpose of the LSP is to teach students how to value and profit from their own thoughts and experiences. The process also helps students to get a firmer grip on their unique identities, to improve their general language and writing abilities, and to heighten their appreciation of the writing of others.

Basic idea: The basic teaching strategy, or paradigm, is built around having students read essays written by class peers. These are treated as important works. The essays are edited, reproduced, and accompanied by comprehension questions and language improvement exercises.

One of the very special benefits in this technique seems to come from students' realization that their work can take on a more durable quality than a typical theme which even the teacher may not get to read. This is a strong source of motivation to think and use language effectively.

Step 1: The LSP should begin with a provocative discussion from which a purpose for expressing (writing) is generated.

Step 2: Depending on the level of sophistication of the students, the teacher either records the oral story (discourse) of the student, or the student writes it as a conventional essay.

Step 3: The teacher selects one or two essays to be edited jointly with the student, being sure the student understands that the next step will involve having the class read the work.

Step 4: The teacher, with the possible help of the student, prepares comprehension questions on the material at a literal, interpretive, and applied level.

Step 5: The teacher, more than likely without the author's input, prepares two or three exercises to improve expression and language. These should be designed to point-up both the weaknesses and merits of the author's style. Three basic types of Language Exercises can be constructed

*(Excerpt from draft manuscript of Manzo, A.V., Kansas City: University of Missouri, 1974.)

346

easily: a) word/phrase/punctuation improvement; b) improving sentence structures and/or mood; c) re-writing small sections, or re-structuring plot and sequence.

Step 6: The class reads the essay and does the comprehension check. Answers are discussed. The author is present during the discussion, but should maintain a low profile to permit uninhibited interaction among class members.

Step 7: Based on the common frame of reference provided by the comprehension check, the class turns to the Language Exercises. The author may participate more openly in discussing the language exercises.

Comments: In our experience, student-authors have tended to be very objective during discussions, critiquing their work, often joining in the criticism in a self-correcting way. Discussions have tended to be very adult, generally light, and sharply analytical. In all, a good experience with language activity.

Example/Sample

The theme shown below was done with an inner city adult in a high school equivalency course. It was stimulated by a discussion about dreams and their interpretation. The instructor worked individually with this student, writing his story for him as he told it. The other members of the class attempted to write their own stories at their desks. The instructor and student edited the theme together until it was to the student's liking.

I Dreamed I Was Green

Author: Frank Cody, Westinghouse Employee, Kansas City, Missouri

1   I fell asleep last night on the couch in front of my TV. I was watching an old movie called the "Boy with the Green Hair."
My body ached from another long day. My stomach was now working on the cornbeef and cabbage, Dynamite! The combination made me dream a strange dream.
5   I dreamed that I woke up and had turned green. God, it was so real! At first I thought it was the light. Then I thought someone was playing a practical joke on me. But none of these things made sense. The kids were fast asleep and my wife had not yet come home from her part-time job. She is a ticket girl at the Waldo.
I called the doctor. The answering service wanted to know what was wrong. I told
10   them. He never called back. I went next door to my neighbor, Bud. He was shocked. He brought me to the hospital. His wife watched our kids.
The doctors said there is nothing wrong with you that we can tell, except that you are definitely green!
Now the dream gets all crazy. All I know is that I find myself planted in the backyard
15   and beginning to look more and more like a tree. Then a lot of time passes. And the house is old and my wife and kids are gone, but I'm still in the backyard. No one seems to notice me. I'm not unhappy. I'm not happy. I'm nothing. I'm just there.
Well, that's not really true, about me just being there, I mean. There are moments when I'm very happy, like when squirrels and birds are playing on my branches. And I
20   really feel good when I turn beautiful colors in the fall. And even though I don't like the winter, it's kind of nice to be covered with blue-white snow. February is worst. Dark and

sad. But then in March I begin to swell on the inside. I feel life stirring inside me, like a woman does long before anyone even knows she is pregnant. Then April showers and then in May I bust out of myself and turn beautiful green.

25   I woke up at about that time. This may sound crazy, but I was a little disappointed that I was not green.

Comprehension Check   Level I

Directions: Decide whether the following statements are consistent with those made in the story. Circle the *T* for true or the *F* for false. You may *not* look back to the story to answer these questions.

    Write the number of the line or lines which helped you answer each question.

T F **1.** The kids woke me from my dream by the racket that they were making. (line _____)

T F **2.** Thank goodness for the help of my neighbor, Frank. (line _____)

T F **3.** My neighbor was shocked to see that I was green. (line _____)

T F **4.** February is best. I love the blue-white snow. (line _____)

Comprehension Check   Level II

Recall   1. What was the man who wrote this article doing when he fell asleep?

Recall   2. What is the first thing this man did when he realized that he had turned green?

Recognition and Conjecture   3. Find the line in the story which tells the kind of work the "green man's" wife does. What is the name of the place she worked at? What kind of place do you think it is?

Translation   4. What is another word for "working" in the sentence below?

"My stomach was now *working* on the cornbeef and cabbage."

Conjecture   5. Why do you suppose the writer of this story dreamed that he was green?

Evaluation and Explanation   6. Do you think that you would like to have the man who dreamed he was green as a friend? Why?

Evaluation and Explanation   7. Did you like this man's story? What part did you like best or least?

Evaluation   8. Does dreaming, in your opinion, serve any useful purpose? Can it be bad for you?

The questions above are arranged in order of increasing difficulty of question type. The higher order questions require deeper thinking and more sophisticated language. This does not mean that a specific question of a recall type, for example, could not be "harder" to answer *correctly* than a "higher" order question. It simply is not as demanding in terms of integrative thinking and language requirement.

Comprehension Check Level III

Carefully consider the statements below. In column *A* answer *yes* if you think the writer of the above story might believe in them or *no* if you think he probably would not really believe in them. In column *B* indicate which line or lines from the story helped you to decide on your answer.

A	B	Statements
Yes/No	Line(s)	

1. I hate boiled food.
2. A man needs friends.
3. Doctors aren't really much good.
4. I am nothing but a vegetable. I'm just there.
5. I really don't like kids much.
6. Nature is refreshing.
7. Only jerks go out of their way to look different.
8. Life has its ups and downs.
9. Dreaming isn't good for you.
10. I sure wish things wouldn't change as much as they do.

Language Improvement Exercises

Choosing More Appropriate Words Level I

Sometimes replacing or modifying a few words in a paragraph can greatly improve the clarity and the value of the expression in a piece. Carefully study the paragraph below. Replace the underlined words with words chosen from the list below.

>   1   2
> I *called* the doctor. The answering service *wanted to know* what was wrong. I told
>   3
> them. *He* never called back. I went next door to my neighbor, Bud. He was shocked.
>   4 5   6
> *He brought* me to the hospital. His wife *watched* our kids.

I 1)_____ the doctor. The answering service 2)_____ what was wrong. I told them. 3)_____ never called back. I went next door to my neighbor, Bud. He was shocked. 4)_____ 5)_____ me to the hospital. His wife 6)_____ our kids.

spoke to	asked	Bud	told
phoned	the doctor	drove	looked after

Improving Mood Level II

"I Dreamed I Was Green" is written in a half-humorous, half-serious vein. That is to say, the language is quite casual.

Decide which of the sentences below best matches the mood of the piece. Underline the words, phrases, and/or punctuations that you think best represent the half-serious mood. Write "I" for improved, "N" for not.

_____ 1. I called the doctor's answering service to see if I could get his opinion on why I might be green.

——— 2. I called the doctor. Naturally, I got some corny answering service.
——— 3. I went next door to my neighbor, Bud. He was shocked!
——— 4. Bud's wife, Martha, volunteered to look after the children while I was at the hospital.
——— 5. You guessed it, the doctor never called back.

Reorganization and Rewriting   Level III

Do A or B.

A. Pretend that you are the author of this article and rewrite the paragragh between lines 16 and 20 in a way that you believe would improve it.

_____

_____

_____

_____

_____

_____

_____

_____

_____

B. Reorganizing. Can you see any means by which this piece can be reordered so that the basic story remains the same, but the effect is more imaginative or stylish. (You may rewrite small sections to accomplish this.)

_____

_____

_____

_____

_____

_____

_____

_____

_____

APPENDIX C
The Cunningham Secondary and Adult Basic Sight Word List[1]

By James W. and Patricia M. Cunningham

First 50 words (according to frequency of occurrence):

the	it	they	all	wlll
of	for	be	were	their
and	on	this	there	can
to	with	had	said	up
a	his	have	by	out
in	as	from	or	an
is	I	not	what	which
that	at	but	when	would
he	are	one	her	him
was	you	she	we	if

Second 50:

so	these	my	over	way
them	no	who	make	just
about	many	than	see	where
do	like	now	down	man
has	your	did	people	after
some	two	first	little	very
then	could	its	me	too
into	time	been	back	get
more	each	new	only	long
other	how	made	may	good

[1]This word list contains the 300 words which occur on both the Atlantic and Pacific Sight Word List (Otto and Chester, 1972) and the Kucera-Francis Word List (1st 500 words) (1967).

Third 50:

much	know	water	say	home
our	even	around	men	look
Mr.	come	because	house	last
go	use	old	also	think
through	work	went	place	away
before	same	take	put	part
day	came	another	again	should
any	well	off	does	number
most	here	three	find	us
must	right	under	still	never

Fourth 50:

great	while	next	few	need
small	Mrs.	end	set	want
thought	don't	children	saw	told
school	left	might	help	different
own	something	took	high	let
why	ask	once	enough	didn't
every	got	word	give	side
big	world	night	those	name
found	year	until	both	along
such	always	head	between	tell

Fifth 50:

line	white	kind	form	today
eyes	began	ever	call	important
without	hand	himself	mother	sure
almost	large	together	car	land
air	room	keep	I'm	gave
city	it's	thing	feet	against
better	often	best	second	miss
far	country	boy	family	across
knew	door	sound	toward	face
show	four	light	young	money

Sixth 50:

nothing	done	cannot	mean	table
whole	hard	five	girl	six
sometimes	order	half	anything	outside
live	soon	run	red	street
heard	open	am	stood	woman
morning	top	ago	black	road
above	change	study	true	start
seen	really	front	town	strong
play	near	short	feel	class
body	turn	behind	leave	gone

References

Allington, R. L. "Improving Content Area Reading Instruction in the Middle School." *Journal of Reading* 18 (1975):455– 461.

Allington, R. L. "Sustained Approaches to Reading and Writing. *Language Arts* 52 (1975):813– 815.

Allington, R. L., Chodos, L., Domaracki, J., and Truex, S. "Passage Dependence: Four Diagnostic Oral Reading Tests. *The Reading Teacher* 30 (1977):369– 375.

Anderson, R. C. "Schema-Directed Processes in Language Comprehension." In A. M. Lesgold, J. W. Pellegrino, S. D. Fakkema, and R. Glaser (eds.), *Cognitive Psychology and Instruction*. New York: Plenum Press, 1978.

Anderson, R. C., Pichert, J. W., Goetz, E. T., Schallert, D. L., Stevens, K. V., and Trollip, S. R. "Instantiation of General Terms." *Journal of Verbal Learning and Verbal Behavior* 15 (1976):667– 679.

Anderson, R. C., Stevens, K. C., Shifrin, Z., and Osborn, J. H. "Instantiation of Word Meanings in Children." *Journal of Reading Behavior* 10 (1978):148– 157.

Aulls, M. W. *Developmental and Remedial Reading in the Middle Grades.* Boston: Allyn & Bacon, 1978.

Baldwin, R. S., and Kaufman, R. K. "A Concurrent Validity Study of the Raygor Readability Estimate." *Journal of Reading* 23 (1979):148– 153.

Barron, R. "The Use of Vocabulary as an Advance Organizer." In H. L. Herber and P. L. Sanders (eds.), *Research in Reading in the Content Areas: First Year Report*. Syracuse, N.Y.: Syracuse University Reading and Language Arts Center, 1969. (monograph)

Beach, D. M. *Reaching Teenagers: Learning Centers in the Secondary Classroom.* Pacific Palisades, Ca.: Goodyear, 1977.

Betts, E. A. *Foundations of Reading Instruction*. New York: American Book, 1946.

Bibliographic Index. New York: H. W. Wilson, 1938– present.

Bormuth, J. R. "Cloze Test Readability: Criterion Referenced Scores." *Journal of Educational Measurement* 5 (1968):189– 196.

Botel, M. *Botel Reading Inventory*. Chicago: Follett, 1978.

Britannica Junior. Chicago: Encyclopaedia Britannica.

Burmeister, L. E. *Reading Strategies for Middle and Secondary School Teachers*, 2nd ed. Reading, Mass.: Addison-Wesley, 1978.

Byars, B. *Summer of the Swans*. New York: Viking, 1970.

Canney, G., and Schreiner, R. "A Study of the Effectiveness of Selected Syllabication Rules and Phonogram Patterns for Word Attack." *Reading Research Quarterly* 12 (1976–1977):102–124.

Chomsky, C. "After Decoding: What?" *Language Arts* 53 (1976):288–296, 314.

Clary, L. M. "Tips for Testing Reading Informally in the Content Areas." *Journal of Reading* 20 (1976):156–157.

Compton's Encyclopedia. Chicago: Encyclopaedia Britannica.

Cooper, C. R., and Petrosky, A. R. "Psycholinguistic View of the Fluent Reading Process." *Journal of Reading* 20 (1976):184–207.

Crist, B. I. "One Capsule a Week—A Painless Remedy for Vocabulary Ills." *Journal of Reading* 19 (1975):147–149.

Cunningham, J. W., and Cunningham, P. M. "Validating a Limited-Cloze Procedure." *Journal of Reading Behavior* 10 (1978):211–213.

Cunningham, P. M. "Decoding Polysyllabic Words: An Alternative Strategy." *Journal of Reading* 21 (1978):608–614.

Cunningham, P. M. "Investigating a Synthesized Theory of Mediated Word Identification." *Reading Research Quarterly* 11 (1975–1976):127–143.

Cunningham, P. M. "Match Informal Evaluation to Your Teaching Practices." *The Reading Teacher* 31 (1977):51–56.

Cunningham, P. M. "Applying a Compare/Contrast Process to Identifying Polysyllabic Words." In Press, 1980.

Cunningham, P. M., Rystrom, R. C., and Cunningham, J. W., "A New Syllabication Strategy and Reading Achievement." In Press, 1980.

Current Index to Journals in Education. New York: Macmillan Information, 1969–present.

Cutter, R., and Fendall, B. *Encyclopedia of Auto Racing Greats.* Englewood Cliffs, N.J.: M. Evans, 1973.

Dahl, P. R. *An Experimental Program for Teaching High Speed Word Recognition and Comprehension Skills*. University of Minnesota, Final Report, Project No. 3–1154. Washington, D.C.: Department of Health, Education and Welfare, 1974.

Dahl, P. R., and Samuels, S. J. "Teaching High Speed Word Recognition and Comprehension Skills. Unpublished manuscript, 1975.

Danziger, P. *The Cat Ate My Gymsuit*. New York: Dell, 1974.

Davis, F. B. "Research in Comprehension in Reading." *Reading Research Quarterly* 4 (1968):499–545.

Duffy, G. G. (ed.). *Reading in the Middle School*. Newark, Del.: International Reading Association Perspectives in Reading, no. 18, 1974.

Earle, R. "The Use of the Structured Overview in Mathematics Classes." In H. L. Herber and P. L. Sanders (eds.), *Research in Reading in the Content Areas: First Year Report*. Syracuse, N.Y.: Syracuse University Reading and Language Arts Center, 1969. (monograph)

Earle, R. *Teaching Reading and Mathematics*. Newark, Del.: International Reading Association, 1976.

Education Index. New York: H. W. Wilson, 1929–present.

Ekwall, E. D. *Diagnosis and Remediation of the Disabled Reader.* Boston: Allyn & Bacon, 1976.

Encyclopaedia Britannica. Chicago: Encyclopaedia Britannica.

Encyclopedia of Educational Research. New York: Macmillan, 1969.

Encyclopedia of Physics. New York: Van Nostrand Reinhold, 1974.

Encyclopedia of World Literature in the 20th Century. New York: F. Ungar, 1967 (and supplements).

Fernald, G. M. *Remedial Techniques in Basic School Subjects.* New York: McGraw-Hill, 1943.

Frederiksen, C. H. "Representing Logical and Semantic Structure of Knowledge Acquired from Discourse." *Cognitive Psychology* 7 (1975):371– 458.

Fry, E. "Fry's Readability Graph; Clarification, Validity, and Extension to Level 17." *Journal of Reading* 21 (1977):242– 252.

George, J. *My Side of the Mountain.* New York: Dutton, 1959.

Glasser, W. *Schools Without Failure.* New York: Harper & Row, 1969.

Goodman, K. S. "A Linguistic Study of Cues and Miscues in Reading." *Elementary English* 42 (1965):639– 643.

Goodman, Y. M., and Burke, C. L. *Reading Miscue Inventory.* New York: Macmillan, 1972.

Goodspeed, P. *Hugh and Fitzhugh.* New York: Platt and Munk, n.d.

Granger, E. *Granger's Index to Poetry.* New York: Columbia University Press, 1973.

Grimes, J. *The Thread of Discourse.* The Hague, Netherlands: Mouton, 1975.

Grove's Dictionary of Music and Musicians. New York: St. Martin's Press, 1954 (and supplementary volumes).

Guinness Book of World Records. New York: Bantam.

Gwynne, F. *The King Who Rained.* New York: Windmill Press & E. P. Dutton, 1970.

Haberlandt, K., and Bingham, G. "Verbs Contribute to the Coherence of Brief Narratives: Reading Related and Unrelated Sentence Triples." *Journal of Verbal Learning and Verbal Behavior* 17 (1978):419– 425.

Hafner, L. E. (ed.). *Improving Reading in Middle and Secondary Schools —Selected Readings*, 2nd ed. New York: Macmillan, 1974.

Haley, A. *Roots.* New York: Dell, 1976.

Harris, A. J. *How to Increase Reading Ability*, 4th ed. New York: Longman, 1960.

Herber, H. L. *Teaching Reading in Content Areas,* 2nd ed. Englewood Cliffs, N.J.: Prentice-Hall, 1978.

Huey, E. B. *The Psychology and Pedagogy of Reading.* Cambridge, Mass.: MIT Press, 1968. (Originally published, 1908, by Macmillan of New York.)

Hultgren, H. A., and Arthur, S. V. "The Case for Heesh, Shis and Shim." *Language Arts* 55 (1978):198– 199.

Hunt, L. "Six Steps to the Individualized Reading Program (IRP)." *Elementary English* 48 (1971):27– 32.

Information Please Almanac. New York: Simon & Schuster.

Juster, N. *The Phantom Tollbooth.* New York: Random House, 1961.

Kieras, D. E. "Good and Bad Structure in Simple Paragraphs: Effects on Apparent Theme, Reading Time, and Recall." *Journal of Verbal Learning and Verbal Behavior* 17 (1978):13– 28.

Kintsch, W. *The Representation of Meaning in Memory.* Hillsdale, N.J.: Lawrence Erlbaum Associates, 1974.

Kohl, H. *36 Children*. New York: Signet, 1967.

Kucera, H. and Francis, W. N. *Computational Analysis of Present-Day American English.* Providence, R.I.: Brown University Press, 1967.

Kulhavy, R. W. "Feedback in Written Instruction." *Review of Educational Research* 47 (1977):211–232.

LaBerge, D., and Samuels, S. J. "Toward a Theory of Automatic Information Processing in Reading. *Cognitive Psychology* 6 (1974):293–323.

Lake, M. L. "Improve the Dictionary's Image." *Elementary English* 48 (1971):363–365.

Macaulay, D. *Cathedral*. Boston: Houghton-Mifflin, 1973.

———. *City*. Boston: Houghton Mifflin, 1974.

———. *Pyramid*. Boston: Houghton Mifflin, 1975.

Mandler, J. M., and Johnson, N. S. "Remembrance of Things Parsed: Story Structure and Recall." *Cognitive Psychology* 9 (1977):111–151.

Manzo, A. V. "Guided Reading Procedure." *Journal of Reading* 18 (1975):287–291.

Marzano, R. J., Case, N., Debooy, A., and Prochoruk, K. "Are Syllabication and Reading Ability Related?" *Journal of Reading* 19 (1976):545–547.

Mathison, S. "Solving Story Problems and Liking it." *The Arithmetic Teacher*. Nov., 1969. 577–579.

McCracken, R. "Initiating Sustained Silent Reading." *Journal of Reading* 14 (1971): 521–529, 582.

Meyer, B. J. F. "Organization in Prose and Memory: Research with Application to Reading Comprehension." In P. D. Pearson (ed.), *Reading: Theory, Research, and Practice*, 26th Yearbook of the National Reading Conference, Clemson, S.C.: The National Reading Conference, 1977.

Michelson, N. I. "Associative Verbal Encoding: A/V/E: A Measure of Language Performance and Its Relationship to Reading Achievement (abstract)." *Reading Research Quarterly* 9 (1974):227–231.

Morley, C. (ed.). *The Shorter Bartlett's Familiar Quotations.* New York: Pocket Books, 1963.

Morris, D., and Morris, I. *Who Was Who in American Politics*. New York: Hawthorne, 1974.

Nash, J. R. *Bloodletters and Badmen.* New York: M. Evans, 1973.

Niensted, S. "Read + Write + Talk = Progress." *Journal of Reading* 20 (1977):305–309.

Otto, W., and Chester, R. "Sight Words for Beginning Readers." *The Journal of Educational Research* 65 (1972):435–443.

Pearson, P. D., and Johnson, D. D. *Teaching Reading Comprehension*. New York: Holt, Rinehart and Winston, 1978.

The People's Almanac. New York: Doubleday.

Raygor, A. L. "The Raygor Readability Estimate: A Quick and Easy Way to Determine Difficulty." 26th Yearbook of the National Reading Conference, 1977:259–263.

Readers' Guide to Periodical Literature. New York: H. W. Wilson, 1900–present.

Resources in Education. Washington, D.C.: National Institute of Education, 1966–present.

Robbins, R. H. *Encyclopedia of Witchcraft and Demonology*. New York: Crown, 1959.

Robinson, F. P. *Effective Study*. New York: Harper & Row, 1961.

Robinson, H. A. *Teaching Reading and Study Strategies—the Content Areas*. Boston: Allyn & Bacon, 1975.

Rockwell, T. *How to Eat Fried Worms*. New York: Franklin Watts, 1973.

Rumelhart, D. E., and Norman, D. A. "Accretion, Tuning, and Restructuring: Three Modes of Learning." In J. W. Cotton and R. L. Klatzky (eds.), *Semantic Factors in Cognition*. Hillsdale, N.J.: Lawrence Erlbaum Associates, 1978.

Schank, R. C. *Conceptual Information Processing*. Amsterdam: North-Holland, 1975.

The Scientific American Resource Library. San Francisco: Freeman.

Searfoss, L. W., and Readence, J. E. *Strategies for Helping Children Read*. Unpublished manuscript.

Silvaroli, N. J. *Classroom Reading Inventory*, 3rd ed. Dubuque, Iowa: Brown, 1976.

Smith, F. *Understanding Reading* 2nd ed. New York: Holt, Rinehart and Winston, 1978.

Smith, R. J., and Barrett, T. C. *Teaching Reading in the Middle Grades*. Reading, Mass.: Addison-Wesley, 1974.

Snyder, Z. K. *And All Between*. New York: Anthaneum, 1976.

Spache, G. D. *Diagnostic Reading Scales*. Monterey, California: McGraw-Hill, 1973.

Spache, G. D., and Spache, E. *Reading in the Elementary School*. 4th ed. Boston: Allyn & Bacon, 1977.

Spiegel, D. L. "Meaning-Seeking Strategies for the Beginning Reader." *The Reading Teacher* 31 (1978):772–776.

Spiro, R. J. "Constructive Processes in Prose Comprehension and Recall." In R. J. Spiro, B. C. Bryce, and W. F. Brewer (eds.), *Theoretical Issues in Reading Comprehension*. Hillsdale, N.J.: Lawrence Erlbaum Associates, 1979.

Stauffer, R. G. *Directing Reading Maturity as a Cognitive Process*. New York: Harper & Row, 1969.

Taba, H. *Teachers' Handbook for Elementary Social Studies.* Reading, Mass.: Addison-Wesley, 1967.

Taylor, W. L. " 'Cloze Procedure': A New Tool for Measuring Readability." *Journalism Quarterly* 30 (1953):415–433.

This Fabulous Century. New York: Time-Life Books, 1969.

Thomas, E. L., and Robinson, H. A. *Improving Reading in Every Class*. Boston: Allyn & Bacon, 1977.

Thorndyke, P. W. "Cognitive Structures in Comprehension and Memory of Narrative Discourse." *Cognitive Psychology* 9 (1977):77–110.

Travers, R. M. (ed.). *Second Handbook of Research on Teaching*. Chicago: Rand McNally, 1973.

Twentieth Century Authors: A Biographical Dictionary of Modern Literature. New York: H. W. Wilson, 1975.

Vaughan, S., Crawley, S., and Mountain, L. "A Multiple-Modality Approach to Word Study: Vocabulary Scavenger Hunts." *The Reading Teacher* 32 (1979):434–437.

The W.E.B.—*Wonderfully Exciting Books.* Ohio State University Reading and Language Arts Department, Spring, 1978.

Who's Who in America. Chicago: A. N. Marquis.

The World Almanac. New York: Doubleday.

The World Book Encyclopedia. Chicago: Field Enterprises Educational Corporation.

Index